With the support of extensive and prodigious multi-archival and multi-source research, Zhu Dandan has written a comprehensive, insightful, and truly original book on one of the most critical turning points in the history of Mao's China, the international communist movement, and the global Cold War. Highly recommended.

—*Chen Jian*
Michael J. Zak Professor of History for US-China Relations
Cornell University

1956
MAO'S CHINA AND THE HUNGARIAN CRISIS

1956
MAO'S CHINA AND THE HUNGARIAN CRISIS

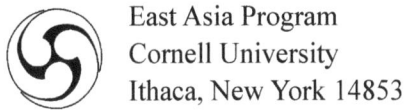

East Asia Program
Cornell University
Ithaca, New York 14853

The Cornell East Asia Series is published by the Cornell University East Asia Program (distinct from Cornell University Press). We publish books on a variety of scholarly topics relating to East Asia as a service to the academic community and the general public. Standing Orders, which provide for automatic notification and invoicing of each title in the series upon publication are accepted.

Address submission inquiries to CEAS Editorial Board, East Asia Program, Cornell University, 140 Uris Hall, Ithaca, New York 14853-7601.

Publication of this work is supported by the Fundamental Research Funds for the Central Universities, China.

Number 170 in the Cornell East Asia Series
Copyright ©2013 by Zhu Dandan. All rights reserved.
ISSN: 1050-2955
ISBN: 978-1-933947-90-7 hardcover
ISBN: 978-1-933947-70-9 paperback
Library of Congress Control Number: 2013938550
Printed in the United States of America

∞ The paper in this book meets the requirements for permanence of ISO 9706:1994.

CAUTION: Except for brief quotations in a review, no part of this book may be reproduced or utilized in any form without permission in writing from the author. Please address all inquiries to Zhu Dandan in care of the East Asia Program, Cornell University, 140 Uris Hall, Ithaca, NY 14853-7601.

Contents

Introduction ... 1

1 **Communist China and the Communist World (1949–1956)** ... 17
   Mao's Communist China in the Making (1949–1953) ... 22
   Small Leap in Socialist Transformation (1955–1956) ... 39

2 **China and the Eastern Bloc: Before and After the CPSU Twentieth Congress** ... 49
   China's Policy toward the Eastern Bloc up to the CPSU Twentieth Congress ... 50
   Political Developments in Hungary and Poland since the CPSU Twentieth Congress with Comparison to Chinese Domestic Political Developments ... 62
   Changes in China's Policy toward Eastern Europe after the CPSU Twentieth Congress ... 73
   China and the Crises in Poland and Hungary to Late October 1956 ... 83

3 **China's Diplomatic and Political Involvement in the Hungarian Crisis (October–November 1956)** ... 115
   Unexpected Crisis: The Chinese Delegation in Moscow ... 116
   Beijing's Efforts to Rescue Bloc Unity ... 135
   Toward a Maoist Formula of Interstate Relationships ... 152
   The Turning Point: 29 October ... 160
   China and the Second Soviet Intervention in Hungary ... 165
   The Chinese Solution: Repairing Communist Unity ... 180

4	**The Impact of the Hungarian Crisis on Chinese Domestic Politics (1956–1957)**	**195**
	The Hungarian Revolt and Chinese Domestic Problems	197
	The Hungarian Revolt and the Rectification Plan	213
	Inviting the Democratic Parties to Participate in Rectification	230
	About Face: From Blooming and Contending to the Anti-Rightist Campaign	247

Conclusion   265

Bibliography   275

Index   301

Introduction

The idea of Europe as the central battlefield of the Cold War as that face-off took shape between the two great powers has to be revised to take account of the emergence into international prominence of events in Asia in the early 1950s.[1] The Asian region, as an "other side" or front of the Cold War, has now started to enter into historiography with the end of the conflict and declassification of Chinese state documents, whose scrutiny promises to cast cold war history in a new light both globally and regionally. The development of the study of Communist China's Cold War history has more than any other historiographical development begun to contribute to a more integral and truly global Cold War history.[2]

---

1. On Europe as the origin and central battleground of the Cold War, see Antonio Varsori, "Reflections on the Origins of the Cold War," in Odd Arne Westad, ed., *Reviewing the Cold War: Approaches, Interpretations, and Theory* (London and Portland, OR: F. Cass, 2000), 281–302. On the emergence of the United States and USSR confrontations in Asia from the Western countries' foreign policy perspective, see Michael Schaller, *The American Occupation of Japan: The Origins of the Cold War in Asia* (Oxford University Press, 1987); Steven Hugh Lee, *Outposts of Empire: Korea, Vietnam, and the Origins of the Cold War in Asia, 1949–1954* (Montreal: McGill-Queen's University Press, 1996). On Cold War origins in Asia, see John Lewis Gaddis, *We Now Know: Rethinking Cold War History* (New York: Oxford, 1997), 54–84. On Communist China's foreign policy and the origin of the Cold War in Asia, see Chen Jian, *Mao's China and the Cold War* (Chapel Hill, NC: University of North Carolina Press, 2001), 1–144; Niu Jun, *Cong Yan'an zouxiang Shijie: Zhongguo gongchandang duiwai guanxi de qiyuan* [From Yan'an to the World: The Origins of the Chinese Communist Party (CCP) Foreign Relations] (Beijing: Zhonggongdangshi, 2008), 224–345; Yang Kuisong, *Zhongjian didai de geming: Guoji dabeijing xia kan Zhonggong chenggong zhi dao* [Revolution in the middle zone: On the success of the Chinese Communist Party in the international setting] (Taiyuan: Shanxi renmin, 2010), 469–541.

2. See the back cover of Gaddis, *We Now Know*. On the recent trends for Chinese scholars to write on the Cold War history on the basis of Chinese and other Eastern and Western sources, see Xia Yafeng, "The Study of Cold War Inter-

In Mao Zedong's words, 1956 was a year of "big events," both at home and abroad.³ The "secret speech" delivered by Soviet leader Nikita Khrushchev to the Communist Party of the Soviet Union's (CPSU) Twentieth Congress had, according to Mao, "opened the lid" on the repressiveness of the immediate postwar Soviet regimes, thereby "making a mess" in ideologically inspiring a wave of de-Stalinization marked by massive demonstrations in Poland and Hungary. These mass movements demanded from their governments the improvement of their countries' living standards and the safeguarding of national independence and political rights in the teeth of the Soviet Union.⁴ The Hungarian events, in particular, were more complicated than either a populist antisocialist protest or a form of anti-Soviet agitation, and the Chinese leaders exerted great effort in trying to apply the lessons of Hungary to their own domestic situation.⁵

The purpose of this volume is to make sense of the inner connection between China's political and diplomatic involvement in the Hungarian crisis and the influence this crisis had on China's domestic policy from late 1956 to 1957. In this short but very crucial period of time, Chinese domestic politics changed dramatically from the rhetorically inclusive and pluralistic "rectification" and

---

national History in China: A Review of the Last Twenty Years," *Journal of Cold War Studies*, 10, no. 1 (2008): 81–115; Zhi Liang, Xia Yafei, and Ming Chen, "ECNU-WWICS Occasional Paper: Recent Trends in the Study of Cold War History in China," Cold War International History Project, Woodrow Wilson International Center for Scholars (October 2012), occasional paper 1.

3. Liu Congwen ed., *Liu Shaoqii nianpu, 1898–1969* (hereinafter *LSN*) [A chronological record of Liu Shaoqi], 2 vols. (Beijing: Zhongyang wenxian, 1996), vol. 2: 809.

4. Wu Lengxi, *Shinian lunzhan, 1956–1966: ZhongSu guanxi huiyilu* [Ten-year polemical debate, 1956–1966: A memoir on Sino–Soviet relations] (Beijing: Zhongyang wenxian, 1999), 6. Wu Lengxi was then director of the New China News Agency and editor-in-chief of *People's Daily*, and he attended several Politburo Standing Committee meetings discussing the de-Stalinization issue. Mao repeated the same claim later on several occasions. Also see Chen, *Mao's China and the Cold War*, 64.

5. See Bo Yibo, *Ruogan zhongda juece yu shijian de huigu* [Review on a Certain Number of Crucial Decisions and Events (thereafter *Huigu*)], 2 vols. (Beijing: Remmin, 1997), 2: 597–99.

"hundred flowers" (HF) campaigns to the repressive and authoritarian Anti-Rightist Campaign, changes in which Chairman Mao's interpretation of the Hungarian crisis of 1956 played an essential role.⁶

This book takes advantage of the wealth of newly available archival material in opting for a domestic-centered method in studying the relations between China and the Hungarian crisis of 1956. Its particular focus lies with how the crisis prompted Mao to adopt a more aggressive agenda in promoting the socialist revolution and [effort of] reconstruction at home, at the same time emphasizing the necessity to keep hierarchical order within the communist camp against the background of the Cold War. This attention, while centrally devoted to China, nevertheless captures an international dimension of the Hungarian crisis to which insufficient attention has as yet been paid.⁷

---

6. For a good and brief introduction to the HF movement and the following Anti-Rightist campaign, see Merle Goldman, "The Party and the Intellectuals," in *The Cambridge History of China*. Vol. 14 (*CHOC* 14). *The People's Republic, Part 1: The Emergence of Revolutionary China, 1949–1965*, eds. Roderick MacFarquhar and John K. Fairbank (Cambridge: Cambridge University Press, 1987), 218–58.

7. Up to the 1990s, the books and articles on the Hungarian Revolution of 1956 written by either the Hungarian scholars or Western researchers rarely touched upon Chinese diplomatic and political involvement in the process of the events, let alone seeking to assess the impact of the October Revolution on the Chinese domestic scene throughout late 1956 to late 1957. János Radványi, a senior official in the Hungarian diplomatic service in 1956, published an article in 1970 recollecting his observation of the Chinese role in the 1956 Hungarian crisis. Radványi provides us with important information on the Chinese embassy's role—that of ambassador Hao Deqing, in particular—in Beijing's final judgment of the nature of the Hungarian events, as may now be confirmed by newly declassified Chinese Foreign Ministry archive. See Radványi, "The Hungarian Revolution and the Hundred Flowers Campaign," *China Quarterly*, 43 (July–September 1970): 127–29. Fortunately, several Chinese and foreign scholars have applied themselves to this topic, after the 1990s, gradually unveiling some of the interconnections between China and the Hungarian crisis of 1956; see Chen, *Mao's China and the Cold War*, 145–62, which is based on a paper with the same title delivered at the international conference "Cold War and Sino–Soviet Relations" in Beijing in 1997. As far as this author knows, Chen is the first Chinese-American scholar to write on the relation between China and the Hungarian October events. Hu Bo in the final chapter of his PhD dissertation dealing with the Hungarian revolt and the Cold War concludes less promisingly that China's role in the Hungarian events was "secondary." See his "Lengzhan yinying xia de Xiongyali shijian" (The Hungarian Crisis

The nature and sequence of the Hungarian Revolution of 1956, a major historical episode in the Cold War, continues to be debated,

---

under the Shadow of the Cold War), (PhD diss., East China Normal University, 1999), 118–27, a line expanded in the book emerging from his PhD dissertation, *Lengzhan yinying xia de Xiongyali shijian: Daguo de yingce yu hudong* [The Hungarian incident in the shadow of the Cold War: Great powers' responses and interactions] (Beijing: Zhongguo shehuikexue, 2004): 231–44. Mercy A. Kuo, meanwhile, argues: "The PRC's involvement in the Hungarian events can be seen as a seal of Beijing's equal footing with Moscow," in her book *Contending with Contradictions: China's Policy toward Soviet Eastern Europe and the Origins of the Sino-Soviet Split, 1953–1960* (New York: Lexington Books, 2001): 95–111. Shen Zhihua has published several essays discussing China's role in the Polish and Hungarian events of 1956 and the October crises' impacts on China's domestic politics up to 1957: "1956 nian shiyue weiji: Zhongguo de juece he yingxiang—BoXiong shijian yu Zhongguo yanjiu zhi yi' " [China's Role and Influence in the Revolts in Poland and Hungary in 1956: Studies on Polish and Hungarian Crises and China, part 1], *Lishi Yanjiu*, 2 (2005): 119–43; "Zhongguo dui DongOu shiyue weiji de fanying he sikao—'Boxiong shijian yu Zhongguo' yanjiu zhi er" (hereinafter "Fanying he sikao") [On the October crises in Eastern Europe: China's reaction and reflection—A Study of the Polish and Hungarian Incidents and China, Part 2], *Shixue Yuekan* 1 (2007): 75–85; "1957 nian Zhengfeng yundong shi ruhe kaishi de" [How was the rectification movement in 1957 started?], *Zhonggong dangshi yanjiu*, 6 (2008): 72–83; "China's Role and Influence in the Incidents in Poland and Hungary in 1956," *Social Sciences in China* 26, no. 3 (Summer 2005): 3–16; "Mao and the 1956 Soviet Military Intervention in Hungary," in *The 1956 Hungarian Revolution and the Soviet Bloc Countries: Reactions and Repercussions*, János M. Rainer et al. (Budapest: Institute for the History of the 1956 Hungarian Revolution, Historical Archives of Hungarian State Security, 2007), 24–37. Also see his book *Sikao yu xuanze: cong zhishifenzi huiyi dao fanyoupai yundong* [Reflections and choices: The consciousness of the Chinese intellectuals and the Anti-Rightist Campaign (1956–1957): The history of the People's Republic of China, Vol. 3] (Hong Kong: The Chinese University of Hong Kong, 2008), 369–608. Péter Vàmos discussed at length the impact of the Hungarian events on Mao's domestic and foreign policy, in his paper "Sino–Hungarian Relations and the 1956 Revolution" and dedicated a whole book to the same topic in Hungarian. See Vàmos, *Kína mellettünk?* [Is China with us?]. Both of Vàmos's publications made extensive use of the newly declassified Chinese foreign ministry archival documents. Lorenz M. Lüthi concludes that regardless of the actual influence the Chinese side had on the Soviet decision-making process in late October 1956, the CCP leadership's self-confidence was enhanced after Polish and Hungarian events. More meaningfully, Lüthi explores Chairman Mao's rejection of Khrushchev's de-Stalinization and peaceful coexistence policies in the wake of the Polish October and the Hungarian Revolution. Lüthi further examines the impact of the Eastern-bloc crises on Chinese domestic politics up to the summer of 1957. See Lorenz M. Lüthi, *The Sino–Soviet Split: Cold War in the Communist World* (Princeton, NJ, and Oxford: Princeton University Press, 2008): 57–74.

with these considerations playing to current attempts to redefine Cold War history more inclusively, pulling into focus interactions between the great powers and local politics. In Hungary, the majority of archival sources on the 1956 Hungarian Revolution are now available to scholarship, joining the post-90s declassification of many other depositories around the globe. In 1989–1990, an institute for the history of the 1956 Hungarian Revolution was established, aiming to draw the attention of local and international historians. Similarly, a number of Polish, Czechoslovak, and Yugoslav archival documents have been discovered and released.[8] Even some Soviet sources, which are of the utmost importance in understanding Soviet decision-making and action during the crisis, have gradually been opened to scrutiny.[9] As a result of declassification trends in East-Central Europe, as well as the release of numerous Western sources on 1956 during the latter part of the 1980s, historians have

---

8. In Hungary, most archival sources on 1956 can be found in Magyar Országos Levéltár (MOL) [the Hungarian National Archive]. Besides the Hungarian National Archive and archives in Russia, Cold War historians can also find useful materials on the Hungarian crisis of 1956 in documents preserved in the Czech Republic, Poland, former East Germany, and the United States: for example, the Military History Archive and Central National Archives of the Czech Republic; der DDR im Bundesarchiv (SAPMDB) [Eastern Germany Communist Archive] in Berlin and the National Security Archive in Washington, D.C. For a collection of documents translated into English on 1956 Hungary whose historical materials derive mainly from Russia, Hungary, and Western democratic countries, see Csaba Békés and Malcolm Byrne, *The 1956 Hungarian Revolution: A History in Documents* (Budapest and New York: Central European University Press, 2002). Making extensive use of archival source materials, scholars have made significant efforts in writing the history of Soviet bloc states during the Cold War, on their relations with the former Soviet Union, and on their foreign policies; see, for example, Gyorgy Gyarmati and Janos M Rainer, *A Captive Nation in the Soviet Empire, 1944–1989* (Boulder, CO: East European Monographs, 2008); Tibor Valuch and Gyorgy Gyarmati, *Hungary under Soviet Domination: 1944–1989* (Boulder, CO: East European Monographs, 2010); László Borhi, *Hungary in the Cold War, 1945–1956: Between the United States and the Soviet Union* (Budapest: Central European University Press, 2004); a complete history of Poland under Communism during the Cold War, see Anthony Kemp-Welch, *Poland under Communism: A Cold War History* (Cambridge: Cambridge University Press, 2008).

9. For an article introducing these archives from the Russian side, see Csaba Békés, "New Findings on the 1956 Hungarian Revolution," *CWIHP Bulletin* (hereinafter *Bulletin*) 2 (1992): 1–3.

already produced books and articles presenting hitherto unknown data, important evidence, and various interpretations.[10] In the introductory essay to his authoritative translation and annotation of the so-called Malin Notes of key Kremlin meetings during the crises, Mark Kramer of Harvard University examines how the Soviet leadership responded to the implicit threat of the dissolution of the communist empire during the 1956 crises.[11] In his analysis of the Soviet decision-making processes before and during the October crises, Kramer found that although the Soviets had made advance preparations in military terms to maintain, defend, or even restore the socialist order in the Eastern European states, the Kremlin leadership became more and more reluctant to use armed force without the utmost certainty that such a course was necessary.[12] In fact, it was Moscow's hesitation over using military

---

10. Alexander Stykalin, "The Hungarian Crisis of 1956: The Soviet Role in the Light of New Archival Documents," *Cold War History*, 2, no. 1 (October 2001): 113-44. On the Soviet decision-making process as illuminated by Russian archives, see Mark Kramer,"Hungary and Poland 1956: Khrushchev's CPSU CC Presidium Meeting on Eastern European Crises, 24 October 1956," *Bulletin*, 5 (1995), 1: 50-56; Kramer, "New Evidence on Soviet Decision-Making and the 1956 Polish and Hungarian Crises," *Bulletin*, 8-9 (1996/1997): 358-84. For a detailed introduction to Hungarian scholars' interpretations and the policies and impact of Western powers on the 1956 Hungarian Crisis, see Terry Cox, ed., *Hungary 1956—Forty Years On* (London: Frank Cass Publishers, 1997); Jenö Györkei and Miklós Horváth, eds., *Soviet Military Intervention in Hungary 1956* (Budapest: Central European University Press, 1999).

11. V. N. Malin, head of the CPSU General Department, attended the Soviet Presidium meetings in the fall of 1956 taking notes, which "constitute [...] the only known contemporaneous record of the key sessions of late October and early November at which Kremlin leaders went back and forth over whether to pull out from Hungary or reintroduce new troops," *Bulletin* 8-9 (1996/1997): 356; for the notes, see V. N. Malin, "Working Notes from the Session of the CPSU CC Presidium on 26 October 1956," *Bulletin* 8-9 (1996/1997): 389-92. The Malin Notes were also published in English in Békés and Byrne, *The 1956 Hungarian Revolution*. For another collection of multinational historical documents on the Hungarian 1956 events, see Békés et al., eds., *The Hidden History of Hungary 1956: A Compendium of Declassified Documents* (Budapest—Washington, DC: the National Security Archive, 1996).

12. Kramer, "Hungary and Poland," 54-56; "New Evidence," 375-84; Kramer, "The 'Malin Notes' on the Crises in Hungary and Poland, 1956," *Bulletin*, 8-9 (1996/1997): 393-410.

means in Hungary that gave Beijing the chance to maneuver the Kremlin leadership into admitting the inequality in Soviet-satellite relations. In doing so, the Chinese side aimed to dent Soviet prestige and power inside the bloc and thus to enhance its own authority and influence internationally.

A range of new findings and interpretations of Hungarian scholars of the 1956 incident can be found in two essay collections published in the late 1990s.[13] *Soviet Military Intervention in Hungary 1956* discloses valuable new material on the organization, command, strategy, and tactics of the Soviet armed forces that invaded Hungary in 1956. On the basis of study of the former Soviet archives, this book has, among other points, helped explain the scale of military operations, precisely documenting the irrationally large size of the forces. Csaba Békés, in his article "The 1956 Hungarian Revolution and World Politics," has attempted to reexamine the reaction of the big powers to the Hungarian crisis, prising open newly accessible West European and former Soviet archives to illuminate their high-level decision-making processes, especially as these bore on considerations of international diplomacy.[14] In his recent biography of János Kádár, Huszár Tibor has reinterpreted the Hungarian crisis of 1956 from 23 October to 4 November by emphasizing Kádár's personal role in the Kremlin's reorientations of view with regard to the riots in Hungary. Tibor's book was enabled by interviews with former diplomats, and the memoirs of diplomats and top party officials, which taken together recontextualize the 1956 revolution through focusing on the influence of a particular Hungarian leader.[15] Further, relevant articles and documents have been published by the Institute for the History of the 1956 Hungar-

---

13. Cox, *Hungary 1956*; Györkei and Horváth, *Soviet Military Intervention*.
14. See Csaba Békés, "The 1956 Hungarian Revolution and World Politics" *The Hungarian Quarterly* 36 (1995): 109–21.
15. Tibor Huszár, *Kádár János Politikai Életrajza* [A political biography of János Kádár] (Budapest: Szabad Tér Kiadó-Kossuth Kiadó, 2001), 300–10. For a good English biography of János Kádár, see Roger Gough, *A Good Comrade: János Kádár, Communism and Hungary* (New York: I.B. Tauris, 2006).

ian Revolution and in the Cold War International History Project Bulletin.[16]

Exploiting previously unavailable primary source material from multiple Eastern Bloc countries and new evidence from U.S. sources, Johanna Granville in her latest volume paints a complex picture of the interaction of internal and external factors in shaping the Hungarian Revolution as it played out beyond the confines of Hungary and the Soviet Bloc. As she points out in the foreword of her book, the Hungarian Revolution was the first large-scale rebellion opposing the Soviet Union within its own communist camp: "the first war" between socialist states and "the first domino" in a process that resulted ultimately in the Soviet Union's loss of hegemony over East Europe in 1989. Granville argues that the Khrushchev leadership was by no means a rational actor in regard to its decision-making during the crisis. In addition, despite the dominant position of the Soviet Union, the East European communist states to some extent and at various times were able to manipulate or influence their boss in the Kremlin.[17] After Poznan, the Polish leadership took the initiative of seeking to forge closer political contacts with the Chinese, soliciting Beijing's support for the Polish leadership's efforts to wrest a greater measure of national self-determination in domestic affairs from the Soviet Union. Before the Chinese leadership came to the conclusion by the end of October that the nature of the Hungarian Revolution was "counter-revolutionary," Mao and his colleagues had identified Poland and Hungary's requirements for internal autonomy as a good opportu-

---

16. Békés, "New Findings," 1–3; Kramer, "Hungary and Poland," 50–56; "The 'Malin Notes,'" 385–410; Vladislav M. Zubok: "Look What Chaos in the Beautiful Socialist Camp! Deng Xiaoping and the Sino–Soviet Split 1956–1963," *Bulletin* 10 (1998): 150–55.

17. Johanna C. Granville, *The First Domino: International Decision Making during the Hungarian Crisis of 1956* (College Station, Texas: Texas A&M University Press, 2004). This is the first English monograph on the Hungarian crisis of 1956 drawing on new archival collections from multiple Eastern-bloc countries. For a comparison of the Polish and Hungarian crises, see Granville, "1956 Reconsidered: Why Hungary and Not Poland?" *The Slavonic and East European Review*, 4 (2002): 656–87.

nity to contest the Soviets' unquestionable authority in the Eastern Bloc.

However thoughtful and resourceful much historiographic work on the Hungarian crisis since the end of the Cold War, few studies from the present period have dealt with the inner connection between China's political and diplomatic involvement in the crisis and the crisis's knock-on effects on Chinese Communist Party (CCP) domestic policy thereafter. This deficiency is doubtless due to the extremely rigid criteria governing the release of party and state documents in China. Moreover, most Chinese scholars and historians seem reluctant to touch upon the Polish–Hungarian crises, the latter in particular, with discussions of the subject in relation to Chinese domestic politics remaining virtually taboo even in the 1990s.[18]

To begin to get a sense of work in this field, in his essay "Beijing and the Hungarian Crisis of 1956" delivered during the 1997 Beijing conference on the Cold War and Sino–Soviet relations (later revised as a chapter of his influential book *Mao's China and the Cold War*), Chen Jian makes the tantalizing suggestion that the crisis of 1956, and Beijing and Moscow's handling of it, exposed profound contradictions between communism as a set of utopian ideals and as practical human experience. The momentum of international communism faltered after Budapest, against Mao's deepest-held beliefs, which had been to advocate and defend Soviet military intervention.[19] Shen Zhihua's essay, "China's Role and Influence in the Revolts in Poland and Hungary in 1956," draws primarily on Soviet archival sources together with the author's interviews with the former Chinese diplomats to Hungary and East European states in the 1950s, to illuminate Chinese involvement in the Hungarian crisis in October 1956 from the inside, as it were. Shen reaches the view that

---

18. The official Chinese definition of the Hungarian Revolution during Mao's era was that the episode represented a "counterrevolutionary" event. For the limited amount of materials or studies on Hungary in history studies in China, see Shen, "1956 nian shiyue weiji," 119–22.

19. Chen, *Mao's China and the Cold War*, 160–62.

"China played a dominant role in both pulling the Soviet troops out of Budapest and subsequently bringing them back."[20]

As Chen Jian has indicated, as far as China's domestic situation was concerned, Beijing's attitude toward the Hungarian crisis reflected Mao's persistent belief that "class struggle continued to exist in a socialist country." In other words, the establishment of a socialist state did not extinguish such struggle, which demanded a ceaseless effort of engagement and structural transformation, or "continuous revolution," on the party as it worked in the fields of politics and ideology.[21] Chen further suggests that the crises in Poland and Hungary also enhanced Mao's and the CCP leadership's consciousness of China as a global exemplar of a large-scale proletarian revolution that had been actually carried through, unlike the apparently incomplete projects in Europe. Promoting a self-defined concept of equality with other nations and polities, Beijing sought to displace Moscow from its central position as embodying the archetypal proletarian revolution.[22]

As far as China's diplomatic and political involvement in the Hungarian crisis goes, Shen's essay views China's involvement in the Soviet decision to "suppress the reactionary elements in Hungary," as the CCP leaders so cast them, as highly significant, even decisive. By "decisive," Shen means less that China tipped the USSR's hand in directing its intervention than that the CCP was able to use the Polish and Hungarian crises as bargaining chips in return for Soviet acknowledgment that the preeminent state had blundered in the past in its conduct of Soviet–East European relations. Once the Chinese formed the view that there was a real danger of Hungary renouncing socialism and withdrawing from the communist camp, Mao and his colleagues swung behind the Soviet military incursion and helped the Kremlin restore hierarchical bloc unity.[23]

While duly examining China's involvement in the Soviet leadership's final decision to suppress the Hungarian Revolt, my analysis

---
20. Shen, "1956 nian shiyue weiji," 119–43.
21. Chen, *Mao's China and the Cold War,* 161.
22. Ibid., 148, 161–62.
23. Shen, "1956 nian shiyue weiji," 130–40.

in this study is more concerned with offering a critical evaluation of Maoist China's interbloc policies in the period from the fall of 1956 to the end of 1957. My argument is that Beijing's advocacy of equality and internal autonomy against Soviet "big power chauvinism" in the communist camp and its call for a movement away from a pattern of Stalinist dependency in interstate relations, represent strategic expedients on the part of Chairman Mao to weaken the USSR's prestige and ultimately accede to the leadership of world communism himself. The apparent desire of the Hungarian people to break free from Stalinist rule led the Chinese most immediately to support the Soviets' military intervention. Chinese efforts to help the Soviets restore bloc unity after the Hungarian crisis demonstrate Mao's perception that communist camp integrity had to be guaranteed by relations of dominance, with the strongest state framing definitions of communism and providing a general pattern of development, which would remain Stalinist in essence. It is conceivable that Mao saw China in the place of this preeminent country. There is no evidence, meanwhile, that the Chairman ever seriously considered that equal interstate relationships were applicable to the communist world. On the contrary, as Mao understood it, the splintering effect the Hungarian revolt had on bloc unity reaffirmed the essential truth that some kind of Stalinist interstate system was a necessity inside the camp.

Chinese domestic politics from late 1956 to the end of 1957 was a period of extreme ideological turmoil in which the CCP's policy underwent changes of direction with a frequency unknown in the late forties and early fifties. The motives for Mao's many changes in policy over these two years can be hard to make out. Some have accused the leader of "a kind of despotic capriciousness and arbitrariness" in seeking to open up the CCP to new influences, judging that Mao was mostly playing a power game involving the balancing of various factions.[24] In this study, I shall argue that Mao's private

---

24. Benjamin Schwartz, "Thoughts on the Late Mao—Between Total Redemption and Utter Frustration," in *The Secret Speeches of Chairman Mao: From the Hundred Flowers to the Great Leap Forward*, ed. Roderick MacFarquhar et al. (Cambridge, MA: Harvard University Press, 1989), 19–22.

analysis of Hungary, whatever his internal factioneering, was highly critical of the Hungarian state, and particularly of Mátyás Rákosi's, its previous leader, inflexible tactics of using coercive means to solve domestic "contradictions" after Hungary's transition to state socialism. Mao further judged that this error arose naturally in the context of any Stalinist state–party governance. Looking back to the Chinese Communist strategies of bringing together a majority to secure certain political goals formulated in the Yan'an era, Mao opted for soft methods, such as party rectification and HF, as putative solutions to domestic problems. With all due respect to Mao's foresight, there is no evidence that he anticipated the undesirable consequences of the Hungarian Revolution, that it would in effect induce leading Chinese statesmen and intellectuals, together with students, to consider the reform of Maoist policies of suppression against certain social groups in the form of mass campaigns, going as far as proposing the overhaul of the means of governance and political system. It turned out that the Chairman could barely tolerate such internal views or their external sources. The way was thus clear for Mao to give up his previous plan of building a socialism with Chinese characteristics through cooperation with the intelligentsia, instead turning to the more doctrinaire and technical production plans of the Great Leap Forward and to long-term campaigns to "remold thought," placing any potential dissident intellectual firmly under the thumb of the communist regime.[25]

This study was made possible by the study of materials from

---

25. The CCP's contradictory policy toward the intellectuals had been present since the Yan'an rectification campaign in the early 1940s; see Gao Hua, *Hongtaiyang shi zenyang shengqide* [How did the sun rise over Yan'an? A history of the rectification movement] (hereinafter *Hongtaiyang*) (Hong Kong: Chinese University of Hong Kong, 2000), 313–427. For an analysis of the party's contradictory approach to the intellectuals, see Merle Goldman, "The Party and the Intellectuals," 218–58. If Gao Hua's *Hongtaiyang* focuses on the "human drama" of "the rise of Mao Zedong" in the process of Yan'an rectification, then Franz Shurmann's writing provides extensive details on the "systematic structures" constituted by the CCP, or on "the New China" constructed with Maoism, the party, and the cadre; see Franz Shurmann, *Ideology and Organization in Communist China* (Berkeley, CA: University of California Press, 1966). Also see Maurice Meisner, *Mao's China and After: A History of the People's Republic* (New York: Free Press, 1999), 31–54.

several countries and archives, China in particular, including party documents and personal collections, Chinese Foreign Ministry archives (CFMA), leaders' papers, contemporary newspapers, and interviews with Chinese diplomats to Eastern Europe in the 1950s and 1960s. From 2004 until the present, the Chinese foreign ministry (CFM) has declassified more than 65,000 items from its diplomatic records for the period between 1949 and 1965, including records of top Chinese leaders' conversations with Eastern Bloc statesmen before and after the October 1956 crises and communications between the foreign ministry and the Chinese embassy in Hungary, which critically informed my understanding of the leading concerns of the CCP's main concerns over Eastern Europe. At the same time, this study also relies heavily on archival materials released in Russia since the early 1990s and on some firsthand Hungarian documents relaying Sino-Hungarian communications. A large number of Russian archives relevant to the Soviet Bloc and the 1956 October crises have been translated into Chinese and have been made available to general readers in an edited collection on Soviet archives.[26]

This volume consists of four chapters, together with an introduction and conclusion. In Chapter 1, I examine how a socialist China had been established in the late 1940s and early 1950s under Mao's leadership largely following the pattern of Stalinist socialism in the Soviet Union and corresponding Eastern European processes of economic Stalinization. The chapter describes in detail certain events in the early phase of the People's Republic of China's (PRC's) transplanting of the Stalinist model to Chinese society, analyzing how Mao made full use of his politically and ideologically dominant status inside the CCP to push forward a radical program of state reconstruction, which largely defied Stalin's own moderate ad-

---

26. Shen Zhihua, ed., *Sulian lishi dang'an xuanbian* [Selected Historical Soviet Archives] (hereinafter as *SHSA*), 34 vols. (Beijing: Shehui kexue wenxian, 2002); also see Shen Zhihua and Li Danhui, eds., *ZhongSu guanxi: Eguo dang'an fuyinjian huibian* (weikan) [Sino-Soviet Relations: Collected Copies of Russian Archives: unpublished version] (Center of Cold War History Studies, China East Normal University, 2002).

vice based on acknowledging the dominance of the paradigm of people's democracy in the period following World War II. Attention also is given to Chinese policies vis-à-vis the Eastern Bloc during Stalin's final years and after; although the Chinese regime wanted to learn from the socialist transformation in the Eastern European states, Chairman Mao also wished to keep the Soviet Bloc at some sort of arm's length both politically and institutionally, preventing outside events from disrupting Chinese socialist transformation. But China's self-imposed distance from the Soviet Bloc also, ironically, signaled Mao's view of his country as a future leader of world revolution. Therefore, after years of efforts to catch up with the people's democracies and the USSR in domestic reconstruction, the basic completion of the socialist form of the state based on a Soviet model by late 1955 meant that, for Mao, the time was ripe for a strengthened China to involve itself more deeply in inner-bloc matters.

Chapter 2 addresses the different effects that Khrushchev's secret speech had on the Eastern Bloc on the one hand, and on Mao's Communist China on the other, reviewing the domestic instabilities in Hungary and Poland before and after the CPSU Twentieth Congress, and weighing the forces and circumstances that gave rise to a new program emphasizing a socialism with distinctively Chinese characteristics after February 1956 (however much it may also have been marked with Chinese limitations). This section begins to consider the domestic political dynamics of China's growing involvement in Eastern Bloc affairs in the post–CPSU Twentieth Congress atmosphere. In taking the temperature of the unexpected (and, to the CCP, unwelcome) consequences of the anti-Stalinist and nationalist foment incited by the CPSU Twentieth Congress in both Hungary and Poland, it provides a detailed analysis of the Hungarian leadership's moves to solve the domestic problems through calling in Soviet power, in strong contrast to the Poles' efforts to keep a hand on the tiller themselves, which consigned the country to a state of disorder and uncertainty that incubated insurrection. On the Chinese side, meanwhile, given the considerable degree of ideological and political autonomy the CCP enjoyed from the Soviet Union, the CCP leadership did not feel personally threatened by the Stalin episode but rather saw it as a good opportunity to strike out for a distinctive Chinese socialism aiming to surpass the achievements of the Soviets and to introduce the Maoist experience to the broader international communist community.

Chapter 3 takes up the story from the Chinese diplomatic and political intervention in the Polish and then Hungarian crises in the second half of October, advancing the view that Mao and his colleagues sought to parlay the events into an opportunity to secure a greater measure of equality with the Soviet Union. The events precipitated a series of unexpected policy changes not only on the Soviet side but also on the part of the Chinese largely due to the pace and complexity of domestic developments in Hungary. These investigations assess the special role played by the Chinese in the Soviet decision to pull out its troops from Hungary, asking how and why Beijing shifted its diplomatic policy from opposing "big-state chauvinism" to advocating a Soviet Bloc unity in such short order in late October 1956. The chapter next explores why it became so important for Mao to emphasize the ultimate value of the Stalinist pattern of interbloc relations as the perception, in Moscow and Beijing, of the potential unruliness of the bloc's ideological and institutional diversity without a proper framework of management brought the two major communist powers closer together.

Chapter 4 turns to the influence of the Hungarian Revolution on the development of Communist China from late 1956 to the end of 1957, a crucial prelude to the famous 1958 "Great Leap Forward" campaign. It examines the domestic circumstances in which Mao gradually become aware of the potential dangers involved in the call for reforms in both economic and political realms even as the Chairman was vigorously advocating for political relaxations, like the HF, with which he most likely harbored serious misgivings at a time of disquiet among the intellectuals over the Hungarian events. In pursuing these issues I examine the party officials' misinterpretation of Mao's purposes in continuing the HF policy and the intellectuals' and students' idealistic hopes of the center's top-down reform. Mao justified his speedy truncation of the permission extended to outsiders to criticize party work with the excuse that some counterrevolutionary elements had conspired to provoke Hungarian-style revolts in China, though it is more plausible that the key element was Mao's own concern that the legitimacy of the unlimited power and ideological correctness of his leadership would start to be called into question.

In the conclusion, I review the main findings of this thesis, arguing that the idea that China sought to reform the Stalinist pattern of interbloc relationships after Khrushchev's denunciation of him is seriously misconceived and fails to square with the actual conduct of Chinese foreign policy in relation to Hungary, as well as with the evolution of Chinese domestic politics between 1956 and 1957. Despite the fact that China's status inside the Soviet Bloc had been significantly enhanced with no diminution in the strength of the Sino–Soviet alliance in the immediate aftermath of Hungary, the radical policies adopted by Mao at home and on the international front after the failure of HF provoked a double crisis in China's relationship with the Soviet-led bloc and in China's domestic path of development. There seems little alternative to the depressing summary observation that the Hungarian events taught the Chairman and his successors that any attempt at political reform was only likely to prompt a collapse of the communist regime.

CHAPTER 1

Communist China and the Communist World
(1949–1956)

The final triumph of the Communists in the Chinese civil war in 1949 significantly strengthened their faith in a teleological conception of history, promising unprecedented levels of abundance and happiness for China and the world. The communists were confident in their ability comprehensively to restructure not merely their former revolutionary base areas but also society as a whole through a wholesale redistribution of power, wealth, and status among China's various social groups. Committed to these utopian principles, as unchallenged top leader of the state and party, Mao Zedong prophesied several months in advance of the founding of the People's Republic of China: "We should not only be capable of destroying an old world; but also be capable of creating a new one."[1]

While the politically successful examples of Soviet socialization and the construction of a basis for socialism in Eastern Europe certainly inspired Mao to frame a Chinese Communist agenda, before the start of the 1950s international pressures and domestic difficulties had constrained the Chairman from taking radical means in aiming to secure revolutionary victory. Externally, Mao was concerned about the imminence of an imperialist attack on China led by the United States, understanding international relations as he

---

1. Tony Saich and Benjamin Yang, *The Rise to Power of the Chinese Communist Party: Documents and Analysis* (New York: M.E. Sharpe, 1996), 1346; see also Feng Xigang, "Maoci shuangbi: Yongxueci yu youyongci" [Two: Praise snow and on swimming], *Suibi* [Essay], 3 (2007), 16.

did through the prism of class analysis.[2] Internally, the domestic situation in Mao's view was highly complicated, with the most pressing task for the new government being to recover from the disastrous social and economic dislocation wrought by the war, particularly in the big cities, where the Communists previously had little direct experience. To Mao, apart from the unfinished military takeover and unsolved socioeconomic problems, the newly liberated areas in the south, together with the cities, posed a political problem insofar as their social structures continued to shelter unreconstructed "imperialists" or remnants of the Guomindang (GMD), who could conceivably rebel against the regime.[3] Therefore, in the years immediately following 1949, Mao prioritized consolidating party power as a preliminary to the further social transformation that would bring in a communist society. In line with Mao's caution, the resolution of the second plenum of the CCP CC Seventh Congress held in March 1949 proclaimed that "our principles must be firm, and we must also have all the necessary and permissible flexibility to realize these principles." These words sanctioned a long-run program of social transformation, defining the 1949 victory as "the first step on a March of 10,000 *li*" in which "the road after revolution" was acknowledged as being "even longer and the work even greater and harder."[4]

---

2. Odd Arne Westad, ed., *Brothers in Arms: The Rise and Fall of the Sino-Soviet Alliance 1945–1963* (Palo Alto, CA: Stanford University Press, and Washington, DC: Woodrow Wilson Center Press, 1998), 167.

3. Junshi kexueyuan et al., eds., *Mao Zedong junshi wenji* [Mao Zedong's selected works on military affairs] (Beijing: Junshikexue; zhongyang wenxian, 1993), 5: 91–92, 670; Zhonggong zhongyang wenxian yanjiushi [CCP Central Committee Document Research Office], ed., *Mao Zedong wenji* (hereinafter *MWJ*) [Collected works of Mao Zedong] (Beijing: Renmin, 1996), 5: 308–9.

4. Saich and Yang, *The Rise to Power*, 1344–46. For a thoughtful comparative study of the state breakdown in Asia in the modern period and a discussion on China's revolution to build a "new" state, see Jack A. Goldstone, *Revolution and Rebellion in the Early Modern World* (Berkeley: University of California Press, 1993), 349–498. For his later critical thinking of the European-centered "early modern" world, a historical view that had significantly affected Communist China leadership's perception of modernization, see "The Problem of the 'Early Modern' World," *Journal of the Economic and Social History of the Orient* 41, no. 3 (1998): 49–56.

Stalin's assessment of the national-democratic nature of the Chinese Revolution, and his advice on the design and construction of the Chinese regime, also played a crucial role in the CCP's adoption of a gradualist line.[5] Stalin's China policy was in fact quite straightforward, in that he presumed that the gradual pattern of political–economic transformation developed in the Eastern Bloc in the mid-1940s would be applicable to China with certain adjustments (such as a firmer unification with the national bourgeoisie in the Chinese case). This general pattern was reflected as early as in April 1948 in Stalin's advice to Mao to settle initially on a relatively moderate economic policy rather than committing to rapid economic socialization before political conditions were mature.[6] In Stalin's mind, China was not ready for socialism *tout court*, not even in the form of the dictatorship of the proletariat. It should first form a multiparty coalition government before establishing an "elected" body that would adopt a written constitution probably with close reference to the experience of the Eastern European countries in founding their states after the Second World War under the guidance of the Kremlin. This in turn, Stalin argued, would provide a legitimate basis on which one-party rule could develop.[7] Given the

---

5. "Liu Shaoqi's Report to the CPSU CC Politburo, July 4, 1949" (with Stalin's handwritten notations) in Westad, *Brothers in Arms*, 304–5, in which Liu clearly conveyed to Stalin that the CCP leadership absolutely agreed with his assessment of the nature of the Chinese new democratic state and the new government. Also see "Liu Shaoqi's Report to the CPSU CC Politburo, July 4, 1949," in Niu Jun, "XinZhongguo waijiao de xingcheng jiqi zhuyao tezheng" [The formation of diplomatic policy in China and its characteristics], *Lishi yanjiu* [History studies] (1999), 5: 8; Liu Jianping, "Sugong yu Zhongguo gongchandang renmin minzhu zhuanzheng lilun de queli" [The communist party of the Soviet Union and the formation of Chinese communist people's democratic dictatorship theory], *Lishi yanjiu* [History studies] (1998), 1: 78–96.
6. "Telegram, Stalin to Mao Zedong, April 20, 1948," in Westad, *Brothers in Arms*, 298–99.
7. Li Hua-Yu, *Mao and the Economic Stalinization of China, 1948–1953* (Harvard Cold War Studies Book Series. Lanham: Rowman & Littlefield, 2006), 3–4; for a comparison of China's pattern of economic planning in the consolidation years with that of the postwar Eastern Bloc states, see Alexander Eckstein, "Conditions and Prospects for Economic Growth in Communist China," *World Politics: A Quarterly Journal of International Relations* 7, no. 1 (October 1954): 255–83. Also see his "Economic Growth and Change in China: A Twenty-Year Perspective,"

CCP leaders' own view of their regime as fragile, Mao and his top colleagues had no reason to buck the practical and ideological importance of "leaning to Moscow" against the background of the Cold War by disregarding the Kremlin's counsel.[8]

The term in which the People's Republic of China was designated, then, was New Democracy, a form of state organization introduced by Mao based on Comintern advice after the beginning of the second phase of the Sino-Japanese war in 1940. This was the same concept formulated in 1945 to define the political identity of the states in Eastern Europe that evolved under Moscow's tutelage. The CCP held back on announcing its intention of establishing a dictatorship of the proletariat, instead stressing a multiclass and multiparty political structure and a mixed economy to bring together all possible resources.[9] In general, the policy of the Chinese Communists in the immediate years before and after the founding

---

China Quarterly 54, no. 1 (1973): 211–41; "National Income and Capital Formation in Hungary, 1900–1950," *Review of Income and Wealth* 5, no. 1 (1955): 152–223.

8. "Liu Shaoqi's Report to the CPSU CC Politburo, July 4, 1949," in Westad, *Brothers in Arms*, 304–5. For the Chinese leadership's efforts in adjusting domestic policies, including party construction and economic planning, in accordance with Stalin's advice for the purpose of establishing a real alliance with the Soviet Union, see Andrei Ledovsky, "Migaoyang de fuhua mimi shiming 1949nian 1–2yue" [Mikoyan's Secret Mission to China in January and February 1949], translated by Li Yuzhen, *Dangde wenxian* [Party Documents] (1995), 6: 81–84; (1996), 1: 90–96; English version: "Mikoyan's Secret Mission to China in January and February 1949," *Far Eastern Affairs*, no. 2 (1995): 72–94; no. 3 (1995): 74–90. For Russian recollection of Liu Shaoqi's visit to Moscow, see Andrei Ledovsky, "The Moscow Visit of a Delegation of the Communist Party of China in June to August 1949 (First Installment)," *Far Eastern Affairs* 4 (1996): 64–86; 5 (1996): 84–97. For the Chinese side's account, see Shi Zhe, *Zai lishi juren shenbian: Shi Zhe huiyilu* [At the side of historical giants: Shi Zhe's memoirs], edited by Li Haiwen. (Beijing: Zhongyang wenxian, 1996), 402–24.

9. Mao admitted that his New Democracy concept had been established on "Stalin's theories" in the 1940s. For a good analysis of China's New Democracy and its connection with the guidance from the Comintern and the Soviet Union, see Yang Kuisong, "Mao Zedong weishenme fangqi Xinminzhuzhuyi-guanyu Eguomoshi de yingxiang" [Why did Mao Zedong give up New Democracy?—On the influence of the Soviet Model], *Jindaishi yanjiu*, 4(1997): 139–53; *Makesizhuyi Zhongguohua de lishi jincheng* [The Historical Process of China's Nationalizing Marxism] (Kaifeng: Henan renmin, 1994), 309–23.

of the new state involved much more caution and concessions to the finely balanced situations both at home and abroad than is apparent from the communist line formally taken from 1952 onward, despite the party's consistent ideological commitment to "the construction of Communism" and their doggedness in seeking to extirpate their class enemies.[10]

It is perhaps possible to stick one's neck out at this point to venture the necessarily ex post hypothesis that, had the Chinese Communists only been able to adhere to the gradualist policies they formulated in the early years, then the Chinese domestic situation in the second half of the 1950s would have been better than that in the Soviet Bloc states, which had seen the imposition by force of a Soviet social structure in the Stalin years. As the history of the PRC over the course of the 1950s in fact demonstrates, however, the Chinese Communist regime soon abandoned its principles of a gradual transition consolidating New Democracy policies, moving instead to a rapid collectivization on the Soviet model. In the second half of the 1950s, the Chinese Communists began to formulate, in their eyes, a better and faster path than the Soviets' toward achieving a decisive socioeconomic and political shift, to which, they believed, the other Communist Bloc states would ultimately aspire. If the Eastern European parties effectively found themselves in a Stalinist "dilemma of the one alternative," the Chinese Communists had greater room for maneuver in professing compliance with the Stalinist model while actually developing it according to a more radical pattern justified by a claim for the national distinctiveness of the Chinese revolution.[11]

---

10. Saich and Yang, *The Rise to Power*, 1373–74. Mao in this article summarized the three main experiences of the party during the previous twenty-eight years: (1) "A party with discipline, armed with the theories of Marx, Engels, Lenin, and Stalin, employing the method of self-criticism and linked up closely with the masses"; (2) "an army led by such a party"; (3) "a united front of various revolutionary strata and groups led by such a party."
11. On Eastern European communist parties' dilemma of "one alternative," see Zbigniew K. Brzezinski, *The Soviet Bloc: Unity and Conflict* (Cambridge, MA: Harvard University Press, 1960), 167; for a later study on the postwar relations between Stalin's Soviet Union and the Eastern European states, see Silvio Pons,

MAO'S COMMUNIST CHINA IN THE MAKING (1949-1953)

Directed by the cautious and gradualist political line defined by the collective CCP leadership and agreed to by the Chairman, much of the economic and infrastructural work led by Mao's second-in-command Liu Shaoqi and Zhou Enlai's government proceeded in orderly fashion typically overseen by officials with some specialized knowledge of economic issues. Yet by late 1952 these cautious and incremental policies were rejected, with the Chairman coming formally to reassess the New Democracy as insufficient to ground Chinese socialism on the Soviet pattern. In order to unite the leadership behind his new thinking, the Chairman launched sharp attacks both on gradualist socioeconomic development programs and on the leaders advocating and supporting them.[12] Liu Shaoqi and his colleagues came under explicit political attack from the newly promoted head of the State Planning Commission (SPC) Gao Gang (also recently raised or "elected" to the politburo) and party organization department chief Rao Shushi. While Mao in the end decided to retain Liu and purge Gao, he successfully leveled a fair amount of criticism against Liu's gradualist policies. The upshot of these disagreements and power struggles was an ambitious "socialist transformation" program that diverged markedly from the New Democracy line in bearing close resemblance to the Soviet type of socialization developed by Stalin in the 1920s and 1930s.

How should we account for the dramatic shifts in Chinese economic and, indeed, general political policy, in the 1950s from a "realistic" line to one that led to overreaching and catastrophe? On this issue, we should note, first of all (taking Mao Zedong's absolute preeminence in the party into account) the evolution in the Chairman's

---

"Stalin and the European Communists after World War Two (1943–1948)," *Past & Present* 210, suppl. 6 (2011): 121–38.

12. Pang Xianzhi and Jin Chongji, eds. *Mao Zedong zhuan (1949–1976)* (hereinafter *Maozhuan*) [Biography of Mao Zedong 1949–1976] (Beijing: Zhongyang wenxian, 2004), 1: 236–68; Jin Chongji, ed., *Liu Shaoqi zhuan* (hereinafter *Liuzhuan*) [A biography of Liu Shaoqi] (Beijing: Zhongyang wenxian, 1998), 2: 611–18, 627–35, 686–93.

mind of how a *new* China should be built, as well as over what timescale and under what social conditions.[13] At the same time, without doubting Mao's crucial role, it is important to take the full measure of the diversity of the characters, personal experiences, and individual worldviews of the other Communist leaders, who may have shared broad ideological and political commitments but held different practical views on how to create a wealthy and powerful state. Third, contrary to pictures of Mao as a moderate or centrist arbiter of policy disputes in this early period, the Chairman in fact indicated his preferences at the outset of the debates over the pace of socialization, which only served to polarize conflicts within the leadership.[14] In terms of the concrete policy disputes of the consolidation years, areas of debate included the degree to which agricultural production would be reorganized into cooperatives and the proper role of trade unions in nationally owned factories. Accord-

---

13. Several factors contributed to Mao's absolutely dominant position among his colleagues and the party: (1) Mao had monopolized power during the Yan'an era by formulating ideological (theoretical) principles stating his own "correct" interpretation of orthodox Marxist–Leninism and offering general guidelines for action programs (i.e., specific policies) oriented by ideological considerations; (2) Mao had gotten the upper hand in arbitrating the party's internal policy disputes by the end of the Yan'an rectification campaign, which in effect removed him from a sphere in which party institutions could control him; (3) Mao's control of and influence over the army and public security forces was absolute and marked a difference from the Soviet Union, where these sectors were more technically constituted and enjoyed some measure of autonomy; Mao had always given attention to controlling the party's military affairs and had closely supervised matters of public security; (4) Mao was able to take personal credit both within and outside the party for directing the CCP's overwhelming success in the civil war. For a stimulating discussion about the relationships between ideology, personality, and decision-making in international relations on the basis of a study of Chinese Communist foreign policy, see Michael H. Hunt, *The Genesis of Chinese Communist Foreign Policy* (New York: Columbia University Press, 1996), 208–10.

14. For arguments that stress Mao's moderate centrist position in dealing with party disputes, that see him as smoothing over others' conflicts, see Frederick C. Teiwes, *Politics and Purges in China: Rectification and the Decline of Party Reforms, 1950–1965* (Armonk, New York: M.E. Sharpe, 1993), 86–87, and Teiwes, "Politics at the 'Core': The Political Circumstances of Mao Zedong, Deng Xiaoping and Jiang Zeming," *China Information* 15, no. 1 (2001): 10, in which the author states, "With few exceptions, little space was left for bold, unprecedented initiatives, and like his colleagues Mao normally played a game of incremental adjustments."

ing to the party's political system, which entrusted large amounts of power to individuals rather than institutions, Mao's perceived wishes were interpreted by hardliners as sanctioning their own bids for power and status, on the thinking that they could then implement the leader's mandate. With his hands full fighting a war in Korea while launching endless campaigns at home, the Chairman redefined the major political tasks of the consolidation years and pressed for policy changes. There was little incentive for his close colleagues to argue against Mao's principles once he had revealed his hand.[15]

Some of Mao's key ideological prescriptions of China's "proper" socialist development differed from those of his closest colleagues. Mao primarily identified himself as a Chinese Marxist–Leninist, that is, an acolyte of Marx, Lenin, and Stalin in believing that communism represented the end of history, holding out the promise of an ideal realization of humans' potential. He further subscribed to the Leninist–Stalinist tenet that the overthrow of capitalism was essential to building a proletariat-dominated society; this at once necessitated the expropriation of the capitalists, the ousting of the bourgeoisie, and the dismantling of bourgeois socioeconomic institutions. His lieutenants agreed, but what made Mao special among the Chinese Communist nation-builders was his ideological and political rigidity in giving priority to the destruction of the old system, mode of production, and culture over economic recovery and the development of China's underdeveloped agrarian economy. Fearing the alienation of his base, or rather their drifting into a deplorable "trade-union consciousness," Mao drew on his analysis of Lenin and Yan'an revolutionary experience to urge a thorough transition from the old to the new. The Stalinist model of socialization, in this context, perfectly fitted his aim of eliminating the capitalist mode of ownership (or private ownership) in rural and urban settings.[16]

---

15. Pang, *Maozhuan*, 242.
16. For Mao's Marxist–Leninist beliefs and the guiding role of orthodox ideology in Mao's perception of the Chinese revolution and state-building, see Ben-

His revolutionary instincts notwithstanding, however, Mao was after all a politician whose task lay in gauging his strength (or his party and state's power) in mobilizing the political forces necessary to bring about a certain historical phase. The basic indices used by the Chairman to judge the existing political situation and therefore to decide or adjust his tactics in steering toward political goals (or even in changing his direction of travel) were his sense of the strengths of different classes and of the character of the people's political consciousness. Mao's sense of historical necessities and contingencies was political and ideological, rather than strictly economic. As the following treatment demonstrates, when Mao saw that the necessary conditions for rapid societal reconstruction were not mature, he endorsed the moderate New Democracy line and left Liu Shaoqi, with his own ultimate say assured, in effective control of party construction and its economic work from late 1948 to the first half of 1951.[17]

The evidence, then, strongly suggests that Mao agreed with Liu's openness to peaceful and moderate economic experiments during the late 1940s without, however, ever acceding to a developed understanding of how and why the "existence and development of urban and rural factors of capitalism" could contribute to national growth. Mao was intellectually formed in the crucible of early twentieth-century politics, specifically China's revolutionary struggle, and took his references primarily not from Marxian economics but from Lenin's and Stalin's interpretations and especially from his reflections on his own experience in revolutionary power-building in remote areas. Neither Lenin nor Stalin had set out the

---

jamin Schwartz, "Marx and Lenin in China," *Far Eastern Survey* 18, no. 15 (1949): 174–78; Yang Kuisong, "Mao Zedong weishenme fangqi Xinminzhuzhuyi?" 141–53.

17. Liu Chongwen and Shaotao Chen, eds., *Liu Shaoqi nianpu (1898–1969)* (hereinafter *LSN*) [The chronicles of Liu Shaoqi (1898–1969)] (Beijing: Zhongyang wenxian, 1996), 2: 164–65, 167–78, 192–210, 215–17; Jin, *Liu Shaoqi zhuan*, 613–18, 623–41, 686–707. For a good analysis of the ideological rigidity and the tactical flexibility of Chinese Communist Party under Mao, see Yang, *Makesizhuyi Zhongguohua*, 121–34, 175–97, 268–309.

economic benefits of capitalism or capitalist contributions to a mixed or generally directed economy.[18] Furthermore, unlike his colleagues Liu Shaoqi, Zhang Wentian, and Zhou Enlai, who all studied abroad as young men, Mao chose to stay in China, which provided him with time creatively to adapt the grand theories of Marxism–Leninism to Chinese circumstances and to distinctively Chinese revolutionary forms of praxis. This, though, allowed Mao very limited access to the outside world or to international discussions of Marxism. If one compares Liu's evaluations of economic policies in the late 1940s with Mao's in the same period, one cannot but be struck by the imprecision of Mao's notion of the benefits that a mixed economy could bring to the development of his country.[19] As a result, the rationality or theoretical thoroughness of the economic principles placed before Mao—for instance, the stress on the full development of new productive forces as a prerequisite for transforming backward relations of production—may have deter-

---

18. See, for example, Mao Zedong, "Xinminzhuyi lun" [On New Democracy], Jan. 1940, *Mao Zedong xuanji* [Selected Works of Mao Zedong] (hereinafter *MXJ*) (Beijing: Renmin, 1991), 2: 666–85; Liu Shaoqi, "Letter to Stalin on Mao's Plan of China's Transition to Socialism" (title added by the author), Zhonggong zhongyang wenxian yanjiushi [CCP Central Committee Document Research Office], *Jianguo yilai zhongyao wenxian xuanbian* (hereinafter *Zhongyao Wenxian*) (Beijing: Zhongyang wenxian, 1992), 3: 367–71. Also see Schwartz, "Marx and Lenin in China," 174–78; Yang, "Mao Zedong weishenme fangqi Xinminzhuzhuyi?", 141–53.

19. Mao repeatedly stressed the importance, with Liu, of allowing "all elements of capitalism in the cities and the countryside that are not harmful but beneficial to the national economy" to exist and develop. As to the reasons for taking such a policy, however, the clearest answers the Chairman provided in this period typically took two forms: politically, "the Chinese liberal bourgeoisie and its representatives often adopt the position of either participating or remaining neutral in the people's democratic revolutionary struggle, owing to the oppression or restrictions of imperialism, feudalism, and bureaucratic capitalism"; while economically, "the still backward situation of the Chinese economy at present" necessitated compromise. Specifically economic terms like "commodity," "business," "commerce," "the market," and "light industry" never appeared in Mao's justification of his New Democracy economic policies. See Mao Zedong, "Resolution of the Second Plenum of the Seventh CCP CC (13 March 1949)," in Saich and Yang, *The Rise to Power*, 1342–44.

mined the thinking of Liu and other top officials but enjoyed relatively little traction with the Chairman. In retrospect, the Chairman and his key economic planners had arrived at a quite different understanding of the criteria of a "thoroughly prepared" socioeconomic transformation and of how to adapt the Stalinist economic model to China, a largely agrarian and preindustrial country. On these questions, Liu Shaoqi in the period of his effective control emphasized the need for China to ramp up its production, seeking to raise people's living standards if necessary by capitalist means (using capitalist industry and commerce) before the party seriously committed itself administratively to socialist transformation.[20] Planning the rehabilitation and development of agriculture and industry, Liu's view was to begin with a focus on agriculture and light industry as the most relevant to people's livelihoods in the context of preparing for a long-term program of industrialization and development.[21] Liu's nonselective and balanced view of economic development (envisaging a cycle of economic activities) distinguished Chinese economic policy from the Stalinist strategy of economic development, which favored heavy capital-intensive development at the expense of consumption and agriculture, a typical emphasis in the Soviet Bloc at the time.

Despite sharing Mao's concern to do things in a gradualist and flexible way, ensuring that every movement was "thoroughly prepared" for, Liu (and other key economic planners) seem to have placed greater store on economic indicators as precursors of socialist development, while the Chairman essentially continued to look to political factors and revolutionary consciousness. Mao's fear was that launching rigid socioeconomic reforms at this stage might

---

20. "Liu Shaoqi's Report Made in the North China Financial and Economic Committee Session," 25 December 1948, *Liu Shaoqi zhuan*, 615–17. Jin Chongji, "Zai Liu Shaoqi shengping he sixiang yantaohui shang de jianghua" [Speech delivered at the closing session of the seminar on Liu Shaoqi's life and thoughts, 23 November 1998], *Dang de wenxian* [Party Documents], 1 (1999): 51–55.

21. Liu Shaoqi, "Zhongguo gongchandang jinhou de Lishirenwu" [The CCP's Historical Tasks from Now on: made in July 1951] *Dang de wenxian*, 6 (1989): 18; also see *Liuzhuan*, 690–91.

jeopardize the nation's path to socialism, especially if the mass of the people remained "unawakened" to its prospects. Further, right up until the late 1940s, the Chairman was prejudiced in favor of the view that the creation of a "modern heavy industrial sector" would represent the principal determinant in building up the nation's power. The Chinese economy would pull itself up by its bootstraps, as the Chairman saw it, essentially in increasing its production through modernizing, by which he doubtless meant developing heavy industry. Mao's aspirations here clearly aped Soviet developmental design, or more aptly the Stalinist strategy of building socialism.[22] Although it still took Mao time to square his ideal of accelerating economic growth through the application of mass mobilization techniques with his conception of the more doctrinaire Stalinist model, after the establishment of the new regime he soon began to feel that Liu and his economists' model was problematic.

Mao Zedong soon became discontented with his lieutenants' prudence in advancing economic transformation. According to the recollections of Deng Xiaoping, the Chairman, whom Deng addresses respectfully as *laorenjia* (the grand old man), "already indicated dissatisfaction with Comrade [Liu] Shaoqi and Premier Zhou [Enlai] in the early post-liberation days."[23] The first ideological clash between Mao and his more economically minded colleagues came

---

22. According to Mao's librarian, the Chairman spoke highly of Stalin's "On a Socialist Economy" while still emphasizing intellectual independence in reading this book when he recommended it to his cadres. See Pang Xianzhi, "Maozhuxi dushu shenghuo wojian wowen: jiangshu zhenshi de Mao Zedong" [The reading life of Mao Zedong: What I saw and what I heard of the real Mao], *Tebie cehua* [Special Report] (2006): 39–43. For the impact of Stalin's "History of the All-Russian Communist Party (Bolshevik): Short Course," see Li, *Mao and Economic Stalinization of China*, 95–116. On the common development design that Communist China shared with the Soviet Union during the first Chinese five-year-plan period, see Anthony M. Tang, "Agriculture in the Industrialization of Communist China and the Soviet Union," *Journal of Farm Economics*, 49, no. 5 (Dec. 1967): 1118–34.

23. Dai Maolin and Zhao Xiaoguang, "Shixi 'Gao-Rao shijian' fasheng de yuanyin" [An attempt on analyzing the origin of the 'Gao-Rao affair'], *Dangshijiaoxue yu yanjiu* [Party history teaching and research], 6 (2003): 65.

over "the question of forming [agricultural producers'] cooperatives (APCs)." Rather than pitting Mao against Liu directly, ideological differences emerged in the form of different perspectives on the proper pace of agricultural collectivization as put forward by the Northeast Bureau headed by Gao Gang and the central leadership represented by Liu from the end of 1949 to early 1950. Gao Gang advocated a step-by-step collectivization of individual agricultural labor, while Liu insisted that at that moment in time the maintenance of peasant private ownership could increase production and therefore could finance industrial development, making it advisable to postpone collectivization until the mechanization of agriculture.[24] There is evidence, however, that Mao became indirectly involved in this early dispute, supporting Gao's proposal to make Manchuria something of a planning laboratory and training ground for the mainland as a whole.[25] In retrospect, these issues of how China could modify the Soviet experience of collectivized agriculture to suit national conditions, and of the relation of technical reform (mechanization) to institutional reform (full nationalization), came to be highly influential for the course of Chinese socialism.

Whatever the differences between Mao and his comrades, the Chairman did not immediately veto the moderate economic policies effected by the central party, still less encourage deviations

---

24. Jin, *Liuzhuan*, 692; Dai Maolin and Zhao Xiaoguang, ibid., 65–66.
25. Bo Yibo, *Ruogan Zhongda juece yu shijian de huigu* (hereafter *Huigu*) [Review on a certain number of crucial decisions and events], 2 vols. (Beijing: Renmin, 1997), 1: 207; also see Dai and Zhao, "Shixi 'Gao-Rao shijian,'" 66. Mao's backing for Gao Gang's radical policies in developing agricultural collectivization soon after the establishment of the regime was not casually given but rather represented a purposeful choice, indicating the Chairman's sense of collectivization as an indispensable step in implementing his grand vision of socioeconomic transformation emulating Stalin in the 1920s and 1930s. "Mao's key contribution to the first session of the critical Senior Cadres' Meetings of 1942–1943 was to rehearse (in a three-day speech) Stalin's twelve conditions for achieving Bolshevism, that many of the key documents for study in the rectification movement were Stalinist tracts," Joseph W. Esherick, "Ten Theses on the Chinese Revolution Modern China," *Modern China*, 21, no. 1 (1995): 45–76.

from the gradualist line.[26] Indeed, the main constraint on Mao's behavior was not the agitation of vanguard socialists within the party, whom Mao could easily face down, but the opposition of largely "uneducated" people who betrayed no dissatisfaction with the political and economic pattern of New Democracy. Throughout this period, Mao acknowledged the Soviet Union as a model of socialism, not being moved to probe the ideological limitations or specificity of the Soviet agricultural collectivization by reflecting on the social contradictions of Chinese society. At the same time, however, at no point did Mao's sense of the means and timetable for achieving socialism coincide with Stalin's. It is unlikely that Mao wished to accept Stalin's moderate policy recommendations for China's socialist state-building, preferring rather to appease him and offer support on purely political expedients (for instance, by falling in line with the suggestion of forming a multiparty government and drafting a constitution).[27] To the consternation of his lieutenants, Mao was ruthlessly prepared to discard the theoretical principles of New Democracy and the contemporary gradualist line when he felt new situations required it.

Mao's assessment of the domestic situation changed, as China was on the verge of plunging into the Korean War. While remaining concerned at the possibility of an American imperialist incursion, the best option for the Chairman in his strategic planning was to

---

26. From late 1949 to the second half of 1950, the Communist leadership concentrated on two important issues: first and foremost the unification of the state by force; at the same time, economic recovery in big cities from the war-torn devastation. Mao was evidently not enthusiastic in expanding and intensifying the counterrevolutionary campaign until late September to early October of 1950, right before the top Communist Chinese leaders reached the consensus to intervene in the Korean War. For Mao's general views on Chinese finance and economy in this period, see Pang and Jin, *Maozhuan*, 69–80; for the CCP's financial and economic policies, see Zhonggong zhongyang dangshi yanjiushi [CCP Central Committee Document Research Office], ed., *Zhongguo gongchandang lishi dashiji, 1919.5–2005.12* [Major events of the Chinese Communist Party 1919.5–2005.12] (Beijing: Zhonggong dangshi, 2006), 151–60.

27. Li Hua-Yu, "The Political Stalinization of China: The Establishment of One-Party Constitutionalism, 1948–1954," *Journal of Cold War Studies*, 3, no. 2 (Spring 2001): 31.

avoid immediate confrontation, however much he might prepare for it. With all due respect to Mao's foresight, there is no evidence that he anticipated the Chinese would fight the Americans on the Korean peninsula. But Mao recognized an international obligation to help the North Korean communists unite their country by force on the peninsula. Bound by this ideological belief, Mao had no choice but to gave the green light to Kim Il Sung's first-attack plan. We now know that he made it clear to Kim that if the "imperialists" intervened and pushed their forces across the thirty-eighth parallel (of latitude), the Chinese would fight them back.[28] After yielding to the necessity of fighting in order to save the communists in Korea and to defend socialism in China and globally, Mao quickly saw in the war an opportunity to shape the thought of the masses at home, for whom the foreign threat became a palpable reality.[29] As one scholar has pointed out, Mao's crisis management in sending troops to Korea aimed not only at safeguarding China and defending the

---

28. Chen Jian, "The Sino-Soviet Alliance and China's Entry into the Korean War," CWIHP Working Paper 1 (Washington, DC: Woodrow Wilson International Center for Scholars, 1992); Yang Kuisong, *Zhonghua renmin gongheguo jianguoshi yanjiu* [Historical study of the formulation of the People's Republic of China] (Nanchang: Jiangxi renmin, 2009), 2: 94–143. Also see Chen, *China's Road to the Korean War: The Making of the Sino-American Confrontation* (New York: Columbia University Press, 1994); Sergei Goncharov, John Lewis, and Litai Xue, *Uncertain Partners: Stalin, Mao, and the Korean War* (Stanford, CA: Stanford University Press, 1993), 168–202.

29. Mao developed a strategy to extend the ethos of war against the Americans into a stronger revolutionary momentum at home during the two months from August to October, since he had already determined that the Chinese should prepare to help the North Koreans in July 1950. As a result, only two days after the central party formally decided to fight the Korean War, Mao had ready a new version of the "Instruction on the Suppression of Counter-Revolutionaries" (also called the "double-ten" instruction as it was issued on 10 October 1950), which framed the terms for a much intensified political campaign nationwide. See Bo Yibo, *Huigu*, 1: 43. For a good analysis of the intensification of the Movement of Suppression of the Anti-Revolutionaries after the Korean War and Mao's relevant strategic and ideological thinking, see Yang Kuisong, "Guanyu Zhongguo chubing Chaoxian de yishixingtai yinsu" [On the ideological factors in China's military involvement in the Korean War], http://www.yangkuisong.net/ztlw/wjsyj/000122_2.htm. accessed on 1 July 2008. This website was totally removed by the end of 2012 for unknown reasons, but this article could easily be found and downloaded via www.baidu.com, a Chinese language search engine.

world revolution but also, and more importantly, fomenting a domestic mobilization that would secure the widest possible acceptance for the CCP leadership and its policies.[30] Mao was a professional communist revolutionary whose avowed goal of transforming the old China in line with his socialist ideals required a degree of flexibility in patiently accumulating power and launching political offensives at an opportune moment. The Korean War thus presented as much an opportunity as a challenge.

In launching this intense mass mobilization, the Chairman felt the time was ripe to push more radical policy changes on the social front than he had hitherto dared. This led him to detach himself from the gradualist line. In the summer of 1951, the Chairman directly intervened after the Shanxi provincial committee proposal for a rapid formation of cooperatives was rejected by the North China Bureau and the central party under Liu Shaoqi.[31] In the early 1950s, the top leaders represented by Liu Shaoqi and Zhou Enlai who continued to advocate the gradualist line thus began to feel implicit political pressure from the Chairman. A two-month-long session of "treatment for health recovery" was scheduled for Liu in November 1951 after Premier Zhou had himself been granted time off for two months. When Liu came back to work in January 1952, he found himself deprived of formal authority to lead economic matters, instead being reassigned to head the "Three Antis" and "Five Antis" campaigns.[32]

---

30. Chen Jian, "A Response: How to Pursue a Critical History of Mao's Foreign Policy," *China Journal*, no. 49. (January 2003): 137–42. For an account of the Chinese Communist experience accumulated in the mass mobilization during the Yan'an era, see Govind S. Kelkar, "The Chinese Experience of Political Campaigns and Mass Mobilization," *Social Scientist*, 7, no. 5 (December 1978): 45–63; for a comparison study of the Soviet and Chinese mass mobilizations, see Thomas P. Bernstein, *Leadership and Mass Mobilisation in the Soviet and Chinese Collectivisation Campaigns of 1929–30 and 1955–56: A Comparison* (Cambridge: Cambridge University Press, 1967).

31. According to Bo Yibo, the Chairman talked Liu and other two economic leaders (including Bo) into accepting the Shanxi "speeding-up of the formation of cooperatives" plan; see Bo Yibo, *Huigu*, 1: 198.

32. Concerning the concrete policy disputes of the consolidation years, apart from the agricultural cooperativization issue, another area of debate entailed

In the summer, as recommended by the Chairman, the central party decided to transfer the regional top leaders to Beijing. Given Mao's high evaluation of Gao, he came to be regarded as the pre-eminent, or literally "the fore horse," of the five regional leaders called to the center to contribute to the formation of policy in late 1952.[33] It was not surprising then that Gao Gang, already a politburo member, was promoted by the Chairman to head the State Planning Commission (SPC) tasked with preparing the five-year plan. In the context of Mao's dissatisfaction with Liu and Zhou, Gao's enhanced status in the center undoubtedly broke an established power balance in Beijing, provoking uncertainty and tension among Mao's subordinate colleagues.

On the international front, Mao successfully parlayed his way to a greater degree of independence in socialist transformation through deferring to Stalin in limiting increases in industrial output from a foreseen 20 to 15 percent and in less important issues (notably, by holding the National People's Congress and drafting the constitution). Although Stalin did caution the leadership to be realistic in setting economic-growth rates, his overall endorsement of the Chinese socialist transformation plan undoubtedly gave Mao a strong support to push the relevant policies from the top to the

---

whether the trade unions in nationally owned factories still represented the interests of the working class and should as such be differentiated from factory administrations. Deng Zihui supported the idea that even after the establishment of a communist state, these two interests were theoretically separate. Gao Gang took the "party" line that the trade unions and the working class had formally identical interests, with Liu Shaoqi weighing in with Deng. In the formative years of the new regime, the Chairman emphasized the need for a united front and advocated concessions in China's public factories. But when it came to October 1951, Mao absolutely supported Gao Gang's position. Therefore, even before the final months of 1951, the Chairman had already clearly expressed his preference for radical policies in both agricultural collectivization and national manufacturing. See *Liuzhuan*, 706.

33. Gao Gang, Rao Shushi, Deng Zihui, Deng Xiaoping, and Xi Zhongxun were the five regional leaders chosen by the central party as the ones to transfer to Beijing in 1953; see Zhang Wenxiong et al., eds., *Jujiao zhuxitai: Zhidianjiangshan (1949–1976)* [Focusing on the rostrum of the Chinese chairman: To set China the right way] (Changsha: Hunan renmin, 2004), 174–83, 192–97.

local levels.³⁴ The Chairman sent Premier Zhou to Moscow in August 1952 with a draft of the Chinese first five-year plan (FFYP) to be commented upon and certified by the Kremlin. When Zhou returned with Soviet endorsement for a program of carrying out the FFYP on 24 September, Mao immediately announced his determination to "make a transition to socialism within 10 to 15 years," setting this goal in the latter part of 1952 in a central party meeting. His view was accepted with no dissent at the top.³⁵ In autumn 1952, as Mao began to plan China's transition to socialism, he instructed Liu to broach the idea of a tightly managed progression with Stalin in Moscow in October 1952. Liu delivered to Stalin a letter explaining the rationale for rapidly developing a nationalized economy in China as the CCP's instrument for effecting a socialist transformation in the country through enlarging the zone of state economic control by peaceful means and long-term efforts.³⁶ Stalin gave his approval to a plan to "carry out the transition to socialism in a gradual manner" as specified in Liu's letter but rejected Mao's follow-up proposal to postpone holding a national people's congress and drafting a constitution until after 1954, the year Stalin had previously recommended.³⁷ The difference between the two leaders was that Stalin rigidly insisted on applying his own established formula in terms of the relationship between social–political and economic reform to every conceivable case, as he had urged with the Eastern European Communist parties in the first half of 1940s, while Mao cleaved to the desirability of adopting Soviet-style transformation on the basis of his understanding of the Chinese characteristics.

---

34. Li, "The Political Stalinization of China," 31.
35. According to Bo Yibo's recollection, Mao's opinion was accepted with no contrary voices from the leaders who attended the meeting: Liu Shaoqi, Zhou Enlai, Chen Yun, Deng Xiaoping, Peng Dehuai, Peng Zhen, Chen Yi, Bo Yibo, Luo Ruiqin, Su Yu, An Ziwen, Yang Shangkun, Rao Shushi, Xi Zhongxun, and Nie Rongzhen. See Bo Yibo's letter to Tian Jiaying [on the situation of the 24 September meeting], handwritten draft, 30 December 1965, cited in Pang and Jin, *Maozhuan*, 241. Also see Bo Yibo, *Huigu*, 1: 221. For Stalin's advice on the FFYP and Mao's acceptance, see Li, *Mao and Economic Stalinization of China*, 64.
36. Zhongyang wenxian, *Zhongyao wenxian*, 3: 367–71, 371 fn. 1.
37. Li, *Mao and the Economic Stalinization of China*, 85.

Knowing that concessions had to be made to secure the Kremlin's noninterference in the domestic affairs that were his priority, Mao had little trouble taking on board Stalin's suggestions in the field of the Georgian's "expertise."[38]

The evidence suggests that, buoyed by Stalin's endorsement, Mao put the finishing touches to his conceptual framework for China's socialist transition in the period between late October 1952 and late February 1953, before proceeding to southern China on a research trip during which he began to propagandize his socialist transformation line among the local party cadres.[39] By early February, Mao's plans to eliminate the capitalist class in a step-by-step manner, while at the same time driving large-scale socioeconomic collectivization and nationalization in agriculture, took shape. These plans involved the rationalization and state absorption of the handicraft industry, other local forms of consumer-oriented manufacture, and commerce. According to Mao's official biography, the Chairman's typical procedure in formulating, then implementing a new policy (such as the later 1955 small leap, or the HF and rectification campaigns of 1956) was to "focus on a very specific problem, thinking about it and at the same time airing his views" initially in his inner central circles, then among groups of local cadres.[40] This procedure apparently allowed the Chairman to approximate "objec-

---

38. As Li Hua-Yu points out, although Stalin's response to Liu's letter neither stated concrete measures nor broached the question of timing for a socialist transition in China, Mao, in line with the whole CCP leadership, chose to interpret Stalin's reply as supportive of his own plan. See Li, *Mao and the Economic Stalinization of China*, 88; also see Pang and Jin, *Maozhuan*, 242–44.

39. Up to November 1952, Mao only talked about his idea of transforming the state into an officially socialist organ in ten to fifteen years within the small circle of his central leadership. But Luo Ruiqing, head of public security, publicized Mao's new policy to a wider range of cadres. Once Luo's behavior had been discovered by the party center, the Chairman not only criticized and punished Luo but also admitted that it was his responsibility to tell his colleagues not to leak the news before everything had been made ready. For Mao's letter to a small circle of central party leaders on 13 November 1952, see Pang and Jin, *Maozhuan*, 236–37; for the formulation of the specific political targets and implementing steps of Mao's socialist transition plan in the period, see Zhongyang wenxian, *MWJ*, 6: 231; Bo, *Huigu*, 1: 221; Pang and Jin, *Maozhuan*, 245–68; Yang, *Makesizhuyi Zhongguohua*, 309–23.

40. Pang and Jin, *Maozhuan*, 245.

tive reality" in the rarefied context of policy formation (the danger of course was that middle- and lower-level officials only offered the Chairman a ready sounding-board for his own views, depriving Mao of the comprehensive information he needed to make plans).[41] In the instance of collectivization, Mao came across local officials passing on peasants' enthusiasm for cooperatives from the very beginning of his tour, very likely emboldening him to step up the campaign nationally. With Stalin out of the way on 5 March 1953, the Chairman was free to mobilize support among the cadres for his plan and at the same time to criticize "the mistaken views" in the center that differed from his own.[42]

Back from his investigative tour in the south, the Chairman bridled sharply when faced with another problem, the newly announced fiscal principle of placing "public and private [enterprises] . . . on an equal footing" in paying taxes, which led to a round of inner-party criticism meetings from the summer of 1953, which openly arraigned Bo Yibo while obliquely directing accusations against Liu Shaoqi and Zhou Enlai. A number of factors seem to have come together in goading Mao on the new tax system. Mao was originally extremely upset by the fact that Zhou Enlai, with the

---

41. Mao also demonstrated great interest in collecting information on successful examples of joint state–private enterprises during his trip, which meant that he was not only eager to promote collectivization in the rural areas but also was serious about nationalization, though in the first stage via joint state–private ownership, of capitalist industrialization in urban areas. Zhonggong hebeisheng dangshiyanjiushi [CCP Hebei Province Party history research office], ed., *Lingxiu zai Hebei* [the leader in Hebei province] (Beijing: Zhonggongdangshi, 1993), 64–75; Zhonggong hubeisheng dangshiziliao weiyuanhui [CCP Hubei Provincial Party Historical Materials Committee] ed., *Mao Zedong Zai Hubei* [Mao Zedong in Hubei] (Beijing: Zhonggongdangshi, 1993), 2–4; Fu Dazhang, "Guanyu Mao Zedongtongzhi 1953nian2yue shicha Anqingshi jianghua de huiyi" [Recollection of Mao's Speech Given in February 1953 during his visit to Anqing], *Lilunzhanxian* [Theoretical Front] 96 (1981): 3; Li, *Mao and the Economic Stalinization of China*, 128–29. For a critical study of Mao's "mass line" strategy in pursuit of his own ideological and political ends, see Liu Yu, "From the Mass Line to Mao's Cult" (PhD diss., Columbia University, 2006): 350–650.

42. Guo Simin, *Wo yanzhong de Mao Zedong* [My Perceptions of Mao Zedong] (Shijiazhuang: Hebei renmin, 1990), 41; Teiwes, *Politics and Purges*, xvii and ft. 7; also see *Mao Zedong zai Hubei*, 2–4.

party's financial officials, had not consulted him on what they deemed a matter of concrete administration, with the result that he had "only become aware of it from reading the newspaper."[43] Moreover, the Chairman soon associated this new tax principle with residual New Democracy thinking among the top, seeing in it the principle that the capitalist class should be continuously reassured during the transitional stage, rather than progressively eliminated even if by gradual means. The policy heightened Mao's circumspection toward Zhou Enlai and Liu Shaoqi, putting in question the socialist orthodoxy of their combined efforts to consolidate the gradualist policies of the early 1950s. In particular, Liu Shaoqi's views on questions like the proper pace of collectivization, the peacefulness of a new democratic phase, and the placation of capitalists seemed to Mao increasingly at odds with the situation as he understood it. Further, Stalin's special fondness for Liu and the latter's obedience to Moscow's moderate line could only compound the Chairman's displeasure. More than three months after the death of Stalin, Mao judged that he could teach his top lieutenants a lesson and further solidify his own authority within the party. As soon as the Chairman began to address this fairly technical policy issue from the perspective of class struggle, the problem to a large extent became a matter of political jostling.[44]

While the story, politically, of the CCP from early 1953 to early 1954 largely concerned Mao's efforts to cement his crypto-totalitarian grip on the party, the origin of these efforts can usefully be traced back to policy differences between Mao and Stalin, as well as between Mao and his highest-ranking executives. Though Mao was

---

43. Mao Zedong's letter to Zhou Enlai and the others, 15 January 1953, Pang and Jin, *Maozhuan*, 251. This new tax system was designed to solve the problem of securing state revenues at a time when ownership was shifting to the state sector; Zhou and the financial leaders regarded it as a concrete government question not requiring the Chairman's attention. Bo Yibo, *Huigu*, 234–35; Teiwes, *Politics and Purges*, xvii.

44. For an analysis of personal power as a key factor in determining the Chinese top leaders' goals, see Benjamin Schwartz, "Modernisation and the Maoist Vision—Some Reflections on Chinese Communist Goals," *China Quarterly*, 21 (1965): 3–19.

far from slavish in his adherence to doctrinaire Stalinism, he wholeheartedly applauded Stalin's prescription of speed in the building of socialism. The simultaneous achievement of the two goals of socialization and modernization represented a heady prospect to Mao, who accepted Stalin's nostrums on the possibility of developing socialism independently of the lack of extensive heavy industry. With the political mass campaigns extended nationwide after China's involvement in the Korean War, Mao believed that a realignment of the power of China's different classes lay within his grasp and should consequently form the top item on the CCP agenda. Neither Stalin's gradualist advice on Chinese development nor the CCP central leadership's early plan for a peaceful and moderate transformation of the mixed economy under the banner of New Democracy any longer accorded with Mao's sense of the political winds. In one sense, the 1953–1954 political struggle as orchestrated by Mao served to dispel any continued enthusiasm for gradualism among the center, bestowing new respectability on Mao's radical line. Mao meanwhile had to maneuver Moscow into supporting important domestic policy initiatives, while concealing the heterodoxy in Stalinist terms of both himself and most of his top leadership. Stalin's stroke and the reorganization of power inside Kremlin in the name of collective leadership in fact released much of the pressure on Mao's Beijing, significantly freeing the Chairman's hands.[45]

With Khrushchev's gradual rise to the dominant position in the Kremlin, both Sino-Soviet relations and Sino-East European relations improved markedly in the period between 1954 and 1955. While Stalin had taken care to keep the independent Chinese Communists at a distance from the Soviet Bloc, Khrushchev was much more receptive to the potential role that Mao's China could play in the communist camp. By making Mao's China an active agent in the politics of international communism, Khrushchev sought to but-

---

45. For Mao's devotion to the Stalinist model as expressed in Soviet texts, especially in Stalin's *Short Course,* see Li, *Mao and the Economic Stalinization of China,* 95–116; see also Benjamin Schwartz, "China's Developmental Experience, 1949–72," *Proceedings of the Academy of Political Science,* 31: 1 (1973): 17–26.

tress his power at home and greatly to improve the ideological and constitutional unity of the bloc, while preserving for the USSR an indisputable leading role. Mao and his colleagues were happy to see the improvements in China's relations with the USSR, especially as they fulfilled aspirations toward closer links between the people's democracies that the Chairman had nurtured since the late 1940s. However, the Chinese prudently refrained from involving themselves too deeply in Eastern Bloc issues, since their primary focus in this period was on domestic socialist transition.[46]

SMALL LEAP IN SOCIALIST TRANSFORMATION (1955–1956)

In the context of China's socialist reform under the CCP's leadership, 1955 was a very important year. After completion of the colossal tasks of founding the new state, consolidating political power at home, and obtaining recognition and prestige in the communist camp through its "victory" on the Korean peninsula over the United States, the country entered into a period of accelerating socialization within the framework of (*mutatis mutandis*) a Stalinist model.[47] In the international arena, the Cold War entered a stable and relatively peaceful phase after the end of the Korean War, arriving at a point of equilibrium given the success of the Geneva and Ban-

---

46. On the CCP side, Mao and his colleagues were trying to avail themselves of newfound opportunities for connecting themselves not only with the USSR but also with the people's democracies in Europe before the final victory over the nationalists was achieved. For a treatment of this apparent contradiction, see Mao, "The Present Situation and Our Tasks," 25 December 1947, *Selected Works of Mao Tse-Tung* (Beijing: Foreign Languages Press, 1969), 4: 172; Lu Dingyi. "Duiyu zhanhou guoji xingshi zhong jige jibenwenti de jieshi" [Explanations of several basic problems concerning the postwar international situation], *Jiefang ribao* [Liberation Daily], 4 January 1947; Liu Shaoqi, 'Guojizhuyi yu Minzuzhuyi' [Internationalism and Nationalism] *Renmin ribao* [People's Daily], 1 November 1948. Ledovsky, "Mikoyan's Secret Mission," 82.

47. The Chinese diplomats' impressions of the Communist China's increasing prestige in the Eastern Bloc states after the Korean War are based on the author's oral interview with Chinese diplomats in those states, 17 April 2004.

dung conferences. Mao and the party proclaimed this stalemate period as the ideal climate for building China's socialist state on a national level.[48]

Socialization progressed quite rapidly after the end of Gao-Rao affair in late 1953, with policy placing agricultural collectivization at the forefront of socialization, while commerce, entrepreneurial forms of capitalism, and handicrafts were all incrementally assimilated to socialism according to a defined nonconfrontational line. Convinced that the greater development of the cooperatives would lead to a rapid rise in production to meet the needs of industrial development, the party center made cooperativization its first priority in 1954. Shortly after conferring with the Eastern European leaders in September, the Central Rural Work Department confirmed a short-term target of six hundred thousand agricultural producers' cooperatives (APCs) by spring 1955, a twofold increase of the level foreseen in April.[49] The center's ambitious targets for socialization seem both to have galvanized the local cadres and activists, while raising concerns among the peasants over whether their interests would be met in collective production.[50] In early

---

48. The Geneva Conference began on 24 April 1954, on the question of the restoration of peace in Korea and Indochina, chaired by the Soviet Union and Great Britain, with representatives from the United States, China, France, the Viet Minh, South Vietnam, Laos, Cambodia, India, Canada, and Australia in attendance. With the assistance of the Soviet and Chinese representatives, the conference reached a settlement on the Indochina War of Independence (1946–1954). The Bandung Conference, held in Indonesia in April 1955, is generally regarded as the first demonstration of the growing diplomatic significance of the Third World. This conference restated China's five principles of peaceful coexistence first set out in the Sino–Indian agreement in Tibet in 1954. See Chen, *Mao's China and the Cold War* (Chapel Hill, NC, and London: University of North Carolina Press, 2001), Chapter 6, fn. 36, 337. A so-called Bandung spirit of cooperation among these nonaligned states developed rapidly, allowing the Chinese to see their role in facilitating postimperial dialogue as that of contributors to world peace.

49. Frederick C. Teiwes, *The Politics of Agricultural Cooperativization in China: Mao, Deng Zihui, and the "High Tide" of 1955* (Armonk, NY: M.E. Sharpe, 1993), 33–34.

50. Many peasants began to manifest forms of passive resistance and foot-dragging over cooperativization. A massive sale and culling of farm livestock followed shortly on the center's APC announcement. See "Circular of the CCP Center on Overhauling and Consolidating Agricultural Producers' Cooperatives" (10

1955, Deng Zihui, head of the Central Committee's Rural Work Department, pointed out existing problems in agricultural collectivization in some areas, arguing that the movement of cooperativization should at that point be consolidated and controlled. Deng's proposal was soon endorsed by the politburo, leading to his issuing a circular reining in the cadres to avoid the escalation of rural tensions.[51]

Mao, to some extent, appears to have agreed with Deng in the early months of 1955 on the need to go slow or adjust his policies of agricultural collectivization. Mao took the enthusiasm of the peasants as a crucial, even decisive, indicator of underlying policy faults, though looking to the masses' opinion as a subjective indicator could hardly lead the Chairman to question the essential correctness of his general line. The reportedly high-handed treatment of peasants by local cadres forcing them to join collectives and the food shortage in the countryside apparently rang a warning bell for the Chairman.[52] Considering his leaders' opinions, as represented by Deng Zihui in conjunction with the politburo's leading economic specialist, Chen Yun, as reasonable, Mao in early March explicitly supported the idea of slowing down the pace of collectivization, suggesting a four and one-half year suspension of new activities permitting the consolidation of existing collectives. This "draw back

---

January 1955) document from the CCP Center to the local cadres, in Teiwes, *The Politics of Agricultural Cooperativization*, 157–58; for social studies on cadre and peasants' behavior under the CCP's radical economic rural policies during the mid-1950s, see Thomas Bernstein, "Cadre and Peasant Behavior under Conditions of Insecurity and Deprivation: The Grain Supply Crisis of the Spring of 1955" in *Chinese Communist Politics in Action* ed., Doak Barnett (Seattle: University of Washington Press), 365–99; Li Huaiyin, "The First Encounter: Peasant Resistance to State Control of Grain in East China in the Mid-1950s," *China Quarterly* 185, no. 1 (2006): 145–62.

51. See Frederick C. Teiwes, "Establishment and Consolidatiäng of the New Regime" in *CHOC*, 14, 114–15. Bo Yibo, *Huigu*, 167–68, 338–46, 353–56, 361–62. For the circular, see Teiwes, *The Politics of Agricultural Cooperativization*, 157–60.

52. For Mao's consciousness of the food shortage in the countryside as informed by a letter from a nonparty intellectual, Huang Yanpei, and on the high-handed treatment of peasants by local cadres from a letter written by local people to one of his guards, see Pang and Jin, *Maozhuan*, 370; Deng Zihui, *Deng Zihui wenji* [Collective works of Deng Zihui] (Beijing: Renmin, 1996), 409, 485.

in order to make a better jump" strategy was sloganized as "halt, shrink, develop."⁵³

It was in May 1955 that Mao changed his attitudes toward the collectives and started to criticize the view of consolidation and stabilization that he had supported in the spring. The direct cause of the "change of May" may have come from Mao's countryside survey as undertaken from April to May in 1955, in which he saw and reported many apparently positive results in the APCs, registering the local cadres' enthusiasm for pressing ahead with socialization. It was true that as a result of earlier campaigns, the common Chinese people had thrown themselves into all manner of socialist activities, generally identifying the party with their own prosperity. Nonetheless, problems of egalitarianism and bureaucracy in the local agricultural producers' cooperatives would eventually give the peasants pause on the matter of socialization.⁵⁴ Mao's information on peasant attitudes and on the success of the collectives may have been unreliable insofar as it derived from local government reports and a limited range of inspection.⁵⁵ Furthermore, in the Chairman's view, it was the relatively wealthier peasants who most resisted common ownership, partly since their competitiveness was eroded by the state's heavy grain purchases. For a rigid Communist revolutionary like Mao, it was both politically and ideologically unacceptable to make concessions to the "backward small peasant" whom he saw as standing in the way of the revolution. After his tour in the latter part of May, Mao drew the conclusion that the masses were in fact crying out for high-speed socialist reform, an inference supported by the evidence of former apparently successful rural campaigns,

---

53. Bo Yibo, *Huigu*, 378; Du Runsheng, "Yi wushiniandaichuqi wo yu Mao Zedong zhuxi de jici huimian" [Recollecting the meetings I had with Chairman Mao Zedong in the early 1950s] in *Mianhuai Mao Zedong* [Recollecting Mao Zedong], ed. Mianhuai Mao Zedong editing group (Beijing: Zhongyang wenxian, 1993), 380–81.

54. For an analysis of the reasons for Mao's "Change of May" see MacFarquhar, *CHOC*, 14: 115; Bo Yibo, *Huigu*, 379; Jin, *Liuzhuan*, 781–82.

55. Bo Yibo, *Huigu*, 379.

however contradicted by the report of the Rural Work Department in the spring of 1955.

Thus, as Mao saw it, the most important task after his tour was to adjust policy in the direction of stepping up the pace of nationalization for agriculture, handicrafts, industry, and commerce. Although Mao was largely successful in shaping a public image as a rational Communist ruler, wisely steering a middle course between right and left, mediating between party rivals and relating the utopian demands of the people to pragmatically achievable programs, he was in fact unable to maintain this role of arbiter for most of the first half of the 1950s. From the middle of 1955, Mao undertook a more focused study than ever before of economic questions, gaining greater confidence in expressing positions narrowly phrased within this discipline. Mao came to understand economic development as a spiral process, in which successive increments in material and human resources combine and reinforce one another to propel movement forward.[56] After May 1955, therefore, Mao launched a new campaign of suppression against the opinion of those with doubts over the rapid expansion of the collectives, whether these were expressed from within the party or outside. This policy found expression in his July speech in a criticism of "some of our comrades (who are) tottering like a woman with bound feet." Deng Zihui's concerns were thus labeled as displaying "rightist" timidity.[57]

Mao clearly identified class struggle as his political priority throughout the phase of transition to socialism, since he believed that only after a general elimination of the bourgeois ideology could the Chinese Communist state move on to its next stage of development. Closely related to the formation of a radical Maoist orientation in the transformation to socialism were cultural campaigns against "bourgeois ideology" in art and literature (which took the form of criticizing Hu Feng's literary views) and a purgative political movement seeking to expel counterrevolutionaries and "bad

---

56. Mao Zedong, *Mao Zedong Unrehearsed*, 31.
57. Bo Yibo, *Huigu*, 346, 356; MacFarquhar, *CHOC*, 14: 116.

elements" from within the party, which came to be known as the *sufan* movement of May 1955. Hu Feng, a left-wing writer who had advocated the individuality of literature and the writer's responsibility to criticize the times in the 1930s and 1940s in GMD-controlled areas, was stigmatized as a leading light of the "Hu Feng antiparty faction" by the center in early May. This Hu Feng affair originated in a long, self-defensive report he wrote on the tension between the party's tight ideological control and artistic creativity in the period of CCP power, which would have infuriated Mao as the prime mover in the drive to political and cultural conformity in the Communist regime since the early 1950s.[58] For Mao, as he made clear in the series of party directives and *Renmin ribao* (*RMRB*, People's Daily) editorials on the Hu Feng "antiparty faction," the political purge would not only enable the party to rid itself of all sorts of elements not identified with the objectives of the Communist revolution, but would also strengthen the political consciousness of the masses (the intellectuals and cadres in particular), encouraging them to "remold" themselves by "searching for and revealing hidden counterrevolutionary elements."[59]

Once the center's main criterion for assigning persons to the "people" or " nonpeople " had been internalized within the mind of the general public, the party should call upon any lurking "bad elements" to unburden themselves to the party organization, an instrument through which China would become a "real unity" in the political awareness of the populace. As the history of Mao's China in

---

58. Hu's report suggested that the degree of control over artistic and personal expression exercised by the CCP "enervated" people, so that the "formalism" (*gongshi zhuyi*) of party doctrine made the content less convincing to readers. Mao may have taken this to heart in his HF campaign in the following period, which we shall discuss further in Chapters 2 and 4. See Pang and Jin, *Maozhuan*, 299–307; Merle Goldman, "Hu Feng's Conflict with the Communist Literary Authorities," *China Quarterly*, 12 (1962): 102–37; Jonathan Spence, "On 'Chinese Revolutionary Literature'," *Yale French Studies* 39 (1967): 215–25.

59. For the Chairman's directives and comments on Hu Feng's "antiparty faction" case, which clearly expressed political considerations in escalating Hu's affair into a nationwide political purge aiming at the reconstruction of the people's political value-system, see Pang and Jin, *Maozhuan*, 302–7.

the first half of 1950s shows, this spiritual transformation, whether conducted through force or propaganda, went hand in hand with socioeconomic change in ensuring the purity and thoroughness of the revolution at home.

In supplanting bourgeois institutions with socialism in China, as Mao understood it, policy had to relate its political and economic objectives to relevant action programs in material and spiritual fields, balancing the development of the country with the more urgent imperative of consolidating the party and sometimes Mao's own personal power. All these factors contributed to Mao's preference for a rapid rather than slower mass campaign, but relatively more stable change. At the same time, the need to deal with party diehards and rightist holdouts in society at large consumed a good deal of energy, highlighting for Mao the need to further "educate" the public, that is, to internalize Chinese Communist philosophy in the popular mind as another front of a bitter class struggle. In an underlying sense, Mao felt it opportune by the second half of 1955 to inaugurate a thoroughly socialist direction for the country, of which, to his thinking, the socialist upsurge in the countryside would only be the initial movement. Following the high tide of agricultural collectivization, the nationalization of private industry, commerce, and handicrafts also made a leap forward between late 1955 and early 1956.[60]

With the basic completion of the institutional reorganization of the Chinese life in socioeconomic terms (collectivization in the countryside and nationalization in the cities), Mao took his task of having brought about socialism on the Stalinist pattern in China as fundamentally achieved. He was no doubt bolstered in this estimate by what he assumed was the general acceptance by various groups of people, the intellectual elites in particular, of the revolution and socialist transformation by the end of 1955. Even compared with

---

60. Up to October 1955, 38 million peasant households had joined collectives, 32 percent of the total. Three months later, by the end of December 1955, this number had reached 75 million, 63.3 percent of the total. See Pang and Jin, *Maozhuan*, 407–8.

the Soviet experience, as Mao recognized, this rapid and stable socialist transformation in China had to be counted as a significant achievement in Communist history, lending Mao the vaunting ambition eventually to surpass the Soviets by carrying off another miraculous (if inevitable from a Marxist perspective) victory in socialist construction (industrialization), the next objective the Chairman defined for his party and people. To ensure that rightist, i.e., conservative in this case, thinking was purged from the party, the center preestablished antirightist guidelines for the projected eighth party congress. From the period between the end of 1955 to early 1956, the Communist Party as a whole was "filled with exaltation," high on its drive for a faster and better path toward modernization as prescribed by Stalinist orthodoxy. There is little evidence that Mao and his colleagues anticipated that Khrushchev's performance (or anti-Stalin speech) in the forthcoming CPSU Twentieth Congress would change their perception of the basic applicability of the Stalinist model to Chinese conditions; neither did the leaders within the Kremlin foresee the possible impact of their de-Stalinization on the domestic affairs of China.[61]

CONCLUSION

The Soviet path to socialism represented a general blueprint for Chinese state reconstruction under the leadership of Chairman Mao; it is impossible to understand China's internal development during the early PRC period without relating Chinese aspirations to the Soviet past and the Soviet and Eastern European present. Despite Mao's repeated emphasis on intellectual independence in adapting Soviet experience to China, he in essence took the Stalinist road to socialism in the 1920s and 1930s as China's own path, in preference to the post–Second World War people's democracy pattern "suggested" by Stalin. The Chairman decided as early as the late

---

61. Bo Yibo, *Huigu*, 1: 526–27, 530–31.

1940s that he had to weigh domestic and external conditions in judging the moment to transform quantitative into qualitative changes, that is say, to cement his immediate displacement of the institutions and practices of bourgeois and imperialist life into a revolutionary overthrow of the mechanisms and consciousness of the old China. Unclear on how long it would take him to achieve this objective, Mao played a waiting game and was content to pass himself off as a centrist. It was in this short period that certain un-Stalinist economic formulae in building socialism emerged in the central party, which could have provided the theoretical and practical justification for the CCP to shift its focus domestically from ongoing political struggles to economic development possibly well into the late 1970s. But given Mao's insistence on political orthodoxy throughout this period, it was inevitable he would condemn as rightist the idea of leaving bourgeois interests standing in the name of developing a healthier or more productive economy. To appease Stalin, the Chairman made concessions in areas he considered less crucial only as a way of safeguarding his domestic policies. To borrow another scholar's epigram apropos of the Yugoslavia leaders immediately after 1945, Mao at this stage was ideologically more Stalinist than Stalin.[62]

The significant influence of the experience of the Soviet Union on China's domestic socialization notwithstanding, Chairman Mao tightened his hand on the tiller of domestic affairs after Stalin's death. The flow of information between socialist parties had been heavily censored by Mao himself in the early 1950s to prevent outside events throwing any sort of spanner in the works of Chinese socialist transformation. Within such an isolated internal environment, Mao met no significant impediment in consolidating his power in the center and uniting the party behind his vision for the country's future. To a large degree, these two purposes were intertwined given that Mao saw himself as the sole creative interpreter of Marxism–Leninism in a new and complex Chinese environment,

---

62. Brzezinski, *The Soviet Bloc*, 38.

requiring a maximum of personal power for socialism's realization. The correctness of the party and nation's development thus hinged on Mao's uncontested dominance. These facts make it hard to draw a clear demarcation between the Maoist vision and Mao's personal pursuit of power, especially without a consideration of the specific political context in which Mao exercised himself.

The Chinese involvement with the USSR and Eastern Europe was highly interconnected with the CCP's perception of its status within the Communist Bloc. The Chairman and his colleagues regarded the Soviets and Communists on the European continent as "brothers" in the Communist camp, of which Mao's China counted itself an integral member. Based on this assumption of the nature of the interbloc relationship, Chairman Mao emphasized the necessity for China and the bloc regimes to help each other by sharing resources, particularly their respective "advanced" experiences of socialization. Notably, this Chinese brotherhood interpretation of the intrasocialist relationships is not so different from the Soviet definition of the hierarchical organization of the Communist commonwealth, given that in Chinese culture brothers are identified by positions in a family hierarchy. But the Stalinist version took the Soviet leading position in the bloc for granted, while the Maoist indicated a possibility for status change: "The junior may one day surpass the senior."[63] In the first half of the 1950s, even after the death of Stalin, the Chinese Communists held themselves aloof from Soviet bloc events, devoting their efforts to catching up with the people's democracies and the USSR in domestic reconstruction. After the basic completion of the socialist form of the state on the Soviet model by the end of 1955, the Chinese leadership, particularly Mao, were taken over by a kind of secular zeal in their perception of China's future potential in socialist modernization, a process they looked for inspiration, both at home and abroad, in hastening by all available means. At the same time, as the following chapter describes, Chinese leaders became more willing to involve themselves in Eastern Bloc affairs.

---

63. Shi Zhe, *Shi Zhe koushu: ZhongSu guanxi jianzhenglu (Jianzhenglu* hereinafter) [Shi Zhe's oral recollection: My own experience of the Sino–Soviet relations], edited by Li Haiwen. Beijing: Dangdai Zhongguo, 2005, 195–96.

CHAPTER 2

China and the Eastern Bloc: Before and After the CPSU Twentieth Congress

The CPSU Twentieth Congress set in train extensive changes to both interbloc relations and domestic developments in Communist China and the East European satellites. Khrushchev's so-called secret speech, which instigated the process of de-Stalinization in the Communist camp, led not to a thaw in the cold war or a revision of socialism but rather to a series of largely noncommunist insurgent movements in the Eastern European republics. Liberal in character and originating in Hungary and Poland, these movements demanded independence and liberation from the Soviet Union. On the Chinese side, the Soviet critique of Stalin and his dogma coincided with the Maoist push to develop a faster and better path to modernization, aiming to outstrip the Soviets. This domestic objective was closely connected with the Chinese leadership's—Chairman Mao's in particular—ambition to begin exporting the Chinese revolutionary and state-construction experiences to other parts of the bloc, redefining the status of China in the Communist camp. Chinese domestic developments turned on Mao's changing interpretations of Eastern Bloc instability, as either pertaining to fundamental contradictions or weaknesses in Communism or rather extrinsic, positive effects associated with the machinations of a few provocateurs. By late 1955 and early 1956, Mao and his colleagues believed that they had cemented a communist state in China and were far more adroit in their management of domestic politics than their Soviet counterparts. At the same time, the problems in the bloc forced Mao and the top CCP leadership to conduct a serious review of their own work.

As the Eastern European states began to angle for enhanced cooperation with China in the autumn of 1956, Beijing was drawn ineluctably into Soviet Bloc affairs. Nevertheless, the European regimes themselves were unable to press the Chinese leadership into support for the Polish and Hungarian aspirations for domestic autonomy. (It is possible that China would have gone further in backing up other, more competent, or stronger leaderships in the USSR's satellite nations.) The third part of this chapter, while affirming the Polish Communists' success in drawing Beijing's attention to the problems caused by absolute Soviet rule in the Eastern Bloc, argues that the Chinese leadership never wavered from its own interests and always prioritized bloc integrity in its international diplomacy in the context of the Cold War.

CHINA'S POLICY TOWARD THE EASTERN BLOC UP TO THE CPSU TWENTIETH CONGRESS

Chinese foreign policy in the early fifties followed three principles set out by Mao Zedong: "lean to one side" (*yi biandao*); "build a new kitchen" (*ling qi luzao*), and "sweep the house clean before inviting guests" (*dasao ganjing wuzi zaiqingke*). These three guidelines on the whole expounded the CCP's firm decision both to develop close links with the Soviet-led Communist camp and at the same time to present a "closed-door" position to the non-Communist world before the consolidation of the new regime. Consequently, the Chinese Communist perspective on external relationships was of necessity a narrow one, focusing on its connection with the Soviet Union first and foremost, and then with the Soviet Bloc. The Chairman's first foreign visit had been as head of a delegation to Moscow after the formal establishment of the People's Republic of China. In retrospect, the Communist China–Soviet alliance had been formalized through a new treaty of "friendship, alliance, and mutual assistance" with two subsidiary agreements, notwithstanding any hidden complications. For the CCP, which had just won control over territorial mainland China, the forging of alliances by formal treaties and more importantly through ideological and political association with the Soviet-led Communist camp represented a likely prerequisite of their future international identity in the Cold War, even before taking into consideration the importance of Communist membership on domestic political and security grounds. The Chinese leadership further assumed that integration into the Soviet Bloc would establish a more stable regional environment, freeing them to concentrate on the domestic tasks of nationwide liberation and economic rehabilitation.[1]

If sheer facts of geography had been sufficient to block any political or military contact between the China and the East and southern Europe for centuries, China's entry into the Communist Bloc on the face of it offered a good opportunity for enhanced cooperation. Following the Soviet Union's lead in extending diplomatic recognition the day after the PRC's founding, the people's democracies in the Eastern Bloc (Bulgaria, Romania, Poland, Hungary, Czechoslovakia, GDR, and Albania) recognized the CCP between October and November 1949. On the basis of the establish-

---

1. For the CCP's leaders' main concern regarding their foreign policy and the international situation see Shao Kuokang, *Zhou Enlai and the Foundation of Chinese Foreign Policy* (Houndmills, Basingstoke, Hampshire: Palgrave Macmillan, 1996), 131–36. For a more open and historically oriented understanding of Chinese foreign relations, the diversity and complexity of Chinese Communist foreign policy, and the origins of Mao's foreign policy, see Michael Hunt, *The Genesis of Chinese Communist Foreign Policy* (New York: Columbia University Press, 1996), 125–250. Yang Kuisong's book focuses particularly on the process of creating ideological orthodoxy among the Chinese Communists from the 1920s to the early 1930s and the efforts the party made to transcend the old orthodoxy as the top leaders shaped policies responsive to the needs of survival and development on the basis of the perceptions of their changing configurations of power in domestic and international politics. No matter how innovative and unique the Chinese Communists seemed during the second half of the 1930s to the 1940s under Mao's guidance, to break an established orthodoxy proved to be more complex and difficult task for them to accomplish. Yang, *Makesizhuyi Zhongguohua*, 1–19, 411–28; for a closely connected historical narrative, see his *Zhongjian didai de geming*, 169–468.

ment of formal diplomatic relations with the Eastern Bloc states, Communist China signed economic and cultural agreements with these countries in the early 1950s, paving the way for extensive barter trade relationships with the East European members of the Soviet-dominated Council of Mutual Economic Assistance, in which China was granted observer status.[2] Insofar as formal measures were concerned, Communist China and the Eastern Bloc were then joined as distant relatives inside the international socialist camp.[3]

However, although Mao and his colleagues had been diligent in establishing a direct connection with the people's democracies before their victory in the revolution, it was Stalin who was in a position to dictate the form of the relationship between China and the Eastern Bloc. The Sino–Soviet deal establishing a "division of labor" between the nations, as introduced by Stalin to Liu Shaoqi during the latter's trip to Moscow in the summer of 1949, represented one of the informal restrictions that the Chinese side was forced to

---

2. "Letters and telegrams on the establishment of diplomatic relationships with various countries," Chinese Foreign Ministry Archives (CFMA hereinafter), File 102-00099-01,1–10. See also Pei Jianzhang, ed., *Zhonghua Renmin gongheguo waijiaoshi: 1957–1969* (hereinafter *Waijiaoshi*) [Diplomatic History of the People's Republic of China: 1957–1969] (Beijing: Shijie zhishi, 1994), 1: 44–77. Hungarian source materials recorded that the Hungarian government took the initiative in developing economic cooperation with the CCP leadership one month before the establishment of the PRC; see "Proposal of the Hungarian Foreign Ministry and the Hungarian Ministry of Foreign Trade to Initiate Economic Negotiations with the CCP Leadership," issued on 5 September 1949, H00001, A Magyar Országos Levéltár [The National Archives of Hungary] (hereinafter MOL), XIX-J-1-j China, 1945–1964, 5. doboz, 26, 566/1949. On general relations with the CCP leadership in the same period, see the Hungarian foreign ministry on Hungary's initial relations with the CCP leadership and the Democratic People's Republic of Korea (DPRK), recorded on 27 September 1949, H00002, MOL, XIX-J-1-j China, 1945–1964, 3. doboz, 4/b, 692/1949.

3. Although Yugoslavia issued a declaration to recognize the new China, the Chinese government made no reply to the Yugoslavian side, considering the Soviet–Yugoslavia schism and China's implicit support of the 1948 Cominform resolution on the Yugoslavia question. The Sino–Yugoslavia diplomatic relationship was established in January 1955, almost two years after Stalin's death. Pei, *Waijiaoshi*, 74–75.

abide by during the Stalin period.⁴ This division marked a clear boundary to the Chinese sphere of influence, which ended in Asia; Stalin was here mindful of the parallels between potential Chinese influence on the Eastern European states and that, historically, of Yugoslavia on the more orthodox Balkan nations.⁵ As a result, the PRC's relationship with the Eastern Bloc states during the Stalin era found itself limited to trade, cultural exchanges, and formal diplomatic connections. No significant (party–party) political relations existed affiliating the Communist parties of China and Eastern Europe.⁶

Stalin's stroke in early 1953 did not lead to an immediate development of political contacts between China and the Eastern Bloc.⁷

---

4. For Stalin's meetings with Liu Shaoqi, see Shi Zhe, *Zai Lishi juren shenbian*, 410–14; on the interpretations of Stalin's division-of-labor proposal, see Vladislav Zubok and Constantine Pleshakov, *Inside the Kremlin's Cold War: From Stalin to Khrushchev* (Cambridge, MA, and London: Harvard University Press, 1996), 58; see also Chen, *China's Road to the Korean War*, 74–75.

5. To head off another Yugoslavia, Stalin decided to divide the communist commonwealth in two, separating China from the people's democracies both institutionally and politically. Mao and the CCP could figure in the international roster of Communism as a leader of the Asian revolutionary process under Soviet supervision. On Stalin's suggestion for an Asian Cominform, see Xu Zehao, *Wang Jiaxiangzhuan* [A Biography of Wang Jiaxiang] (Beijing: Dangdai Zhongguo, 2006), 302; *Wang Jiaxiang Nianpu 1906–1974* [A Chronicle of Wang Jiaxiang 1906–1974] (Beijing: Zhonggong zhongyang wenxian, 2001), 371–72.

6. It has to be pointed out that Communist China's relations with Poland in political, economic, and social aspects were evidently much closer than with other Soviet Bloc members. To some extent, Poland provided an opening for revolutionary China to maintain meaningful contact with the outside world, such as Europe, Latin America, and later, as we know, the United States. "Documents on the establishment of Sino–Polish diplomatic relationship" (5–7 October 1949) CFMA, 109-00009-01, 1–3; "On Polish Delegation's visit to China," 109-00009-01, 6. Shen also concluded in his article on Sino–Polish relationship in the early 1950s that the bilateral relations of the two should be regarded as special and close among the Soviet Bloc states, in his "1956nian de ZhongBo guanxi-Laizi Zhongguo de dang'an wenxian he neibubaodao" [The 1956 Polish Crisis and Sino–Polish Relations: Sources from the Chinese archival documents and inside reports], *Eluosi yanjiu* [Russian Studies] 3 (2006): 45–46.

7. Up to 1954, the Chinese government had signed cooperation agreements in fields such as science and technology, and radio communication with the Soviet Bloc states. "Sino–Hungarian Agreement on Scientific and Technical Cooperation," issued on 3 Oct., 1953, H00006, MOL, XIX-J-1-j China, 1945–1964, 34. doboz; "Sino–Hungarian Agreement on Cooperation in Radio Communication,"

That year was crucial for Mao Zedong and his colleagues, a year in which the party committee under his direct control had its hands full planning its "general line for the socialist transition period," i.e., the Chinese formal adoption of the 1930s Soviet model in moving toward nationwide socialization. Despite some obvious erosion of the validity of the verbal deal confining Chinese Communist influence to South and Southeast Asia with Stalin's demise, the CCP leadership kept its head down by dealing with domestic political and economic problems, choosing not to offer any views on the troubles afflicting the other nations in the Soviet Bloc. At the same time, uncertainty over the succession of the Soviet leadership probably also encouraged the Chinese leadership to cultivate a wait-and-see attitude toward the events in Hungary and East Germany. It was also possible that Chairman Mao deliberately blocked the news about the partition of Berlin domestically since any news of ongoing problems with socialization in Eastern European states could hardly do any good for the Chinese Revolution. Rather, Mao simply passed on a Soviet interpretation of the Eastern Bloc uprisings, blaming a Western conspiracy against socialism and thus presenting the events in a political, rather than economic perspective.[8]

[date missing; should be in 1953 based on the Chinese document of this agreement], H00007, MOL, XIX-J-1-j China, 1945–1964, 12. doboz, 9/a, 00865/1954. Also see Pei, *Waijiaoshi*, 44–77.

8. The Chinese foreign ministry archives declassified material catalog has no reports on the East Berlin crisis, which may suggest that these materials are still classified. In fact, a lengthy report on the June uprising was sent back to Beijing via a Xinhua journalist in the form of *Neibucankao* [Inner circle information] (*Neican* hereinafter). See *Neican*, no. 213 (11 September 1953): 128–65, cited in Li Hua-Yu, *Mao and the Economic Stalinization of China*, 42–43. Looking at Chinese propaganda dealing with the bloc from early 1953, Li finds many expressions of the superiority of the economic systems of the Eastern European regimes, as built on the Stalinist pattern, compared to their predecessors. Li interprets these reports as the center's efforts to convince the common people of the merits of socialism in the run-up to a wholesale social transformation. See ibid., 123–24. Xinhua News Agency journalists sent abroad were authorized to submit reports, commonly entitled *Neican*, on key issues directly to the party's central committee members, including Mao himself. This type of report was selected and compiled into an inner-circle information journal to circulate only among high-level CCP cadres, whose publication was started in 1949 and ended in 1964. *Neibu cankao* is an inner-circle

Its fraternal ideological connection with the Eastern European socialist states, however, prompted the Chinese government to provide food and material support immediately after receiving a letter of request from the government of the GDR. The Chinese side made it clear in July 1953 that contract terms for this freight could be discussed later, and that the East Germans need not concern themselves with any date of return.[9]

Sino-Soviet relations entered into a honeymoon period with Khrushchev's ascendency. Khrushchev was busy deploying both domestic and foreign resources to consolidate a power base. The first secretary of the CPSU viewed China as an important player in creating cohesion among the socialist camp nations, believing that greater Communist interstate unity would play into his hands in Moscow. Beijing reacted positively to Khrushchev's overtures, with Premier Zhou Enlai inviting the Russian dignitary to a celebration of the fifth anniversary of the establishing of the Chinese Communist state, one of the most important events in the Chinese Communist calendar in the early 1950s.[10] Khrushchev reciprocated by granting China economic aid and concessions, reversing a Stalinist policy toward the end of his rule.[11] Khrushchev's rhetoric in this period stressed how deleterious Stalin's heavy-handedness had been for Sino-Soviet relations: "Stalin spoiled our relations with China.

---

journal on both domestic and foreign events edited by the Xinhua News Agency for reference purposes among the high-ranking CCP cadres only. The author would like to thank Shen Zhihua, professor of Huadong Normal University, for sharing his personal collection of the copies of the journal series, obtained from the China Study Service Center, Hong Kong Chinese University.

9. Zhonggong *Zhongyang wenxian yanjiushi* [CCP Chinese Central Committee Document Research Office], ed., *Zhou Enlai nianpu, 1949–1976* [A chronological record of Zhou Enlai, 1949–1976] (hereinafter *ZNP*) (Beijing: Zhongyang wenxian, 1997), 1: 315.

10. Vladislav and Pleshakov, *Inside Kremlin*, 170–72; Pei, *Waijiaoshi*, 43.

11. During Khrushchev's first visit, the Soviets signed a series of agreements with the Chinese, including the return to China of military bases in Lushun, along with their equipment; giving up Soviet shares in four Sino-Soviet ventures; providing China with loans totaling 520 million rubles; and offering China technology transfer on 156 key industrial projects for the first five-year plan of the PRC; for details, see Westad, *Brothers in Arms*, 257.

... In general he was insensitive to the Chinese," promising far greater conciliation with Kruschchev at the helm.¹² Mao and the other high-ranking leaders had a range of reasons for backing Khrushchev's climb to the top. First of all, Khrushchev's emphasis on the importance of Communist China diplomatically opened up a prospect for the CCP to be treated as equals on the world stage. Georgi M. Malenkov, by contrast, had leaned toward the West in stating pragmatically the USSR's shared interest with its enemies in averting a nuclear catastrophe; at the same time, Molotov's personal conservatism made him unreceptive to any idea that deviated too far from doctrinaire Stalinism.¹³ Khrushchev, the dark horse in the race for Soviet preeminence, wanted to rid Chinese nostrils of the bad odor left by Stalin's cynical imperialism, making Khrushchev a natural choice for Chinese support. Further, the inexperience of the new Soviet elite both in fomenting revolution and constructing socialism encouraged Mao to think that he would enjoy at least a ten-year period of peace and noninterference in implementing his construction plan in China. Mao was keen to inform these projects with a sense of the lessons learned from the Eastern European experience, which he reckoned the Soviets would

---

12. Nikita Khrushchev, *Khrushchev Remembers: The Glasnost Tapes*, transl. Jerrod L. Schecter with Vyacheslav Luchkov (Boston: Little, Brown, 1990), 142–43. For the latest Chinese scholarship on the Soviet aid to the CCP and later the new regime in the late 1940s, see Shen Zhihua, "Dui ZhongSu tongmeng jingji Beijing de lishikaocha" [A historical investigation into the economic background of the Sino–Soviet Alliance—Studies on Sino–Soviet economic relations, 1948–1949, Part I], *Dang de wenxian*, 2 (2001): 53–64; "XinZhongguo jianlichuqi Sulian duihua jingjiyuanzhu de jibenqinghuang-laizi Zhongguo he Eluosi de dang'an cailiao" [Basic information regarding Soviet economic aid to China in the early years of New China—Archival material from China and Russia], Parts I & II, *Eluosi Yanjiu* [Russian Study], 1 (2001): 53–66; 2 (2001): 49–58; "Jianguochuqi Sulian duihuayuanzhu de jibenqinghuang" [The Soviet economic assistance to Communist China in its early years: A general introduction], *Dangshi yanjiu ziliao* [CCP History research materials], 3 (2001): 1–16; *Sulian zhuanjia zai Zhongguo, 1948–1960* [Soviet Experts in China, 1948–1960], 2nd ed. (Beijing: Xinhua, 2009).
13. Vladislav and Pleshakov, *Inside the Kremlin*, 78–109. For Chinese top leaders' impression of Molotov's stubbornness and inflexibility on foreign policy in dealing with the Western powers, see Wu, *Shinian lunzhan, 1956–1966: ZhongSu guanxi huiyilu* [Ten-Year polemical debate, 1956–1966: A memoir on Sino–Soviet Relations]. Beijing: Zhongyang wenxian, 1999: 10–11.

not be too proprietary in interpreting.¹⁴ With Stalin out the way, it became much easier for the Chinese to project a socialism with distinctively Chinese characteristics, even if this rested on the basis of the Stalinist model. Stalin's death also allowed the Chinese and Eastern Europeans to talk to each other without the fear of being overruled by Moscow.

As a result, from 1954 onward, the Chinese government initiated closer contacts with the Eastern European states. Through these contacts, Mao strove to learn from fellow bloc nations with a view to fine-tuning Chinese socioeconomic reforms; as Mao put it during the process of compiling the PRC's first constitution: the party should not be afraid to adopt useful sections of other states' systems so long as it adapted these to Chinese conditions, while also taking heed of the reactionary or unsuccessful aspects of other forms of socialism.¹⁵ After the Geneva conference, Zhou Enlai, China's top diplomat as well as premier, paid visits to the GDR and Poland. Zhou's speech in Warsaw further expressed the CCP's intention of learning from the people's democracies: "Poland in the fields of the economy and culture is more advanced than China. We should learn a great deal from Poland in these respects."¹⁶ The Chinese delegation was also impressed by the ardor and courtesy of their hosts, who were clearly thrilled to receive high-level Chinese guests.¹⁷ The upshot of the Chinese delegation's visit would seem to have been a strengthened willingness on the part of the CCP to cultivate relations with the Eastern Bloc states now that China had emerged as a recognized power in the Communist camp.

In September 1954, high-level delegations from the Eastern Bloc states gathered in Beijing on the invitation of the Chinese gov-

---

14. Shi Zhe remembers Mao stating words to this effect on 12 October 1954, see Shi Zhe, *Jianzhenglu*, 195–96.
15. Mao had been prepared to draw on a range of sources, from Chinese to foreign, and from socialist and capitalist states, in writing the first Chinese constitution of 1954; see Pang and Jin, *Maozhuan*, 317–20.
16. Zhongyang wenxian, *ZNP*, 404–5; Pei, *Waijiaoshi*, 59.
17. "On the Polish Delegation's Visit in China," CFMA, File 109-00403-06, 30–36.

ernment for the fifth anniversary of the PRC. Almost simultaneously with the high point in the Sino–Soviet relationship signaled by Khrushchev's first visit to China, the CCP held a series of direct talks with the leaderships of the people's democracies of Hungary and Poland in the capital. Briefly meeting the Hungarian ambassador on 22 September, Mao asked about the Hungarian language, particularly its differences from Romanian and German, and the typical features of the Hungarian people. Mao's questions suggest that his knowledge of Hungary had barely advanced since 1949.[18] Yet when he met the Hungarian leaders on 26 September, he took the keenest interest in the progress of socialization in the Central European country, enquiring especially closely into the development of agricultural socialization. After hearing the presentation of the head of the Hungarian delegation, András Hegedüs on the topic, Mao praised Hungary's achievements in this area, which were well ahead of China's. Premier Zhou then introduced Deng Zihui, the head of the central rural work department for overseeing Chinese agricultural cooperativization as established in early 1953, to Hegedüs, suggesting they could exchange accounts of their experience in agriculture and water conservation. In essence, the Chairman understood the situation in the Eastern European states primarily through the prism of international Communism, judging states on the basis of their degree of Stalinist socialization. Preoccupied with the question on how to bring about a rapid agricultural collectivization in 1954, Mao was impressed by the achievements in the Eastern Bloc states and determined that China's social and economic transformation should catch up and then in time surpass that of the European republics.[19]

One special detail worth noting is that, before the meeting

---

18. "Record of Chairman Mao's Meeting with Szikládan, the Hungarian Ambassador in Beijing," CFMA, 117-00353-02, 1–4. For the Hungarian archival record of the meeting between Mao and Szikládan in May, see "Hungarian Embassy in Beijing on the Ambassador's Meeting with Mao Zedong, 17 May, 1954," H00009, MOL, XIX-J-1-j China, 1945–1964, 1. doboz, 12, 00973/1954.

19. "Record of Chairman Mao's Meeting with the Hungarian Government Delegation and the Hungarian Ambassador to China," CFMA, 109-00409-01, 1–9.

ended, Mao specifically told Hegedüs to send his greetings to Comrade Rákosi, who had been invited by the Chinese government but could not make the trip.[20] As Rákosi later recalled, after the Hungarian delegation returned to Budapest, the head of the delegation (whom Rákosi did not recall, but should by rights have been Hegedüs) passed on Mao's regret that he had not been able to meet the Hungarian top leader in Beijing. Mao actually had met Rákosi in 1949 during his first visit to Moscow, on the occasion of the celebration of Stalin's seventieth birthday, when the two heads of state had chatted twice during coffee breaks. Rákosi had quickly began to acquaint Mao with his country and suggested that Hungarian industry could send some supplies to China. The Chairman had warmed to this suggestion of industrial cooperation immediately, asking Rákosi to put in a formal proposal.[21] Though the transfer never got off the ground, the likelihood is that Mao was much interested in any possible cooperation on Hungary's part in China's industrialization, also warming to Hungary's positive disposition toward China.

Thereafter, on 28 September and 9 October, Mao Zedong twice met with the Polish delegation led by Boleslaw Bierut in a similarly fraternal atmosphere. On 1 October, the Chinese side also arranged a meeting between Deng Zihui and Bierut to exchange notes on agriculture.[22] During the first meeting Mao again praised the Polish party's achievements, suggesting that the first Chinese constitution had in some respects taken the Polish Constitution as a model. Mao proposed to Bierut a certain formula for the states' prospective cooperation: you first help us with industrialization, then, after we have industrialized, "let us be your aid." The Chinese, that is, professed friendship but (given the current state of their resources) no

---

20. Ibid, CFMA, 109-00409-01, 9.
21. "Rákosi's Account of Rajk's Case and the Inner Struggle of the Hungarian Party," in Shen Zhihua ed., *Sulian lishidangan xuanbian* [Selected Historical Soviet Archives, *SHSA*] (Beijing: Shehui kexue wenxian, 2002), 26: 193.
22. "Minutes: Deng Zihui's Meeting with Bierut, 1 October 1954," CFMA, 109-00403-03, 11–12.

material aid.[23] Mao's proposal and wording is consistent in terms of the Chairman's desire to prove his capacity to build China into a superior socialist power, particularly in the post-Stalin era. The supposed achievements in agricultural collectivization of both Hungary and Poland thus lent a significant impetus to Mao's demand for a greater speed of social and economic transformation at home. In all this Mao was seeking faster socialization and economic growth, which could help him to realize his underlying ambition: to be in a position where he could hold up China as a model socialist state, capable of aiding others in Europe and elsewhere.

In retrospect, as a result of the softer methods used by the post-Stalin Soviets in managing the international socialist movement and China's growing interest in learning from the Eastern Bloc, relations between China and the Eastern European states toward the end of 1954 were closer and more amicable than ever before. Nevertheless, the Chinese side to some degree harbored reservations about its involvement with the Soviet-controlled Eastern Bloc organization. According to Shi Zhe, during his long tour around China in 1954, Khrushchev mooted the suggestion of inviting China to join the Council for Mutual Economic Associate (CMEA)—the official equivalent to the Comecon established in 1949 as an entity corresponding to the Western European Organization for Economic Co-operation. Mao's reaction to this proposal, as conveyed by Shi Zhe, was firmly negative, leading to his rebuffing Khrushchev face to face two days later, with the words, "It is not at all necessary [for us to join the CMEA] since it would have no significant meaning for the Chinese construction of socialism. On the contrary, it would be problematic for us to get entangled in [the CMEA], which could only hinder the development of [our own socialist] construction." Khrushchev immediately withdrew his plan.[24] Mao's refusal was clearly motivated by a reluctance to subordinate China formally to a Soviet-led organization, especially in view of China's difficult

---

23. "Summary of Chairman Mao's Meeting with Bierut, 9 October 1954," CFMA, 109-00403-05, part 1. See also Pei, *Waijiaoshi*, 60.

24. Shi Zhe, *Jianzhenglu*, 200–201.

birth pangs as a Communist nation. Mao may also have had in mind the complicated relations between the Eastern Bloc states and the Soviet Union, which had the potential to redefine state economics subversively, possibly putting in jeopardy China's ability to adhere to its own principles in developing a Chinese socialism.

In general, the improved relationship between China and the Eastern Bloc states from 1954 to early 1956 was marked by a development of relations focusing as much on the exchange of experiences in the socioeconomic sphere as on the cultivation of specific political contacts.[25] On the one hand, with the USSR as the leading figure inside the Communist camp, the people's democracies in Europe were viewed by the Chinese Communists as cases parallel to their own revolutionary enterprise. The Maoist regime had its own internal and external reasons for pursuing closer interstate relations. On the other hand, despite Khrushchev's attempt to draw China into closer formal or institutional ties with the people's democracies under Soviet leadership, the Chinese had insisted on their independence within a post-Stalin interstate system. In regard to domestic politics, the more rapid domestic Stalinization in the Eastern European states urged on the Chinese leadership, Mao in particular, stimulating them to further accelerate domestic socioeconomic transformation in the second half of the 1950s. If Mao doubted that Soviet social transformation could be emulated or overhauled over a short period, the degree of collectivization and

---

25. For China's foreign policy toward the Eastern European countries, see Pei, *Waijiaoshi*, 1: 52–77. In the politburo session of the Hungarian Worker's Party, the attendees suggested that Rákosi, in representing the Party Center, write a letter to Mao Zedong expressing their appreciation of financial support received from the Chinese government. In the same meeting, the Politburo members decided to provide technical assistance to a Chinese machine-tractor station in March 1955; see "Session of the HWP Politburo on Hungary's proposed technical assistance to a Chinese Machine-Tractor Station (10 March 1955)," H00011, MOL, M-KS 276.f. 53.cs. 221.0e. With full awareness of the value of improved Sino–Hungarian relations in economic and technical exchanges, the Hungarian party's leadership issued a formal instruction on widening cooperation with Chinese in the fields of trade, economy, and industry on 31 August 1956; see "Session of the HWP Politburo on the Widening of Sino–Hungarian Economic and Technical Cooperation (16 November 1956)," H00012, MOL, M-KS 276.f. 53.cs. 301.0e.

industrialization in the Eastern Bloc states could be taken far more readily as an achievable benchmark. Mao was, after all, acutely conscious of the necessity of building socialism and developing China's economic power in order to enhance his country's stature in the world at large. All this in turn reinforced Chairman Mao's radical view in emphasizing a rapid implementation of socioeconomic reconstruction supplemented by ideological remolding and political purges, which he believed would ensure systematic, solid foundations for Chinese socialism.

POLITICAL DEVELOPMENTS IN HUNGARY AND POLAND SINCE THE CPSU TWENTIETH CONGRESS IN COMPARISON TO CHINESE DOMESTIC POLITICAL DEVELOPMENTS

In the first year and a half after Stalin's death, the Kremlin's so-called collective leadership started to steer a New Course economically, moving away from heavy capital–intensive development toward managed consumption and agricultural reforms. A shift of focus to light industry and trade aimed to boost the incomes of collectivized farmers and make available a wider range of goods to customers. In the political realm, however, the Kremlin envisaged restricting adaptations of the Stalinist system to a minimum.[26] Khrushchev, a leader rooted in the revolutionary age, broadly rejected the New Course formula, in favor of maintaining a program of development especially by jump-starting agricultural productivity. Khrushchev's thaw in domestic politics extended to the rehabilitation of Marshal

---

26. Hope M. Harrison, *Driving the Soviets up the Wall, Soviet-East German Relations, 1953–1961* (Princeton, NJ: Princeton University Press, 2003), 28; Brzezinski, *The Soviet Bloc*, 156–65. For Khrushchev's interpretation of the political purpose of the "New Course," see Khrushchev, *The Glasnost Tapes*, 163. For Hungarian politics between 1947 and 1953 see Gyula Szvák, *Magyar századok: Gergely Jenö–Izsák Lajos, A huszadik század története* [Hundred years of Hungary series: Jeno Gergely–Lajos Izsak, history of the twentieth century] (Budapest: Pannonica Kiadó, 2000), 306–42.

Tito in Yugoslavia and to fence-mending with other socialist nations. Throughout late 1954 and 1955, Khrushchev's regime loosened Stalinist political orthodoxies, unwittingly opening up a Pandora's box that called Stalin's infallibility in politics and interbloc relationships in question.[27]

The signal, even ritual, event in this process of ideological enfranchisement was Khrushchev's so-called secret speech delivered at the end of the CPSU Twentieth Congress. On the morning of 25 February, as a representative of the CPSU, Khrushchev denounced Stalin's crimes to the party delegates in a closed session, requesting as a final salvo (perhaps not entirely sincerely) that this dressing-down remain private. The speech was read out with deliberate slowness to Eastern European Communist leaders during the night of 25–26 February, allowing note-taking.[28] Despite the stunning vigor of its condemnation of Stalin's malfeasance, Khrushchev's speech was careful to single out Stalin's political purges, his extreme personality cult, incompetence during the war, and alienation from the people; it did not disavow the state infrastructure of Communism or ideological underpinnings of the party. Stalin's treatment of the people's democracies also escaped mention; Khrushchev may have wanted to be a Stalin in one respect at least.[29]

Intentionally or not, Khrushchev's speech shook the power of the already wobbly incumbent Stalinists in Eastern Europe. The Soviet leaders wanted to shore up a revised Communism by enforcing international-bloc unity, thereby constraining changes within the socioeconomic sphere. However, after only one year of the New Course, a head of opposition to state parties and to Moscow's ultimate lead had built up among the rank and file and wider public in the people's democracies.[30]

---

27. For an argument treating Khrushchev's rise to power as a recapitulation of the Stalinist experience, see Brzezinski, *The Soviet Bloc*, 168.
28. The Hungarian delegates had about three hours to listen to sixty reels' worth of the secret speech. "Rákosi's Account of Rajk's case and the Inner Struggle of the Hungarian Party," Shen, *SHSA*, 26: 196.
29. Brzezinski, *The Soviet Bloc*, 179; Lüthi, *The Sino–Soviet Split*, 48–49.
30. See Kramer's three-part "The Early Post-Stalin Succession Struggle and

In Hungary specifically, the difficulties of a much-hated Stalinist leader, Mátyás Rákosi, in facing down widespread public discontent in 1956 were only compounded by Khrushchev's denunciation of Stalin.[31] Increasingly changing direction according to local conditions, Rákosi rehabilitated László Rajk on 27 March 1956, besides making other concessions.[32] Rákosi's belated moderation, however, only raised the hopes of Hungary's youth and intellectuals, who an-

---

Upheavals in East-Central Europe: Internal–External Linkages in Soviet Policy Making," *Journal of Cold War Studies*, 1, no. 2 (1999): 3–38. The Hungarian nationwide disorders, more severe than those in 1953, reerupted between 1955 and 1956; see Kramer, "New Evidence on Soviet Decision-Making and the 1956 Polish and Hungarian Crises," *CWIHP Bulletin*, 8–9 (1996/1997): 363.

31. Mátyás Rákosi was prime minister of Hungary from 14 August 1952 to 4 July 1953. For a brief biography of Rákosi, see László Izsák, *Magyarorszag miniszterelnökei: 1848–1990*, [The prime ministers of Hungary: 1848–1990] (Budapest: Cégér Kiadó Kft. 1993), 187–91. Mátyás Rákosi, Ernő Gerő, József Révai, and Farkas Mihály formed a "gang of four" in the HWP during the Stalin era.

32. As an important organizer of the Hungarian Communist Party in the second half of the 1940s, László Rajk replaced Imre Nagy as minister of internal affairs in 1946. In this post, he organized the State Protection Authority (ÁVH), an organization analogous to the KGB, and prohibited and liquidated several religious, national, democratic, and maverick establishments and groups. He also put on the first show trials. Following the announcement of Yugoslav's expulsion from the Cominform, the Soviet Union launched a series of measures to purge any elements of "nationalist deviation" from the ranks of Eastern European Communist parties. In 1949 Rajk fell victim to Stalinist purges orchestrated by Rákosi, who saw the influence and popularity of Rajk among the Hungarian Communists as a threat to his own authority. Rajk was accused of being a Titoist spy, and he confessed to all the charges that were brought against him for an acquittal promised by the authorities during his imprisonment. However, the Soviets and the Hungarian Communist leadership under Rákosi had already determined to use Rajk's case to initiate the famous anti-Titoist purges. As a consequence, Rajk, together with seven other men who stood trial with him, was sentenced to death after the show trial held in September 1949 and was executed three weeks later. Richard John Crampton, *Eastern Europe in the Twentieth Century—and After* (London: Routledge, 1997), 263; Richard Frucht, *Encyclopedia of Eastern Europe: From the Congress of Vienna to the Fall of Communism* (London: Taylor & Francis Group, 2003), 651. For an excerpt from Rajk's indictment, see Jussi Hanhimäki and Odd Arne Westad, *The Cold War: A History in Documents and Eyewitness Accounts* (Oxford and New York: Oxford University Press, 2003), 63–65. For the official announcement of Rajk and his associates' rehabilitation, see *Szabad Nép* [Free People, one of the most influential national newspapers in Hungary], 27 March 1956; the announcement was broadcast by Radio Budapest on 31 March 1956. See Charles Gati, *Failed Illusions: Moscow, Washington, Budapest, and the 1956 Hungarian Revolt* (Stanford, CA: Stanford University Press, 2006), 48–49.

ticipated the more moderate Nagy's accession to the premiership. But when Nagy, an ethnically Hungarian agricultural scientist, became prime minister with Soviet blessing, Rákosi remained party general secretary, leaving in place a disgruntled rump of opposition to the New Course. Nagy's initial economic reforms began to question Stalinist orthodoxies of social transformation and heavy-handed state violence, both previously areas of Rákosi's political responsibility. It seems that Nagy was too idealistic or naive to sense the discontent in the senior politburo and secretariat, buoyed by a spirit of reformism in the lower party echelons. Rákosi chose his moment to act immediately after Khrushchev announced his neo-Stalinist economic program, denouncing Nagy's deviationism and ousting him in April 1955. In November 1955, Nagy was finally expelled from the party. Khrushchev later censured the Hungarians for not having consulted Moscow before the expulsion, given that the former leader would have been a highly useful figure during the unrest of mid-July.[33] After returning to the citizenry, Nagy involved himself into the life of the common people, maintaining his popularity at an exceptionally high level and retaining the ear of the masses, especially the young. A wistful Marxist–Leninist theoretician, Nagy spent his internal exile formulating post-Communist ideas in which Hungary would take up a neutral position in the Cold War.[34]

---

33. Veljko Mićunović, *Moscow Diary*, trans. David Floyd, intro. George Kennan (Garden City, NY: Doubleday Books, 1980), 88.

34. For the Kremlin's support to appointing Nagy as Hungarian prime minister in mid-June 1953, see Békés Csaba and Malcolm Byrne, *The 1956 Hungarian Revolution: A History in Documents* (Budapest and New York: Central European University, 2002), 16. For Nagy's self-conception as a Marxist–Leninist scientist, see Meray Tibor, *Thirteen Days That Shook the Kremlin: Imre Nagy and the Hungarian Revolution* (New York: Praeger, 1959), 19; for Rákosi's efforts to stigmatize Nagy inside the Kremlin, see Charles Gati, *Failed Illusions*, 115; for Khrushchev's account of the Hungarians' failing to consult Moscow about Nagy's expulsion, see Mićunović, *Moscow Diary*, 88, backing up "Hao Deqing's talk with the Soviet ambassador on the Hungarian political situation, 16 August 1956," 109-01040-01, 49–51, CFMA. For a recent general study of the Hungarian Revolution of 1956, see Paul Lendvai, *One Day That Shook the Communist World: The 1956 Hungarian Uprising and Its Legacy*, transl. Ann Major (Princeton, NJ: Princeton University Press, 2010), 5–240.

This intensifying ferment among Hungarians helped the Petőfi Circle, a discussion group originally set up by Rákosi's government in honor of the famous nineteenth-century patriotic poet, transform itself by June 1956 into a prominent organ of opposition.[35] In close contact with Nagy and emboldened by the thaw in Hungary and the Poznan riots, the circle began to think that civil society could force Rákosi out.[36] The 30 June Hungarian Workers' Party (HWP) Central Committee resolution, Rákosi's last-ditch Stalinist response to the unrest, accused the Petőfi Circle of "turning the debates into group attacks against the People's Republic," connecting "anti-Party elements" and "a certain group which has formed around Imre Nagy with the intention of making the whole story a 'Nagy conspiracy.'"[37] Rákosi's proposal of suppressing Nagy and his literary outlets, though, was deemed too risky by party commissars more attuned to the public mood than Rákosi himself. Ernő Gerő, a traditional Stalinist allied with Rákosi's faction, went over his leader's head in informing the Soviet embassy that "severe complications could unexpectedly emerge" at the forthcoming plenum of 18 July on account of Rákosi's weakened position and central party disunity. Andropov duly cabled Moscow, drawing the Soviets once more into Hungarian domestic politics in lobbying for a clear endorsement of the 30 June resolution, seeking to mend rifts in the HWP.[38]

There is little doubt that in the first half of 1956 the entire CPSU presidium supported Rákosi, notwithstanding Khrushchev's later

---

35. The Petőfi Circle was formed in March 1956 as a debating club within the framework of the Federation of Working Youth. The members of this club strongly criticized the crimes and mistakes of the Rákosi regime, greatly contributing to the ferment that eventually exploded in the Hungarian revolt.

36. The Poznan Uprising of June was a workers' demonstration, and was put down at a cost of fifty-three deaths. See Duncan Townson, *A Dictionary of Contemporary History: 1945 to the Present* (Oxford: Blackwell, 1999), 152; for the Petőfi Circle's response to Poznan, see Brzezinski, *The Soviet Bloc*, 220–21.

37. Radio Budapest, 30 June 1956; for an English version, see Brzezinski, *The Soviet Bloc*, 221.

38. "Shifrtelegramma," from Yuri V. Andropov to the CPSU Presidium and Secretariat, 9 July 1956 (Special Dossier–Strictly Secret), in Arkhiv Prezidenta Rossiiskoi Federatsii (APRF), f. 3, op. 64, d. 483, ll. 151–62, cited in Kramer, "New Evidence," 362.

repudiation of him post-October as someone "lacking the most elementary understanding of what needed to be done" to the extent that "it had been a great mistake to have relied on that idiot."[39] Even before Mikoyan's departure for Budapest, Khrushchev maintained the desirability of alleviating Rákosi's personal situation.[40] Mikoyan began to induce the Kremlin to change its mind after a conversation with Rákosi on 26 June even prior to his arrival in Hungary; Rákosi was terrified of the masses rounding on him for his show trial of Rajk and the Soviets turning against him for normalizing relations with Tito so back-handedly.[41] Mikoyan's follow-up meetings with Rákosi, Gerő, and other top Hungarian leaders in Budapest convinced him that Rákosi was the problem. Gerő's briefings had laid before the envoy the full extent of the popular ferment, suggesting that the central party had to pull together, which they could not do with Rákosi in charge. Perhaps Gerő here just wanted to unseat his colleague.[42]

Facing a sea of enemies, Rákosi had the presence of mind to defend himself, contending that no single Communist had to have a "fundamental solution." He had not earlier cracked down on the counterrevolutionaries because "the situation [in Hungary] is so intense and complicated that the arrest [of anti-Party elements] won't

---

39. Mićunović, *Moscow Diary*, 135–36, 140; Kramer, "New Evidence," 362. On Moscow's reasons for backing Rákosi in mid-July, see Mićunović, op. cit., 87.

40. The literal translation of Khrushchev's Russian is, "There must be an easing of the situation, Rákosi," an ambiguous rendering somewhere between "We must alleviate Rákosi's situation" and "Rákosi must alleviate the situation," the second suggesting the Soviets' increasing dissatisfaction with the Hungarian leader. According to Mićunović's diary on 15 July, Khrushchev pledged support before backing off that commitment to Tito the same day. The Soviets were wary of growing Yugoslav influence over the bloc and would likely have understated the expedients they had planned for intervening in Hungary. For the Malin Notes, see Center for the Storage of Contemporary Documentation (TsKhSD), f. 3, op. 12, d. 1005, ll. 2–20b, English version translated and annotated by Mark Kramer, "The 'Malin Notes' on Crises in Hungary and Poland in 1956," *CWIHP Bulletin*, 8–9 (Winter 1996/1997): 385–410; see also Mićunović, *Moscow Diary*, 88–91.

41. "Mikoyan's Report to the CPSU Presidium on 26 June, 1956," in Shen, *SHSA*, 27: 207.

42. "Summary of Mikoyan's meeting with Rákosi and others, 13 July 1956," ibid., 211.

help things at all. . . . After we arrest one group of them, there will be another, and then the third, endless."⁴³ From the Soviet perspective, these words only betrayed weakness. The presidium members, Khrushchev especially, had begun to feel that their dissociation from Stalin had been too abrupt. As a self-exculpatory maneuver, though, the Soviet leadership preferred to attribute the unrest in the bloc to the "subversive activities of the imperialists," meaning that, applying a restrictive understanding of the events, "when the head ached, they dealt with the head," sacrificing Rákosi for the HWP's unity.⁴⁴

With Mikoyan's strong sponsorship, Rákosi's first secretary post went to Gerő, and several imprisoned Communists, most prominently János Kádár, were recalled to party positions.⁴⁵ Whatever the rebalancing of elements within the HWP, the July solution met international exigencies in appeasing Tito and keeping in power a regime fully committed to the Soviet Union.⁴⁶ The Soviet leadership began to posit a common foundation for the Communist parties, which supposedly rested on the Soviet economic model and were (unlike Tito or Nagy's outlooks) unambiguously aligned with the USSR in the Cold War. Far from allowing leeway to intraparty political dissent, this framework, as Mikoyan explained, justified a resumption of party discipline, since "the relaxation of international tensions and the slogan of coexistence [as proclaimed at the CPSU Twentieth Congress] do not presuppose but, on the contrary, exclude ideological concessions and any accommodation to hostile views."⁴⁷

---

43. Ibid.
44. For Khrushchev's ideas of the genesis of the Polish and Hungarian turmoil, see the Malin Notes, TsKhSD, f. 3, op. 12, d. 1005, ll. 2–20b, *CWIHP Bulletin*, 8–9: 388.
45. Kramer, "New Evidence," 364 and fn. 63. On the eve of the plenum, Mikoyan also held talks with key members of the HWP Central Leadership, canvassing for Gerő.
46. Brzezinski, *The Soviet Bloc*, 222.
47. "Mikoyan's Telegram from Budapest to the CPSU Presidium," Shen, *SHSA*, 27, 233; Kramer, "New Evidence," ft. 66; his source is "TsK KPSS," 18 July 1956, Osobaya papka, in APRF, F. 3, Op. 64, D. 483, L231.

In fact, Rákosi's caution that his removal would not avert a meltdown proved correct. Gerő's appointment, together with unhelpful Soviet suggestions over party management, presided over an intensification of social turbulence aggravated by the central party's failure to reach "a unified position among the members of the Politburo" by early September.[48] The new first secretary had unenviably to restore order "without a clear-cut conception of what his policy, even basic assumptions, ought to be."[49] At his wits' end, Gerő left for Moscow in September looking for further assistance, inexplicably staying one and one-half months in the USSR as the domestic situation deteriorated unchecked.[50] The Kremlin, meanwhile, exasperated with the July compromise and feckless Hungarian leadership, all the while coming to an alternative diagnosis of the troubles' root causes, took up Andropov's advice to strengthen its contacts with the Hungarians by inviting the leadership to Moscow, while taking credit for refloating Hungarian industry. Meanwhile, Khrushchev arranged a meeting between Gerő and Tito in the Crimea, hoping that a step forward in the process of a Hungarian–Yugoslav rehabilitation would provide a shot in the arm for the beleaguered HWP.[51]

These Soviet efforts, though, only stoked the anti-Soviet mood of ordinary Hungarians. As Gerő told Andropov on his return from Moscow, the Hungarian populace could not now be conceivably reconciled to Moscow; Hungary domestically had become more "complicated and turbulent," with potentially "serious problems" lying in wait "throughout the country." "Acute discontent had extended to the workers, not counting those anxious peasants who are demanding the dismissal of the Agricultural Cooperatives." The Rajk's internment backfired on the party leadership as opposition

---

48. Kramer, "New Evidence," 365, fn. 67.
49. Brzezinski, *The Soviet Bloc*, 223.
50. "Summary of Andropov's Conversation with Gerő, 2 September 1956," Shen, *SHSA*, 27, 258; Kramer, "New Evidence," 365, fn. 68.
51. "Andropov's report to the CPSU Presidium, 27 August 1956," Shen, *SHSA*, 27, 246; For the Yugoslav perspective on Khrushchev's arranging Gerő's Yugoslavia visit in early October 1956, see Mićunović, *Moscow Diary*, 116–18.

forces pressed for further concessions; many agitated openly for Nagy's return.[52] Nagy put Moscow on the horns of a dilemma. On the one hand, the HWP was besieged by calls for his reinstatement, which could serve to pacify public unrest. On the other, Nagy's identification with the new nationalist policies put him beyond the pale of the CPSU presidium. Gerő maintained that Nagy stubbornly refused to admit error on every point of contention throughout the period of his leadership.[53] To Moscow, Nagy's nationalism was politically toxic, so that the Kremlin never seriously countenanced his return to power. However, Gomulka's ascendancy in Poland and the Kremlin's own evolution gave the Hungarians false hope. This tide of discontent reached a critical mark between 15 and 22 October.[54]

Polish restiveness with Soviet domination had followed a similar course to that in Hungary. A large number of intellectuals' discussion groups had convened as early as 1955, rapidly convening into illegal forms of political assembly weighing political alternatives. But a significant difference from the Hungarian state of affairs lay in the fact that provided the regime was not threatened, Polish political members typically welcomed opportunities to diminish Poland's dependence on the Soviet Union, nursing still-fresh memories of the Soviet's forced dissolution in the late 1930s of the Polish United Workers' Party (Poland's governing Communist Party from 1948 to 1989). In this atmosphere, Wladyslaw Gomulka, ex–"right-wing" deviationist secretly released from prison in 1954, represented a more palatable option than the Kremlin loyalist Boleslaw Bierut.

---

52. "Andropov's Report from Budapest to the Soviet Foreign Ministry, 12 October 1956," Shen, *SHSA*, 27, 267; "Shifrtelegramma," 12 October 1956, from Yuri V. Andropov to the CPSU Presidium, in APRF, F. 3, Op. 64, D. 484, L1. 64–75.

53. "Andropov's Report from Budapest to the Soviet Foreign Ministry, 12 October 1956," Shen, *SHSA*, 27, 267.

54. Khrushchev set out the clear view in this session: "We should recruit Nagy for political action. But until then we shouldn't make a chairman of the government." See TsKhSD, f. 3, op. 12, d. 1006, ll. 4–40b, compiled by V. N. Malin, *CWIHP Bulletin*, 8–9: 388–89. However, without asking Soviet advice, the Hungarian central committee elected Nagy the new premier in the plenum held on 23 October as a last throw of the dice to appease domestic anger. See Kramer, "Hungary and Poland, 1956: Khrushchev's CPSU CC Presidium Meeting on East European Crises, 24 October 1956," *CWIHP Bulletin*, 5 (Spring 1995): 52–53.

Not beset by either internal splits or direct Soviet interference, the party could develop a much more gradualist line of policy relaxation than in Hungary. The CPSU Twentieth Congress threw everything in the air, jeopardizing the ability of the Polish Communists to move toward a recognition of the primacy of domestic concerns while consolidating itself and the executive institutions of socialism.[55]

Following Bierut's fatal heart attack in Moscow, Khrushchev backed the Stalinist Edward Ochab. The PUWP, for its part, jockeyed for its legitimacy by conceding that living standards had fallen during the Stalin years, while arguing that the state political apparatus allowed for economic reform. By the summer, popular ferment had reached the working classes, leading to demonstrations demanding systematic wage reform in Poznan. The army killed fifty-three people and inflicted over three hundred serious injuries.[56] The Soviet leadership anxiously warded off the possibility of a "domino" of insurrection in the Eastern European states by postulating imperialist provocation;[57] at the same time, leaders started to redefine acceptable forms of state socialism around a common core of Soviet doctrine.[58] The Soviets preferred political measures, rather than controlled concessions, as a means of pressuring the Poles to get control of the situation.

After Poznan and the Soviet strong-arm tactics, the formerly united Polish leadership split over the issue of Polish–Soviet relations and Gomulka's role in the party. The Soviets had not opposed Gomulka's return to public life, with Khrushchev even suggesting to Ochab that Gomulka might come to Moscow for recuperation. As

---

55. Brzezinski, *The Soviet Bloc*, 239–40.
56. See "Opinions on the Poznan Violence, 25 July 1956," CFMA, 109-00761-01, 1–13; Townson, *A Dictionary of Contemporary History*, 152. For a special study on Poznan of 1956, see Edmunda Makowski, *Poznański Czerwiec 1956: Pierwszy Bunt Społeczeństwa W Prl* (Poznań: Wydawn. Poznanskie, 2001).
57. "Khrushchev's Wording during the CPSU Presidium Meeting Held on 12 July," Kramer, "New Evidence," *CWIHP Bulletin* 8–9: 385; for public commentaries on the Poznan events, see the official newspaper of the Central Committee (CC) of the CPSU, *Pravda*, 1 July 1956.
58. *Pravda*, 16 July 1956; relevant analysis see Brzezinski, *The Soviet Bloc*, 245–46.

far as it is possible to reconstruct Khrushchev's motives, it seems he considered that the inclusion of Gomulka in the politburo in a relatively unimportant role, far from being a threat, could even be of service in appeasing the uprisings. Domestically, Gomulka had increasingly become a national symbol of Polish reconciliation, around whom different interest groups could gather. The final decision to invite Gomulka back to the politburo, however, was made after Ochab's Beijing visit in September, during which he told the Chinese leadership that he was inclined to bring Gomulka back to the center (the Chinese role in his return is discussed in a later section).[59]

In early October, then, the top Polish leaders rehabilitated Gomulka by granting him the position of general secretary of the Polish United Worker's Party (PUWP). The PUWP under Gomulka's leadership promulgated an alternative line to the CPSU's official assessment of the Polish uprising, proclaiming that the party, not the insurgents, should take the major responsibility for Poznan. In the debate among the party hierarchy, Defense Minister Marshal Rokossowski, a Polish-born Russian citizen sent to Warsaw by Stalin in 1949, lost his place in the new politburo. The Soviet leaders thus entertained a strong suspicion that Gomulka, if unchecked, would be instrumental in elaborating an independent Polish line. On 19 October, a top-ranking Soviet leadership delegation led by Khrushchev flew into Warsaw without any prearrangement with the PUWP, with Soviet troops simultaneously surrounding the Polish capital. These dramatic moves could even be seen as portending full-blown Soviet military intervention.[60]

---

59. For a good analysis of the Polish top leadership's debates on Gomulka's role and relevant Soviet attitudes from late July to mid-October, see Brzezinski, *The Soviet Bloc*, 242–60; for Ochab's recollection, Rozmowa z Edwardem Ochabem, Teresa Toranska, Oni, Warszawa, 1989, s. 217, cited in Shen Zhihua and Li Danhui, "The 1956 Polish Crisis and Sino–Polish Relations: Sources from the Chinese Archival Documents and Inside Reports" (conference paper delivered to "The October 1956 Events in Poland in International Relations," October 2006, Warsaw); Shen and Li, "1956nian de ZhongBo guanxi," 45–48.
60. Kramer, "New Evidence," *CWIHP Bulletin*, 8–9: 360.

To sum up, although by early 1956 Polish domestic conditions were better than those in Hungary, where the regime was plagued by internal splits and a discontinuity in policy, both largely due to the Hungarian leadership's dependence on Moscow, the anti-Stalinist and nationalist atmosphere produced by the CPSU Twentieth Congress in both countries in effect placed them in a similar position: top leaders had to weigh their alternatives in considering whether to restore controversial nationalist figures (Nagy in Hungary, Gomulka in Poland) and how to define their role in the center, keeping a lid on domestic disturbances. At the same time, both Poland and Hungary had to bear in mind possible Soviet responses to any of their domestic actions, given the leaders' personal vulnerability and their de facto semisubordinate status to the USSR. The Polish central party moved first to include Gomulka in the regime, then granted him a position of real power. The more independent posture adopted by the Polish center under Gomulka on domestic affairs was soon taken by the Soviets as a threat to their ultimate dominance in Poland and possibly within the Communist camp as a whole. By the second half of October 1956, Polish domestic moves and the Polish–Soviet relationship had thus attracted the attention of the Soviets, the Chinese, and other inner-bloc members. Nevertheless, in hindsight, the Hungarian domestic situation was in fact more unstable than that in Poland at this point, as almost no efficient measures had been taken by the local regime to appease the buildup of popular resentment, leaving the whole country in a state of disorder and uncertainty and thereby sowing the seeds of insurrection.

CHANGES IN CHINA'S POLICY TOWARD EASTERN EUROPE AFTER THE CPSU TWENTIETH CONGRESS

The Chairman's reservations about Khrushchev's idea of a peaceful transition notwithstanding, to a great extent, Mao had from the outset subscribed to the Soviet reassessment of Stalin. It is no overstatement to suggest that Mao had expected, some day, that the legend of Stalin would be shattered.[61] It was thus an optimal outcome for Mao that the Kremlin had lifted the lid on its own initiative. Mao himself saw an opportunity in the speech, since it left China freer to follow its own path within the international socialist camp. Nevertheless, Khrushchev's speech on Stalin astounded Mao and his colleagues in the vigor of its condemnation. Within the top ranks of the CCP, many officials were concerned that the fortunes of Communism could suffer worldwide as a result of Khrushchev's denunciation. The openness of Khrushchev's condemnation of Stalin "made a mess" in the sense of provoking serious ideological confusion within the Communist camp.[62] The Chairman sensed that it was time for the Chinese regime to voice its independent opinions not only on the problem of Stalin but also on a wider range of issues, such as a proper reevaluation of history of the Chinese Revolution and socioeconomic reconstruction. From 12 March up to early April, Mao shifted much of his focus from domestic briefings to the Soviet problem, studying and talking throughout the CPSU Twentieth Congress in group meetings and with various individuals.[63] The upshot of these meetings was Mao's suggestion on 24 March to publish an article presenting the CCP's own balanced

---

61. Mao had reservations over Khrushchev's claim that under certain favorable circumstances, socialism might be established by nonviolent parliamentary means, a conjunction abbreviated under the phrase "peaceful transition" by the Chinese. This "peaceful transition" notion jarred with the Maoist theory and practice of socialist transition, which held that the capitalist class and all its devices and thoughts had to be progressively and decisively crushed so as to pave the way for a new structure. But as Shen Zhihua concludes, in his work on the period, Mao's disagreement with the Kremlin's peaceful-transition line did not become a major issue at this time; see Shen Zhihua, "Sugong ershida feisidalinhua jiqi dui ZhongSu guanxi de yingxiang," 58.
62. Wu Lengxi, *Yi Maozhuxi: wo qinshen jingli de ruogan Zhongda lishishijian de pianduan* [Memory of Chairman Mao: Some important historical incidents of which I have firsthand knowledge] (*Yi Maozhuxi* hereinafter) (Beijing: Xinhua, 1995), 4–5.
63. Pang and Jin, *Maozhuan*, 495–96; Wu Lengxi, *Yi Maozhuxi*, 5–7; Chen Jian and Yang Kuisong, "Chinese Politics and the Collapse of the Sino–Soviet Alliance," in Westad, *Brothers in Arms*, 260–61.

view of Stalin, implicitly rectifying the mistakes of the CPSU Twentieth Congress statements and Khrushchev's secret report.[64]

In the meantime, far from restricting fallout from the Stalin denunciation in China, the Chinese leadership was (perhaps studiedly) careless in disseminating the upshot of the CPSU Twentieth Congress and Khrushchev's secret words at home. *RMRB* quickly reprinted the CPSU Twentieth Congress documents, including the Mikoyan speech made on 16 February exposing Stalin's purges during the 1930s. Having obtained notes of Khrushchev's speech, the center had it read to the party members, making pamphlets of the text and handing them out with *Cankao ziliao* (Reference Materials), a collection of important international information for high-ranking party cadres. At the same time, *Cankao xiaoxi*, an internally circulated Xinhua newspaper specializing in international developments available to party cadres, covered a large quantity of foreign responses and reactions to the CPSU Twentieth Congress, airing problems in assessing Stalin that were current during this period. The foreign-language book store in Beijing, well-known for its large-scale collection of foreign books and materials, even offered a number of the American Communist Party newspaper, *Worker's Daily*, in which a complete version of Khrushchev's secret report was published. All the papers soon sold out, having been passed out among college students in Beijing. After years of indoctrination and mass mobilization in support of essentially Soviet models, it is reasonable to assume that the people from various groups in the Middle Kingdom would be taken aback by any criticism of the rationality and efficiency of the Stalinist political project in any form, not least because of its relevance to all forms of socialist transformation and planning at home. Not surprisingly, therefore, the effect of these de-Stalinization materials was so shattering that provincial cadres, intellectuals, non-Communist party members, and businessmen were said to be "surprised and confused" by

---

64. Since no written records of the series of meetings held from 18 to 23 March were retained, Wu's recollection of the meetings was the only material serviceable in this connection; see Wu, *Yi Maozhuxi*, 7; Pang and Jin, *Maozhuan*, 497.

the sudden developments, with some even questioning the accuracy of the translation of these articles.⁶⁵

In light of the Chairman's emerging idea in this period that rigid approximation to Stalinist models was becoming an impediment to the achievement of Chinese domestic and external objectives, and his positive reception of Soviet efforts to deconsecrate Stalin, the CCP's "careless" handling of the congress speeches becomes very meaningful. It has to be remembered that in early 1954, Mao and his top colleagues still made every effort to limit information on the Soviets' changing assessment of Stalin to the center, voicing far greater dissent from the Soviet line in private than they were willing, for the time being, to make broadly public. After all, the domestic socialist transformation, which rested on a reprise of Stalinism, was still supposedly in process, meaning it was best for the party to profess strict adherence to the Soviet experience in general to avoid any ambiguity that might jeopardize implementation of the master plan. But when it came to early 1956, particularly after the Soviet critique of Stalinism, Mao was apparently more relaxed in having the Chinese public informed of Stalin's mistakes, especially now that the issue of seeking innovative means to surpass Soviet socialism was at the top of his political agenda. All this, however, was only possible because the CPSU Twentieth Congress coincided with the announcement of the socialist transformation in China, which encouraged the Chairman to advance more ambitious projects yet. Given Mao's historical record in manipulating popular opinion either by controlling or relaxing the flow of information, it seems therefore plausible that the Chairman arranged the leaking of new developments in the USSR to a wider Chinese audience, in the anticipation that the ideological and political confusion in the CCP would soon settle of its own accord. If not, an authoritative statement of the Chinese view on Stalin could be offered to allay both domestic and international concerns.⁶⁶

---

65. Shen Zhihua, "Sugong ershida," 51–53.
66. Li Shenzhi interpreted Mao as not being implacably opposed to the leaking of the secret speech through various channels in his article, "Mao zhuxi shi

Once the first draft of this article was ready, beyond circulating the draft within the politburo, the central party asked Chinese embassies and representative offices to report on local media responses to the Soviet denunciation of Stalin.[67] Separate telegrams were sent to embassies in the Eastern Bloc (to Hungary, Romania, Bulgaria, Albania, and Mongolia), urging embassy staff and Xinhua journalists to send feedback by 3 April, two days before the publication of the editorial.[68] Through the local media's responses to the secret speech, the Chinese leadership possibly wanted to make judgments of various governments' official reactions to the Stalin problem by gauging the tone of their mainstream media editorials. At the same time, information collected by Chinese embassy staff and Xinhua journalists from mainly nonofficial channels could provide Beijing with a general picture of social and popular responses to the secret speech within the camp. With these two types of intelligence, the central party could therefore carry out a final revision of its formal announcement based on the investigation of the other socialist states' official stances and an informed sense of the social repercussions of Soviet de-Stalinization. In contrast with the roughness and ambiguity of Khrushchev's secret speech, the Chinese leadership was intent on a comprehensive assessment of Stalin summarizing the historical experience of the dictatorship of the proletariat in the

---

shenme shihou jueding yinshe chudong de" [When did Mao decide to draw a snake out of its hole?], in Niu Han and Deng Jiuping, ed. *Liuyuexue: jiyizhong de fanyoupai yundong* [Snow in June: Remembering the Anti-Rightist Campaign] (Beijing: Jingjiribao, 1998), 117. For an example of Mao's manipulation of public responses via information control in the case of the reassessment of Beria and the East German uprising, see Li, *Mao and the Economic Stalinization of China*, 41–43. For the central party's notice demanding that local party committees lead party insiders and outsiders to study the "On the Historical Experience" editorial one day before its formal publication, see Shen, "Sugong Ershida," ft. 137, 68.

67. "The Central Party's Telegram to Chinese Ambassadors and Chargé d'Affaires, Requesting Them to Make Reports on the Local Media's Responses to the Soviet Denunciation of Stalin during the Twentieth Congress before 3 April, 31 March 1956," CFMA, 109-00971-02, 7.

68. "The Foreign Ministry and Xinhua News Agency Requested the Embassies in Albania, Bulgaria, Hungary, Romania and Mongolia to Collect Information on Responses to the CPSU Twentieth Congress by Various Actors, 31 March 1956," CFMA, 109-00971-02, 6.

most pellucid theoretical terms. Apparently, the Chinese authors, Mao in particular, had expected to win huge prestige internationally by issuing a more persuasive and clearer statement of Stalin's problems to a wider audience within the Communist camp.

On 5 April, an editorial titled "On the Historical Experience of the Dictatorship of the Proletariat" came out in *RMRB* with a title annotation specially added by Mao to underline the piece's authority, noting the article was written by *RMRB* staff on the basis of discussions held in an enlarged session of the CCP.[69] The core of this article, on which Mao himself had expended great editorial effort, was an evaluation of Stalin's achievements and mistakes. Mao insisted on a so-called seventy-thirty ratio in balancing Stalin's contributions and faults, obviously resulting in an affirmative appraisal of Stalin in general. Nonetheless, Mao's specific procedures for framing this seventy-thirty ratio demand further study.[70] In fact, after an opening admission that many mistakes were bound to occur in the process of realizing the proletariat dictatorship, Mao tactically phrased his assessment of Stalin's contribution to Marxism–Leninism in this way: "The man who showed the Soviet people the way to these achievements was Lenin. In the struggle to carry out Lenin's principles, the Central Committee of the Communist Party of the Soviet Union, through its vigorous leadership, earned its credit, in which Stalin had an ineffaceable share." Further: "After Lenin's death, Stalin, as the chief leader of the Party and the state, creatively applied and developed Marxism–Leninism."[71] This esti-

---

69. Editorial article on the front page, 5 April 1956, *Renmin ribao* [People's Daily] (hereinafter *RMRB*); Zhonggong zhongyang wenxian yanjiushi [CCP Central Committee Document Research Office] ed., *Jianguo yilai Mao Zedong wengao (Diliuce)* [Mao Zedong's manuscripts since the founding of the People's Republic of China] (hereinafter *JMW*) (Beijing: Zhongyang wenxian, 1992), 6: 59.

70. It is now possible to read some of the hidden lines of this article for more information on the sources, and the course of editorial work on this key text has now been made known. The meetings held from 18 March to late April left no official records so Wu Lengxi's memoirs, including *Yi Maozhuxi* and *Shinian luanzhan*, are the major sources to study on the course of editorial work of this article and the Chinese leadership's real intentions. See Pang and Jin, *Maozhuan*, 496.

71. "Mao's Revisions of and Comments on the 'the Historical Experience of the Dictatorship of the Proletariat,'" *JMW*, 6: 59–67.

mation of Stalin's ideological position in essence did not diverge from the Soviet reevaluation of Stalin's theoretical contribution, which conceptualized the projection forward of basic Marxist–Leninism into advanced Stalinism. The article also reiterated its statement of the mistakes made by Stalin in the latter part of his career in a way consonant with the Soviet denouncement. In this respect, Mao did agree with Khrushchev's method of destroying Stalin's infallibility.

Nevertheless, the Chairman could not agree with the strictures passed upon the role of a charismatic Communist leader simply on the basis of specific abuses of power carried out by Stalin in his old age. From Chairman Mao's perspective, it was "utterly wrong to deny the role of individuals, the role of forerunners and leaders" simply because of the personality cult that Stalin had cultivated around himself. Mao concluded that the origin of Stalin's individual cult was a form of subjectivism or one-sidedness, representing a deviation "from objective reality and from the masses." As early as in his famous speech delivered in Yen'an in 1943, Mao's definition of "correct leadership" had formed an integral part of his famous mass line: "All correct leadership is necessarily from the masses, to the masses." In order to practice this mass line, Mao had persisted in immersing himself in his revolutionary base, traveling nationwide on tours in which he sought to take account of popular views. "When any leader of the Party or the state places himself over and above the Party and the masses ... when he alienates himself from the masses," for Mao, he was bound to make mistakes "even [if he were] so outstanding a personality as Stalin." Mao refused to budge one inch from the orthodox Marxist–Leninist position that leaders play a large role in history, only, as he admitted later, concerning himself with distinguishing what he perceives to be "correct" from "incorrect" personal cults.[72] However tactical and circumspect Mao's treatment of Stalin's personality cult, his conclusion to some extent

---

72. Chen and Yang, "Chinese Politics and the Collapse of the Sino–Soviet Alliance," 262; personal collection of Mao's conversations with foreign delegates, "Mao's Meeting with Voroshilov," in 1957.

parted company with that of Khrushchev: for Khrushchev, Stalin's errors stemmed from his personality and faults incident to human nature, while for Mao they were more a matter of his deviation from objective reality and from the masses. Neither critique fundamentally impugned the communist system itself insofar as that system depended upon a highly centralized power structure controlled by one party and ultimately one person. Present-day theoretical understandings, both for Western liberalism and within the CCP, have thus advanced from both the Mao and Khrushchev views.

In engaging with the secret speech, Mao and other Chinese leaders were also concerned to contest what they viewed as improper interference on the part of the CPSU in the Chinese Revolution and subsequent Soviet high-handedness toward the Chinese. Notably, Khrushchev's speech contained no references to Stalin's erroneous treatment of China, which the Chinese side certainly interpreted as a serious flaw in content. Only, it thought, by denouncing Stalin's wrongdoings toward the Chinese Communist Revolution could the Chinese party substantially break with Soviet superstition and begin to place more stress on the correctness of a specifically Chinese adaptation of Marxism to China. The integration of the universal truths of theoretical Communism with the actual situation in China, a backward agrarian country, the article claimed, "opened up boundless vistas for the development of Marxism–Leninism."[73] Instead of criticizing Soviet neglect in failing to pick up on Stalin's incorrect treatment of the Chinese revolution, an evidently injudicious course in light of China's strategically fraternal relationship with the USSR, the official article underscored the need to sum up the domestic experience of Communism in such a way as orient it continuously against dogmatism. Mao himself on several occasions added a review of the CCP's historical mistakes to the article's final draft. The actual purport of this passage was to suggest that the history of the

---

73. "On the Historical Experience of the Dictatorship of the Proletariat," Harvard University, Center for International Affairs, and East Asian Research Center, Harvard University, *Communist China 1955–1959: Policy Documents with Analysis* (Cambridge, MA: Harvard University Press, 1962), 10: 149.

CCP had been one of continuous struggle in trying to take the correct line in the face of doctrinaires inside the party and interference from outside. These so-called doctrinaires indicated "some comrades [who] crudely applied this formula of Stalin's to China" and were either directly sponsored by the Soviets or merely enthralled by the Soviet theoretical model.[74]

Another notable aspect of the sanctioned article was Mao's bold attempt to use the theory of contradiction, whose applicability had previously been restricted to the Chinese experience during the Stalin era, to explain the source of some of the mistakes committed by the leader of a party in any form of socialist society. Mao had already formulated his theory of contradiction in "On Contradiction" in 1937. But while, as a prominent scholar points out, "There [is] to be sure ... substantial continuity in the philosophical core of Mao Zedong's thought, from 1937 to the early 1960s at least," Mao initiates a variant here in filling a new bottle with old wine—or rather greatly expanding the scope of his concept of contradiction to apply to the genesis of the socialist state in the broadest terms.[75] Mao's philosophical generalization of the problems of socialist societies points in several directions. Mao's basic idea is that, unless particular steps are taken, the leaders of the revolution find themselves in the contradictory position of being alienated from the masses whose interests they supposedly embody; they owe this position merely to their prominence in the party hierarchy. In advancing this diagnosis, the Chinese Communist leaders staked out a new, more confident claim for the superiority of the theoretical pattern of the Chinese Communist movement, which was presented as having certain advantages over those of the other socialist states, including the Soviet Union and, to a greater extent, the Eastern Bloc states. Mao's growing confidence in this theoretical framework also encouraged him to adapt the theory to forms of political and economic management in attempting to develop a Chinese model of

---

74. Ibid.
75. Stuart Schram, *The Thought of Mao Tse-Tung* (Cambridge: Cambridge University Press, 1989), 93.

socialization, as we will discuss later. Viewing China as an independent and more liberal Communist power within the camp, the Eastern European regimes began to show great interest in China's experience, turning to Beijing for pointers as to what they could hope for with the development of local forms of socialism.

The aftermath of the CPSU Twentieth Congress subjected the Communist camp to its severest test. Khrushchev's secret speech had different effects on the Soviet Eastern Bloc than those it had on Mao's Communist China. For some of the Eastern European states, such as Hungary and Poland, the dissipation of Stalinism occurred at an unfortunate phase in their development—in the immediate aftermath of the most difficult stage of industrialization and collectivization but before new social institutions could take root, meaning that these states' capacity to resist redoubled external and internal pressures came under extreme pressure. Objectively speaking, China was in a stage of socialist transition similar to that of Eastern Europe. Yet, unlike all the other Soviet Bloc states, Mao's China enjoyed a considerable degree of ideological and political autonomy from the Soviet Union. In consequence the Chinese leadership did not feel personally threatened by the Stalin episode. The Chairman's emphasis on a socialism with distinctively Chinese characteristics allowed China to escape being tarred with the brush of Stalinism in the fallout from Stalin's death; furthermore, Mao saw the Soviet reassessment of Stalin and consequent confusion in the Communist camp as a good opportunity for the Chinese Communists to introduce their theoretical articulations to the broader international Communist community. Mao's efforts in reevaluating Stalin's mistakes in the CCP's own language should be viewed as integral parts of a Chinese initiative to take a more leading role, however limited in the ideological and theoretical realm, in the international Communist movement.[76]

---

76. Of course, Mao at this stage still thought it would be wise to camouflage his strong ambitions skillfully; Wu, *Yi Maozhuxi*, 7.

CHINA AND THE CRISES IN POLAND AND HUNGARY TO LATE OCTOBER 1956

The Chinese official response followed Khrushchev's secret speech after one and one-half months. During this period, Khrushchev's policy of undercutting the Stalinist myth, without, however, promoting a clearly defined substitute, had provoked sharp doubts among the Eastern Bloc leadership as to their own security and ideological legitimacy. The very ambiguity of the Kremlin's policy toward the Eastern Bloc, meanwhile, encouraged a greater scope of independent action and interpretation on their leaders' part, with the result that countries found themselves adopting more diverse perspectives, which threatened the unity of the socialist camp.

At the same time, Yugoslavia was restored to the position of an active agent in the politics of the camp through Khrushchev's efforts in rejecting Stalin's earlier conception of the Yugoslav role inside the camp and the cooperation of Khrushchev and Tito in the wake of the CPSU Twentieth Congress. In order to eliminate any remaining obstacles to Khrushchev's plan of restoring to the Soviet Bloc the unity it had before 1948, the Soviet leadership placed common party bonds between the Yugoslav and other Eastern European socialist states above practical differences in conducting collectivist policies. The failure to settle a number of outstanding historical and diplomatic issues with Yugoslavia threatened many Eastern European Communist regimes, especially as it appeared that the secret speech and history in general had vindicated the Yugoslav stance of 1948, which had set it strongly against the revival of hardcore Stalinism and against the rest of Eastern Europe, indeed conscripting many de-Stalinizing elements within its own party platform. The Eastern European leaders, essentially still Stalinist, found themselves between a rock and a hard place with a de-Stalinizing Communist movement on the one side and a fractious, dissatisfied citizenship on the other.[77]

---

77. For Soviet–Yugoslav rapprochement as a result of Khrushchev's efforts to

Compared to the influence of the USSR and affiliated European states like Yugoslavia, the Chinese impact on the region was still limited in the period following the CPSU Twentieth Congress. Nevertheless, the Chinese party's detached position among the people's democracies, together with its legendary history of nation-state liberation and autochthonous socialist construction, undoubtedly added luster to the Chinese Communist perspective on international Communist problems, which gained in authority and the appearance of neutrality after Stalin's death. China's successful domestic consolidation and its role in the outcome of the Korean War further boosted its international prestige. Further, as noted before, Communist China's foreign relations with the Eastern Bloc states had broadened after 1954, effectively promoting China as a plausible candidate as a socialist role model following the discrediting of Stalinism.[78]

In this troubled context, the people's democracies were understandably interested to know the formal Chinese response to Khrushchev's speech. The Western media had even ascribed the Chinese reluctance to declare their hand after the CPSU Twentieth Congress to their inability to fall in line with the new Soviet position.[79] The Hungarians, ranging from top party leaders to lower-level cadres, were reportedly very concerned about the length of the Chinese silence over the Congress.[80] According to Chinese journalist reports from Warsaw, the Poles also took the Chinese statement seriously. In arguing issues of leaders' personality cults and of peaceful

---

bring Tito and his country back into the Soviet Bloc after the Soviet leader gradually ascended to the top from 1954 on and the Eastern Bloc's complicated responses to the rehabilitation of Yugoslavia in the second half of the 1950s, see Brzezinski, *The Soviet Bloc*, 182–90, 193–203. For an analysis on the influence that Yugoslav "national communism" had on Hungary since 1955, see Ferenc Fehér and Agnes Heller, *Hungary 1956 Revisited: The Message of a Revolution—A Quarter of a Century After* (London: George Allen & Unwin, 1983), 37–38.

78. For China's growing connection with the Eastern Bloc states, see the first section in this chapter.

79. "Hungarian Journalist Quarters at Beijing on the Situation after the Twentieth Congress, 9 April 1956," CFMA, 109-01040-01, 17–18.

80. "Hao Deqing's Talk with the Hungarian Foreign Minister on the Situation in Hungary after the Twentieth Congress," CFMA, 109-01040-01, 16.

democratic-to-socialist transition, many Poles reportedly said that they would hold off on their opinions until Mao Zedong, the most authoritative world leader on these matters, had delivered his verdict.[81]

Eventually, the Chinese programmatic statement on the CPSU Twentieth Congress and Stalin's reassessment came out in April, with an immediate effect on the Communist commonwealth. The Chinese statement was categorical in stressing three factors vis-à-vis Stalin: the issue of the dictatorship of the proletariat, the diagnosis of Stalinist errors, and the Chinese's own experience of antidogmatism. Had the Poles and the Hungarians been able to read between the lines of the Chinese statement, they would have been able to see that all three lines of argument bore closely on the question of the legitimacy of the Stalinist regimes, so challenged recently in Hungary and Poland, and also sought to bolster the prestige of the Chinese model in the socialist camp. The Polish and Hungarian reformists, however, instead understood the Chinese communiqué as urging a tacit form of encouragement by virtue of the relative autonomy of the Chinese in the camp and the stress on the indigenous nature of their socialism. These factors deepened their impression that the Chinese actually supported their de-Stalinist aspirations.[82]

In Hungary, Chinese influence was reflected in the ideology of emerging Hungarian nationalist communists, particularly in Imre Nagy's admiration of China's five principles of coexistence. After his removal in 1955, Nagy grew increasingly certain that the five Bandung principles of international affairs—national independence, sovereignty, equality, noninterference, and self-determination—as

---

81. *Neican* (5 March 1956): 17–19; (28 June 1956): 719–20.
82. The Polish and Hungarian perception of China's support to indigenous socialist development can be demonstrated by Nagy's borrowing five Chinese-initiated Bandung principles to establish his ideal foreign policy in his country and more evidently by the Polish regime's efforts to pursue the Chinese central leadership's understanding of and help for their domestic politics and relationship with the Soviets. See following discussion in this chapter.

promoted by the Chinese, should apply equally to the Soviet camp.[83] It is likely that Nagy misinterpreted the Chinese articles as also tending to this interpretation. Nagy sensed the coming political storm in his forced resignation from the party, penning a lengthy thesis titled "In Defense of the New Course" in late 1955 and early 1956. The paper, later published as a book in the West under the title *On Communism*, addressed four major issues: industry, agriculture, political terror, and foreign policy. In the chapter on foreign policy, Nagy adopted China's five principles of coexistence as the pillars of his theoretical framework defending Hungarian national sovereignty and independence from the Soviet Union, especially through his appeal to the dicta of respecting nations' territorial integrity and signing pacts of nonaggression.[84] The five principles had initially emerged in a communiqué signed between China and India in 1954, being formally proposed by Zhou Enlai at the 1955 Bandung conference in Indonesia as an alternative code of international relations for third-world states emerging from the experience of European colonialism. The official Chinese statement of these principles was typically accompanied by the restrictive phrase, "between states of different social systems," intended to allay the noncommunist Asian countries' fear that China would export revolution to their territories, while leaving unclear the mandate of the Soviet Union or other dominant socialist states to intervene in the affairs of international Communism. Nagy entitled his foreign policy chapter "The Five Basic Principles of International Relations and the Question of Our Foreign Policy," not only using the five principles as the overarching thesis of the chapter but insisting that they "must extend to the relations between the countries within the democratic *and* socialist camps."[85]

---

83. Imre Nagy, *On Communism: In Defence of the New Course* (New York: Praeger, 1957), 20–23.
84. Ibid.
85. Cheng Yinghong, "Beyond Moscow-Centric Interpretation: An Examination of the China Connection in Eastern Europe and North Vietnam during the Era of De-Stalinization," *Journal of World History*, 15, 4 (December 2004): 487–518; Nagy, *On Communism*, 23. The HF policy was formulated in early 1956, be-

Meanwhile, Mao's secret speech on Ten Relationships, together with his "Let a Hundred Flowers Bloom, Let a Hundred Schools Contend" (HF) policy were interpreted in Hungary and Poland as harbingers of future Communist diversity.[86] On 19 June 1956, several days before the outbreak of the Poznan uprising, the Polish side explained its country's intellectual and political relaxation to Chinese delegates by saying, "We must not suppress [people's criticisms]; that could only hinder the development of criticism." Instead, the leadership needed to reinforce state control, relying on the provision of balanced information to the masses to quell unrest.[87] It seemed that there was a great similarity between the quasidemocratic atmosphere in Poland and the spirit of latitude in Mao's call for a "hundred flowers," which inevitably led to the convergence of the Eastern European and Chinese socialist experiences.

Chinese foreign policy in Eastern Europe was marked by three trends preceding the summer of 1956. First, China had sought to establish closer relationships with the people's republics, expanding economic and cultural exchanges over the head, as it were, of the

---

fore the CPSU Twentieth Congress, and was built on a basic reassessment of conditions in China: with the means of production (ownership of capital and resources) now largely in the hands of the state or collective units, the victory of socialism over capitalism had been basically decided. This situation called for a fundamental shift in the party's priorities for economic development. The broad range of social forces could now be rallied behind the development effort and this HF policy was designed to encourage creative inputs by China's intellectuals. Mao's speech on Ten Relationships emerged in April 1956 and embodied the results of the central leadership's reevaluation of the Soviet model on the basis of politburo discussions with leading personnel from thirty-four economic departments. Although Mao and his associates had aimed to make more significant modifications in the Soviet pattern, it was not until the Communist leaders inside the Kremlin revealed some shortcomings of Stalin's model that the Chinese Communists in the center began to examine the Stalinist mode of social development in a more self-consciously critical manner. For more details, see MacFarquhar, *CHOC*, 14: 122–29.

86. The Hungarian embassy in Beijing had obtained the tenth section: China's relationship with foreign countries in April 1956; Sándor Szobolevszki and, and István Vida, eds., *Iratok a Magyar-Kínai Kapcsolatok Történetéhez: Magyar-Kínai Kapcsolatok: 1956–1959; Dokumentumok* [Hungarian–China relations, 1956–1959: Documents] (Budapest: MTA Jelenkor-kutató Bizottság, 2001), 40–42.

87. "Summary of Wang [Binnan] Ambassador's Visit to the Soviet Ambassador [in Warsaw], 6 June 1956," CFMA, 109-01141-01, 18–21.

USSR. Second, the Chinese leadership had a growing interest in observing political developments in the region, sharpened by the increasing prospect of China's coming to play more of a leading role in the post-Stalin Comintern (however much, at this stage, Chinese insight into Eastern European countries remained limited). Third, China was genuinely open to learning from the lessons of the Eastern European socialist experiences, especially after Khrushchev had put a hold on the theoretical potential of Stalinism. The latter two trends became much more obvious when the Eastern Bloc exploded in a number of de-Stalinist campaigns after the CPSU Twentieth Congress. The violence in Poznan had the initial effect in China of alerting its leaders' attention to political problems in the bloc, beginning first of all with Poland.

The initial Chinese line taken in response to the Poznan strikes in no way diverged from Soviet and Polish public assertions that Poznan represented a foreign counterrevolutionary and internal reactionary plot. A lengthy *RMRB* editorial warning readers to "Guard against Imperialist Intrigues and Domestic Reactionary Activities" flagged so-called imperialist subversive activities in the Socialist Bloc, which had begun to be visible with the earlier East Berlin and Czech Pilsen crises. Though this article took its inspiration from the Poznan strikes, its main concerns were with the Chinese domestic situation, in relation to which the piece pointed out two distinct lessons: (1) the party should correctly carry out its work among the masses and in other fields to avoid being "sabotaged" by "enemies"; and (2) it would be naïve to imagine that class struggle and the antipathy between the working and owning classes had been definitively superseded by the development of socialism.[88] The Chinese party drew these conclusions against a backdrop of uncertainty in terms of what was actually happening both in Eastern Europe and among the Soviet leadership. Mao and the Chinese leaders' reflexive

---

88. "Jingti diguozhuyi Yinmou he guonei fangeming Huodong" [Guard against imperialist intrigues and domestic reactionary activities], *RMRB,* 12 July 1956, 1.

belief that "class struggle continues to exist in a socialist country"[89] embodied Mao's persistent sensitivity, sharpened by his Marxist-Leninist formation, to the potential threat posed by antagonists, which was always stronger than his half-skeptical and short-lived acceptance of the idea in 1956 that class struggle was withering away.

It should be noted at this point that decision-making on major policy issues, both foreign and domestic, was highly concentrated within China. Consideration of the 1956 events and riots in Eastern Europe was reserved for the attention of a small group of top leaders, who alone carried responsibility for weighing the risks, merits, and practical constraints of alternative courses of action. Mao Zedong, as party chairman, continued to call the shots in responding to an evolving situation about which the leaders knew they were only partially informed. Apart from the official reports of other socialist states and Western news reports, the Chinese party had its own de facto intelligence in the Eastern Bloc, which had begun to flow to the Center in the form of Soviet and Polish official analysis, informal exchanges with other socialist leaders, and the measurement of mass reaction, from late June.[90] According to currently available Chinese materials, Mao had recourse to three major information channels on Poland: the Chinese embassy in Warsaw, Xinhua News Agency journalist reports and more in-depth information (*Neican*) circulated only to top leaders, and Western news journalism.[91] From the second half of July until October 1956 the

---

89. Wu, *Yi Maozhuxi*, 16–17.
90. "Some Comments on Poznan Incident Collected in Poznan, 2 July 1956," 109-01141-01, 25–28; "Record of Yu Shen, the Chargé d'Affaires's visit to the Polish Party International Department Vice Minister, June 1956," CFMA, 109-00761-04, 20–21; "Summary of Wang [Binnan] Ambassador's Visit to Kirylok, the Polish Ambassador to China (7 July 1956), 109-01018-04, 16–17.
91. In point of fact, the Chinese government had already begun to expand its intelligence network in the Eastern Bloc in 1956 by sending Xinhua journalists to some key Eastern European socialist states, including Poland, though not yet to Hungary, for routine and in-depth reports. Wu Lengxi, head of Xinhua at that time, had been allowed to sit in on the standing committee meetings of the politburo since 1956, and Mao would usually turn to him for the latest news on crucial international issues. See Wu, *Shinian lunzhan*, 1–91; Li Shenzhi, *Fengyu canghuang*

CCP top leaders gradually came to understand more about the Polish crisis, especially as they were increasingly able to factor Chinese intelligence reports into their estimates. After Poznan ceased to be an immediate threat, Stanislaw Kiryluk, the Polish ambassador to Beijing, admitted to his Chinese counterpart that the workers had had justifiable grievances, briefing China on the background, of economic difficulties and political uncertainties following the CPSU Twentieth Congress, which precipitated the strikes. He further explained that the radical Polish response to Khrushchev's secret speech arguably had its inception in the humiliating fate in nationalist terms of the Polish Communist Party in 1938. Further, for Kiryluk, the disturbances testified to the harmful consequences of doctrinarism, which for instance had enflamed public opinion by purging Gomulka; this emphasis, conveniently for the Chinese, agreed with a leading line of the CCP article's analysis of the riots. Finally, Kiryluk expressed his appreciation of Mao Zedong's "Ten Guidelines" (Ten Relationships), offering the view that "the CCP was the first [Communist] party to draw conclusions about the problems posed by the Soviet [Twentieth] Congress." He amplified this endorsement by suggesting that of all the national parties, the Chinese was the one that made the fewest mistakes during the Stalinist era.[92] Kiryluk's words, though probably unrepresentative of the entirety of the inner Polish party, which was split after Poznan, demonstrated an intention on the part of the Polish Communists to draw the CCP into European problems, probably for the sake of claiming financial assistance or diplomatic support. In its situation of detachment from the Eastern Bloc, China enjoyed a wide scope of ideological autonomy, which it could conceivably exercise to the benefit of plural strands of international Communism.

The Polish explanation of the origins of Poznan, and of Poland's difficulties at the time, diverted the CCP's attention away from the

---

wushinian—Li Shenzhi wenxuan [Fifty Years of Upheaval and Chasm—Selected Texts by Li Shenzhi] (hereinafter *Fengyu*) (Hong Kong: Mingbao, 2004), 107.

92. "Summary of Wang [Binnan] Ambassador's Visit to Kirylok, the Polish ambassador to China, 7 July 1956," CFMA, 109-01018-04, 16–17.

subversion of imperialists and toward Poland's genuine domestic problems. In responding to the main concerns of the central party, both the Chinese embassy and Xinhua reports from Warsaw sent back in-depth analyses of the social roots of the Poznan violence. The two reports came to a similar conclusion: although in essence the violence had been provoked by imperialist and reactionary agitation, correct analysis should focus on the "serious difficulties and problems" existing within the Polish party and government.[93] The Chinese inner party always took the violence seriously as indicating the political, ideological, and operational weakness of the Polish socialist regime within the bloc. To Mao, as architect of the Chinese model of socialization, certain questions in the wake of the Polish turbulence seemed unavoidable: What were the shortcomings and flaws of the Community parties and of governments in the Eastern Bloc? What were the origins of the Soviet Bloc's problems? How could the Chinese avoid their mistakes and head off comparable crises in China? Lessons adopted wholesale from Soviet analy-sis seemed insufficient to answer all these questions, forcing the Chinese to expend great effort on extrapolating the lessons of the Eastern European experience to their own situations, as will be discussed in detail in later chapters.

The Polish message in relation to Gomulka, however, did not receive an immediate response from the Chinese side. Both Chinese embassy and Xinhua reports took the view that the Polish leaders had sufficiently recognized the people's legitimate discontent, adopting measures to alleviate public unrest; as they supposed the situation was improving, they neglected to mention Gomulka or any specifically political factors, with the embassy communiqués noting that the CCP article was implicitly Soviet-oriented on this issue.[94] Even after Gomulka's rehabilitation, and the retraction of previous criticisms, in August, after which he acceded to a deter-

---

93. "On Poznan Military Riots: Edited by the Chinese Embassy in Poland," CFMA, 109-00761-01, 1–13; Xie Wenqing, "On the origin of the outbreak of Poznan military riots," *Neican* (28 July 1956): 591–604.
94. Ibid.

mining position in the future of the PUWP and the state, Chinese intelligence in Warsaw failed to refer explicitly to Gomulka's symbolic importance.[95] Partly this was due simply to ignorance on the part of the Chinese.[96] Nevertheless, if we dig a little deeper, it is evident that Chinese intelligence could easily have inferred Gomulka's significance, especially given the Polish initiative of leaking information about him in early July. Chinese information-gathering seems to have been directed by Mao and the central party, who apparently chose to ignore or downplay questions of Gomulka's status in the PUWP until late August at least, on the basis that Mao had no desire to participate in domestic Polish politics.

At this juncture, in order to begin to dissociate themselves from Moscow's influence, the Poles turned to Beijing for inspiration under the pretext that the CCP regime was independent of Soviet rule and receptive to the principle of equality within the socialist camp. Before Ochab left Warsaw traveling through Moscow to attend the CCP CC Eighth Congress in September 1956, he invited Wang Bingnan, the Chinese ambassador, for a banquet. That evening, Ochab told Wang Bingnan that besides expressing his goodwill toward the Chinese people and strengthening the ties of unity between the two countries' parties, he was coming to China to learn from the experience of the CCP. Ochab claimed a particular interest in the resolutions that China had "courageously" passed after the CPSU Twentieth Congress, most probably the Ten Relationships. Although these resolutions emerged out of a domestic Chinese en-

---

95. Ochab's recollection: Rozmowa z Edwardem Ochabem, Teresa Toranska, Oni, Warszawa, 1989, s. 214–17, quoted in Shen and Li, "The 1956 Polish Crisis and Sino-Polish Relations," 45–48. Also see Anderzej Werblan, "1956nian de Bolan shiyue: Chuanshuo yu xianshi [October 1956 in Poland: Legends and realities]," transl. Wang Yan, *Lengzhanguojishi yanjiu* [Cold War International History Studies], 4 (Fall 2006): 81–89. Werblan's article is translated from Jan Rowiński, ed., *Polski Październik 1956 W Polityce Światowej* (Warszawa: Pism, 2006), 13–40.

96. Wang Bingnan, the Chinese ambassador to Poland, asked about Gomulka during one meeting with the Soviet ambassador held in mid-June, "Summary of Ambassador Wang [Bingnan]'s Conversation with the Soviet Ambassador, 15 June 1956," 109-01141-01, 17–18. There is no report in CFMA currently declassified documents of 1956 on further Chinese consultation on the situation of Gomulka either from the Soviet or from the Polish side.

vironment, the PUWP believed some of them might apply to its own situation. Ochab also informed Wang Bingnan that he might have to return to Warsaw ahead of schedule due to "the complicated situation at home."[97]

Ochab's delegation arrived in Moscow first on 12 September. During his meetings with the Soviet leaders, Ochab said that the PUWP Central Committee had requested the departure of the Soviet advisors attached to Polish public security. It is less clear whether Ochab also told Khrushchev of the PUWP CC's intention to restore Gomulka to the politburo. In either case, it is now known that, to ensure Chinese support, Ochab fully briefed the Chinese central leadership in Beijing of this plan. As Ochab recalled, the Chinese leaders "entirely sympathized with the Polish situation," bolstering his implicit faith in Sino–Polish party relations.[98] Whatever the degree of Sino–Polish deepened communication, though, the two sides did not broach the question of Poland's relation with the Soviet Union, with Ochab even taking steps to dissimulate about the coming confrontations with the USSR by assuring Mao that the Soviet ambassador had accompanied him all the way on his trip. Ochab's chief concern here seemed to be to regulate the flow of information about Poland to the Chinese himself, forestalling interpretation by the Soviets.

On the day he left, Ochab finally took the opportunity to intimate that all was not well in his country's relations with its senior partner in Communism. After Ochab's flight fortuitously "malfunctioned" on the runway, Zhu De boarded the plane to see Ochab. Ochab confessed that marked anti-Soviet tendencies existed in Po-

---

97. "Summary of Ambassador Wang (Bingnan)'s Conversation with the Polish Party Delegation during the Reception before Its Departure to Attend the CCP CC Eighth National Congress, 10 September 1956," CFMA, 109-01141-01, 58–61.

98. Leszek Głuchowski said in his paper on the Soviet–Polish crisis that Ochab had informed Khrushchev of the Polish initiative to restore Gomulka to the leadership. See his "Poland, 1956: Khrushchev, Gomulka, and the 'Polish October,'" *CWIHP Bulletin*, 5 (Spring 1995): 47, ft. 6. Shen Zhihua points out that Ochab did not mention a word about Gomulka's rehabilitation to the politburo to Khrushchev when he was in Moscow; see Shen Zhihua and Li Danhui's conference paper, "The 1956 Polish Crisis and Sino–Polish Relations," 48.

land, though the Poles were by no means yet prepared to break their alliance with the Soviets. Rather, the Poles merely sought autonomy in dealing with domestic issues within the current socialist framework.[99] Ever since the Chinese party had aired its response to the CPSU Twentieth Congress, emphasizing the need to work through its own socialist plan accentuating distinctively Chinese characteristics, the Poles had understood the Chinese model as validating their own stress on autonomous domestic patterns. Ochab and his colleagues believed that China's qualitatively different relationship with the socialist bloc and its leverage in the Kremlin through Moscow–Beijing cooperation in the Krushchev era made the "independent and autonomous" Chinese regime the best candidate for coordinating an international socialist response and subtly applying pressure on the Soviet Union, in the event that the CPSU could not come to an agreement with the Poles.[100]

As for the Chinese response to Ochab's overture, the French newspaper *France-Soir* reported Mao's support for Poland's aspirations, suggesting that China was emerging as a counterweight to the USSR in the international Communist movement.[101] The U.S. newspaper *The New York Herald* even claimed in a headline to detect "Soviet Restraint on Poland Because Of China: Mao Zedong Was the First to Send Congratulation Message to Wladyslaw Gomulka."[102] In fact, judging from the currently available Chinese and Polish source materials, there is still insufficient evidence to determine Mao and the Chinese leadership's immediate reaction to the Polish problem and Gomulka's reinstatement.[103] Nevertheless, in contrast

---

99. Rozmowa z Edwardem Ochabem, s. 219–21, cited in Shen and Li, "The 1956 Polish Crisis and Sino–Polish Relations," 45–48.
100. Ibid.
101. *Neican* (17 October 1956): 1042–44.
102. *Neican* (27 October 1956): 1283–84.
103. Ochab only said that the Chinese were "very sympathetic" to the Polish situation, without making any clear statement of the leadership's response to his overtures in his memoir; see Shen and Li, "The 1956 Polish Crisis and Sino–Polish Relations," 47–48. As of yet, China has not declassified the records of the Chinese leaders' meetings with the Polish delegation (Ochab). As far as I know, Mao, Zhou Enlai, and Liu Shaoqi received the Eastern European leaders separately during the

to its earlier construction of Polish issues principally in relation to domestic problems, it was evident that from late October the Chinese leadership had been actively discussing Soviet interference in Poland and intervening themselves on the Eastern European scene.[104] The active role later played by the Chinese in mediating between the Soviets and the Poles was quickly interpreted by Poles, Hungarians, other socialists, and even some Western observers as endorsing the Polish position, namely, that local diversity should be respected within Communism. The actual picture was more complex, both with regard to the Chinese leadership's changes of attitude toward Poland and its perception of shifts in Sino–Soviet relations, the two leading themes in the evolution of Chinese foreign policy.

On 30 June the CPSU CC issued a declaration in response to some of the anti-Stalinist criticisms of the Soviet system. This declaration met Soviet efforts to define the limits of the anti-Stalinist aftermath in seeking to posit some common foundations for interstate socialist unity, which seemed more needed than ever in the face of the Poznan riots, which broke out in late June. While taking stock of these disturbances, the Soviets were also extremely wary of Yugoslavia's growing influence in Eastern Europe, especially in Hungary and Poland. In the course of negotiating the second Soviet–Yugoslav declaration, Khrushchev had realized his fundamental differences with Tito on the key issue of the unity of international Communism. As Veljko Micunovic correctly pointed out, Tito's refusal to assume any obligations with regard to the socialist camp or to sign any statement on ideological unity significantly

---

CCP Eighth Party Congress. *Maozhuan* reports that during the congress Mao met the delegations of socialist parties or other workers' parties from twenty-nine countries, with several paragraphs devoted to reports from these meetings (with the East German, Yugoslavian, British, Italian, Bulgarian, and French parties); however, the meeting with Ochab is not even mentioned. Mao met Mikoyan on 18 September to discuss how to treat correctly those colleagues who had committed mistakes. According to a prominent scholar, Mao said to Mikoyan that Rákosi was a good comrade. See Pang and Jin, *Maozhuan*, 536–43.

104. Wu Lengxi, *Shinian lunzhan*, 34–48.

alarmed the Russians.[105] Alerted by Yugoslav ambition and the possibility of regional instability and rebellion, the Soviets naturally moved to stress the common aims and outlook of international Communism, which could be implemented through an available Soviet model defined as determining the conditions under which specific adaptations would be tolerated. Although the Soviets meant to issue warnings to the whole socialist camp, unsurprisingly their message resonated particularly in the ears of the Chinese regime, the only socialist regime which operated autonomously within the framework of the international socialist camp.

Furthermore, the Soviet leaders had obtained a report on Mao's April Ten Relationships speech by the end of August 1956, despite its not yet having been published and having been kept secret from China's socialist allies. The report dwelled on the Chinese tendency critically to utilize Soviet experiences in the first six months of 1956, a course suggested by Mao himself.[106] The Soviets, conscious of Yugoslav ambition and the instability of its subordinate Eastern European regimes, cared less about China's development of distinctive socialist features and more about its potential role as a rival and power-broker within the bloc. Aiming to mitigate Chinese influence in this sphere, Mikoyan flew to Beijing to attend the CCP Eighth Congress. Moscow (or Khrushchev) probably felt quite justified in making a statement of Soviet primacy within the camp, timing their statement to shore up the USSR's indisputable authority. The statement on 30 June nevertheless caused the Chinese leadership extreme discomfort.

An article coauthored by two prominent Chinese scholars points to Mao and his comrades' dissatisfaction with the Soviet manner of handling Khrushchev's secret speech as nearly the sole origin of the CCP's criticism of Soviet "big power chauvinism."[107] In

---

105. Mićunović, *Moscow Diary*, 73.
106. "B. Likhachev's Report to the CPSU CC on Mao Zedong's Ten Principles" (Ten Relationships, added by the author); for a Chinese translation, see Shen Zhihua and Li Danhui, eds., *ZhongSu guanxi*, 11: 2690–2708.
107. Chen and Yang, "Chinese Politics and the Collapse of the Sino–Soviet Alliance," 260.

fact, it is more likely that, as early as the beginning of March, Deng Xiaoping, Zhang Wentian, and Wang Jiaxiang had argued that the Soviets would have difficulty in curbing their traditional big power behavior even though Stalin was no longer their leader (though their opinions may also reflect Mao's position). While obviously uncomfortable with Khrushchev's exposure of Stalin and denigration of his mistakes, without advance consultation with Beijing, Mao placed much less weight on the thesis of Soviet chauvinism at this time. Relevant documents and materials from February to September betray no evident discontent on Mao's part with the development of Sino–Soviet relations under Khrushchev. Khrushchev's secret speech, from Mao's perspective, rather helped the CCP to break with the theoretical and practical patterns of socialist industrialization formulated by Stalin (or so-called Stalinist superstitions), potentially widening the sphere of theoretical and ideological Chinese influence across the international socialist camp. Alongside Khrushchev's secret speech, Mikoyan's plan to diminish the value of China's specific revolutionary experience in the CCP Eighth Congress struck Mao as more of an open or intentional affront to him and his country.

Addressing the CCP Eighth Congress, Mikoyan bluntly observed, "Assuredly, each country has its distinctive features and brings its own specific elements to bear in making the transition to socialism. But, as Lenin pointed out, these features can relate only to something relatively unimportant."[108] According to Shi Zhe, Mikoyan spent most of his speech exalting Soviet Russia, even claiming that each positive achievement or progressive step of the CCP derived from its emulation of the Soviet model. Mao took personal offense at Mikoyan's arrogance and apparent theoretical naivety, stopping him one day before the end of the Congress to complain at the unequal relations between the Soviet Union and China and to take issue with the former Comintern and CPSU for their heavy-handed paternalism in treating the CCP as some form of er-

---

108. Brzezinski, *The Soviet Bloc*, 204.

rant child.[109] In Mao's eyes, China's revolutionary achievements under his leadership deserved a respect lacking in Mikoyan's haughty and quite open claims. However, even if the Chairman was unhappy with Mikoyan, cooperation between the Chinese and Soviets was not necessarily impaired at this stage. Especially given his legendary short temper and habits of command, it is likely that Mao intended to do no more than scold Mikoyan for his impertinence.

Although Mao had spoken out against the Soviets' "father–son" mentality in his talk with Mikoyan, the two sides were committed to working closely together in involving themselves in the internal politics of other Communist member states. In the course of the Eighth Congress, Mikoyan, together with Peng Dehuai, flew to Pyongyang to intervene in factional struggles within the Korean Workers' Party.[110] Before Mikoyan's departure, Mao hosted a dinner for him, Pavel Fedorovich Iudin and other Soviet delegates, during which they discussed Mikoyan's mission to Pyongyang and the situation in both Hungary and Poland. The Chairman mainly focused on the Korean issue, suggesting Mikoyan mediate discussions between Kim Il-Sung and his party critics. With Mikoyan receptive, Mao specifically agued, "We have to prepare for one thing, that Kim Il-Sung may say that we are intervening in their own affairs and ask us to withdraw our troops [the Chinese Voluntary Army still stationed in North Korea]," a course to which he was reluctant to assent given that the "Americans are in the South; Syngman Rhee's force is strong." Agreeing that the Koreans were resistant to Soviet and Chinese interference in party matters, Mikoyan put forth the case that it was absolutely appropriate for the socialist parties to

---

109. See Wu Lengxi, *Shinian lunzhan*, 32; Shi Zhe, *Zai lishi juren shenbian*, 608–13. Shi Zhe, as the simultaneous interpreter of Mao's talk to Mikoyan, had provided a detailed description of the conditions and a record of Mao's talk.

110. For a discussion on the origin and development of the inner-party power struggle in North Korea based on archival source materials, see James F. Person, "The Myth of Factional Struggle within the Korean Workers' Party, 1945–1956" (preliminary draft delivered in International Workshop on The Cold War and the Korean Peninsula: The Domestic Politics and Foreign Relations of North and South Korea, Beijing University, PRC, 18 May 2007).

advise or criticize each other. Interestingly, at this point Mikoyan moved to the topic of Hungarian events and used his decision to remove Rákosi as an example that the Soviet interference in Hungarian affairs had been beneficial to Hungarians in jump-starting an adequate domestic response to social problems. Mao was not necessarily sold on the analogy between Korea and Hungary as records suggest he replied only briefly, while Mikoyan had spoken at length. Furthermore, the Chairman does not seem to have assigned a high priority to the Hungarian developments at this stage, worrying more about Kim and Korea. Mao's words—"Rákosi is a good comrade with a high Marxist ideological level. He can quit. But Kim is a man hard to deal with"—seem to betray a double standard with regard to intervention into other socialist states' politics. Evidently, the Chairman shared the Soviet position to remove Stalinist leaders like Rákosi who were in his judgment handicapping the local parties in regaining popular support in the Eastern Bloc. It was a satisfactory result for Rákosi to accept the Soviet arrangement for stepping down while Kim was making trouble in the Asian region by insisting on his independence in domestic affairs. While Chairman Mao had consistently insisted on his autonomy in domestic politics, he in essence felt both ideologically and politically justified for the more "advanced" Communist states to lead the "less developed" ones.[111]

Even if piqued by Soviet paternalism, Mao saw the strategic value for the Chinese of stability in the Communist camp, as assured by Sino–Soviet cooperation. As long as these two factors—international unity and the Chinese perception of Soviet attitudes toward the PRC—were not contradictory, the Chinese leadership was in no hurry to throw down any sort of challenge to the Soviets. Mao had been taking a principled line in telling Tito that the Chinese "support[ed] the Soviet Union as the center insofar as this was beneficial to the socialist movement," even as he regretted that "there are still certain figures in the Soviet Union who doubt that

---

111. "Record of Chairman Mao's Conversation with Mikoyan, September 1956," China Central Archives (CCA): 138–43, personal collection.

our socialist construction can be successful and assert our Party to be fake."[112] Clearly discontent among the Chinese had been building at the Soviet's big-power chauvinism, which to some extent underlay Chinese encouragement at Polish aspirations to greater autonomy. In Eastern Europe, the turning point of the Polish situation came in early October. The Polish leadership stated its reasons for believing that Polish Communism had reached a dead end, preparing the way for the return of Gomulka. In his reappearance in the politburo, Gomulka set out a political prospectus, which included the return of his associates to both the politburo and the secretariat and the ousting of Rokossowski and other pro-Soviet members.[113] The Soviet leaders were shocked to learn of this sidelining of "the people on whom they depend,"[114] especially as they had not even been consulted. Primarily concerned for the sake of Soviet military security to dampen nationalist and anti-Soviet emotions in Poland, the Kremlin determined to apply both political and military pressure to compel the Poles under Gomulka to back down. To avoid confusion inside the camp, the CPSU presidium issued telegrams to the other socialist parties on 18 October. One day later, on 19 October, a powerful delegation led by Khrushchev headed for Warsaw simultaneously with a battalion of armored troops.[115] The situation had suddenly escalated to a point of imminent danger.

In late October, a few days before the outbreak of the Hungarian upheaval, Beijing's diplomatic attention was taken up by the dis-

---

112. For Mao's words during his meeting with the Yugoslav delegation during the CCP Eighth Congress, see Zhongyang wenxian, MWJ (Beijing: Renmin, 1999), 7: 122–23; for an English translation, see Zhang Shuguang and Chen Jian, "The Emerging Dispute between Beijing and Moscow: Ten Newly Available Chinese Documents," *CWIHP Bulletin*, 6–7 (Winter 1995/1996): 148–52.
113. Głuchowski, "Poland 1956," 38–39.
114. Khrushchev greeted Marshal Rokossovsky and other pro-Soviet generals at the airport and told the Polish leaders in Russian: "These are the people we relied on;" quoted from "the Polish United Workers' Party (PUWP) Politburo Announcement, 19 October 1956" in Shen, *SHSA*, 27, 28; for the English version, see Głuchowski, op. cit., 40.
115. Kramer, "New Evidence," 35; Granville, "From the Archives of Warsaw and Budapest; A Comparison of the Events of 1956," *East European Politics & Societies*, 16, no. 2 (Spring 2002): 548–49; Györkei and Horváth op. cit., 9.

turbances in Poland and tensions in Polish–Soviet relations.[116] During the enlarged meeting of the CCP politburo standing committee and the enlarged politburo convention meeting from 21 to 22 October 1956, the top Chinese leaders considered the anti-Soviet feeling in Warsaw and Soviet intervention on the basis of the telegram sent by the CPSU and their own source materials from Warsaw.[117]

On 19 October, Soviet ambassador to Beijing, Pavel Iudin, forwarded the CPSU presidium telegram to Liu Shaoqi. According to Shi Zhe, who was present as interpreter for Liu, the Soviet ambassador indicated to the Chinese the serious divergence on fundamental policies that had emerged inside the Polish party. Officials of the PUWP intended to reshuffle the politburo to expel Marshal Rokossowski. Shi Zhe interpreted Iudin as expressing a fear, on the part of the Soviets, that the PUWP Eighth Plenum would confirm an incipient tendency of Polish deviationism away from the socialist camp and toward the capitalist world. Liu then learned that the Soviet delegation was already en route for Warsaw.[118] Comparing

---

116. For a general introduction to the Polish crisis and China's response, see MacFarquhar et al., *Secret Speeches,* 8. For a good description and analysis, see Chen, *Mao's China and the Cold War,* 146–50; Shen Zhihua, "1956 nian shiyue weiji," 123–27; Shen and Li, "The 1956 Polish Crisis and Sino–Polish Relations," 46–47.

117. Zhongyang wenxian, *ZNP,* 630; According to Wu's memoir, one enlarged meeting was held in the afternoon of 20 October on the topic of the Polish crisis. For a good description of this meeting see Chen, *Mao's China and the Cold War,* 147. In *ZNP,* however, only the meetings on 21 and 22 October feature. Mao and other members of the politburo agreed that the Soviets wanted to intervene on the strength of their big-power chauvinism, a mindset that violated the egalitarian spirit of international Communism.

118. The Soviet delegation, led by Khrushchev, flew to Warsaw at 7 A.M. on 19 October. Negotiations went on until the morning of 20 October (Warsaw time; in Beijing time the afternoon of 20 October). According to Wu Lengxi, a politburo meeting was held in the afternoon of 20 October to discuss the Soviet notice, in which the CPSU canvased Chinese opinion on a possible military resolution of the Polish crisis. Mao said that the Soviets were on the brink of military intervention yet pulled back from making a final decision. At this point the Soviets' own meeting with the Poles had broken off without agreement. There is some uncertainty as to whether the Soviets actually forewarned the Chinese as to their military plans. There is no corresponding Soviet record that they did so, and the timing of the communication—after the end of meetings in Poland—would suggest that consultation with the Chinese could carry no influence on the Soviet course of action.

the content of Iudin's talk to Liu with that of the Soviet telegram, it appears the ambassador said no more to the Chinese than what had been committed to paper. Notably, Shi Zhe pointed out in particular that Iudin betrayed no inkling of the impending Soviet siege of Warsaw.[119] The earliest reports from Warsaw (either from the embassy or the Xinhua journalist) were sent on 20 October. Wang Bingnan, the Chinese ambassador in Warsaw, reported the rumor of the Soviet movement toward Warsaw, which was explained by the Soviet ambassador Ponomarenko as "several soldiers taking a walk."[120] The Chinese side also obtained news from Associated Press in Warsaw, which offered the analysis that the Soviet troop movement was surely mandated by the top Soviet leaders before they left for Warsaw.[121] Even if the time lag in receiving these reports is ignored, there is no way that the Chinese leadership could have guessed at Soviet military action before 20 October 1956, let alone checked it.[122]

Meanwhile, on 19 October, before the Soviet delegation met Polish representatives, the situation, in Khrushchev's own words, became "somewhat bleak."[123] In the field, the Soviet troops encountered Polish soldiers who had been revolting against Rokossowski and other Soviet-aligned generals. These rebellious Poles were al-

---

Alternatively, it is possible that the CCP got wind of Soviet plans from the Chinese embassy in Poland. The Chinese were definitely behind events in Warsaw during their meeting, which sought ways to prevent an outbreak of interstate violence in Warsaw. See Wu, *Shinian lunzhan*, 37–39.

119. TsKhSD, f. 3, op. 14, d. 67, ll. 25, 104; Chinese version, see "The CPSU CC Presidium's Decision to Send a Delegation to Poland, 18 October 1956, top secret," *SHSA*, 27, 26. The official biography of Mao also adopted Shi Zhe's memoirs to represent the history. Shi, *jianzhenglu*, 220; also see Pang and Jin, *Maozhuan*, 601–2.

120. "Main points of Wang Bingnan's meeting with Ponomarenko, 20 October 1956," CFMA, 109-01141-02, 77–78.

121. *Neican* (22 October 1956): 1087.

122. Even telegrams from Chinese intelligence abroad, whether in Eastern Europe or the West, normally took at least a day to arrive. For a good analysis of the Chinese role in the Soviet threat to the Poles, see Shen, "1956 nian shiyue weiji," 119–43.

123. Nikita Khrushchev, *Khrushchev Remembers: The Last Testament*, trans. and ed. Strobe Talbott (New York: Bantam Books, 1974), 203.

ready on a war footing against those who remained loyal to Rokossowski. The situation was so pressing that "for a brief while, Poland appeared to be on the verge of civil war as well as a conflict with the Soviet Union."[124] The Soviet leaders, however, were not prepared to intervene by force of arms without the utmost certainty that such a course was necessary. Even at this late juncture, the Soviets still expected that a combination of political pressure and military threats would bring the Poles back into line, at least to the degree that a political accommodation could be arranged. Further, the unsettled state of the Polish army made Khrushchev believe it would be easy to start an armed conflict with the Poles, but hard to vanquish every army faction decisively. Judging that the Gomulka regime was still backed by Polish troops out of Rokossowski's control and would not budge under Soviet pressure, the Soviet delegation returned to Moscow.[125]

While the Soviets had paused, however, affairs in Poland took on a revolutionary character. Tensions mounted on 20 and 21 October, with anti-Soviet campaigns spreading throughout the country. Under the pressure of this mounting unrest, both the Soviet and Polish sides preferred peaceful resolution rather than direct military confrontation. On 21 October Khrushchev suggested in the presidium that "in view of the situation we should give up on armed intervention and show our patience." Most presidium members present at the meeting agreed. The Soviet leadership was forced to make concessions to Poland in "refrain[ing] from military intervention" and "display[ing] patience" for the time being.[126] In order to appease public feeling in Poland, the Soviets addressed a letter to the Central Committee of the Polish Communist Party agreeing to the withdrawal of the Soviet advisory group attached to the Polish

---

124. Kramer, "New Evidence," 361.
125. For Khrushchev's estimation of the possible consequence of using military intervention in Poland and the Polish side's efforts in convincing the Kremlin leaders of their unchanged commitment to Communism and wishes to maintain their allied relationship with the Soviets, see Kramer, "New Evidence," 360–61.
126. "Working Notes from the Session of the CPSU CC Presidium on 21 October 1956," *SHSA*, 27, 43.

security department and the recall of Soviet advisers in the Polish armed forces.[127] Meanwhile, on the Polish side, Gomulka immediately took action to appease the army and public, sending a clear message to Moscow about the new Polish regime's commitment to Marxism–Leninism and to close relations with the USSR. Faced with snowballing demonstrations across Poland and Gomulka's posture of cooperation, the Soviet leadership took the path of least resistance, tolerating Gomulka's independence in domestic affairs for now and relegating the prospect of military intervention to a last resort.

On the question of how to deal with the aftermath of the Polish crisis and how to stabilize the Soviet Bloc, the Soviet leaders remained at a loss. Seeking to shore up unity, the CPSU presidium convened a meeting to be attended by leaders from the GDR, China, Czechoslovakia, Bulgaria, and Hungary on 23 October. A letter to the central committees of these countries' parties was also agreed, featuring a single substantive sentence: "In view of the situation in Poland, we would like an exchange of views." Khrushchev and his colleagues took special care to fetch the Chinese comrades in a Soviet aircraft.[128] In the aftermath of the Polish crisis, the immediate task for the Soviets was to win the support of the other socialist parties, especially the CCP, in order to prevent the national diversity of the camp from developing into international splits. China's detached relationship with the Eastern Bloc and the recent experience of coordination with Beijing in dealing with interbloc affairs for unity (Kim's North Korea, for example) probably convinced Khrushchev that the Chinese could be more useful in mediating the Soviet–Polish relations than those East European satellites. How-

---

127. TsKhSD, f. 3, op. 14, d. 67, ll. 1, 4, 5; for the Chinese version, see "The CC CPSU Presidium Decision to Send a Letter to the PZPR CC on the Issue of Soviet Advisors in Poland," *SHSA*, 27, 47.

128. TsKhSD, f. 3, op. 12, d. 1006, ll. 1–3; op. 14, d. 67, l. 129; op. 14, d. 67, ll. 1, 4, 5; for the Chinese version, see "the CPSU CC's Decision to Send Telegrams to Chinese, Czechoslovak, Bulgarian and East Germany Central Parties and Letter to Gomulka, 21 Oct. 1956," *SHSA*, 27, 45.

ever, what if Chairman Mao wanted to do more than the Kremlin leader wanted him to do in the politics of the Eastern Bloc? By the evening of 21 October, the Chinese side was well aware of the Soviet military movements in Poland.[129] More importantly, on 20 October, after the Soviet delegation had already left, Xie Wenqing, the *Xinhua* journalist stationed in Warsaw, sent a telegram to the central party, reporting on splits in the Polish party and on the general political complexion in Poland in the run-up to the CCP Eighth Plenum. Because of Xie's personal experience of participating in some of the students' and workers' demonstrations, he made the following judgments: (1) the demonstrators (both workers and students) publicized their commitment to Communism and to a fraternal Polish–Soviet relationship; (2) the Poles stressed their autonomy in seeking to establish socialism their own way, calling for interstate equality and for Gomulka's restoration to the leadership. The Polish people were very unhappy with the Soviet delegation's visit to Warsaw, construing this as unreasonable Soviet interference in Polish domestic politics. Xie finally pointed out that "it was said" that Gomulka's domestic line was to pursue independent foreign and economic policies.[130] At the same time, Beijing received reports from the Chinese embassy concerning Wang Bingnan's meetings with the Soviet ambassador P. K. Ponomarenko, in which the Soviet ambassador expressed the deep anxiety of the CPSU CC presidium regarding the anti-Soviet propaganda rife in Poland and the possibility of Polish deviation away from the socialist bloc.[131] Evidently, the Xinhua journalist report and the embassy briefing reflected two different perceptions of the same crisis, the first that of the Polish grassroots, the second that of the Soviet leadership. The crux of the

---

129. "Telegram on the Recent Development of the Polish Party, Telegram from the Chinese Embassy in Warsaw" sent on 19 October 1956, CFMA, 109-00762-03, 15–17.
130. "Xie Wenqing's report on the Polish Party Divergences," CFMA, 109-00762-03, 18–20; *Neican* (22 October 1956): 1075–76, 1079–80.
131. "Minutes of Wang Bingnan's talk with Ponomarenko," CFMA, 109-01141-02, 76–78.

matter was which side the CCP leadership, especially Mao, would take.

On the evening of 21 October, Mao summoned a politburo standing committee meeting to discuss the Polish issue after receiving the Soviet letter inviting a Chinese delegation to Moscow. After hearing an introductory presentation on the Polish situation compiled from foreign reports from Wu Lengxi, head of the New China News Agency, Mao stated his view that the Soviet intention of intervening stemmed from big-power chauvinism, and as such violated the basic principles of international relations.[132] Insofar as the new Polish leadership under Wladyslaw Gomulka had made clear that its allegiances in the Cold War lay unambiguously on the socialist side, the Chinese officials opined that it would be wrong for the Soviet Union to use military means to interfere in the domestic affairs of Poland. Mao declared the Polish situation urgent, counseling haste in crafting the Chinese position.[133] The meeting's participants reached consensus on an emergency resolution, firmly opposing Soviet military intervention in Warsaw, and indeed ascribing the Soviet incursion to big-power chauvinism: "[Soviet military intervention to Poland] is [a case of] serious big-power chauvinism, which should not be allowed in any circumstances."[134] After the meeting and late on 22 October, Mao, accompanied by Zhou Enlai, Deng Xiaoping, and Liu Shaoqi, met with the Soviet ambassador, Pavel Iudin, to deliver the CCP CC unanimous view that Soviet armed intervention in Poland was against the internationalist principles of the proletariat. Their text read: "If [the Soviet side still] insists [on military interven-

---

132. Zhongyang wenxian, *ZNP*, 630; Wu Lengxi also referred to Mao's criticism of the Soviet military threat to Poland as big-power chauvinism in his memoir; see Wu, *Shinian lunzhan*, 38–39. The problem is that Wu stated the Politburo meeting was held on 20 October, with quite a few mistakes in his recollection. Currently, the available Chinese official historical publications, such as *ZNP*, *LSN*, and Pang and Jin, *Maozhuan*, all recorded the first politburo meeting on Poland being held on 21 October.
133. Wu, *Shinian lunzhan*, 35.
134. Zhongyang wenxian, *ZNP*, 630; Wu, *Shinian lunzhan*, 35–36; Chen, *Mao's China and the Cold War*, 147.

tion], the Chinese government is prepared to denounce [any Soviet steps toward invasion]."[135] Iudin immediately phoned Khrushchev to inform him of the Chinese position. Mao's message at this stage, however, apparently played no significant role in influencing Soviet decision-making on Poland. As mentioned above, when Mao's message reached Khrushchev, the Soviet leadership had already decided to make concessions to Gomulka and the Poles.

The Chinese leadership was not necessarily abreast of developments on the Polish issue inside the Kremlin, complicating its efforts at mediating between its Communist partners. Soon after their discussion with Iudin, Mao Zedong, Liu Shaoqi, Zhou Enlai, and Deng Xiaoping reconvened at around 3:00 A.M. to frame the agenda for the Chinese delegation invited to Moscow. They defined its mission as interceding between the CPSU and the PUWP, intending on the one hand to rebuke the CPSU's big-power chauvinism and, on the other, to persuade their Polish comrades to desist from breaking from the overall interests of the socialist camp. It appears that the Chinese were ready to act as power-brokers, foreseeing a series of bilateral negotiations as the context in which to effect these diplomatic maneuvers.[136] Late in the evening of 22 October, another CCP CC standing committee meeting gathered to continue the discussion on Poland. By then, more information on the latest developments had been sent to Beijing. The situation in Poland seemed to have stabilized, with Soviet troops beginning to withdraw. Yet the final settlement was left open, to a large extent pending the result of the PUWP Eighth Plenum.[137]

After the politburo meeting, Mao met with Iudin again. Most likely already aware of the dissipation of tension, Mao addressed

---

135. Zhongyang wenxian, *ZNP,* 631: The meeting ended at 12:40 A.M., and Mao met with Yudin at 1:00 A.M. It was evident that Mao's conversation with Yudin had a hidden message for Moscow, warning against its big-power chauvinism.
136. Ibid.
137. *Neican* (22 October 1956): 1075–80; also see "Xie Wenqing's Telegram to the New China News Agency via Foreign Ministry on the Inner-Split of the Polish Party," CFMA, 109-00762-03, 18–20.

the ambassador in a calmer and more moderate tone than he did the previous day. Mao confirmed that the Chinese would send a delegation to Moscow, adding that independent sources of information available to the CCP suggested that the reactionaries (in the Soviet view) had been joined by many members of the masses theoretically well-disposed toward Communism. Therefore, "It seems that the Poles were not on the immediate verge of breaking from the socialist camp, yet they were determined to reshuffle the Politburo." In dealing with the Polish issue, in Mao's view, no more than two measures suggested themselves as plausible, one "hard," the other "soft": the hard one was to suppress dissidence by force, and the soft one to persuade the Polish to back down. If persuasion did not work, Mao's view was that it would be preferable for the Soviets to reconcile themselves to certain concessions, admitting the legitimacy of Gomulka's regime, continuing economic assistance, and cooperating on equal terms than to jettison the Poles from the Socialist camp.[138] Having clearly discerned the growing weakness of the Soviet-dominant Communist system, the Chairman's explicit opposition to Soviet chauvinist intervention in Polish domestic affairs and his "kind" suggestions to the Kremlin to treat the Poles on more equal footing for unity implicitly intended to make a gradual change of the Soviet leading role in the Communist world.

Notably, the Chairman at this point broached a related but sensitive topic: the correct assessment of Stalin. On this matter, Mao stressed his sense of the necessity of criticizing Stalin, but only according to certain methods, noting that the Soviets and Chinese disagreed on these. For Mao, it was only legitimate and strategically desirable to repudiate elements of Stalin's legacy under the condition of protecting his overall reputation. Mao reemphasized his seventy–thirty or even eighty–twenty ratio in rating Stalin's achievements as far more significant than his mistakes, which originated from his subjectivism rather than anything related to his personal-

---

138. Shi, *Jianzhenglu*, 221–22; "Boxiong shijian yu Liu Shaoqi fangsu" [The Polish–Hungarian Incident and Liu Shaoqi's trip to Moscow] (hereinafter "The Polish–Hungarian Incident"), *Bainian Chao* [Hundred-Year Tide] 2 (1997): 12.

ity. (This may have been a reference to Stalin's supposed crude style or personal rusticity). For Mao's purposes, Stalin and his image represented a weapon to be used to fight against the imperialists and various other enemies. The Soviet denunciation of Stalin risked discarding this weapon simply because Stalin had made some mistakes. But what if our common enemies used the weapon to kill us? "We had lifted a rock only to drop it on our own feet."[139] The Chairman's words indicated his increasing awareness of the danger in repudiating Stalin and his dogma, whose essential ideological and political elements had already been part of the Communist practice for decades. In Mao's judgment at this stage, a careless rejection of the orthodoxy, even if it had been proved to be imperfect, could be channeled by the class enemies against the legitimacy of the Communist enterprise in general, a consequence that the Communist Mao felt responsible to keep from happening. Iudin duly conveyed Mao's words to Khrushchev after their meeting.

The top Chinese leaders' discussions on the Polish crisis and the Soviet–Polish relationship, together with Mao's talks with Iudin prior to the delegation's trip to Moscow, reveal Beijing's major concerns during the Polish unrest and in the run-up to the Hungarian events.[140] First of all, the Chinese wanted to signal their divergence from the big-power approach deployed by the Soviets, which they considered responsible to a major degree for the crises' outbreak. This difference was furthermore understood by the top Chinese leaders as a pretext for adjusting the general principles regulating relations between the fraternal parties, challenging the taken-for-granted seniority and superiority of the USSR in the Communist hierarchy. China justified this formula of socialist equivalence as

---

139. Shi, *Jianzhenglu*, 222; Chen, *Mao's China and the Cold War*, 149–50. Deng Xiaoping repeated Mao's words during his meeting with the Soviet delegation in July 1963; for an English translation, see "Meeting of the Delegation of the Communist Party of the Soviet Union and the Chinese Communist Party, Moscow, 5–20 July 1963," *CWIHP Bulletin,* 10 (March 1998): 176, sources from the Russian side.

140. The Hungarian crisis turned out to be of a different nature as time went on. However, at this stage it still satisfied Beijing's initial concerns.

the best way to prevent similar crises from happening again. Nevertheless, it should be noted that Chinese advocacy of a more equitable adjustment between Soviet interests and those of the other members was primarily guided by its own political concerns. After Mikoyan's open speech in the CCP Eighth Congress, Mao and his comrades' suspicions of the opportunism of the new Soviet leaders (incubated at the time of the CPSU Twentieth Congress) deepened. The Chinese were always wary of any Soviet intention to downgrade the importance of the CCP and thus to constrain Chinese freedom of action. The Soviet military threat to the Poles had in effect provided Mao and the CCP with a good opportunity to express their discontent with the unequal relations between China and the Soviet Union (even if these were one-sidedly defined by Mao and his colleagues, as the Soviets took their dominant position inside the camp for granted). In other words, Chinese discomfort at Soviet big-power chauvinism and its father-son mentality applied predominantly to China itself, however it might have been construed in Eastern Europe. The Polish anticentralist campaign and subsequent unrest in the socialist camp offered China a pivot on which it could seek to redress the balance of relations among the Communist states more favorably to the PRC.

This assessment of the priorities of the Moscow missions, however, does not mean that Mao directly intended to challenge the dominant Soviet position within the international Communist movement.[141] It is undeniable that Mao had already felt the pull of a strong aspiration toward ideological and political primacy immediately prior to late 1956, sometimes acting as if he had become the "new emperor" of the international Communist movement.[142] Moreover, the Chairman's awareness of China's future potential as a great power probably also affected his strategies to an unprecedented degree. Nevertheless, at least by early October 1956, Mao

---

141. For the account given by some Chinese scholars, see Shen and Li, "The 1956 Polish Crisis and Sino–Polish Relations," 48–52.

142. Chen and Yang, "Chinese Politics and the Collapse of the Sino–Soviet Alliance," 263–64.

considered that China under his leadership remained deep within a process of internal socialist development, such that it was not ready to accede at once to international leadership. Realistically, the Soviets' leading position was indisputable, not so much in political and ideological terms as on its dominance in military buildup and heavy industry, achievements that China could not hope to outstrip any time soon. China's interests meanwhile lay on the side of Communist camp unity, which went a long way to securing Chinese ideological ambitions and economic plans.

CONCLUSION

The CPSU Twentieth Congress and Khrushchev's secret speech marked a turning point in domestic politics in both Eastern Bloc states like Hungary and Poland and in Mao's China. For the Hungarian and Polish Communist regimes, the dissipation of Stalinism occurred at an unfortunate phase in their development—in the immediate aftermath of the most difficult stage of industrialization and collectivization, but before new social institutions could take root, meaning that these states' capacity to resist external and internal pressures came under extreme pressure. Objectively speaking, China was in a stage of socialist transition similar to that of Eastern Europe. Yet, unlike all the other Soviet Bloc states, Mao's China enjoyed a considerable degree of ideological and political autonomy from the Soviet Union. In consequence the Chinese leadership did not feel personally threatened by the Stalin episode. The Chairman's emphasis on a socialism with distinctively Chinese characteristics allowed China to escape being tarred with the brush of Stalinism in the fallout from Stalin's death. In Mao's estimate, therefore, the Soviet de-Stalinization movement took place at an opportune moment, allowing the Chinese Communists license to seek a faster path to industrialization after the first success of their socialist transition, which could be informed by the Stalinist experience but would not be slavishly bound by it; furthermore, Mao saw the Soviet reassessment of Stalin and consequent confusion in the Communist camp as a good opportunity for the Chinese Communists to introduce their theoretical articulations to the broader international communist community. Mao's efforts at reevaluating Stalin's mistakes in the CCP's own language should be viewed as integral parts of a Chinese initiative to take a more leading role, however limited in the ideological and theoretical realm, in the Communist international.[143]

This freedom to tap on Chinese heritage permitted Mao to hold out the hope of projecting a socialist method of a genuinely global significance. Notably, one significant difference between Mao's understanding of a characteristically Chinese method of socialist construction before and after the Soviet denunciation of Stalin was that, from the end of 1955 to early 1956, the Chairman positively agitated for a big leap forward in industrial production with the regional leaders; in the aftermath of Khrushchev's secret speech, Mao's being able to subscribe to a reassessment of Stalinist mistakes caused him to trim his previously radical development line into a relatively gradualist one despite his constant desire for rapid economic development. Given that it enjoyed a far greater measure of political and ideological autonomy from the Soviet Union than bloc states like Hungary and Poland, the Chinese Communist regime may have imagined it had its eye on a distinctive and liberal road to socialism that other camp members could only admire. But, as we shall deal with in the next two chapters, the question remained how far China would be able to revise the Stalinist model that had essentially served as a blueprint and road map for Mao's successful achievement of socialism. The aftermath of the October Hungarian Revolution would subject the Chairman's un-Stalinist policy adjustments in both political and economic realms to their severest test.

---

143. Of course, Mao at this stage still thought it would be wise to camouflage his strong ambitions skillfully; see Wu, *Yi Maozhuxi*, 7.

In contrast to the Gerő regime's heavy reliance on Soviet leverage to contain domestic instability, the PUWP's top leadership, at least the dominant figures, realized the great danger in echoing the Soviet line and requiring direct Soviet backing in the revolutionary atmosphere of post-Poznan. The CCP's official statement in response to the CPSU Twentieth Congress and Chairman Mao's "On Ten Relationships" gave the Eastern Bloc states the impression that the Chinese Communists favored an interbloc relationship based more on equality and autonomy than the Stalinist hierarchical pattern. The Poles evidently took the initiative in setting up bilateral diplomatic and political contacts with Mao's China aiming to tap the latter's support for their non-Stalinist and autonomous socialist development at home. As far as China's attitudes toward the Polish intention to reshape its relationship with the USSR is concerned, Mao and his colleagues' perception of the nature of the Polish October and their understanding of the balance of relations among Communist states were two key factors in deciding China's hardline interbloc policy throughout late 1956. It is conceivable that the Chairman and his lieutenants regarded the Polish request for more independence in domestic affairs as a good opportunity to redress the Soviet-dominant politics inside the camp. At the same time, they acknowledged the usefulness of bloc unity and integrity to their national interests, coming down on the side of bailing out the Soviets' decision to restore order.

The Chinese also knew that their experience in dealing with the Eastern Bloc states was limited alongside that of Moscow, recommending for China the role of an arbiter, rather than that of the center of international proletarian solidarity or final decision-maker reserved for the Soviets. Furthermore, up to this point, namely, by the latter half of October 1956, Mao already began to realize that to denounce the Stalinist doctrine in general would have meant to deny the Communist leaders like himself and the figures in Moscow, Warsaw, Budapest, etc., a crucial source of strength. As a result, whatever their disagreement with the Russians over the Chinese contribution to world revolution or Soviet policies as imposed on Hungary and Poland, the top Chinese leaders prudently acknowledged their junior status with respect to the Soviets to other member states and planned to persuade the Soviet leadership to revive the legitimacy of Stalinism even if seeking greater equality with (or respect from) the USSR.

CHAPTER 3
China's Diplomatic and Political Involvement in the Hungarian Crisis
(October–November 1956)

The initial purpose of Khrushchev's inviting the Chinese delegation to Moscow was definitively to win Beijing's backing for the Kremlin's policy in the Eastern Bloc and to ask the Chinese to induce the Poles to bow to Soviet domination. Although the Soviets had made advance preparations in military terms to respond to a crisis in Hungary, they do not seem to have anticipated the outbreak of the Hungarian riots immediately following the Polish events. The violence in Hungary, then, caught both Russians and Chinese by surprise. Further, Beijing had very limited information on Hungary, meaning that it was questionable whether the basic principles they had brought with their diplomatic mission to Moscow could apply or answer to the new situation. When the Hungarian crisis broke out on the day of the Chinese delegation's arrival, the Chinese leaders had to decide quickly which factors in the newly emerging Hungarian case were crucial in their political assessment of the revolt's character, and also how best to play their cards in maximizing Chinese influence in the Kremlin.

Although the analysis in this chapter will assess the special role the Chinese did or did not play in the Soviet decision to pull out troops from Hungary, before sending them back in to suppress the October revolution, the focus bears rather on the rationality of the Chinese leadership's decision-making in regard to the events. To a large extent, Beijing's limited knowledge of Hungary and the Chinese leadership's, chiefly Mao's, optimistic estimation of Hungarian developments had prevented China from acting rationally in relation to the events. Coming to believe that the bloc was splitting, Mao and his colleagues were forced to reorient their political objectives from challenging the Soviet-centered order to advocating bloc unity in blunt neo-Stalinist terms. In studying these shifts in Chinese diplomatic and political objectives from the end of October through early November, we can see that Beijing selected its line of upholding the Bandung principles, namely, national independence, sovereignty, equality, and noninterference in internal affairs, for reasons of expediency. Once it felt that bloc unity and integrity were in real danger after Hungary, the CCP decisively reasserted the necessarily hierarchical patterns of interstate relations in Communism. In the final analysis, the Chinese leadership's sense of basic, structuring laws in defining orthodox socialist revolution and construction, and basic laws relating the unity of all socialist states, drew heavily on the Stalinist pattern.

UNEXPECTED CRISIS: THE CHINESE DELEGATION IN MOSCOW

The Chinese delegation arrived on the afternoon of 23 October. According to Shi Zhe, its interpreter, the group was immediately puzzled as to why they were welcomed personally at the airport by Nikita Khrushchev without any retinue or intermediaries. As we now know, a Soviet presidium session held before the Chinese delegation's arrival had determined that Khrushchev and other leaders should greet the Chinese at 11:00 A.M. on 24 October.[1] Khrushchev was motivated by a desire to win over the Chinese to whatever

---

1. Khrushchev held a session with the Presidium members, in which they decided to meet the Chinese on 24 October, TsKhSD, f. 3, op. 12, d. 1006, l. 5. For the Chinese version, see "Working Notes of the CPSU CC Presidium Session," in Shen, *SHSA*, 27: 49.

course of action the Soviets chose in Eastern Europe. At the airport, he struck the Chinese delegation as "extremely nervous," reciting a litany of complaints in relation to the crisis as well as expanding on domestic affairs to Liu Shaoqi as soon as they reached the group's guesthouse. The delegates received the impression that Khrushchev was desperate to secure Chinese support on various matters, especially the Eastern Bloc revolts and CPSU inner party issues.[2]

With regard to the Polish crisis, Khrushchev outlined to the Chinese the Soviets' initial plan of intervening militarily in Warsaw, in order to preempt the Poles' "treason" or departure from the socialist camp. However, Khrushchev informed Liu that the USSR had backed down from this last-ditch policy after a full day of negotiation and trust-building with the Poles. The Kremlin was thus now in a position tentatively to acknowledge the new Polish leadership. Knowing that his Chinese comrades enjoyed greater credit among the Poles than the Soviets did, Khrushchev expressed the wish that the Chinese delegation could prevail on the Poles to keep up strong ties with Moscow. In the course of discussion, according to Shi Zhe, Khrushchev also criticized his previous actions, though exactly what he said on this matter is not recorded. Liu and Deng, despite their reservations as to the Soviet conduct, took the view that Soviet Polish policy was already in accordance with the CCP's

---

2. Shi Zhe did not make clear what problems Khrushchev kept complaining about on the way to the guesthouse. It could be inferred from the later talk between Khrushchev and the Chinese delegation that he mainly discussed ethnic problems, the chaos in Eastern Europe, and inner-party cadre issues. In regard to what these ethnic problems and inner-party cadre issues were, Shi Zhe is silent. See Shi, "The Polish–Hungarian Incident," 13. In his other memoir, *Wo de yisheng* [My Life], ed. Shi Qiulang (Beijing: Renmin), 2001: 468–69, Shi Zhe says that Khrushchev had already told Liu Shaoqi of the anti-Communist nature of the Hungarian crisis on the way to the guest house from the airport on 23 October. This seems impossible given that Khrushchev still had no clear idea of the Hungarian turmoil at the time of his welcoming the Chinese delegation, according to currently available Soviet documents on the Hungarian crisis of 1956 (see, for example, Malin Notes). Shi Zhe's article published in "The Polish–Hungarian Incident" therefore should be treated as the most reliable record of the Chinese delegation's stay in Moscow by far. Also see Jin, *Liuzhuan*, 804.

guidelines and fell in line with the policy agenda previously arranged with Mao, promising Khrushchev their backing.³ However, when Khrushchev moved to wind up the talks, apparently in raptures of delight, Liu Shaoqi asked him to stay on as Liu introduced a more important topic: the problem of Stalin. This was a theme that the Chinese had been intending to broach after the sequence of political disturbances took place in the Eastern Bloc in the second half of 1956. As Shi Zhe recalled, Liu Shaoqi said to Khrushchev that given that Lenin and Stalin were two swords (of world Communism), one of them (i.e., Stalin) should not be thrown away.⁴ Obviously, Mao and his colleagues considered their divergence with the Soviets over the evaluation of Stalin and Stalinism a very serious issue, pledging themselves to efforts that would bring Khrushchev around to their standpoint during the delegation's visit. Nevertheless, the Chinese leadership was cautious enough to negotiate with Khrushchev on this issue solely via private meetings, preventing an open challenge to Khrushchev's treatment of Stalin either in front of the Soviet leaders or in public.

During his talks with the Chinese, Khrushchev received a phone call from Ernő Gerő, the new HWP leader appointed by the Soviets to displace Rákosi several months prior, asking for permission to cancel his visit to Moscow given the turbulence of Hungarian domestic affairs.⁵ In fact, Gerő and other key figures had been away for several months, only returning one day before the first demonstration took place, and they lacked any action plan to deal

---

3. Shi, *Jianzhenglu*, 223.
4. Shi, "The Polish-Hungarian Incident," 13; Jianzhenglu, 225.
5. Shi, "The Polish-Hungarian Incident," 13; also see Kramer, "Hungary and Poland, 1956." As András Hegedüs recalled, Gerő had remained in contact with Moscow through Andropov through the evening of 23 October before the escalation of the upheaval in the Hungarian capital. See András Hegedüs, *Hegejusi huiyilu* [Hegedüs's memoir], trans. Chen Zhiliu and Chai Pengfei (Beijing: Shijie Zhishi, 1992), 291. For a Hungarian version, see Hegedüs, *A Történelem A Hatalom Igézetében: Életrajzi Elemzések* [In history and struggles, memoir of Andras Hegedüs] (Budapest: Kossuth, 1988). Hegedüs was named the first vice prime minister by the Hungarian party's central committee on 23 October 1956 to assist Nagy's work. See Izsák, *Magyarország Miniszterelnökei*, 197–200.

with such an emergency. By the time Gerő talked to Khrushchev over the phone, the Hungarian turmoil had already reached a breaking point and was moving beyond the control of the top Hungarian leaders. Strangely, although Gerő had already appealed for Soviet military assistance through the Soviet attaché in Budapest, he chose not to enlarge upon the current Budapest events directly to Khrushchev. Gerő most likely feared for his job in failing to communicate to Khrushchev the full extent of the disturbances; the Kremlin leader had a reputation for harshness and impulsiveness and could well have dismissed Gerő summarily.

Shortly afterward, Khrushchev received two phone calls from Marshal Georgy Zhukov, reporting a severe mass riot and relaying the request of the Hungarian government to mobilize the Soviet forces stationed outside Hungary. The Chinese delegation was thus inadvertently present during Khrushchev's conference with Zhukov on this issue. Both Khrushchev and Liu Shaoqi were surprised by Zhukov's report, as Gerő's earlier call had given no hint of impending insurrection. Putting down the phone, Khrushchev said immediately that since the Chinese representatives knew nothing about the Hungarian issue, he would not ask for their input at this point. He then invited the Chinese delegation to the CPSU presidium session to be held the following day for further information. With regard to the Stalin question, Khrushchev seemed not to grant it any great significance and simply replied, "It was right to abandon the sword of Stalin since it was already useless." The development of events in Hungary then forced Khrushchev to abbreviate his discussion with the Chinese and rush off.[6]

Having left the Chinese delegation's guesthouse in haste, Khrushchev summoned an urgent Presidium plenary session to consider a Soviet response to the Hungarian events. As the Hungarian crisis had come upon the Soviet leaders while they were still locked in deliberations over the Polish case, a divided Kremlin quickly appreciated it could hardly afford another fissure in its Eastern Euro-

---

6. Shi, "The Polish-Hungarian Incident," 13.

pean front.⁷ Against the backdrop of the Cold War, as Khrushchev later recalled, the double upheavals on the Soviet Eastern European front could in the worst case precipitate a serious crisis in both the military and geopolitical sense if the Soviets found themselves cut off from their forces in the GDR.⁸ Khrushchev immediately proposed sending troops to Budapest; most of the presidium members agreed. Only Mikoyan advocated political measures such as delegating the management of the situation to Nagy and the Hungarians, while reserving force as a last resort after political measures had failed.⁹ Other Soviet officials doubted Nagy's ability to take control when "the government is being overthrown," further taking the view that "there's no comparison [between the Hungarian case and] Poland." In Poland the Gomulka leadership clearly held the reins of power, while Gerő was making a direct request for Soviet military intervention since the events in Budapest were moving at too fast a pace for the HWP to deal with on its own. Eventually, the presidium had to make a decision to send troops to Hungary without unanimity. Seeking to nip unrest in Eastern Europe in the bud, Khrushchev ordered a first military intervention in response to the Hungarian's informal call for Soviet assistance.¹⁰

---

7. All the top leaders except Mikoyan favored a military resolution. Mikoyan's dissenting view advocated political measures, insisting that troops should be used only if it became necessary. The original note does not mention the time of this session, though according to the research of the working note author, it seems to have started after 10:00 P.M. (running until 11:00 P.M.). Therefore, Khrushchev would have summoned this session after he left Liu Shaoqi's lodgings; "Working Notes from the Session of the CPSU CC Presidium on 23 October 1956," *CWIHP Bulletin*, 8–9: 388–89.

8. Khrushchev, *Khrushchev Remembers*, 199, 225.

9. Mikoyan advised "trying political measures, then sending troops"; *CWIHP Bulletin*, 8–9: 388–89.

10. Khrushchev insisted that the Hungarian government should send a request for military assistance. (See *CWIHP*, virtual archive, "Account of a Meeting at the CPSU CC, 24 October 1956, on the Situation in Poland and Hungary," accessed 15 December 2012, http://www.wilsoncenter.org/digital-archive.) Gerő did not draft one and it was Hegedüs who eventually signed a letter requesting Soviet troops, which arrived in Moscow on 28 October via Andropov; "Andropov Report, 28 October, 1956," *CWIHP Bulletin*, 5 (Spring 1995): 30. For an introduction to these documents, see Janos Rainer, "The Yeltsin Dossier: Soviet Documents on Hungary, 1956," *CWIHP Bulletin*, 5 (1995): 22.

The Soviet leadership had in reality become aware of the signs of a general crisis in Hungary implicit in Hungarian society's demands for radical change long before incidents eventually broke out. As early as July 1956, the Soviet Special Corps in Hungary began to draft a plan for "the maintenance, defense, and—if need be—restoration of the socialist order of society" by way of Soviet military force, an expedient given the code-name Volna (Wave).[11] The plan included a special order, which determined key sites to be protected in possible cooperation with Hungarian national defense organizations and the people's army, together with the number of firearms available. The formulation of Volna at this stage represented a defensive gesture, indicating that Soviet leaders wanted a reliable fallback option in the event that their attempts to bolster political stability in Hungary did not work out.[12] In mid-October, the Soviet ambassador to Hungary, Yuri Andropov, and the commander of Soviet forces in Hungary, Lieutenant General Pyotr Nikolayevich Lashchenko, sent letters to the CPSU and the Soviet general staff, calling their attention to possible emergencies in Budapest. In the middle of October, considering the political situation to be worsening, Lashchenko ordered his commanders to be ready to take the necessary measures. Lieutenant General Evgenii Malashenko, who helped command the operation in Hungary in 1956, arrived in Budapest on the evening of 22 October to examine the

---

11. The Soviet troops stationed in Eastern Bloc states were reconstituted in September 1955 (in the so-called Special Corps). The purpose of the Special Corps was to close down and defend the Austrian frontier and to safeguard lines of communication in case the Soviet troops were withdrawn. In July 1956, a group of high-ranking Soviet officials visited Hungary to inspect the Special Corps stationed there. These officials helped the command staff of the Special Corps in Hungary draw up plans for possible anti-riot and counterinsurgency operations in Hungary. See Kramer, "New Evidence," 365; Miklós Horváth, "Soviet Aggression against Hungary in 1956: Operations 'Wave' and 'Whirlwind,'" in Lee Congdon and Bela Király, *The Ideas of the Hungarian Revolution, Suppressed and Victorious, 1956–1999* (Bradenton FL: East European Monographs, 2003), 66.

12. Alexander Kirov, "Soviet Military Intervention in Hungary, 1956" in Györkei and Horváth, *Soviet Military Intervention*, 132; also see Shen, "1956nian shiyue weiji," 133–34; Miklós Horváth, "Soviet Aggression against Hungary," 67–69.

state of affairs on the ground in person.[13] Therefore, before a formal request for military aid from the Hungarian government was made and a decision taken inside the Kremlin, the Soviets already had detailed action plans at hand.[14]

Despite the 23 October decision to send troops to Budapest to be ready to carry out the stringent security measures planned by the Soviets several months earlier, Khrushchev did not entirely give up on the prospect of solving the Hungarian problem through largely political means. It was in order to offer an escape valve for political pressure that Khrushchev resolved to restore Nagy to political life, though he was not willing at this stage to rehabilitate him to the degree of letting him lead the Hungarian government. Sending his two key political allies in the presidium, Mikoyan and Suslov, as envoys to Budapest, Khrushchev seems to have held out the hope, as suggested by Mikoyan in the 23 October presidium session, that Nagy could do in Hungary what Gomulka had done in Poland for the Soviets.[15] But if Khrushchev was prepared to take a chance on Nagy, the newer Kremlin leaders had been of two minds about the Hungarian from the very beginning. Nagy was viewed with suspicion on account of his label as a New Course reformist and supposed nationalist; Rákosi, Gerő, and some Soviet diplomats had also to a large extent succeeded in painting Nagy as variously rightist, opportunistic, stubborn, and idealistic, someone "not an enemy, but with 'very dangerous thoughts.'"[16] Aiming to hold the situation in check, Khrushchev therefore told Gerő to pass on to every Hun-

---

13. Yevgeny I. Malashenko, "The Special Corps under Fire in Budapest: Memoirs of an Eyewitness," in Györkei and Horváth, *Soviet Military Intervention*, 221; Shen, "1956nian shiyue weiji," 133.

14. Györkei and Horváth, *Soviet Military Intervention*, 221; Shen, "1956nian shiyue weiji," 133–34; Horváth, "Soviet Aggression," 66.

15. It was Zhukov who suggested sending a CC Presidium member to Budapest; Khrushchev chose Mikoyan and Suslov, his closest allies, to carry out the mission. See "Working Notes," *CWIHP Bulletin*, 8–9: 388–89.

16. "Andropov's Telegram to the Soviet Foreign Ministry, 12 October, 1956," in Shen, *SHSA*, 27, 274. For a good reference to a study on archival materials, see Granville, *The First Domino*, 19–24; for Rákosi's account of Nagy in his memoir, see Shen, *SHSA*, 26, 196.

garian party leader that the Hungarian Workers' Party (HWP) CC plenum could not be held until the demonstrations were suppressed.[17] But this order notwithstanding, Gerő and his colleagues had already held a party plenum to discuss the riots, selecting Nagy, the most likely appeaser of the masses, as the new premier on the night of 23 October.[18] As events unfolded, the Soviets' marked ambivalence over Nagy and their suspicion of his ability to alleviate the Hungarian conflict would become crucial factors in their final decision to replace the regime with pro-Soviet elements.

Meanwhile, on the Chinese delegates' side, Liu Shaoqi made a phone call to Mao after Khrushchev left the guesthouse, giving an account on the situation in Budapest. Beijing thus indirectly received news of the Hungarian crisis at almost the same time as Moscow. Nevertheless, the process of the top Soviet leaders' evaluation of and decision-making with regard to the Hungarian incident undoubtedly remained closed to the Chinese. Liu's knowledge of the Hungarian Crisis on 23 October was too shallow to act as a base for any detailed evaluation on the part of the Chinese. In fact, Beijing did not obtain corroborating reports on the latest developments in Budapest from its own resources or from foreign reports until 25 October.[19] It is likely that the Chinese would have harbored doubts that the Hungarian standoff could exacerbate so quickly, seeing its coincidence with the high-water mark of the Polish unrest

---

17. "Account of a Meeting at the CPSU CC, 24 October 1956," *CWIHP*, virtual archive.

18. Shen, "1956nian shiyue weiji," 127; his source is from АВПРФ, ф. 0122, оп. 401956г, п. 336, д. 10, л. 108, Орехов, События 1956 года, ИРИРАН, Советская внешняя политика, с. 234.

19. As previously noted, the Chinese leadership mainly relied on routine reports from the Chinese embassy in Budapest to get firsthand information from that country. The situation did not improve until November 1956, when two New China News Agency journalists were sent to Budapest after the Soviet second intervention in Hungary. TASS (the Telegraph Agency of the Soviet Union) reported the Budapest riots on 24 October, together with the Hungarian government's request of Soviet military assistance to restore order. This report was reprinted in the 26 October version of *Neican,* suggesting that the Chinese's earliest news of the riots in Budapest could only have come from Liu Shaoqi in Moscow. See *Neican* (26 October 1956): 1242–43.

as suspicious.[20] As one scholar has pointed out, Mao definitely had reason to be unhappy with Moscow's first military intervention in Budapest in late October, considering the Kremlin's decision hasty, irresponsible, and arbitrary.[21] Without being factually well-informed, however, Mao and Liu held back from any clear statement in relation to the Budapest case either at home or in Moscow.[22]

In the meantime, the Chinese leaders also seemed to fear that unless they were properly settled, the major problems in Soviet–satellite relations would threaten the unity of the Communist camp. The Chinese thus adopted the line of helping the Soviets restore unity and moderating their criticisms of Soviet mistakes at this juncture. Having contacted Mao on the night of 23 October, Liu Shaoqi, together with Deng Xiaoping, next met the Chinese diplomats from Warsaw, who had been called to report on the latest developments in Poland. After considering their reports, Liu states,

---

20. The Chinese embassy in Budapest sent a telegram comparing the Hungarian events to the aftermath of the PUWP's Eighth Congress, which would necessarily suggest to the Chinese leadership that the Hungarian demonstrations were stirred up by developments in Poland. This telegram was sent on 23 October before the demonstration and reached the central Chinese leaders by noon, 24 October; see "Chinese Embassy in Hungary's Telegram to Foreign Ministry and the Central Party on the Great Impact the Polish Party's Eighth Congress Had on Hungarian Domestic Politics" *CFMA,* 109-01041-01, 1–2.

21. Yang Kuisong, *Mao Zedong yu Mosike de en'en yuanyuan* [Past kindness and grudges between Mao Zedong and Moscow] (Jiangxi: Jiangxi Renmin, 2002), 390. With a relatively vague picture of what was happening in Budapest, Liu Shaoqi phoned Mao to solicit his opinion on Moscow's decision to intervene in Hungary. Mao thought it better not to give a clear answer on this matter. Yang says further that it was obvious that Mao was not onboard with Moscow's first intervention in Budapest. Yang's statement here is remarkable in light of what we can reconstruct of Beijing's major concerns at this moment. Unfortunately, Yang does not provide any reference to support his account, but the Chinese official declaration, "More on the Historical Lessons of Proletarian Revolution," which did not agree with the Soviet first military intervention, corroborates his claim.

22. Shen Zhihua's personal collection, Liu Shaoqi's "Report at the 1st Meeting of the 2nd Plenary Session of the Eighth Central Committee" in his article "Fanying he sikao," 75–85. It seems clear that the Chinese news reports on Hungary took the form of brief informative summaries without any official comment or special political coloring; this was the case up to 28 October 1956. See Xinhua tongxunshe [New China News Agency] edited, *Xinhuashe xinwengao* [New China news report draft] vol. 2322 (Beijing: Xinhua, 1956): 42–48.

"The Central Committee decided [that the Chinese delegation in Moscow should] comment merely on Soviet big-power chauvinism, [as] too many criticisms at one time would be difficult for the Soviet side to accept." Liu also told his colleagues that enforcing conformity within the Eastern Bloc through Soviet high-handedness would only speed the bloc's tendency to disintegrate, but that the Soviets did not understand the value of a more arm's-length relationship.[23] The latter part of Liu's words demonstrated that the Chinese leadership, Mao in particular, had already begun to conceive of a pattern of Soviet Bloc unity different from that established by Stalin.

In relation to the Polish developments, Deng Xiaoping emphasized knowing the changes in personnel in the Polish politburo after its eighth plenum reshuffle, laying special weight on the positions of Gomulka and Rokossovsky, respectively. He told the representatives of the Chinese embassy in Poland: "[We] should make more efforts in Soviet–Polish mediation. It needs to be noted, however, what [we] say to one side is very likely to be transferred to the other. Therefore, any view [of our side] that we judge improper to be known by either side [the Poles or the Soviets] should not be expressed. Despite the current situation of relations between the two parties being difficult, we should keep in mind that their relationship is likely to improve later."[24] In general, the Chinese delegates followed certain guidelines set by the CCP CC in dealing with Eastern Bloc conflicts, as Liu was later to recall in November: "first of all," the Chinese worked to advance "Sino–Soviet solidarity; "second," they sought "to do [their] work smoothly," in other words, to

---

23. The diplomats sent to Moscow on 23 October 1956 from the Warsaw Chinese embassy were Yu Zhan, then counselor, and Luo Yisu, interpreter in the embassy. Notably, the Chinese delegation did not raise the Stalin question again after the 23 October private meeting with Khrushchev. Luo Yisu, "1956nian 'Bolan shijian' he Zhongguo de zhengce [The 1956 "Polish Incident" and the Chinese Policies]," *Waijiao xueyuan xuebao* [Chinese foreign affairs university bulletin], issue 3 (1997): 41–42; also see the author's interview with Luo Yisu, April 2004.

24. Luo, ibid., 41–42. In Wu Lengxi's memoir, Mao said similar things in the discussion before the Chinese delegation was sent to Moscow; see *Shinian lunzhan*, 44–45.

avoid conflict either with the Poles or the Soviets, or indeed between these parties; and "third," they were "careful [in the way they] made suggestions to fraternal parties." This line was dictated by the perception that stability in the Communist camp and a general fraternal and stable relationship with the USSR were for the Chinese the preconditions of their own security and development during the Cold War.[25]

On 24 October, another Soviet presidium session was held with the Chinese in attendance.[26] Liu Shaoqi, the Chinese representative, hoped the discussion would gravitate toward the issues of big-power chauvinism and bloc unity (as discussed above, the reappraisal of Stalin would be temporarily laid aside) underlying their mission; at any rate, he used the convening of the presidium members as a chance to meet all of its members. As the meeting in fact played out, the presidium was devoted to a narrow and urgent consideration of Poland and Hungary.[27] In describing the Hungarian situation, Khrushchev said that the Soviet troops had entered Budapest, basically restoring social order and solving all but a few residual problems, such as the rebels' possession of a small number of strongholds. The Hungarian people had welcomed the Red Army and the Soviet tanks. He begged the Chinese comrades to understand this drastic measure on the grounds of its absolute necessity. Khrushchev further explained to Liu that the situation in Hungary had demonstrated "a counterrevolutionary tendency" of a completely different character from that in Poland, whose problems were constrained within the party. He stressed that the presidium members had reached unanimity over the use of military means in the Hungarian case and that the presidium had already dispatched Mikoyan to Budapest. It is plausible that Liu received an impression of the situation in Hungary as perplexing but still not entirely out of

---

25. Transcript of Liu Shaoqi's report at the Second Plenum of the Eighth Central Committee of the CPC, 10 November 1956. Quoted from Shen, "Fanying he sikao," 75.
26. ЦХСД, ф. 3, оп. 12, д. 1006, л. 5, 506; Chinese version, Shen, *SHSA*, 27, 49.
27. "Working Notes," *CWIHP Bulletin*, 8–9: 389; Jin, *Liuzhuan*, 805.

hand at this stage. To Khrushchev, the Chinese had a certain utility both in possibly soothing the Poles and as a counterweight in Soviet domestic politics to revanchist elements calling for the reassertion of Stalinist controls. As long as he could handle the Hungarian case without much difficulty, the Soviet first secretary would seek to retain primacy in decision-making inside the Soviet Bloc, rather than genuinely consulting the Chinese for their suggestions. Nevertheless, Khrushchev felt it was necessary to justify the Soviet military intervention in Hungary and to emphasize the substantial differences between Hungary and Poland to the Chinese to ensure their support.[28]

Despite speaking in session for over two hours that included interpreting time, Liu Shaoqi, following his directions from Beijing sent the previous night, did not set out an unambiguous Chinese position in the Soviets' first military intervention into Hungary. Instead, Liu spent much of his time analyzing the Polish events in their essence, pointing out that the divergence between Warsaw and Moscow was a matter of interpretations of socialism, not a conflict between revolution and counterrevolution. In the CCP's judgment, the Polish party under Gomulka's leadership was only asking for autonomy, and not trying to dissociate itself from socialism, with the implication that Poland intended to remain a socialist country inside the Communist camp. Had the Soviet decided to use military force in settling a dispute between two socialist countries, to the Chinese this would have amounted to a major error. Having conveyed Beijing's support of Moscow's decision to solve the Polish dispute through negotiations, Liu thus stressed the ne-

---

28. Shi Zhe, "The Polish–Hungarian Incident," 13; also see Chen Jian, *Mao's China and the Cold War*, 152. For the Russian record see ЦХСД, ф. 3, оп. 12, д. 1005, л. 52; for the Chinese version, see *SHSA*, 27, 52–53. It should be noted that the Russian record says nothing further than that the Soviet and Chinese sides exchanged views on the Polish–Hungarian crises (Comrades Khrushchev, Kaganovich, Bulganin, Molotov, Malinkov with Comrade Liu Shaoqi) omitting any account of what Khrushchev told Liu vis-à-vis current developments in Hungary. Since Malin Notes were served as keynote references to high-ranking officers, it is understandable that most of them were only memos of key points rather than anything more detailed.

cessity of analyzing the origins of the tensions emerging between the Soviet Union and the Eastern Bloc states, such as Poland and Hungary.²⁹

Liu's speech, then, centrally expanded on a theme he dubbed Soviet big-power chauvinism. He attributed tensions between the Soviets, Poles, and Hungarians primarily to overweening Soviet habits of interference and "hegemonizing" in the Stalin era.³⁰ Liu's broad-brush approach meant he did not deal with the Hungarian situation in detail, nor advance a view with regard to Moscow's direct military intervention, even though these two issues obviously formed the very crux of the matters under discussion at the meeting. Rather, Liu asked the Soviets to consider whether the nationalist sentiments in Poland and Hungary were essentially created by Stalin's chauvinism, which had spawned abnormal interstate relationship inside the socialist camp.³¹ It seems that the Chinese delegation decided before the meeting to limit its discussion to the topics preselected in Beijing on 23 October, concerning in general terms the basis of fraternity on which all socialist nations should henceforth deal with each other. If this theme had a practical reference at all, it was not to Hungary but to the Soviet action, which the Chinese meant to commend, in defusing the Polish Crisis through un-Stalin-like negotiations.

---

29. Shi, "The Polish–Hungarian Incident," 14; *Jianzhenglu*, 225–28; Jin, *Liuzhuan*, 805; for a detailed account of Liu's speech, see Chen, *Mao's China and the Cold War*, 153.

30. Shi, ibid.; Jin, ibid.

31. It should be pointed out that in Shi Zhe's article "The Polish–Hungarian Incident," 11–17, also in Chen, *Mao's China and the Cold War*, 52, Liu Shaoqi is described as having offered no separate appraisal of the Hungarian incident. Liu only pointed out that both Polish and Hungarian crises were, to some extent, caused by Soviet big-power chauvinism. In Shi Zhi's *Wo de yisheng*, 471, however, Liu is described as saying that the Hungarian incident had external as well as internal causes. This seems to be a reference to Soviet interference on one side and the domestic difficulties of the Hungarian party on the other. Shi Zhe's oral recollection, *Jianzhenglu*, also adopted the account of the article in "The Polish–Hungarian Incident." Li Haiwen, a trained historian who recorded and compiled Shi Zhe's memoirs, represents a more reliable source than the details offered in *Wo de yisheng*.

In denouncing big-power politics, Liu said that the Chinese party had already openly raised the issue of anti-chauvinism and anti–narrow-minded nationalism in the CCP Eighth Congress with the view of bringing these matters to the attention of the masses. Seeking to capitalize on Khrushchev's own denunciation of Stalin to warn the Soviets against further blunders in foreign affairs, Liu told the Soviet leaders outright what the Chinese thought of Soviet behavior in the past. The Soviet manner of dealing with other socialist states, according to Liu, had imposed its own will insensitively; it would be better, Liu said, if the Soviets sought to "bring round the other party to your view; otherwise, they are the target of your attack." But it was improper, given a truly international vision of socialism, for the Soviets openly to attack other parties, as they had in their articles against the Japanese Communist Party in 1950. Mao's second-in-command added that he saw *Pravda*'s recent accusations against the Polish media in the same light.[32] "It is terribly wrong to consider only one's own interest while totally ignoring that of others, [something] which would bring grave harm to our shared Communist undertaking." To right interstate relationships within the bloc, Liu recommended that the Soviets embark on a course of post-Stalinist self-criticism, learning how to negotiate and cooperate properly with other socialist states.[33]

The Soviet presidium members, according to Shi Zhe, were much agitated by Liu Shaoqi's direct critique of the Soviet Union, even if it was couched in the same terms that Khrushchev had used in critiquing Stalin. Khrushchev simply listened with his head bowed. Yekatrina Furtseva, the CPSU central committee secretary, could so little tolerate Liu's wording that she tried to walk out of the meeting room, only to be compelled to take her seat again by a sharp glance from Khrushchev.[34] After returning to China, Liu's re-

---

32. The article against the Japanese party was *Pravda*'s "On the Japanese Situation" of January 1950; see Shi, *Jianzhenglu*, 227; the latter is most likely referring to "Antisovetskaya Kampaniya V Pol'Skoi Presse," *Pravda*, 20 October 1956.
33. Shi, "The Polish–Hungarian Incident," 14; *Jianzhenglu*, 227.
34. Ibid.

port, as delivered during the second plenary session of the CCP Eighth Congress in November 1956, noted, "In my speech [to the Soviets], I criticized their big-state, big-power chauvinist tendencies in dealing with relations with foreign countries, and in particular with fraternal communist parties. I also pointed out some mistakes and errors they had made in [handling] several specific matters. On this occasion, we finally expressed our views in a frank way."[35] He did not say whether the Soviets construed his criticisms to refer to their Hungarian misadventure. Apparently, however, a hidden purpose of the Chinese side to mention Stalin's past unequal treatment of the bloc member states was to remind Khrushchev and his colleagues not to make the same mistake in dealing with Polish and Hungarian issues.

Nonetheless, Liu made it very clear during the meeting that in any circumstance, "The center [of the international movement] can only be the Soviet Union." "Comrade [Palmiro] Togliatti introduced a 'multicentrality' thesis," Liu Shaoqi stated, "but we told the Italian comrade that we oppose[d] that thesis."[36] The CCP set out to align itself with the CPSU within the parameters of a robust debate. In other words, in light of the fear of the imperialists that the Soviet Union and China would bind together, the unity of the two parties (the CCP and the CPSU) stood as the essential principle of international relations to be preserved before all else. As Shi Zhe recalled, some of the Soviet leaders certainly bridled under his Chinese straightforwardness, even though he had laid great stress on the CCP's recognition of the Soviet leadership within the camp. More anecdotally, Shi Zhe's memoirs suggest that many Russians thought it unacceptable that the Chinese Communists should determine Communism for them, jibing "So you [Chinese] then are the real

---

35. Transcript of Liu Shaoqi's report quoted from Jin, *Liuzhuan*, 805. Also see Zhongyang dang'anguan [Central archives], ed., *Gongheguo wushinian zhenguidang'an* (hereinafter *Zhenguidang'an*) [Fifty years precious archival collection of the People's Republic of China] (Beijing: Zhongguodang'an, 1999), 1: 15–18.

36. Palmiro Togliatti, Secretary General of the Italian Communist Party (PCI), 1926–1964. For Liu's words, see Shi Zhe, "The Polish–Hungarian Incident," 14; *Jianzhenglu*, 227.

Marxists." Any hidden complications notwithstanding, Khrushchev stated his view at the end of the meeting that the Soviet side agreed with Liu's opinions and were open to hold another discussion on big-power politics with the Chinese.[37]

In what is now available from the Russian archives, the Soviet side kept a very brief note of the meeting on 24 October penned by V. N. Malin, head of the CPSU General Department, with one or two sentences for every key point. The main course of the meeting, judging from the materials preserved by both sides, was dominated by Liu Shaoqi's speech. Careful comparative study of Shi Zhe's recollections and the Soviet presidium session record reveals that the Soviet version, though much shorter than Shi Zhe's memoir, retains the major points of Liu's speech as conveyed by Shi Zhe's account, notably the Chinese acceptance of the peaceful resolution to the Polish question and China's support of a hierarchical organization for the Communist camp with the Soviet Union as the center. Malin's notes does touch on Liu's attestation that "there are mistakes [on the Soviet side], which needed to be overcome." Malin also comments or annotates, "On some occasions, [we] did impose [our] views on the others." It is significant that in the Soviet record, all specific incidents mentioned by Liu were left out; further, all traces of Chinese criticism in the *Pravda* article and any suggestion of a new relationship between the socialist states has been effectively expunged.[38] No conclusive judgment can be made concerning whether the Soviets omitted any treatment of the substantive matters of Liu's speech because Malin Notes were typically short or because they were unhappy ideologically with the Chinese line. One thing for certain was that it was unprecedented for the top Soviet leaders to face such direct criticisms by another socialist party

---

37. ЦХСД, ф. 3, оп. 12, д. 1005, л. 52; for the Chinese version, see Shen, *SHSA*, 27, 52–53; Shi, "The Polish–Hungarian Incident," 15; *Jianzhenglu*, 228; Jin, *Liuzhuan*, 805; Chen, *Mao's China and the Cold War*, 337.

38. Shi, *Jianzhenglu*, 225–28; for the Russian record see ЦХСД, ф. 3, оп. 12, д. 1005, л. 52 (TsKhSD, f. 3, op. 12, d. 1005, l. 52); for the Chinese version, see Shen, *SHSA*, 27: 52–53. Words in brackets are added by the author on the basis of a comparative study of the material from the Chinese and Soviet sides.

within the Kremlin, making it understandable if Malin chose to omit these unpleasant words (at least to the Soviets) from his notes.[39]

In Shi Zhe's much more detailed account of the session, Khrushchev showed enough patience and modesty to hear out the Chinese criticisms of Soviet mistakes. As far as it is possible to reconstruct Khrushchev's motives, it seems that Khrushchev needed to ensure Chinese political support for his project of shoring up Eastern Bloc unity. As long as the Chinese criticisms of big-power chauvinism restricted themselves to Stalin's mistakes, the first secretary was resigned to accepting them. Of course, Khrushchev's willingness to bear up under the Chinese list of Stalin's mistakes was also rooted in his portrayal of himself as innocent of Stalinist crimes and as a reformist of the Stalinist legacy. In Khrushchev's own words, "A normalization of relationship[s with the other socialist states] must be established on a new base" different from the Stalinist one. The first secretary of the CPSU therefore claimed: "We had to learn to listen to unpleasant criticisms, learn to understand people complaining about the Stalinist measures," and "We had to eat the sour vegetable soup cooked by Stalin."[40] Interestingly, although Khrushchev largely got what he wanted from Mao's regime, namely mediation and support, his meek manner to the Chinese, however sincere, played a subtle but crucial role in making the CCP imagine it had made a significant achievement in inducing the Soviet leadership to recognize its mistakes in dealing with other socialist states and furthermore wielded some influence in changing the Soviet position of absolute dominance in dealing with the interbloc issues that had been legitimized by the Stalinist system.

---

39. It is impossible to say definitively that Shi Zhe's recollection of this meeting is the most reliable and least likely to be clouded by exaggerations, distortions, and retrospective face-saving. Yet comparative studies of Shi Zhe's words and the Malin Notes establish the reliability of the key part of Shi Zhe's recollection of the Chinese delegation's visit to Moscow.

40. Nikita Khrushchev, *Heluxiaofu huiyilu, quanyiben* [Nikita Khrushchev, Khrushchev remembers, a complete version], 3 vols. (Beijing: Shehui kexue wenxian, 2006), 3: 2269.

On 26 October, members of the Chinese delegation attended another meeting held by the CPSU presidium. Given that Khrushchev had given the nod to another discussion on the theme of 24 October, namely great-power politics, Liu Shaoqi and his comrades had supposed they would be getting another chance to air their views on big-power chauvinism, preparing for a whole-day session on the twenty-fifth. However, Khrushchev deliberately steered discussion away from the theme of great-power politics, instead raising the questions of Poland and Hungary. Khrushchev apparently had little appetite for another round of discussion of former and present Soviet wrongdoings as alleged by the Chinese, possibly caused by the Kremlin collective leadership's opposition to repeat these topics. Moreover, despite the fact that Khrushchev had agreed with Liu's opinions expressed on 24 October, the post-Stalin leaders were evidently annoyed at the explicit manner in which the Chinese had criticized Soviet behavior, while also holding serious reservations with regard to the Chinese suggestion of establishing equal relations inside the camp.[41]

Therefore, noting that Khrushchev and his colleagues shied away from the sensitive question of big-power politics, Liu made the decision to swerve away from the "big issues" designated by the Chinese, instead stating Chinese views on Polish–Hungarian issues and helping the Soviets preserve bloc unity. During the 26 October meeting, Liu Shaoqi told the presidium that, in the opinion of the Chinese, the Polish treatment of Rokossowski represented the central question in terms of the cohesiveness of Polish–Soviet and, by implication, bloc relations. In Liu's view, Rokossowski should remain in his post of Polish state defense minister.[42] It would not be appropriate, Liu said, for Gomulka to retaliate against those who had put him on trial or placed him under arrest.[43] The Soviet lead-

---

41. Shi Zhe, *Jianzhenglu*, 229.
42. See "Working Notes from the Session of the CPSU CC Presidium on 26 October 1956," *CWIHP Bulletin*, 8–9: 389; Shi, *Jianzhenglu*, 229.
43. In Malin's working notes, it is recorded as: "Gomulka is taking this to EXTREMES," *CWIHP Bulletin*, 8–9: 389.

ers could not agree more, but told Liu that awkwardness between the Soviets and the Poles had prevented them from conveying this idea to Gomulka themselves. Liu volunteered the Chinese for the role of mediator, provided an opportunity arose. The CPSU first secretary then made the suggestion that Liu Shaoqi visit Warsaw, a proposal to which Liu was amenable provided he had Mao's authorization and an invitation from the Poles.[44]

The Chinese had actually expected the Soviets to ask them to intervene with the Poles given that a far more damaging crisis was threatening to flare up on the Hungarian front. But with the Polish–Soviet standoff to some extent unresolved, Liu was forced to be even more cautious in his criticism of previous Soviet mistakes. While the Chinese delegation failed to adopt a policy line vis-à-vis Hungary, they were extremely conscious of the dangers involved in successive upheavals inside the Soviet Bloc. In the eyes of the Chinese Communists, the most dangerous tendency of these events was the increasing political disunity of the Communist camp, which could only be exploited by the Western powers to attack world Communism. It is therefore conceivable that at this stage the Chinese favored a peaceful settlement of the Polish–Soviet conflict partly through their own diplomacy, hoping that the readjustment of Polish–Soviet relations within the framework of Soviet Bloc unity could serve as a model for Hungary and other states inside the Communist camp. Most likely on this basis, Beijing sent a message to Warsaw shortly after the 26 October CPSU presidium meeting via its own channel, asking to send a Chinese delegation led by Liu Shaoqi to Poland. The Polish leaders knew that the Chinese vice chairman and other CCP key leaders had been in Moscow for days and had turned down the Chinese request, probably on the grounds that the Chinese would be no more than emissaries of the Soviets.[45] After being refused once, Chairman Mao decided to take up matters in person.

---

44. Shi, *Jianzhenglu*, 229. Malin's notes for the same incident do not record the Soviet suggestion of Liu's visit to Warsaw.
45. Author's interview with Luo Yisu, April 2004. According to Luo, Liu Shaoqi later said this himself.

Liu, in representing the CCP leadership, clearly expressed his disagreement with the move to oust the Soviet appointee Rokossowski from his Polish military post during the CPSU presidium session of 26 October. His attitude reflected top Chinese leaders' misgivings regarding the possible chain effect of the Polish example on other bloc states and the region as a whole. Interestingly, as late as 24 October, the Chinese took the line that the major problem in Soviet–satellite relations was the danger of a return to Stalinism, meaning that their consistent advice to the Soviets was to hold to a principle of "noninterference in others' domestic politics."[46] By 26 October, however, one can detect signs that the Chinese regime was becoming increasingly concerned over the disintegrative effects that Polish intransigence might have on the other bloc states, in the first instance, Hungary. Before examining Mao's specific steps in seeking to persuade the Poles to make concessions, there are several questions we should try to clear up: Why and how did the Chinese shift their focus from requests for a more equal pattern of relations to a concern with possible disintegration in Eastern Europe? Why did they not understand these considerations as contradic-tory?[47] To meet these points, it is necessary, first and foremost, to look at Beijing's reaction to the dramatic outbreak of the Hungarian Revolution and to the Chinese leadership's reconceptualization of the situation inside the bloc.

BEIJING'S EFFORTS TO RESCUE BLOC UNITY

In fact, Mao summoned a series of politburo standing committee, politburo, and politburo enlarged sessions from 24 October (Bei-

---

46. Shi, *Jianzhenglu,* 227.
47. Although in Mao's view Soviet chauvinism was serious and worth coming to grips with, an attempt on the part of the Poles to wreck the basic unity of the socialist camp risked a possible domino effect, which would certainly not be in the best interests of the Chinese. Mao had already framed the terms of the Chinese delegation's mission before it set out for Moscow; the party would mediate between the Soviets and Poles under a precondition of socialist camp unity and would also seek to make other political gains for the Chinese.

jing time) through to 31 October. It appears that these meetings were convened very shortly after Mao had heard from Liu on the evening of 23 October, Moscow time, that Hungary was in open revolt.[48] The Chairman and the central party paid close attention to the Polish and Hungarian crises guided by both domestic and external considerations. As Bo Yibo recalled, the leadership attacked these crises intellectually as holding within them various contradictions, or more specifically unsolved problems, persisting under the socialist system.[49] This understanding led the Chinese unavoidably to associate the Polish and Hungarian crises with domestic unrest among students, peasants, and workers that China had itself suffered in 1956 (an in-depth analysis of Chinese domestic considerations is offered in Chapter 4). Equally importantly, there was a new need to reexamine Soviet–satellite relations given the urgent need

---

48. Discussions of the Hungarian crisis followed Mao's normal pattern of dealing with domestic and external events: when a situation was still not clear to him, he would hold an enlarged session soliciting various views and ideas; as the state of affairs kept getting clearer, Mao would confine the topic within a smaller circle, say the politburo; when things became even clearer and Mao had made a judgment, he would hold a wider-range discussion again. The central committee meetings on the Polish Crisis began on 21 October; from 21 October to 9 November, 1956, thirteen to fourteen enlarged politburo sessions sat on the Polish and Hungarian crises and relevant issues. See Bo, *Huigu,* 595–600; *ZNP,* 632: 27, 29–31 October 1956. According to Wu Lengxi, then head of the New China News Agency, who sat in most of the politburo meetings, the members led by Mao had been mainly working on the talks held in Moscow on Polish–Soviet relations from the twenty-third to the thirtieth. At the same time, the delegation cabled a daily report on the progress of the Sino–Soviet and the Sino–Polish talks. However, a key problem with Wu's recollection is that the Polish leadership under Gomulka in fact remained in Warsaw instead of being present at Moscow meetings during the period of the Chinese delegation's appearance at the Kremlin. It was, therefore, impossible for the Chinese representatives in Moscow to hold talks with the Poles and Soviets separately and write reports back to Beijing. See *CWIHP* Digital Archives, "Account of a Meeting at the CPSU CC: On the Situation in Poland and Hungary, 24 Oct. 1956"; "On 23 Oct. 1956 Comrade Gomulka told the CPSU CC that he would accept the invitation and that he would arrive after 11 Nov. 1956." http://www.wilsoncenter.org/digital-archive, accessed 6 January 2013.

49. This trend is arguably reflected in the *People's Daily* editorials issued after the Soviets' second intervention into Hungary and China's announcement of its position on 1 November; see the section "China and the Second Soviet Intervention in Hungary" in this chapter. See also Wu, *Shinian lunzhan,* 71–72, 83–91, and fn. 118.

to restore Soviet Bloc stability and unity in the more volatile post-twentieth congress atmosphere.

As far as we can make out, the position adopted at this stage by the PRC was highly ambiguous, reflecting both the uncertainty of the Chinese leadership over the basic character of the Hungarian incident and its inherent caution. The first Soviet response to the sudden crisis in Budapest, in contrast to its wavering over Poland, was fast and effective. Soviet troops had already entered the Hungarian capital on the morning of 24 October, within twelve hours of the situation's unraveling. The Chinese were at this stage without a position, though it is important to note that they had, simultaneously with the uprisings, underlined their opposition to Soviet big-power politics, which might be taken to imply that their sympathies were on the side of the rebels.[50] At the same time, China's political and ideological interests lay in the consolidation of the Communist camp, in particular the Eastern Bloc states' bond with the Communist camp and China's bond with the Soviet Union.[51] The outbreak of violent opposition in Hungary presented the Chinese with both an opportunity and a threat. They could use the crisis as a stick with which to beat Soviet chauvinist traditions (as Liu Shaoqi had done successfully in Moscow), but this line risked jeopardizing the total solidarity and security of the international Communist camp, which the Chinese acknowledged depended on Soviet hegemony. Without enough information to make assessments of the origin and nature of the Hungarian revolution, the Chinese leadership apparently refrained from either endorsing or rejecting it.

From the initial worsening of the situation in Budapest on 23 October up to the end of the month, Beijing had de facto three major channels to obtain information on Hungary: Chinese intelligence sources in the Eastern Bloc, the delegation in Moscow, and news reports (from both West and East). The New China News Agency offered its first foreign news roundup on the development

---

50. Pang and Jin, *Maozhuan*, 603.
51. See, for example, Mao's conversation with Tito in September 1956; Liu's speech delivered on 24 October in the CPSU CC presidium session quoted above.

of the Hungarian situation on 25 October, forwarding the report of Nagy's election by the Telegraph Agency of the Soviet Union (TASS) as the new premier and the failure of the "antipeople" disturbances in Budapest. Until 25 October, to the best of Chinese knowledge, the major Western news media had made almost no detailed reports of the Hungarian tension.[52] The CCP was very much averse to basing its evaluation of the events solely on a Soviet definition of the riots, leading them to place much more weight on independent sources and feedback from their own delegation.

Aiming to get to the bottom of the Hungarian situation, the foreign ministry, under the direction of the party center, cabled the Chinese embassy in Budapest for prompt information "on the Hungarian domestic political situation and the standing of members of the Hungarian Central Party, that of Imre Nagy in particular."[53] In the meantime, the ministry also requested the Chinese embassies in the neighboring Eastern Bloc states (Czechoslovakia, Romania, Bulgaria, the GDR, and Albania) to report local feedback on the Hungarian situation.[54] In the telegram sent to Budapest, the foreign ministry stressed the need for relevant materials from the embassy to be "objective as to avoid by all means the repetition of others' views." Moreover, Chinese diplomats in Budapest "should not rashly express views or draw hasty conclusions with regard to the Hungarian political situation when meeting with their Hungarian or other socialist country counterparts."[55] This message, stressing independent judgment and caution in dealing with the Hungarian case, was

---

52. UPI (United Press International), the U.S. news agency, published a news report on Radio Free Europe intensifying its attempts to broadcast to the Eastern Bloc states. The United Kingdom and the United States meanwhile were still devoting more attention to Poland, criticizing the relationships between the Soviet Union, Poland, and other socialist states. *Neican* (25 October 1956): 1232–45; (26 October 1956): 1243–45.

53. "Foreign Ministry Telegram to the Chinese Embassy in Hungary: For a Quick Report on the Current Hungarian Domestic Political Situation and the Hungarian Party's Status, 24 October 1956," CFMA 109-01041-01, 9.

54. "Request for Collecting Local Feedback to the Polish–Hungarian Incidents, Telegrams to Embassies in GRD, Czechoslovakia, Bulgaria, Albania," CFMA 109-00972-01, 8.

55. "Foreign Ministry's Telegram to Chinese Embassy in Hungary in Urging

causally related to the central party's critical comment on the pro-Soviet attitude of the Chinese embassy in Poland.[56] Forewarning their Budapest colleagues against uncritical alignment with Moscow, the center also sought to inform itself on Imre Nagy, who presented certain parallels with Gomulka in Poland and was becoming the focal point of domestic aspirations from all sides in Hungary. Nagy's ability to restore order to his country, while bringing Hungary back into the Communist fold, became, for the CCP leaders, the litmus test determining the formation of Chinese policy toward Hungary.

Unfortunately, it seems that Beijing's instructions never reached the Chinese embassy in Budapest. Since there was no radio or telephone hotline over which the Chinese diplomats could get in touch directly with Beijing, they were forced to rely on routine contacts made through the Hungarian public telecommunication system (both telephone and telegram). However, since 23 October, communications between Beijing and Budapest had been disrupted by the paralysis of lines out of Hungary.[57] For example, the two cables arriving in Beijing on 25 October were actually delayed by more than half a day, even taking into account the seven-hour time lag between China and Hungary. These two telegrams, which reported Gerő's speech and the student demonstration, respectively, were

---

It to Send Back Reports on the Current Hungarian Domestic Situation and the Condition of the Hungarian Central Party," *CFMA* 109-01041-01, 9.

56. "Foreign Ministry's Telegram to Wang Bingnan," *CFMA* 109-00762-02, 8. The telegram sent to Budapest was worded almost identically, cautioning against this improper way of "echoing others' views," despite being sent on 24 October, one day later than that to Warsaw.

57. Hungarian foreign telecommunication connections were temporarily cut from midnight of 23 October, reconnected during the afternoon of 25 October but became completely paralyzed on 26 October. The Chinese embassy thereafter used the Hungarian foreign ministry connection between Budapest and its Beijing embassy to send ciphered telegrams to and from the Chinese party center. From 23 October to 4 November, communication between Beijing and Budapest via telegrams was delayed on average by one and one-half or two days, though normally there was a seven-hour time difference between Budapest and Beijing to be counted in the time gap between sending and receiving. See "Reasons the Chinese Embassy Was Not Able to Send Reports Promptly," *CFMA* 109-01041-01, 16; interview with Xia Daosheng, 16 April 2004.

useful in helping the top leaders understand the initial aims of the college student demonstration, namely, to express support for the Polish revolution and to demand similar democratic changes in Hungary.[58] Events as they unfurled, though, were too fluid to be evaluated on a basis of news reports more than one day old, meaning that the CCP leaders could place little faith in updates from Budapest. The time lapse between sending and receiving messages necessarily contributed to the Chinese floundering for a response to the crisis in its first two days.

While Beijing was effectively left on its own, the Chinese embassy in Budapest, according to its attaché Xia Daosheng, followed the dramatic developments on the ground throughout the night of 23 October. In the evening, Hao Deqing, the ambassador and a Communist who had joined the party in 1928 and had long experience in carrying out party propaganda work at the provincial level, held a plenary meeting to assess what the party knew of the disturbances. To its knowledge, one group of Hungarians had marched to Stalin square (today's Város Liget) chanting the slogan "Russians Get Out" before proceeding to tear down Stalin's statue. According to Chinese eyewitnesses, a thick iron chain had been looped round Stalin's neck while the statue's base was sliced through with a welder's torch. A crane then appeared in the square, it was attached to the iron chain and toppled the statue. The masses immediately converged on the statue, kicking and dragging it across the ground.[59]

---

58. See "Report on the Student Demonstrations in Budapest," *CFMA* 109-01041-01, 3–4; "Gerő's Radio Speech Delivered at Night of 23 October," *CFMA* 109-01041-01, 4–5.

59. According to the Soviet record, Khrushchev also raised the issue of Stalin's statue in the CPSU CC politburo meeting of 24 October, which the East German and Bulgarian leaders also attended. Khrushchev's account of this incident, however, was slightly different from that of the Chinese embassy. Khrushchev said, "The bandits wanted to tear down the statue of Stalin. But when they were unsuccessful in this task, they seized a welder's torch and cut the statue to pieces, and then disposed of the whole thing." The Soviet report suggests less forethought on the part of the rioters than the Chinese report. "Account of a Meeting at the CPSU

Hao and his colleagues formed the view that this action must have been premeditated rather than spontaneous.

Furthermore, the protesters had apparently shouted "Koreans Out" at Asian-looking passersby. Told that these people were Chinese, the Hungarians then called "Chinese Out." The veracity of these claims, it should be stressed, rests entirely on the reliability of the accounts by Chinese embassy staff in Budapest. Taken aback by the nationalism of the Hungarians, the Chinese judged it unsafe to venture out after dark. At around 9:00 P.M., gunshots were fired, precipitating a free-for-all. Violence spread throughout Budapest, with the city's police station, gunpowder magazine, and railway station all seized by the rebels. Having led efforts at political indoctrination in the provinces for almost twenty years, Hao immediately sensed the potential danger of these demonstrations; even if they were caused only by hot-headedness, the riots were extremely liable to be manipulated later by "reactionaries," and the evidence suggested a serious controlling intelligence targeting sites of military and political significance. Hao and his colleagues therefore concluded that initially peaceful anti-Soviet demonstrations had mutated into a counterrevolutionary putsch, conveying this judgment in a telegram to Beijing on 24 October.[60]

Meanwhile, Hao Deqing's actions were primarily concerned with ensuring the safety of his staff in the face of a deteriorating situation. He locked the front door of the embassy and gathered most of the staff in the lodging house, with only a few personnel charged with guarding the office block. Beyond further securing a diplomatic delegation and Chinese exchange students in Budapest,

---

CC, 24 October 1956: On the Situation in Poland and Hungary," *CWIHP* Digital Archives, http://www.wilsoncenter.org/digital-archive, accessed 6 January 2013.

60. Interview with Xia Daosheng; for the telegram sent on 24 October, see "Briefing on the Reactionary Riots in Budapest, Telegram to the Foreign Ministry and the Central Party," *CFMA* 109-01041-01, 10–11; "List of the Hungarian Party and Government Leaders' Reshuffle," 109-01041-01, 8; "The Formation of the Hungarian Temporary Tribunal," 109-01041-01, 12; "On the Safety of Our Personnel after the Budapest Reactionary Riots," *CFMA* 109-01041-01, 7.

however, Hao refused to involve himself in Hungarian politics without the authorization of the central party.[61] On 31 October, when officials from the previous Rákosi regime came to the Chinese embassy seeking asylum, Hao Deqing had a guard direct them to the Soviet embassy.[62] There was almost no contact between the Chinese embassy and the new Hungarian regime after the outbreak of the riots, with Chinese diplomatic connections with other socialist state embassies also interrupted by violence in the capital. The ambassador's action in battening down the hatches was successful in safeguarding Chinese nationals, but had the evident drawback of cutting the Chinese off from all sources of information regarding events outside. Previously, in the Polish case, a constant stream of communications between the Chinese mission and high-ranking Polish and Soviet officials, together with in-depth reports from Xie Wenqing on the economic, political, and social background of the troubles, had yielded for Beijing a tolerably comprehensive picture of the Polish October. The Chinese embassy in Budapest was in another situation altogether. It had not established a close working relationship with its Soviet counterpart and was compelled to allow its contact with the Hungarian leadership to drop almost entirely after the outbreak of the demonstrations. As a result, the Chinese embassy mainly relied on broadcasts and leaflets to follow the course of the events, a task further complicated by the fact that of-

---

61. "Foreign Ministry's Telegram to Chinese Embassy in Hungary in Urging It to Send Back Reports on the Current Hungarian Domestic Situation and the Condition of the Hungarian Central Party," *CFMA* 109-01041-01, 9.

62. Interview with Xiao Daosheng; Radványi, "The Hungarian Revolution and the Hundred Flowers Campaign," *China Quarterly*, 43 (1970): 122–23; "On the Safety of Our Personnel after the Budapest Reactionary Riots," *CFMA* 109-01041-01, 7, which also reported that the delegates and exchange students were out of harm's way; see also Hao Deqing, "Waijiaogongzuo sanshinian" [Thirty years of my diplomatic career], in *Dangdai Zhongguo shijie waijiao shengya* [Diplomatic careers of contemporary Chinese envoys], ed. Pei Jianzhang (Beijing: Shijie Zhishi, 1995), 65; "Telegram from the Chinese Embassy in Budapest to the Foreign Ministry and the CCP CC: On the Rejection of the Request of the Former General Secretary of the Hungarian Party to Borrow a Car from the Chinese Embassy," *CFMA* 109-01041-01, 70.

ficial newspaper publications has been suspended for several days even prior to the riots. In making its final decisions, therefore, the central party leadership had to make do with particularly thin knowledge provided by their Hungarian informants.[63]

Messages sent on 24 October from the Chinese embassy in Budapest arrived in Beijing early on the morning of 26 October.[64] The same day, the New China News Agency journalist in Prague sent back a news report, corroborating the Budapest embassy's claim that the unrest had been stoked by reactionaries, who had taken advantage of initially peaceful popular parades to stir up Soviet and anticommunist feeling. According to the Prague briefing, the protests had already passed the point where they had become fullblown armed civil disturbances.[65] Before noon on 26 October, the CCP's leaders were aware of the complexity of the Hungarian uprising, at least insofar as they believed that basically popular events had taken on a counterrevolutionary character as a result of dissatisfaction with the Soviet Union and Rákosi's regime being brought to a head by provocateurs. The Budapest telegram read: "Gunshots

---

63. According to János Radványi, a high-ranking official in the Hungarian foreign ministry in charge of Asian affairs with close ties to Hao Deqing, the Chinese ambassador in Budapest, the Chinese embassy had established a very effective information network within the HCP and the government. The embassy even gained the reputation of the best-informed foreign post in the capital. Hao's caution in dealing with the Hungarian events can possibly be explained by his understanding of the complexity of the Hungarian domestic situation and uncertainty of the real nature of the Nagy regime. See Radványi, "The Hungarian Revolution and the Hundred Flowers Campaign," 121–29.
64. CFMA, 109-01041-01, 10–11, 8, 12, 7.
65. This date was the exact time for the completed draft to be cabled. Usually news would be published in the newspaper at least one day later than this date. In fact, this piece apparently featured in the newspaper on the twenty-seventh. According to the report, reactionaries had piqued anti-Soviet and anti–people's democratic feelings in an initially peaceful students' march, before laying on well-organized armed riots. See "Budapeisi dengdi xuesheng juxingyouxing, fangemingfenzi liyong youxing zhizao baoluan" [26 October 1956 New China News Agency Cabled from Prague]; "Budapeisi baoluan shangwei pingxi: Xinhuashe bulage dian" [The riots in Budapest have still not been suppressed], News Drafts of New China News Agency: 28 October 1956, Xinhuashe xinwengao, 48, 42.

continued the whole night . . . part of the Hungarian state security (ÁVH) forces joined the reactionary side and fired on the Public Security force . . . the Soviet troops had already entered the city."[66] Even worse, "the reactionaries broke into public places and houses and killed some public security personnel and common people." Yet it appeared that the response of the reshuffled Hungarian party and government was to look entirely to Soviet troops to quell the situation after having made no preparation to combat any form of disturbance.[67] It was thus difficult for the CCP to grasp what was happening in Hungary, but obviously equally difficult for them to approve the Soviets' flagrant invasion of a fellow socialist state.

The Chinese could not have made a decision approving the incursion without the utmost certainty that the Soviets' military intervention was necessary and efficient. It was not clear to the Chinese leaders how badly out of hand events in Budapest had gotten; to some extent, they would have inferred, disturbances had been brought under control by the Soviet presence. However, there were also contrasting reports that, far from stopping the violence, the Soviet invasion had actually escalated hostilities in Hungary.[68] Force alone, it appeared, could not resolve the problems in the Eastern Bloc. After Poznan, the Chinese leadership was fully aware of the domestic difficulties in the Eastern Bloc states bequeathed by Stalin-era inflexibility. With the Polish October as a precedent, the Chinese side judged a certain degree of domestic institutional diversity acceptable so long as the local Communist regime maintained control of its own countries' situation. The Chinese were wary of attributing the Hungarian uprising to counterrevolutionary activity; the Soviets' heavy-handed mismanagement of their relations with weaker partners seemed in many ways a more plausible cause. And the Chinese had very recently sought to prevail on the Soviets not to repeat the errors of Stalin-era big-power chauvinism.

It is noteworthy, however, that there were two interacting con-

---

66. *CFMA* 109-01041-01, 10–11.
67. *CFMA* 109-01041-01, 12.
68. Ibid., 13.

ditions for the Chinese to recognize the possibility of limited local diversity. First of all, any anti-Soviet campaign or disturbance in these countries could not translate into an internal challenge to Communist party dominance or to the wider cohesion of the Eastern Bloc; and second, the local Communist party should be strong enough to keep a grip on events without having to call on Soviet military assistance. Both of these conditions seemed to have been breached by the Hungarian events. The weakness of the Hungarian regime, furthermore, alerted Mao and his comrades to the possible presence of residual class enemy elements stirring insurrection perhaps across the whole Eastern Bloc.

The course of the Chinese leadership's discussion on its response to the Hungarian violence has never been made public. But judging from Liu Shaoqi's comments on the Polish treatment of Rokossowski at the 26 October session, it is clear that the Chinese leaders were principally concerned that an excessively nationalist policy on the part of the Poles would exacerbate tensions in other bloc states by licensing anti-Soviet feeling. In any sense, it would pose too much of a risk for the Chinese to support an individual state's bid for independence at the price of the Communist camp's security and consolidation. Mao and his colleagues, in fact, were disturbed by Gomulka's insistence on Rokossowski's dismissal from the national defense ministry, which would encourage requests for Soviet military withdrawal in Hungary and probably in other bloc states. Consequently, the Chinese side took it upon itself to salvage the Eastern European scene through political and diplomatic negotiations with the Poles. After the first attempt to send a Chinese delegation to Warsaw was rejected by the Poles, Mao decided to intervene in person.

On the twenty-seventh of October, at 2:00 A.M., Stanislaw Kiryluk, the Polish ambassador to Beijing, was invited for an urgent meeting with the top Chinese party leaders, including Mao Zedong, Zhou Enlai, and Chen Yun, with Zhang Wentian also in attendance. The consultation went on for three hours. It is likely that the decision to summon Kiryluk was made during the enlarged politburo session held the same day as the Chinese delegation's first rebuff.⁶⁹ According to Kiryluk's telegram sent to the Polish party immediately after the meeting, Chairman Mao, who apparently dominated this meeting, asked Kiryluk to explain to him the genesis of Poland's domestic problems as they emerged in the period from 1949 to 1956. In answering Mao's question, Kiryluk discussed party missteps in regard to both political and economic policy while acknowledging the harm done to Poland by the Beria phenomenon, that is, the domination of politics and society by a secret police organization.⁷⁰

Notably, Kiryluk emphasized two points in relation to the current situation in Poland: first, that the Polish party's eighth plenum had been extraordinarily successful in setting in train a process of democratization, and second, that the process of "Polish democratization was meant to improve the friendship and alliance between the Polish and Soviet Parties and the people of the two countries." Kiryluk's aim seems to have been to get the Chinese and Soviets to back off, insisting that Gomulka's regime was fully able to deal with domestic affairs. But the Soviet and Chinese alliances, he hastened to add, had nothing to fear from increased Polish autonomy. Kiryluk's words seem to reflect Gomulka's views at that time: that the Poles needed to be able to chart a distinct domestic course without relying on the Soviet Union.⁷¹

On the domestic program planned by the United Polish Worker's Party (PZPR) eighth plenum, Mao Zedong, representing the Chinese politburo, expressed his hearty support of the Polish reform. Mao said that the CCP politburo was already acquainted with Gomulka's speech and the eighth plenum resolution, and that the Chinese party was "absolutely supportive of the political line of the

---

69. On 27, 29, 30, 31 October 1956, enlarged politburo sessions were held on the Polish and Hungarian crises. See *ZNP,* 632.

70. Anderzej Werblan. "Chiny a Polski Pazdziernik 1956," *Dzis,* no. 10 (1996): 124–26. Thanks to Shen Zhihua for his generosity in sharing a Chinese version of this article with the author; for similar content see also Werblan, "1956nian de Bolan shiyue," 85–87.

71. Ibid.

Central Committee of the PZPR." The Polish party's new economic program set up on the basis of an assessment of the achievements and mistakes of its forerunner found large favor with Mao. "The Chinese comrades regard our [Polish] way [of reform] as correct and give strong backing to us with full confidence," Kiryruk told Gomulka in his letter. "When asked by the Soviets [for their attitude on the Polish October], the Chinese comrades said that they were affirmative to the Polish reform." The Chairman also told the Polish ambassador that a Chinese delegation led by Liu Shaoqi, Deng Xiaoping, and Wang Jiaxiang arrived in Moscow to take up a Soviet invitation to consult on the Polish October. After negotiations with the Russians, the Chinese delegates successfully persuaded Khrushchev to approve Gomulka's domestic line and to support the Polish party and its leaders. The Kremlin had already invited a Chinese delegation to Moscow, and "if it is possible," also wanted to "send a Chinese delegation to Warsaw."[72] Mao obviously had his reasons for playing up the effectiveness of the Chinese in wringing support for Polish domestic autonomy from the Soviets; he wanted the Poles to assent to China as a mediator and arbiter, for which they needed to be convinced that the Chinese were on their side. Even though the idea of sending a Chinese delegation to Warsaw had come from Moscow, the Chinese were the main movers in bringing the plan to fruition.

However straightforward Mao was with the Poles, it is conceivable that at this stage the Chinese Communists favored redressing the balance of relations among Communist states by allowing limited diversity. "Although the Kremlin still has reservations on the Polish right for free action," Mao asserted, "it goes without saying that the Poles should have the freedom to manage their own affairs and that outdated styles of dealing with other states in the socialist camp should be abolished by the Soviet Politburo anyway." Mao further reiterated his earlier warning against "big Russian chauvinism," suggesting that a Polish–Soviet party relationship of coopera-

---

72. Ibid.

tion should be "reestablished on new principles" in the forthcoming working session between the Polish and Soviet parties on 8 November 1956. Chairman Mao seemed determined to set up a new pattern of Soviet–Eastern Bloc relations for the Soviets and the Eastern Europeans.[73] This Chinese-designed pattern of socialist camp relations, however, came with the proviso that it should respect above all broader unity and stability of the Communist camp. Such a reservation opened the way to varying interpretations of the acceptance of unity, which, depending on time and circumstance, would inevitably impel the Chinese to alter their position with regard to Eastern Bloc country aspirations.

At this juncture, when events in Hungary had developed into a perplexing revolution, or reactionary campaign as the Chinese saw it, the Chinese leadership apparently became concerned with the consequences of the Polish insistence on Rokossowski's complete dismissal and the possible Soviet military withdrawal from Eastern Europe. In conveying the Soviet leadership's message to the Poles, the Chinese informed Kiryluk that the Soviet leaders would not agree to the Polish request of repatriating Soviet military advisors and offices from Poland. At the same time the Kremlin leaders also expressed their anxiety over the political consequences of "the possible Polish decision to remove Marshall Rokossowski from the national defense ministry post." In fact, Mao was trying to persuade the Polish Communist leaders not to go too far in pursuing political independence at home.[74] The Soviets, Mao explained, were not reassured by Gomulka's promise to remain a loyal ally and member of the Warsaw Pact, as attested by his order that the Polish army should cease considering the prospect of a complete withdrawal of the Soviet Northern Group of Forces from Poland.[75] The Soviet leader-

---

73. See Liu's comments to Chinese diplomats from Warsaw: "Liu further told his colleagues that the Soviets did not realize that too strict a pattern in managing the Eastern Bloc would only lead to a trend of disorbition, together with heavier burdens and obligations. Lifting the control over [the bloc states] would instead turn the scales." Luo, "The 1956 'Polish Incident' and Chinese Policies," 41–42.

74. Werblan, "Chiny a Polski Pazdziernik 1956," 124–26; "1956nian de Bolan shiyue," 85–87.

75. Kramer, "New Evidence," 361–62.

ship, once it had decided to "display patience" for the time being on 24 October, must have wanted to avoid a final showdown and battle of wills with Poland. In its own diplomacy, therefore, the Chinese leadership used the cover of referring to Soviet anxieties as a way of introducing its own misgivings over Polish policy.

With respect to the Soviet military presence in the Eastern Bloc, Mao Zedong actually verbalized why the Chinese leadership was against the Polish request for a complete withdrawal of the Soviet forces: "The Soviet withdrawal [would have to be] of a much more widespread and profound nature," meaning that if it were mismanaged, the whole socialist camp would be "in severe danger." According to Mao and the Chinese top leaders, although they trusted the Polish party with the domestic situation in Poland, now that ferment had spread into Hungary and threatened other socialist states, the whole Soviet Bloc needed the safeguard of a rapidly mobilizing Soviet military apparatus. If Poland got its way, other socialist states, "whose power was still not strong enough to take hold of the situation," might also agitate for Soviet withdrawal, and indeed "Nagy's demands [for a Soviet pull-out] during the struggle with the counterrevolutionaries have confirmed the above argument." To emphasize its position, the Chinese side completely agreed with Gomulka's assessment of the necessity for Soviet forces to stay in the GDR. What the Chinese feared the most was "the possible Soviet military withdrawal from the GDR following that from Poland, which posed a severe threat to our [Communist] camp." Mao Zedong thus asked the Poles to think over their request for Soviet military withdrawal, which would shake the Warsaw Pact to its foundations.[76]

In sum, Mao was preoccupied with two major tasks in his urgent meeting with Kiryluk: to convince the Poles that the CCP was supportive of Gomulka's regime and would not intervene in its domestic reforms and to persuade the Polish leadership to give up on its requests for Soviet military withdrawal. The degeneration of the

---

76. Werblan, "Chiny a Polski Pazdziernik 1956," 124–26; "1956nian de Bolan shiyue," 85–87.

Hungarian events into "reactionary riots" warned the Chinese of the possible collapse of a people's democracy following the leadership's failure to curb a popular spirit of anti-Soviet nationalism. As the Chinese saw it, the Polish October offered a possible template to the Hungarians of a new form of socialist international equality with the Soviets. Only if Polish nationalism restricted itself to domestic affairs would, in the Chinese opinion, a further spillover of unrest to Hungary and other possible "weak points" inside the bloc be arrested. As a result, Mao's concluding suggestion was that, on the problem of the Polish domestic reform, "We [the Chinese and the Poles] should unite to persuade the Soviets to accept our view," while on interparty relations and the anti-Soviet feeling in the bloc, "We [referring to the Poles in particular] should demonstrate understanding and tolerance in relation to party–party relations . . . and we . . . never allow enemies to make use of rifts inside our camp." Mao was finally clear about the Chinese's own signature policy of noninterference: "No Chinese delegation will visit Poland without the invitation of the local party. This way, we will avoid giving the imperialists an excuse to accuse [the Chinese of intervening in Polish politics]."[77] This does not quite state the facts of the case, in that Mao had already resolved that, invited or not, he would send a delegation to Warsaw to bring the Poles around to the presence of the Red Army.

Kiryluk's cable reached Gomulka and the other politburo members at 8 P.M., 27 October (Warsaw time).[78] Gomulka had no great difficulty in acceding to Mao's request in that his line had been from the start to restrict the nationalist outcries of Polish Communists to domestic affairs, placating the Soviets with pledges of friendship and continued socialist allegiance. Even if a number of military officers thought it time to ask for the Soviet military to pull out, Gomulka saw the Soviet Army's encampment on Polish soil as essential to the Warsaw Pact. With regard to Rokossowski's removal, this was rather an issue of symbolic significance that had been granted

---

77. Werblan, ibid.
78. *Dzis*. "Kiryluk's Telegram to Gomulka: Mao Zedong's Attitude to the Polish Events." *Dzis*, no. 10 (1996): 124–26 (Chinese translated version).

to satisfy popular demand. In the politburo meeting held the next day to consider the Chinese offer, the Polish party readily welcomed the CCP delegation, writing a letter immediately to invite the Chinese for a visit. In light of Chinese opposition to the immediate dismissal of Rokossowski, the Polish leadership compromised by giving him a holiday. The visit of the Chinese mission was penciled in for November, just after the Polish–Soviet talks. Furthermore, the Polish politburo leaders were at pains to clarify that they had never meant to make an unambiguous request for the withdrawal of the Soviet military from their land.[79] Receptive to the idea implicit in China's diplomatic overtures that the PRC would play a more prominent role in socialist interstate relations, the Poles made certain concessions in the expectation that Soviet hegemony would be to some degree displaced with Chinese involvement and that bloc affairs would soon be more multilateral.

In retrospect, however, this line constituted a misreading of Chinese intentions. The outbreak of the Hungarian violence just after the Polish October had in fact led the Chinese leaders to take more seriously the possible effect of Polish divergence in sapping bloc unity. Before the Chinese had obtained reports on Hungarian domestic developments through its own channels on 26 October, Mao and his colleagues felt themselves in the dark over the nature of the disturbances there. Their immediate strategy was to use the crises in the Eastern Bloc to challenge the monolithic Stalinist formula of interbloc relations, for instance, urging a more flexible approach through their delegation in Moscow. When telegrams from both Budapest and Prague on 26 October suggested to Mao that the socialist leadership in Hungary had allowed things to spiral out of control, with the events taking on a counterrevolutionary character, Mao and his men began to place the emphasis on wresting concessions from the Poles to ease their strained relations with the Kremlin. Mao may still have seen some play in finessing the Polish–Soviet conflict as a

---

79. Leszek Głuchowski, "The Soviet–Polish Confrontation of October 1956: The Situation in the Polish Internal Security Corps," CWIHP Working Paper 17, Woodrow Wilson International Center for Scholars, 1997, 81–82.

means to redefine Soviet–satellite relations. We can see from the following section that the Chinese attitude to the October crises in the bloc had already changed before the Polish party's reply reached Beijing. This change was prompted by the rapidly evolving situation on the ground, so far as the CCP leadership could understand it, between 28 and 29 October in Budapest.

TOWARD A MAOIST FORMULA OF INTERSTATE RELATIONSHIPS

The Kremlin, meanwhile, was itself surprised by the difficulty of managing the Budapest events after giving a green light to military intervention. Debates raged among the CPSU CC presidium members over the significance of the pervasive anti-Soviet violence inside Hungary and for the best way of dealing with the events as these were reported back to the Soviets in a series of incoherent telegrams.[80] Judging from the course of those presidium sessions held on 26 and 28 October, the position adopted at this stage by the USSR equivocated just as much as the Chinese line, reflecting deep-seated uncertainties and conflicts within the Soviet leadership. The Soviet indecision on the Hungarian problem up to 29 October in fact gave the Chinese a window of opportunity in which they could take a hand in the issues affecting the East European Bloc.

Mikoyan and Suslov, Khrushchev's envoys, arrived in Budapest on 24 October, before the great efflorescence of the troubles.[81] Their initial telegram to Moscow described a pacified but still uncertain

---

80. Mikoyan and Suslov, KGB chief Ivan Serov, and Gen. Mikhail S. Malinin arrived in Hungary on 24 October. Mikoyan and Suslov then went into Budapest to reconnoiter the latest developments. Mikoyan, Suslov, and Serov kept the Soviet leadership in Moscow well informed of the situation in Budapest and Hungary through telegrams and secure telephones. See Shen, *SHSA*, 27, 282.

81. The CPSU CC presidium decided to send Mikoyan and Suslov, KGB chief Ivan Serov, and General Mikhail S. Malinin to Hungary for on-the-spot inspections, the former two representing the highest level of the Soviet leadership with a special mission to direct the Hungarian party and government to resolve the domestic conflict.

scene: "All the fortified points of the insurgents [had] been crushed" except for a holdout in the radio station, from which the rebels were requesting Gerő's removal as the condition of their surrender. With the Hungarian government flatly refusing, the Soviet command center "was assigning tasks for the liquidation of the fortification tonight." Mikoyan and Suslov took the view that Gerő in particular, along with other top Hungarian top leaders, was "exaggerating the strength of the opponent and underestimating their own strength." In their assessment, "A turning point in the [Hungarian] events had occurred," in the sense that support was draining away from the rioters; it was now time to rely more heavily on local forces and to emphasize the role of the Hungarians themselves in quashing the revolt. As recorded in the telegram, Gerő told Mikoyan and Suslov via phone before their arrival in Budapest that the situation, in his judgment, was contradictorily "improved and at the same time worse" in the wake of Soviet intervention, since the Soviet action had "negative effects on the mood of the residents, including workers."[82] Mikoyan and Suslov regarded Gerő's words as pessimistic and possibly strategically motivated—that is, as a way of pinning responsibility for crushing the protests on the Soviets.

The Kremlin received Mikoyan and Suslov's report on 24 October via telephone, giving the Soviet leaders the impression that order in Budapest had been restored, with a total stabilization due the next morning. The minds of the politburo now turned to the issue of how to evolve some form of interstate tie to replace the former Stalinist controls and prevent manageable Eastern Bloc diversity from developing into irreconcilable splits. Notably, in a CPSU CC presidium meeting on 24 October, Khrushchev claimed that the Hungarian uprising appeared to have been fomented by writers and supported by students; the population at large had been neither active participants nor hostile to the USSR. If this were true, he rejected GDR leader Walter Ulbricht's suggestion of using Eastern

---

82. Archive of Foreign Policy, Russian Federation (AVP RF) f. 059a, op. 4, p. 6, d. 5, l. 1–7, translated by Johanna Granville, *CWIHP Bulletin,* 5: 23, 29; see also "Mikoyan and Suslov's Telegram to the CPSU CC," in Shen, *SHSA,* 27, 282.

Bloc party propaganda to "expose all the incorrect opinions." The first secretary of the CPSU CC explained to the East Germans and Bulgarians in attendance that "we are not living as we were during the Communist International [in Stalin's era], when only one party was in power." The CPSU could no longer, as Khrushchev had learned from the Polish-Hungarian cases, operate its relations with the other socialist parties "by command" since "polemics between fraternal parties," including propaganda battles between ruling establishments, would inevitably "lead to polemics between nations."[83]

Beyond promising an undefined if limited measure of political autonomy in the Soviet Bloc, Khrushchev also emphasized the importance of socioeconomic development across the socialist camp. The people in Poland and Hungary, as Khrushchev understood, were striking not out of any ideological confusion or anti-Soviet emotion but because "basic economic and social issues had not been resolved." The Soviet leader put this idea in a straightforward and simple way: "Ideological work itself will be of no avail if we do not ensure that living standards rise. It is no accident that the unrest occurred in Hungary and Poland and not in Czechoslovakia. This is because the standard of living in Czechoslovakia is incomparably higher." In his view, as long as the stomachs of the Polish and Hungarian people were full, they would have no cause for complaint about the local Communist regimes and Soviets. Unity among the bloc would thus come about for Khrushchev as a combined effect of improved ideological and propaganda work and economic management.[84] The Soviet party first secretary, rooted in his experience of peasant life, stressed the primacy of the economic on the political stability of Eastern European regimes, in a way congruent with the claim made by the Soviet model of socialist construction to raise the masses' standards of living. However, Khrushchev's emphasis seems also to have underestimated the extent of the alienation and

---

83. "Account of a Meeting at the CPSU CC, 24 October 1956: On the Situation in Poland and Hungary," *CWIHP* Digital Archives, http://www.wilsoncenter.org/digital-archive, accessed 6 January 2013.

84. Ibid.

hostility, long simmering over the Stalin era, felt by ordinary Poles and Hungarians toward socialism.

On the Hungarian side, Soviet participation in the fighting had provoked another spasm of violence in 25 October after a temporary truce. As Mikoyan and Suslov reported, "Fighting again escalated at noon after stabilization since daybreak." According to the Hungarian leaders, tension had built up in other major cities such as Miskolc, Pécs, and Szeged, which had seen separate demonstrations appealing to the government for reform.[85] In effect, the Soviet intervention invited by Gerő forced the Hungarian leadership to confront some hard dilemmas. In calling for aid against the counterrevolutionaries, Gerő set himself against a new regime, which, however inchoate at the time, would inevitably be headed by Nagy. When the troops arrived, Nagy had already been elected as the new premier without Soviet agreement. Problematically, though, Gerő remained head of the party with Nagy the nominal leader of the government. Had the call for Soviet military intervention been even briefly delayed, there would have been a chance, however slender, for the Hungarian leaders to remove Gerő and to seek to exploit Nagy's symbolic cachet to quiet the upheavals. The presence of the troops, however, immediately became a major source of national anger, making Nagy's return to power almost irrelevant. A large-scale spirit of revolution with a strong anti-Soviet flavor, now even joined by the Hungarian officer corps and workers, was spreading throughout the country.[86]

Pressure mounted accordingly for immediate action and, thereby, implicitly for a restatement of the regime's Soviet policy. One of the newly elected politburo secretariat members, Kobol

---

85. "Mikoyan and Suslov's Telegram to the CPSU CC, 25 October," in Shen, *SHSA*, 27, 286.

86. The Chinese embassy reported, "It has been confirmed that most of the Hungarian people's army had joined the reactionary armed forces to fight against the Soviets, the Hungarian police and the rest of the people's army troops" and that "the fight went on for 16 hours and is still ongoing," "in Miskolc, new Pecs and other cities in the east of the country, 'people's committees' have been established under the control of state local authorities." "On the 26 October Situation in Budapest, Telegram to the Foreign Ministry and the Central Party," *CFMA* 109-01041-01, 23.

(head of the first department of the CC MSP, who had recently spoken out sharply against the politburo)[87] suggested that the Hungarian government should ask the Soviet troops to remove themselves from Hungary after social order had been restored. Mikoyan and Suslov, who were present, strongly opposed this proposal, opining that "the question of Soviet military pull-out cannot be raised by any means, since it would amount to a U.S. military pull-in." The diplomats' last negotiating position was that "the Soviet troops would return to their bases once order in Budapest was restored." With the Soviets clearly not open to discussion on the question of withdrawal, none of the other HWP politburo members backed up Kobol. In an effort to stabilize the situation, the HWP politburo decided to replace Gerő by Kádár as the leader of the party and to depute Nagy, as a representative of the government, and Kádár, the new party head, to appeal for order.[88]

However this meeting panned out, though, the Soviets soon found that the Hungarians had acted against Soviet wishes. Without Soviet agreement, Nagy addressed the public via radio on 25 October, declaring that "the Hungarian government [was] requesting negotiations between the Hungarian and Soviet governments on a bilateral interstate relationship following the principle of internationalism," in which it would consider "the problem of Soviet armed forces' departure from Hungary." Mikoyan and Suslov were bewildered by Nagy's declaration, which the Hungarians explained to their guests simply as an expedient to "control the situation and maintain [the party's] legitimacy among the workers." This incident provoked strong suspicion among the Soviets over the credibility of Nagy and his regime.

In a telegram from Budapest to Moscow on 26 June, Mikoyan and Suslov, while filling the Kremlin in on Nagy's broadcast, still

---

87. "Account of a Meeting at the CPSU CC, 24 October 1956: On the Situation in Poland and Hungary," *CWIHP* Digital Archives, http://www.wilsoncenter.org/digital-archive, accessed 6 January 2013.

88. "Mikoyan and Suslov's Telegram to the CPSU CC, 25 October," in Shen, *SHSA*, 27, 286.

considered the HWP CC to be reliable and recommended political means, rather than military intervention, as the solution to Hungary's problems. Mulling over their response after receiving the message, the Kremlin leaders came to the view in an evening session that further concessions to the Hungarian reactionaries would be taken as weakness, strongly advocating the forceful suppression of the demonstrations as a sign of strength.[89] Most of the presidium session participants, except for Khrushchev, blamed Mikoyan for his softness in dealing with Hungary and called for a policy of force. While Khrushchev had been on the side of entering Budapest on 23 October, he still held out a certain hope for Mikoyan's political measures, so that the criticism of his political ally within the Kremlin placed him in a situation of some embarrassment. This was all the more acute given Khrushchev's likely analysis that rearguard leftist elements in the politburo were using the Hungarian events as a pretext for veiled attacks on his own leadership.[90] Khrushchev was forced to defend his colleague without abandoning his earlier line that violence should be faced down with force.[91]

With the mushrooming of new popular demonstrations across Hungary, however, the Soviet leaders soon found that events were moving beyond their control and that of their army. Hungarian workers' support for the agitation forced the Kremlin to reclassify the Hungarian events as something other than a counterrevolutionary uprising. The Hungarian leadership, including Kádár, was inclined to hold negotiations with the revolutionaries, if the alternative was sending in the tanks.[92] To make matters worse for the Soviets,

---

89. "Working Notes," *CWIHP Bulletin,* 8–9: 389.

90. Kramer, "New Evidence," *CWIHP Bulletin,* 8–9: 367.

91. The 26 October session decided that the Politburo was out of step with the Hungarian government and that reinforcements should be sent (Molotov, Zhukov, Malenkov). It also suggested establishing contact with Hegedus and writing an appeal to the troops. See "Working Notes from the Session of the CPSU CC Presidium on 26 October 1956," *CWIHP Bulletin,* 8–9: 389.

92. "Cde. Khrushchev—the matter is becoming more complicated. They're planning a demonstration. Kádár is leaning toward holding negotiations with the centers of resistance"; see "Working Notes from the Session of the CPSU CC Presidium on 28 October 1956," *CWIHP Bulletin,* 8–9: 389–92.

Nagy's position was itself precarious given the distrust in which he was held by some of the rebels.[93] At this point, the Americans together with several other Western states proposed the discussion of the Hungarian case before the UN Security Council, condemning the Soviet intervention as a violation of the peace treaty they had themselves signed with the Hungarians. The worse possible upshot of these international deliberations would be for "UN troops [to] move in on the proposal of the USA and for a second Korea to take place."[94] The Soviet government therefore exerted all political and diplomatic efforts to stop Hungary from appearing before the Security Council.[95]

Brought to this pass, the CPSU CC held an emergency meeting on 28 October on how to deal with these changes. Argument in the presidium members reached a standstill over which line to take in relation to Nagy. Voroshilov, Kaganovich, Bulganin, and Mikoyan (back from Budapest on 28 October) insisted that it was necessary to form a new regime backed up by the Soviet military forces since the current government had failed to cope with the situation under the envoys' guidance. Meanwhile, Malenkov and the former hardliner Zhukov began to call for greater political flexibility since "the situation has unfolded quite differently [from the way we expected] when we decided to send in troops." This switch of allegiance undoubtedly helped Khrushchev to defend Mikoyan and to lead the meeting to a common position. In Khrushchev's view, they had two options: either to support the current Hungarian government's action, mean-

---

93. "Mikoyan and Suslov's report from Budapest," APRF, f. 3, op. 64, d. 484, ll. 131–34; for a Chinese version see Shen, SHSA, 27, 297.

94. "Telegram from the Budapest KGB Station Concerning the Latest Developments in the City Following the Popular Uprising," TsKhSD, f. 89, p. 45, d. 10; for a Chinese version, see Shen, SHSA, 27, 305.

95. "Report from the Soviet Foreign Ministry to the CPSU CC (No Later Than 28 October 1956): Several Western Big Power States Were Planning to Raise 'the Hungarian Situation Question' in the United Nations Security Council, Suggestions for a Soviet Response on This Issue," in Shen, SHSA, 27, 301. An emergency session of the UN Security Council on Hungary was eventually convened in the mid-afternoon on 28 October (New York time, i.e., Moscow time at night). For a historical analysis on United Nations and the Hungarian events of 1956, see Bela Király, "The United Nations Organization and the Hungarian Revolution," 142–66.

ing, as "this might soon be completed," "Nagy will demand a ceasefire and the withdrawal of [the Soviet] troops," or if they resolved on intervening, accepting that "Nagy will turn against us." Khrushchev apparently preferred the first course, stating that "the formulation of a Soviet-controlled committee to take over power" from the current regime represented a last resort. In the end, the presidium members agreed to support the current government, giving the go-ahead to the withdrawal of the troops on the condition of a ceasefire.[96] On the same day, the Soviet Military Command in Hungary issued an order to prepare a plan for the Soviet troops' withdrawal from Budapest, at which point their duties would pass to the Hungarian army. In the plan later developed, the Hungarian army would move into position between 8:00 P.M. on the twenty-ninth and 6:00 A.M. on the thirtieth of October.[97] Moreover, to win the Hungarians over to a ceasefire, the CPSU CC presidium members decided to request the intercession of fraternal parties, namely the Chinese, Bulgarians, Poles, Czechs, and Yugoslavs, to prevent further bloodshed.[98] The apparent Soviet willingness to consult the Chinese on Hungary, as we now know, unintentionally encouraged the CCP to take up an active role to solve the Hungarian dilemma and begin to have some say on Soviet policymaking. In fact, on the one hand, Beijing still had a special interest in pressing the Soviets to admit their Stalinist mistakes in dealing with satellite relations; on the other, the Chinese central leadership was doubtless fully aware of the need to guarantee bloc unity. Compared to the Polish case, the Hungarian events turned out to be more complicated and unpredictable for the Chinese Communists. Therefore the CCP's changing perception (Mao's in particular) of the domestic developments in Hungary to a large extent deter-

---

96. Except for Voroshilov, who preferred to maintain the troops under a firm and powerful committee, Saburov was the only other voice urging the Soviet forces to remain in place. See "Malin Notes from the Session of the CPSU CC Presidium on 28 October 1956," *CWIHP Bulletin*, 8–9: 389–92.
97. Györkei and Horváth, *Soviet Military*, 70–71.
98. "Malin Notes," *CWIHP Bulletin*, 8–9: 389–92. In line with this decision, the CPSU CC Presidium immediately sent out messages to the Poles and Yugoslavs.

mined that the Chinese position taken in solving the Soviet Bloc events throughout this period could be anything but consistent.

THE TURNING POINT: 29 OCTOBER

During the evening of 29 October, Khrushchev, Molotov, and Bulganin met with Chinese delegates in their guesthouse on the Hungarian issue. Under discussion was the Hungarian request that the Soviet military retreat. According to Shi Zhe, Liu Shaoqi believed that the troops should remain in both Poland and Hungary for the purpose of consolidating the Warsaw Pact, a policy in accordance with the Chinese position expressed on 26 October. Hard on the heels of this deliberation, Liu also talked about the necessity of protecting General Rokossowski from "reactionary" vengefulness or backsliding. At this point, Mao called from Beijing with an apparent reverse of position: as Liu Shaoqi reported to the Soviet leaders, political and economic equality should be granted to the Soviet's Eastern European satellites, even if this meant allowing them a greater measure of autonomy. Mao further asserted that the Soviets should pull out and allow the Eastern Bloc states to be independent and self-determining. In theoretical terms, Mao was formulating a response to the "big issues" of domination and equality in international relations, rather than a detailed policy line for Hungary. However, even if Mao had in mind a new framework for left internationalism after the Polish Crisis, the question remains as to why he and his Beijing colleagues thought it appropriate to push the Soviets to accept their ideas on 29 October?[99]

In retrospect, the development of the Hungarian situation possibly had a significant influence on Mao's strategic thinking. On 27

---

99. One of the Chinese delegation's major tasks in Moscow was to rebuke Soviet big-power chauvinism and call for the Soviets to declare a new type of relationship among the socialist states. Liu Shaoqi had already expressed this Chinese intention on 24 October during the CPSU CC presidium session. Mao's meeting with Kiryluk on the twenty-seventh had also outlined the need to rebase Soviet-satellite relations.

October, Nagy announced the formation of a new government consisting of Communists neither tainted by the Rákosi excesses nor persecuted under Rákosi. By 28 and 29 October, Beijing had already received telegrams from the embassy in Hungary (as well as from Eastern Bloc states) on the reformulation of Nagy's government and the improving situation in Budapest; the "counterrevolutionaries," the news was, "had been generally suppressed."[100] A Xinhua journalist in Prague reported Nagy's 28 October reshuffle without comment. The next day, 29 October, at the same time that Mao weighed in on the resolution of the Polish and Hungarian crises with Moscow, the Prague wire praised Nagy's new government, suggesting that it represented a new hope for socialism.[101] Notably, the *RMRB*, the Chinese party's mouthpiece, was also positive on the twenty-eighth and twenty-ninth about Hungarian developments, claiming that a large number of rebels had laid down their arms on government entreaties, and that the leaders of the unrest were seeking a negotiated settlement under a temporary ceasefire.[102] It seemed that peace had been restored.

It is unlikely this endorsement originated from Mao himself, since Mao later criticized the 29 October comment as an instance of an inability to "keep calm" when the actual situation was not clear.[103]

---

100. "The Hungarian Reactionary Armed Forces Have Generally Been Suppressed, Telegram to the Foreign Ministry and the Central Party," *CFMA* 109-01041-01, 24; "Resumes of the Hungarian [New] Ministers," 109-01041-01, 25; "On the Hungarian Government's Measures to Suppress the Riots," 109-01041-01, 31–32.

101. "Xiong zucheng xinzhengfu," 28 October 1956, New China News Agency news draft cabled from Prague, published 29 October 1956 by Xinhua tongxunshe [New China News Agency], vol. 2322, 33. This news draft says that "the Hungarian government commanded the rebels to stop resistance and [up to now] large groups of rioters have already laid down their arms. The rioters asked for negotiation and a temporary ceasefire is achieved in Budapest. The Government and people are trying to restore peaceful life. . . . the negotiations [between the government and the rebellions] are processing." Also see *RMRB*, 28, 29 October 1956.

102. *Xinhuashe xinwengao*, 29 October 1956; *RMRB*, 28, 29 October 1956.

103. On the question of the speed of news, Mao said: "We should conduct concrete analysis of concrete problems, and the same applies to the speed of news. In the case of Imre Nagy's coming to power during the Hungarian incident, we

It is certain, though, that whoever authorized the *RMRB* to express the Chinese view on Nagy's government would have been confident that Mao was at least optimistic about developments. At this stage, Mao probably envisaged the reformulation of Nagy's government as a turning point, proving that the Hungarian Communists were as able to bring the riots to heel as Gomulka was in Poland. In Mao's estimation, now was the moment for the Chinese to press the Soviets critically to reexamine their relations with the satellite states, since no shattering ideological challenge had issued out of the Polish and Hungarian moves toward a more national mode of socialism.[104] These thoughts were likely uppermost in Mao's mind during his call to Liu in Moscow on 29 October. Besides urging a relaxation of Soviet dominance, it is possible that Mao now offered his view of *Pancha Shila* as a new paradigm of interstate relations.[105] In contrast to the circumspect Chinese line taken on 27 October to avert the dissolution of the Warsaw Pact should Soviet forces have to pull out from Poland, Mao now recommended that Moscow consult with the Eastern European countries on its terms of the pact's functioning and even on whether it was still necessary.[106] The stabilization of the situation in Hungary appears to have emboldened the Chinese to question the legitimacy of the Warsaw Pact, the single most important formal commitment binding the Eastern Europe states to the USSR in the post-Stalin era.

---

were not clear about what was happening but weren't able to stay calm and quiet either, so we published the news three days too early. As a result we published the news on day one without saying whether Nagy was good or bad. On day two's news, we said he was good. On day three, we said he was bad. So the masses became confused. Since the original situation was not clear, we really didn't have to say anything." See MacFarquhar et al., *Secret Speeches*, 266.

104. Liu Shaoqi had already raised this prospect with the Soviets without securing their approval. See Shi Zhe, *Jianzhenglu*, 227.

105. *Pancha Shila*, or the five principles of peaceful international relations, included (1) mutual respect for sovereignty and territorial integrity, (2) nonaggression, (3) noninterference in another country's internal affairs, (4) equal and mutual benefit, and (5) peaceful coexistence. These principles were introduced in a joint statement by Indian prime minister Jawaharlal Nehru and Chinese premier Zhou Enlai in New Delhi in June 1954 and remain at the core of the PCC's foreign policy.

106. Shi Zhe, *Jianzhenglu*, 229–32; Yang Kuisong, *Mao Zedong yu Mosike de en'en yuanyuan*, 391.

According to Chinese material, Khrushchev and his colleagues received Mao's suggestion badly, uncomfortable at his implication of an inequality between the Soviet Union and the Soviet Bloc states. Liu explained that Mao only wanted to consolidate camp unity since "they [i.e., the Soviet Bloc states] would get closer to you [the USSR] and become more supportive of your primacy if you withdraw to a distance."[107] After a long discussion, Khrushchev seemed to come round to Mao's view: "[Mao's] suggestions were correct, we should show our courage and establish our [the Soviet] relations on a new base."[108] Liu Shaoqi further asked whether the Soviets could issue a public declaration of their newfound commitment to reformed relationships with the other socialist states. The two sides agreed on the immediate drafting of a Soviet government declaration, "Principles of Development and Further Strengthening of Friendship and Cooperation between the USSR and Other Socialist Countries," with the Chinese themselves promising a declaration in support of the Soviet announcement.[109] The fact that such a declaration on Soviet relations with other socialist states originated from Mao, not Khrushchev, symbolized, for the Chinese, their increasing leverage in shaping the order of the socialist camp.

In brief, the reformulation of Nagy's government and the seemingly stabilized domestic situation in Hungary to a large extent prompted Chairman Mao in Beijing to shift the CCP's position from striving to repair the Soviet-centric bloc unity via its own resources to pressing the Soviets to set up a new pattern of inter-

---

107. Shi Zhe, "The Polish–Hungarian Incident," 15: Liu Shaoqi received a phone call from Beijing in the course of the meeting on 29 October. He conveyed Mao's opinion to the Soviet leaders immediately.

108. In Khrushchev's memoir, he recalled that the two sides discussed the Hungarian issue for a whole night, with both sides stating views for and against keeping troops in Budapest. Eventually, according to Khrushchev, they agreed that Soviet troops should pull out from the city. See Khrushchev, *Heluxiaofu huiyilu*, 3: 2945–47.

109. Shi Zhe, *Jianzhenglu*, 229–32; "Zhonghua renmin gongheguo zhengfu guanyu Sulian zhengfu 1956nian 10yue 30ri xuanyan de shengming" [Statement by the People's Republic of China on the Soviet Declaration of 30 October 1956, 1 November 1956], *Xinhua banyuekan* [New China semimonthly] 23 (1956): 103. Also see Noble Freeland ed., *Documents on International Affairs 1956* (Oxford: Royal Institute of International Affairs, 1959), 476–77.

Communist state relationships on the basis of *Pancha Shila* on 29 October 1956. At first glance, it seems that Mao and his Communist regime represented all the other Communist countries, especially the small and weak ones like Poland and Hungary, in challenging the old interbloc pattern established by Stalin, one in which all member states had to subordinate their interests to those of the USSR and be under the absolute and ultimate leadership of the Soviet Union. The Chairman's behavior in suggesting to apply the five basic principles of international affairs, i.e., national independence, sovereignty, equality, noninterference in internal affairs, and self-determination, to Soviet–satellite relations might further convince the Eastern Bloc that China intended to introduce a more scientific and truly equal state-to-state relationship pattern within the Soviet bloc. With enough knowledge of Mao's long-range perception of world politics and interbloc relations, however, the above interpretations were merely misreadings of Chinese intentions. As would soon be proved by Beijing's reaction to Nagy government's nationalist independence requests in the following days, Mao's suggestion of applying the five principles to interbloc state relationship should only be seen as the political means to alter the old Stalinist formula, which established the USSR's unquestioned dominance in the Communist camp, rather than an end in itself. In the Chairman's understanding of relations among Communist-ruled states, he had never really doubted the legitimacy of an ultimately power-centralized Communist order, in which the strongest "fraternal socialist country" naturally plays the leading role, sets up the principles, and guides other members' behavior. The root of Mao's abrupt shift in policy should be seen from the perspective that the Chairman by this point saw China's future potential as the most powerful Communist regime and recognized the improvement of the Hungarian domestic situation on October 29 as a rare good chance to manipulate the weakening Soviets to abdicate the leading position and give room to what he saw as better men. With all due respect to Mao's political skills, however, there is no evidence that he anticipated the nationalist emotion among the people and Nagy's eventual independence appeal to the Communist camp in the following days, which eventually would force Mao to readjust his own policies.

CHINA AND THE SECOND SOVIET INTERVENTION IN HUNGARY

The situation in Hungary, however, was already spinning out of control as Khrushchev and his colleagues were discussing a declaration with the Chinese. According to Serov's 29 October report on the latest developments in Hungary, "on 27–28 October, 8,000 prisoners were freed, with many of them looting weapons [from their jails] ... strong anti-Communist feeling was aroused among the masses and in several regions armed men search[ed] the apartments of communist [officials] and gunned them down." After the government bowed to popular pressure and declared the dissolution of the state protection authority (Államvédelmi Hatóság or ÁVH), the ministry of the interior (Belügyminisztérium) and the remaining internal security operations fell prey to despondency and paralysis. The ministry of the interior personnel remained, however, under the threat of death by armed groups.[110] Furthermore, Moscow received new telegrams from Mikoyan and Suslov from Budapest on 29 and 30 October, communicating their concern over the situation. The Hungarian "comrades have failed to win over the masses," they said, while "the anti-Communist elements are acting with impunity." Mikoyan and Suslov also feared for the ÁVH officers after the organization was disbanded.[111] In

---

110. TsKhSD, f. 89, p. 45, d. 11; trans. Johanna Granville, *CWIHP Bulletin*, 5: 31–32.
111. "Shifrtelegramma: TsK KPSS," 29 October 1956 (Strictly Secret-Urgent), from A. Mikoyan and M. Suslov, in *AVPRF,* f. 059a, op. 4, p. 6, d. 5, ll. 13–14; quoted from "Working Note of the Session of the CPSU CC Presidium on 30 October 1956," *CWIHP Bulletin*, 8–9: 392–93. The Chinese embassy in Budapest also sent a telegram back to Beijing on Nagy's 28 October declaration, in which Nagy announced the setting up of new police to replace ÁVH. See "A Complete Version of Nagy's 28 October Declaration (Received on 30 October)," *CFMA* 109-01041-01, 34–35.

their estimation, "The situation [on 30 October] [was] not getting better; it was getting worse" with "the party organizations . . . in the process of collaps[ing]" as violence escalated. Nagy's negotiations with the insurgents were at an impasse after they refused to put their guns down until the Soviet troops had left Budapest and Hungary.

In Mikoyan and Suslov's opinion, the matter of most pressing concern was the attitude of the Hungarian troops, since the possibility existed that "the Hungarian units sent to suppress the insurgents would eventually join the rebels, and then it would be necessary for the Soviet forces once more to undertake military operations." The Hungarians had caught wind of the latest Soviet army maneuvers, obliging Nagy to negotiate on two fronts, with the masses, promising the Soviets' withdrawal, and with the Soviets, asking for the infantry to be held off. Mikoyan and Suslov were of the mind that it was advisable to give Nagy breathing space by keeping troops out of territorial Hungary. Part of their motivation was that "this [increased level of Soviet troops in Hungary] could trigger a change in Hungarian policy in the [UN] Security Council." At the same time, the envoys insisted that the USSR "had to make a fundamental reassessment of [their] tactics were the situation to worsen any further."[112] The optimism of the diplomas vis-à-vis the Hungarian riots had evaporated by the time of their telegrams to Moscow on 30 October, at which point the situation was more clouded than ever and all prospects of a simple solution had disappeared.

Not long after Khrushchev, Molotov, and Bulganin left the Chinese delegates, another CPSU CC presidium convened on 30 October to discuss Hungary. The session kicked off with a reading of the Budapest wires of the twenty-ninth and thirtieth, with Khrushchev following this up with an account of discussions with the Chinese. Some form of action was clearly imperative. Khrushchev suggested,

---

112. Mikoyan and Suslov's telegrams from Budapest to the CPSU, 29 October 1956: *AVPRF,* f. 059a, op. 4, p. 6, d. 5, l1. 13–14; 30 October 1956: *AVPRF,* f. 3, op. 64, d. 484, l1. 122–24. For an English translation see *CWIHP Bulletin,* 8–9: 404; for a Chinese version, see *SHSA,* 27, 308, 312.

"We should adopt a declaration today on the withdrawal of troops from the people's democracies (considering these matters further at a session of the Warsaw Pact), taking account of the views of the countries in which our troops are based. The entire CPC CC Politburo supports this position." Even if the presidium regarded Mao's internationalist proposal as a good suggestion, they were more immediately preoccupied with Hungary and seemed to see Mao's idea of a statement of principles as a means of settling a specific issue. While the hardliners Molotov, Bulganin, and Kaganovich had reservations about the Chinese *Pancha Shila*, all the presidium members eventually agreed to issue just such a declaration as a means of putting the Hungarian problem to bed.[113] The Soviet leadership thus approved and issued the document on the same day.[114] In Shi Zhe's account, the content of the Soviet declaration's final draft was broadly identical with Liu's views expressed the night before, with Liu's own words and turns of phrase appearing in several places in the document.[115] Malin Notes of the presidium session, meanwhile, suggest that the Soviet leaders were making amendments to a draft declaration, which itself would form the basis of negotiation with the Chinese delegates.[116] After the adoption of this document, however, modified and hedged with implicit caveats concerning the Polish and Hungarian cases, Khrushchev had it cabled to Mikoyan and Suslov, requesting its transmission to the Hungarian government as a peacemaking clarification of the Soviet attitude on the Hungarian issue.[117]

The Soviets' declaration of noninterference was not as successful

---

113. "Working Notes from the Session of the CPSU CC Presidium on 30 October 1956," *CWIHP Bulletin*, 8–9: 392.

114. Ibid., 393.

115. Shi Zhe, *Jianzhenglu*, 231.

116. In Malin's notes on the CPSU CC presidium session held on 24 October, he wrote that "they had brought a draft announcement." The author considers "they" could refer to the Chinese delegates and that the draft announcement probably was very first version of the draft declaration mentioned later by Shi Zhe. See "24 October 1956 CPSU CC Presidium session" *SHSA*, 27, 52.

117. "Working Notes from the Session of the CPSU CC Presidium on 30 October 1956," *CWIHP Bulletin*, 8–9: 392–93.

as Mao had hoped in defusing suspicion of the big power in the bloc. The Chinese and Soviets immediately understood the edict as framing their relationship in different ways. The USSR had been willing to sign the 30 October declaration on the understanding that their primacy in the socialist bloc would be taken for granted and would not come under any threat from an adjustment of official policy. Mao and his colleagues, on the other hand, while preaching unity and hailing the Soviets' leadership, had a special interest in setting up a new pattern for Soviet-satellite relations. For Beijing, Moscow's declaration on 30 October held great importance, representing a significant step forward in the Chinese quest for equality of standing with the Soviet party, a goal it had pursued since the establishment of the PRC. China effectively used the Polish and Hungarian crises as bargaining chips in return for Soviet acknowledgment that Soviet–East European relations had been plagued by mistakes, and that Moscow had committed rampant violations of the principle of equality with fellow socialist countries. More importantly, the declaration pledged that in the future the Soviet Union would scrupulously observe the full sovereignty of every socialist state.[118] The Soviet presidium was only kept on board by the prospect that the 30 October document, once ratified by China, would lead to the immediate cessation of the upheaval in Hungary.[119] As they understood it, the situation was deteriorating all the time, so that whatever their reservations on the five principles or the relaxation of the Warsaw Pact, they pledged unanimously to a remedial course of action. The expectation that the riots would cease, however, set the bar too high for what the communiqué could achieve at this juncture. The Soviets were faced with options ranging from the end of the socialist experiment in Hungary, an ignominious pull-out of troops, to a hot war imposing socialism on a resisting population.[120]

---

118. Wu Lengxi, *Shinian lunzhan*, 47; Kramer, "New Evidence," *CWIHP Bulletin*, 8–9: fn. 89, 381.
119. "Working Notes from the Session of the CPSU CC Presidium on 30 October 1956," *CWIHP Bulletin*, 8–9: 392.
120. Hu Bo, *Lengzhan yinying xia de xiongyali shijian*, 40; "Working Notes

At this stage, the Chinese delegation in Moscow obtained access to Mikoyan and Suslov's cables from Budapest via the Soviets.[121] The delegation was shocked by the envoys' reports of a heated anti-Communist atmosphere in Budapest, and by the suggestion that the Hungarian government, after the retreat of the Soviet forces, had succumbed to a hardening of its position. The Chinese thus spent 30 October discussing Mikoyan and Suslov's communications, unable to reach a unanimous decision between two options: whether to accept the retreat of Soviet forces from Budapest or urge the return of Soviet forces to Budapest. Liu Shaoqi thus made an evening phone call to Chairman Mao, who suggested that the delegation could put forth both alternatives to the Soviets for discussion. Mao himself inclined to the Soviet Red Army's intervention, yet was prepared to wait until the reactionaries were exposed, partly so that any reprisal against them would carry a greater measure of popular support.[122] In general, although the Chinese leadership was leaning toward Soviet intervention at this point, Mao still thought it better to defer the final decision a little longer. However, one thing was clear: whether in Budapest or not, there was a need for Soviet troops to stay in Hungary. Under Mao's direction, Liu Shaoqi and Deng Xiaoping immediately contacted Khrushchev to ask for a meeting to convey the revised Chinese position.

After receiving the Chinese request, Khrushchev left the session to meet the Chinese delegates around midnight on 30 October. Liu Shaoqi described two possible roads the Soviets could follow, namely, intervention and retreat, and made clear the Chinese party's opposition to the withdrawal of the Red Army from Hungary. The Chinese now saw the Hungarian events as fomented by an "international imperialist plot," from which it was necessary to extricate the satellite by force. This Chinese volte-face, given that they

---

from the Session of the CPSU CC Presidium on 30 October 1956," *CWIHP Bulletin*, 8–9: 392–93.

121. Shi Zhe, "The Polish–Hungarian Incident," 16. The Soviet side sent the cables to the Chinese delegation on 30 October.

122. Shi Zhe, ibid. Liu asked for instructions from Mao on the evening of the thirtieth (Moscow time).

had previously urged the pull-out of troops,[123] put Khrushchev in a quandary, leading to his bringing Liu Shaoqi to the presidium session to consult with other presidium members.

Before Liu Shaoqi appeared at the session, he spoke again to Iudin, toward the end of their encounter firing off several questions bearing directly on the issues that worried the Chinese: "Will Hungary leave our camp? Who is Nagy? Can he be trusted?"[124] China's main concern at this point seems to have been the weakness of the Hungarian party and government, especially given a perceived bias on Nagy's part to nationalism. As a matter of fact, the Chinese embassy sent Beijing a series of reports on the worsening Hungarian situation from 28 to 30 October. In one telegram, sent as early as 11:00 A.M. on 28 October from Budapest, the Chinese embassy warned: "Ever since the outbreak of the Hungarian riots, it is notable that there are many politically dubious points [in the current government] to judge from various [official] announcements and measures broadcast by Hungarian radio."[125] The embassy also asked Beijing's permission to send a counselor back to report on the latest developments in Hungary.[126] Unfortunately all these important telegrams, which would have helped the Chinese leadership form a judgment of the local regime, did not reach the foreign ministry and central party until 31 October. In evaluating Nagy, the Chinese leaders had to fall back on Soviet reports, which they programmatically mistrusted.[127]

---

123. Shi Zhe, *Jianzhenglu*, 233. For an in-depth description of this meeting, see Chen, *Mao's China and the Cold War*, 157; Wu Lengxi, *Shinian lunzhan*, 53.

124. "Working Notes from the Session of the CPSU CC Presidium on 30 October 1956," *CWIHP Bulletin*, 8–9: 392–93.

125. Beijing did not receive this information until the afternoon of 31 October (the telegram was ciphered and the printed version was not ready until 7:50 P.M.). See "More Reports on the Hungarian Riots, Telegram to the Foreign Ministry and the Central Party," *CFMA* 109-01041-01, 42–43.

126. "Whether to Send the Embassy Staff Back to Report the Situation," *CFMA* 109-01041-01, 55. This telegram was sent on 29 October yet printed out in Beijing at 9:25 A.M., 1 November 1956.

127. Hungarian events were raised at the end of the discussion between Liu Shaoqi and Iudin on 30 October. Liu on this subject only said that "the events in Poland and Hungary should serve as a healthy lesson for the whole communist

After meeting with Yudin, Liu Shaoqi and Deng Xiaoping went into the session room to see the members of the Soviet presidium.[128] Liu repeated the CCP CC's opinion that Soviet forces should stay in Budapest and Hungary.[129] Perversely, the new Chinese suggestion went down worse than their earlier, apparently more anti-Soviet line. Molotov said that "we should issue the Declaration and explain our position," thus setting relations with the Nagy government on a workable footing. The presidium still looked to the declaration to effect some sort of outcome, especially if it meant an accommodation with the West over Hungary. According to Liu's records of the meeting on his return to Beijing, the members of the Soviet presidium resolutely opposed the Chinese delegation's suggestion, being convinced of the necessity of retreat.[130]

---

movement." "We communists," he stated, "needed to generalize our experience theoretically, as Marx in his day generalized and analyzed the reasons for the defeat of the Paris Commune, and Lenin the reasons for the defeat of the bourgeois-democratic revolution in Russia." According to Péter Vámos ("Is China with Us? Chinese Diplomatic Records on Hungary, 1956," Budapest: MTA Történettudományi Intézete, 2008), Liu's words may be read as an indictment of Soviet policy, without commenting either on the Soviets' first or possible second intervention in Hungary. The Soviet source of the time, Malin's Notes, only include a few keywords on Yudin's report ("What's the situation: will Hungary leave our camp? Who is Nagy? Can he be trusted? About the advisers," quoting from Vámos's paper. In this author's estimation, Liu's words to a large extent reflected the Chinese side's uncertainty of the Hungarian political situation under Nagy, and Liu at this stage did not receive clear direction from Mao specifically with regard to the Hungarian issue.

128. "Working Notes from the Session of the CPSU CC Presidium on 30 October 1956," 393, records the names of the presidium members present. "Zapis besedy s tovarishchem Liu Shaoqi, 30 oktyabrya 1956 goda," Archiv Vnesnei Politiki Rossiyskoi Federacii, fond 0100, opis 49, delo 9, papka 410, pp. 202–3. English translation of a document kindly provided by Lorenz Lüthi.

129. Ibid., 392–93; also see Wu Lengxi, *Shinian lunzhan*, 53; Jin Chongji, *Liuzhuan*, 806. Wu Lengxi records that Liu spoke harshly during the session, saying that if the Soviet troops retreated from Hungary, the Soviet Union would betray the Hungarian people (and the whole proletarian enterprise) and the Soviet leaders would be looked back upon as "historical criminals." Shi Zhe, "The Polish–Hungarian Incident," 17, however, only recorded that the Chinese delegation (Liu and Deng) expressed its opinion on the Hungarian crisis very clearly: the Hungarian revolt was already of a different nature from that of the Polish. Hungary had to be pulled out of its reactionary crisis.

130. For a good description of the meeting, see Chen, *Mao's China*, 157; Wu Lengxi, *Shinian lunzhan*, 53.

Condemning "the leadership of the CPSU [who] at one time tried to leave socialist Hungary to the mercy of fate," Deng Xiaoping later in July 1963 asserted of the meeting, "You [i.e., the Soviet side] know that at that time we spoke out against your position. Such a position was tantamount to capitulation."[131] Khrushchev's recollection of the meeting is somewhat different, suggesting that the two sides held an all-night meeting, eventually deciding not to use military force in Hungary and to let affairs develop naturally.[132] It is difficult to deny that the Chinese clearly expressed their opinion that the Soviet troops should remain in Hungary. Yet, as the Soviet leaders had already reached a consensus, Liu did not insist on the Chinese position.[133] This Chinese concession, in retrospect, was reasonable because, as stated above, the Chinese leadership was still of two minds over Nagy's regime and thus was not absolutely certain that an immediate military suppression of the revolt was in order.[134] Had Beijing received telegrams from Budapest outlining Nagy's suspicious policies more promptly, Mao would have been much more decisive in pushing the Soviets toward military involvement.[135]

The situation changed again as the Chinese delegation was pre-

---

131. Vladislav Zubok, "Deng Xiaoping and the Sino–Soviet Split, 1956–1963," *CWIHP Bulletin*, 10 (Spring 1998): 154, fn. 18.

132. Khrushchev, *Heluxiaofu huiyilu*, 3: 2266–67.

133. Shi Zhe, *Jianzhenglu*, 233.

134. Hao Deqing called Beijing to check up on his judgment of the Hungarian crisis on 31 October as Beijing had been incommunicado since the twenty-eighth. Hao informed Beijing about Nagy's change of political system in Hungary, suggesting that the current government "was already not communist but was looking toward the capitalist united government of 1945." It was thus not until 31 October that Mao and his colleagues came to the view that the Soviet Union would be committing a blunder if it abandoned its satellite to a reactionary uprising, sacrificing Hungarian state socialism to the opposing camp. "Hao Deqing's Phone Call on 31 October," *CFMA* 109-01041-01, 66–67.

135. In an executive committee session of the Hungarian party held on 16 November 1956, Kádár reported to his colleagues that Hao Deqing, the Chinese ambassador, had told him in a recent meeting that "they [the Chinese leadership] considered the situation in Hungary to be severe once they got to know the policies of Nagy's administration" and "they are very happy to know that we [the current Hungarian leaders] have taken measures [to solve the problems]. "Session of the HSWP Executive Committee on the Chinese Leadership's Advice to the Hungarian Leadership with Regard to the Political Consolidation of the Kádár Regime," H00014, MOL, M-KS 288, f. 5, cs. 2, oe. p. 2.

paring to return to Beijing on 31 October.[136] During their send-off by the presidium at the airport, Khrushchev informed Liu that they had decided on the continued stationing of Soviet troops in Hungary, helping the Hungarian people defend socialism in that country. Khrushchev then offered a multiplicity of reasons as to why the Soviet troops could not retreat from Hungary, in the Chinese view almost identical to those put forward by the Chinese delegation the day before. Liu told Khrushchev: "What you're saying is identical to what we said yesterday." Khrushchev responded that the Soviet declaration was still good, and that it was not contradictory to use force just after the communiqué had been published. In the Chinese record, Liu raised the question of timing: first of all, the troops should be sent in by governmental invitation; and second, the Hungarian people should evidently agree with the decision. Only when the counterrevolutionary features of the Nagy government were completely exposed to the masses, would the people forgive the Soviet intervention.[137] In Khrushchev's recollection, Liu said nothing of the kind, only agreeing with the decision to send in the troops. Khrushchev is emphatic that the final choice of sending the army back in was made by the Soviets independently with absolute support from the Chinese side.

What caused the Soviets to reverse their policy? Did Chinese involvement play a key role in their decision? While the line consistently taken by the Soviets is that they made up their own minds with the promise of absolute Chinese support, CCP leaders believed that the Chinese intervention may have swung Khrushchev's final choice to "suppress the reactionary elements in Hungary."[138] An extensive scholarly literature has not been able to settle the point.[139] As

---

136. Wu Lengxi, *Shinian lunzhan,* 53. It should be mentioned that Wu's book has the date of the delegation's leaving Moscow as 1 November. According to *LSN,* p. 378, they actually left on the evening of 31 October. Also see Shi Zhe, "The Polish-Hungarian Incident," p. 15. The Soviet Presidium decided to intervene in Hungary at its session on 31 October; see *CWIHP Bulletin,* 8–9: 393–94.

137. Chen, *Mao's China,* 157; Jin Chongji, *Liuzhuan,* 806; Wu, *Shinian lunzhan,* 53; Shi Zhe, "The Polish-Hungarian Incident," 15.

138. Ibid.

139. Shen Zhihua concludes that the decisive factor for the renewed Soviet armed intervention was the change in Mao Zedong's attitude toward the Hungar-

we know, the Chinese suggestion that the Soviet troops should stay on continuously in Hungary came at a point when the Soviet leaders were trying to avoid an occupation. Something had changed, then, in the political complexion of the Hungarian events from the day before, when the Soviets had bowed to the political concessions to the Chinese as a prelude to a peaceful solution to the crisis. The Soviet leadership issued a declaration, "On Friendship and Cooperation between the Soviet Union and Other Socialist States," immediately after the 30 October session, ignoring the Chinese suggestion to postpone its publication until the Hungarian situation could be seen in its true light—that is, either as a reactionary uprising or a manageable revision of socialism. Insofar as the CCP had already made its views clear on stationing troops in Hungary, the Chinese took no further exception to the 31 October actions of the Soviets in suppressing the Hungarian crisis. Liu Shaoqi in fact ended his meeting with the Soviet presidium in a relaxed atmosphere, with the CCP delegation leaving for Beijing the next day no further request was made to discuss the Hungarian issue.[140] There are thus good grounds for being skeptical of the large claim that Mao's change in attitude toward Nagy's government on 30 October was the decisive factor impelling the Soviet volte-face.[141]

Rather, the tipping-point may have been Nagy's restoration of a multiparty system on 30 October. The next day, Nagy raised the ante yet further by announcing Hungary's withdrawal from the Warsaw Pact. At the same time, the breakout of the Suez Canal crisis and the Soviet fear of a spillover from Hungary were instrumental in pushing Moscow to act decisively to deploy military force.[142] The American assurance that it did not regard Hungary as its ally—

---

ian crisis or, to be more precise, toward Nagy's government on the night of 30 October. Péter Vámos, meanwhile, argues that the Chinese played no role in the Soviet's decision to send troops to Hungary again. See Shen Zhihua, "1956 nian shiyue weiji," 141; Péter Vámos, "Evolution and Revolution: Sino–Hungarian Relations and the 1956 Revolution," 38.
    140. See Shi Zhe, "The Polish–Hungarian Incident," 17.
    141. Shen Zhihua, "1956nian shiyue weiji," 141.
    142. Kramer, "New Evidence," 369–70.

and thus would not come to its aid—further defused the Soviet anxiety over a potentially cataclysmic conflict that had perhaps previously stayed their hand when weighing the pros and cons of intervention.[143] In comparison with these factors, the role of the Chinese delegation was necessarily slight in changing the Soviet attitude on 31 October. Nevertheless, the fact that Khrushchev and his colleagues informed the Chinese delegation of their decision to intervene at least shows the seriousness with which the Soviet leaders entertained the Chinese suggestion of a troop presence. Moreover, in the Soviet presidium deliberations on intervention, it is plausible that hardliners like Kaganovich would have appealed to the Chinese opinion in arguing against Mikoyan for the use of force. In the event, Mikoyan was the only presidium member to oppose military intervention.[144] Although the Chinese were not kept current on the Soviet inner debates on the final decision, they obviously received the impression that the Soviets had listened to them and looked for their support in resolving their dilemma.

The Hungarian crisis by 31 October, as the CCP's leaders saw it, took the form of an anti-Communist riot stoked by imperialist powers and a few exiled and internal reactionaries.[145] During the last two days of the month, a series of reports and phone calls from the Chinese embassy in Budapest had put the Chinese leadership's

---

143. This assurance refers to U.S. ambassador Bohlen's statement to the Soviet government that the United States did not regard the new Hungary as its ally, reemphasizing the same statement made by John F. Dulles, the secretary of state, on 27 October 1956. The next day, the U.S. representative repeated the assertion during a session of the UN Security Council. Eisenhower himself reemphasized the U.S. position on 31 October in a televised speech. See Györkei and Horváth, "Additional Data," in *Soviet Military*, 31–32; Shi Yinhong, "The Hungarian Incident and American Policy," *Nanking University Journal*, 1 (1998): 97–111, 122.

144. Mikoyan returned from Budapest to attend this session after the presidium had already effectively decided to use force in Hungary. He was alone in his support of Nagy's government. Kaganovich is reported as coming back at him: "The discussion was complicated. The Chinese said we should not withdraw troops.... We can't wait long. The reactionary forces are attacking and we are attacking." "Working Notes from the Session of the CPSU CC Presidium on 1 November 1956," *CWIHP Bulletin*, 8–9: 394–95.

145. See the Chinese announcement in response to the Soviet declaration issued on 1 November.

minds to rest on the true character of Nagy and his regime. Not having received any feedback from Beijing since 28 October, Hao Deqing made an urgent call on 31 October (at 6:00 P.M.; Beijing time 1:00 A.M., 1 November), finally getting through to report the latest situation in Hungary. Hao informed Beijing of Nagy's change to the political system in Hungary, taking the line that the current government "was already not communist but had come back to the capitalist united government of 1945."[146] Just at the point at which he had sanctioned political pluralism, Nagy and his colleagues turned to the Chinese for help in what turned out to be a misguided effort to prevent a second Soviet military invasion. Nagy summoned Hao Deqing to his office late in the evening of 1 November to explain the origin and complexity of the current events in Hungary. The Nagy leadership's major purpose was to ask Ambassador Hao "to send word to Chairman Mao and Premier Zhou to interfere in the issue of Soviet military withdrawal"—that is, to get them to call off the tanks.[147] The Hungarian leaders apparently still pictured the Chinese as major advocates for the tolerance of diversity and national independence within the socialist bloc, relying that they would take a stand against a Stalin-style Soviet military intervention.[148]

Nagy's attempt to conscript the Chinese against the Soviets, though, backfired. Its apparent effect was to provoke the Chinese embassy to adopt an even more radical position toward his "proto-

---

146. "Hao Deqing's Phone Call on 31 October," *CFMA* 109-01041-01, 66–67.
147. Ibid., 90–91.
148. The Hungarian newspaper *Zhenshi* (Chinese translated from Hungarian) published an article citing sources in Warsaw suggesting that the Chinese saw the Soviet crackdown as an act of imperialist aggression against the Hungarian uprising. Raising the possibility that the article was libelous, the Chinese embassy in Budapest cabled back to Beijing for directions on how to respond. "On the Hungarian Newspaper Libeling Our Announcement," *CFMA* 109-01041-01, 89. This telegram from Budapest demonstrated indirectly the Hungarian (and Polish) misinterpretation of the Chinese announcement made on 1 November, seeming to take it for granted that the Chinese would oppose the second Soviet military intervention.

capitalist" regime. In a summary of the latest situation in Hungary sent to Beijing around half a day after Hao's meeting with Nagy, the Chinese embassy reached the conclusion that the HCP's leadership "had degenerated and that Nagy was especially suspicious politically. He is at the very least a careerist, which has become apparent judging by his words and action after the outbreak of the crisis."[149] The Chinese embassy's evaluation undoubtedly played a key role in forming Beijing's final attitude to the Soviet second intervention. In a meeting with the Hungarians held on 5 May 1959 in Beijing, Mao asserted to Ferenc Münnich that it was "the Ambassador [Hao Deqing, who was present at the meeting] whose reports and recommendations" had helped the Chinese leadership the most "in assessing and dealing with the rapidly developing situation in Hungary during 1956." Mao recalled that the Chinese embassy reported that "the counter-revolution was gaining more and more ground and had warned that if the Soviet Union should fail to liquidate the Imre Nagy Government, the restoration of capitalism in Hungary would be unavoidable."[150] Reports sent from Budapest and other source materials received from the East European Communist parties emboldened the CCP to express its appraisal of the crisis in the most unambiguous terms.[151]

---

149. "On the Current Hungarian Political Situation, Telegram from the Chinese Embassy to the Foreign Ministry and the Central Party," *CFMA* 109-01041-01, 93–94.

150. János Rádvanyi, "The Hungarian Revolution and the Hundred Flowers Campaign," 123, 126. The specific report Mao referred to in this conversation must be the telegram sent to Beijing on 2 November. In this report, the Chinese embassy concluded that "the reactionary restoration [of capitalism] would be destined to come if there were no foreign intervention." See "On the Current Hungarian Political Situation," *CFMA* 109-01041-01, 93–94.

151. In Rádvanyi's recollection, Mao told Münnich that "on the basis of this and other information received from the various East European Communist Parties, he had sent an urgent message to the Kremlin asking Khrushchev to take quick military action against the Hungarian revisionists," which indicated that Mao urged Khrushchev to take decisive military action in early November. The present author has not been able to secure any hard evidence confirming Rádvanyi's recollection. For an editorial issued on 3 November defining the official

After the Soviet leaders' decision to intervene was made on 31 October, Soviet troops in Romania and the Ukraine advanced on the country. The Soviet embassy had János Kádár and Ferenc Münnich sent to Moscow where the Soviet leaders were waiting to discuss the formation of a countergovernment.[152] Nagy resorted to the UN in calling for negotiations between the Soviet Union and his country, imploring the great powers to work through this institution to recognize Hungary's neutrality. At the same time, Khrushchev and his comrades negotiated with Romanian, Bulgarian, and Czechoslovak leaders over the terms of Soviet intervention in their neighbor.[153] On 4 November, the suppression of the Hungarian "reactionary riots" began. At 4:00 A.M., Soviet troops attacked Budapest. Three days later after the deaths of an estimated twenty-five-hundred Hungarians, a Soviet-backed Kádár government had been set in place to the satisfaction of Mao and the CCP leadership.[154]

In an *RMRB* editorial published on 3 November, the Chinese leaders accepted that the origin of the Hungarian crisis was profoundly international and that Western countries had been instrumental in fomenting unrest in Hungary.[155] The final aim of this conspiracy was to unsettle the leading socialist state, the Soviet

---

Chinese response to the Hungarian events, see *Xinhua banyuekan* [New China semimonthly], 23 (1956): 104–5: "Shehuizhuyi geguo de weida tuanjie wansui" (Long live the united bloc of socialist countries), *People's Daily* editorial, 3 November.

152. Kádár and Münnich attended the Soviet presidium sessions on 2–3 November, and Kádár was appointed by the Soviets as the head of the countergovernment, see *CWIHP Bulletin,* 8–9: 395–98. Also see *Magyarország Miniszterelnökei,* 209; Ferenc Münnich, *Magyar Századok: A Huszadik Század Története,* 394.

153. Micunovic, *Moscow Diary,* 135, 138–39.

154. See Liu's talk for CCP leaders' continuing belief in their significance in Moscow's decision for a second military intervention in Budapest on 1 November at Yiniantang, see Wu Lengxi, *Shinian lunzhan,* 58. Beijing expressed its support to Kádár and his colleagues' policies in dealing with Nagy and his men, see "Session of the HSWP Executive Committee on the Chinese Leadership's Advice to the Hungarian Leadership with Regard to the Political Consolidation of the Kádár Regime (16 November 1956)," H00014, MOL, M-KS f. 288, cs. 5, oe. 2.

155. *RMRB*, editorial, 3 November 1956.

Union, which they intended to destroy after picking off its allies, one by one. The Chinese government had therefore completely changed its standpoint vis-à-vis the need for socialist cohesion under the most stringent interpretation of Warsaw Pact terms.[156] China in effect claimed that as long as NATO existed, the Warsaw Pact should remain in force as a unified front sheltering its member nations from capitalism. The imperialist power, together with a few reactionaries inside and outside Eastern Europe, was seen by China as making mischief in provoking anti-Soviet sentiment at every possible opportunity. Adopting, then, a marked Cold War mentality, without overlooking or entirely exonerating the errors of the former Hungarian leaders, the top CCP leadership concluded that only socialism could bring about freedom, independence, and welfare at the level of the state.[157] After the primacy of the HWP had been so shaken in the Hungarian crisis, in turn putting great strain on the unity of the international socialist bloc, Beijing moved its focus from seeking to alter the pattern of relations in the Communist camp to emphasizing the shared ideological background of all the bloc states and conceding the bloc's Soviet leadership.[158]

---

156. Mao's attitude changed from the time of his "good suggestion" to Moscow on 29 October; see Chapter 1.

157. The Chinese government made this statement about Hungarian socialism on several occasions: *RMRB*, editorial, 3 November 1956; "Celebrating the Great Success of the Hungarian People," *RMRB*, editorial, 5 November 1956. In the latter piece, the importance of Soviet assistance in the Hungarian crisis as well as the role of people's dictatorship had been emphasized.

158. The Hungarian side passed along the record of Kádár's meeting with Khrushchev on 11 November 1956 (English translation) via its embassy in Beijing to the Chinese major media, *RMRB*, and Xinhua Press, for publication. However, the Chinese media did not respond until the Soviet version appeared to the public through TASS two days later. The Hungarian embassy reported home about the Chinese reluctance to adopt several Hungarian wordings of the Hungarian events, such as Kádár's definition of the Hungarian crisis as "revolution" and "Rákosi-Gerő faction." The Chinese news coverage of this meeting by *RMRB* and Xinhua later strictly followed the content published by TASS. See "Hungarian Embassy in Beijing to the Hungarian Foreign Ministry about China's Evaluation of the Hun-

THE CHINESE SOLUTION: REPAIRING COMMUNIST UNITY

Although the second Soviet military suppression of the Hungarian uprising had seemingly brought the Communist camp back to order, the doubts and the disagreements stimulated by Khrushchev's policy of undercutting the Stalinist myth de facto intensified in the aftermath of the Warsaw and Budapest crises. The Polish October and the Hungarian Revolution had occasioned even more confusion in the Communist camp than the secret speech of February, throwing into doubt the degree of orthodoxy and indeed the adherence to Soviet Russia expected of ruling and (especially) nonruling Communist parties.[159] Tito made a speech at Pula in November on the international situation in the aftermath of the Hungarian crisis, condemning the Stalinist model and the Stalinist leaders inside the camp and speaking authoritatively on matters involving the policies of the Soviet Bloc, provoking a heated debate among the world socialist parties. Different countries' parties found themselves at odds over the nature of Stalin and his and his followers' excesses, the place of personality cults in socialism, the possibility of arriving at socialism by many paths, the form of the Communist party system, and many fundamental tenets of Marxist-Leninist theory, including the dictatorship of the proletariat and the problem of class struggle.[160]

Despite his allegations about the Stalinist system and the cult of personality, Tito's speech took an ambivalent position on the Hungarian uprising, condemning the first Soviet intervention as "absolutely wrong" but giving qualified endorsement to the second

---

garian Events," 15 November 1956, H00013, MOL, XIX-J-1-z Beijing, 1945–1964, 12. doboz, 4811/1956.

159. See MacFarquhar et al., *Secret Speeches*, 9.

160. Tito delivered this major speech on 11 November 1956 at Pula to define his policy in the face of the new circumstances; see "Tietuo tongzhi zai pula fabiao yanshuo he geguo gongchandang de fanying (Zhaiyao)" ["Tito's Pula speech and the reactions of the Communist parties (Abstract)"], *Xinhua banyuekan* 1 (1957): 141–52.

one.[161] Furthermore, the Yugoslav Communist leader quite bluntly criticized the Nagy regime for "doing nothing to stop the brutal actions of the reactionaries." For Tito, Nagy's action in "making an announcement to withdraw the Warsaw Pact and declaring national independence had been meaningless in context and impotent in saving Hungarian Communism." "Viewing the current development in Hungary from the perspective of whether socialism or counterrevolution" then held, Tito though came down on the side of socialism, praising the Soviet-sponsored Kádár government for doing the best of a bad job and keeping the faith in Communism. The second military intervention had been unfortunate for Tito but there was still hope that good could come of it. Tito set out a nuanced position in this speech, hoping to maintain workable relations with Khrushchev and offer support to Gomulka and Kádár while displacing Stalinism from the norm governing relations among the Communist states.[162]

---

161. In his Pula speech on 11 November, Tito said: "We are against interference and the use of foreign armed forces . . . [but] if it meant saving socialism in Hungary, then . . . the Soviet intervention was necessary"; see Johanna Granville "Hungary, 1956: The Yugoslav Connection," *Europe–Asia Studies* 50, no. 3 (1998): 515, ft. 86.

162. "Complete version of Tito's Pula speech" (translated in Chinese), Zhongguo renmin jiefangjun guofang daxue dangshi dangjian zhenggong jiaoyanshi [National Defense University of the Chinese People's Liberation Army], ed., Zhonggong dangshi jiaoxue cankao ziliao (hereinafter *Cankao ziliao*) [CCP Party history teaching and research materials] (Beijing: Guofang Daxue, 1986), 21: 588–600. Khrushchev and Malenkov went to Brioni Island to meet with Tito on the Hungarian issue during 2–3 November and informed the Yugoslav side of the Kremlin's decision to employ military force in Hungary in order to oust the Nagy government and "defend socialism." Tito, to the "pleasant surprise" of Khrushchev and Malenkov, immediately expressed his agreement with this plan since, in Tito's opinion, the Hungarian events had headed off in the direction of "counterrevolution." See Leonid Gibianskii, "Soviet–Yugoslav Relations and the Hungarian Revolution of 1956," *CWIHP Bulletin*, 10 (1998): 140. In a letter to the CPSU on 8 November 8 replying to the Soviet inquiry about Yugoslavia's decision to provide shelter to Nagy and his group at the Yugoslav embassy, the Yugoslav side again expressed its agreement that Nagy's government was weak and that it was desirable to form a new government under Kádár, possibly uniting the "honest communists" of Nagy's government. See "Letter of the CC UCY to the CC CPSU with an Exposition of the Views of the Leadership of the UCY on the Events in Hungary," *CWIHP Bulletin*, 10: 145–47.

Moscow likewise had to perform a difficult balancing act in evaluating Tito's speech. On the one hand, Tito's attitude toward Hungary was a sign of his commitment to a common outlook and to common practices, which made Khrushchev unwilling entirely to consign him to the reactionaries; on the other, it was necessary to cut the Yugoslavs down to size for having dared attack Stalinism and assert their sphere of influence in Eastern and Southeastern Europe. In any case, Tito's Pula speech (and later the speech of Yugoslav Vice President Edvard Kardelj) complicated Soviet-Yugoslav relations however much Tito disavowed this as his ambition.[163] The other Communists weighed in—with leaders in Tirana, Prague, Sofia, and East Berlin having been sharply accused by the Yugoslav Marshal of being "stubborn Stalinists" joining in with Soviet critiques of Tito and defense of Soviet socialism.[164] For the Communist world at this juncture, as Moscow understood it, the most pressing need was to restore the bloc's ideological and political unity with the USSR at the center. Nevertheless, in forsaking many elements of its Stalinist past and involving itself militarily in Hungary, the Soviet leadership had tied its hands when it came to setting the terms of international socialist cohesion. The Chinese thus found themselves in an advantageous position to propose a new formula of unity.

---

163. "I did not want to complicate in any way Soviet-Yugoslav relations." Tito's words are quoted from Granville, "Hungary, 1956: The Yugoslav Connection," 498. The Soviet reply came on 23 November in the form of a *Pravda* article, entitled "To Consolidate Further the Forces of Socialism on the Basis of Marxist-Leninist Principles," in which the Soviets rejected Tito's charges against the Soviet system and the cult of personality and criticized some Yugoslav contentions, such as the applicability of the Yugoslav model to other socialist states. Belgrade accordingly pressed for granting all socialist states full equality with the USSR as the major retrenchment from Stalinism. For a full English translation of the *Pravda* article, see the *New York Times*, 24 November 1956; for a quotation of Belgrade's reply, see Brzezinski, *The Soviet Bloc*, 233.

164. The satellite leaders in Czechoslovakia, East Germany, Albania, Bulgaria, Poland, and Mongolia sprang into an attack on Tito and his party through their party organs. The Italian and French Communist party leaders also wrote articles or filed reports to criticize Tito's position. The Chinese side later published these articles on the 11 December 1956 edition of *RMRB*.

The consideration uppermost in the minds of Chinese leadership was the long-range implication of existing political and ideological diversity in the aftermath of the Polish and Hungarian events. Faced with Tito's allegations that a Stalinist-type bureaucratic system would risk a wave of anti-Communist unrest across the world, Mao and his comrades went through the motions of praising the Soviet system and Stalinism in the strongest possible terms. Whatever the residue of Mao's own relationship with Stalin and the Chairman's bad memories of Stalin's mistaken attitudes toward the Chinese revolution, the Chairman regarded the unified socialist ideology of Leninism and Stalinism and the principles of the October Revolution as the essential moral basis of the Chinese socialist regime, indeed of the international Communist movement in the context of the cold war. Almost every maxim and goal of socialism was related to the Stalinist model and to the Leninist construction of a party-state. For Mao and his comrades, challenging the Stalinist basis of the socialist enterprise could only possibly be divisive and demoralizing, creating an ever larger threat to the possibility of realizing socialism than any war in Hungary.[165]

Furthermore, the CCP's growing perception of the Hungarian crisis as uniquely counterrevolutionary in character and its hostility to "Western imperialism" made it imperative for the Chinese leadership to emphasize the importance of a disciplined and hierarchical unity against dark forces undermining socialism from outside. In the first draft of the Chinese statement, the writers, Mao's two secretaries, Hu Qiaomu and Tian Jiaying, and the head of New China News Agency Wu Lengxi, included the judgment that the Hungarian popular demonstrations could have been avoided had Hungary's domestic social and economic problems been better dealt with by the local regime. This could have happened, they suggested, had the

---

165. The official record of the series of politburo sessions of the CCP held from late November to early December has yet to be made publicly available and quite probably is not extant. Wu Lengxi, who attended the meetings as a nonvoting delegate, made detailed notes on the discussions, which may represent the historical evidence of these important decision-making processes. See Wu, *Shinian lunzhan*, 62–82.

Soviet model not been mechanically transplanted to the satellite state.[166] It seems overwhelmingly likely that this point had been heavily discussed and agreed to in the Chinese context in their previous sessions on Poland and Hungary. By mid-December, however, Mao had changed his mind, making the decision to omit this idea since in his own words, it "oversimplified the essence of the Hungarian events." Preoccupied with the problem of Communist rule, whose legitimacy had been challenged within a Communist state for the first time in Hungary, the Chairman formed the thesis that residual class elements continued to represent enemies and potential counterrevolutionaries to the established socialist order. The Hungarian experience, then, was instrumental in Mao's development of the thesis of the persistence of class struggle after the victory of Communism. Although Mao admitted that the Hungarian affair was the result of various causes, both internal and external, he increasingly laid more emphasis on the external imperialist plot and on local class struggles, diverting attention away from economic problems caused by radical Stalinist polices even where these bore close comparison with Chinese issues. Mao's view of the Soviet crackdown in Hungary was that the purge was regrettably justified; it was necessary to defend socialism even though numerous party members had been discarded in the events' aftermath. The power of the state to some degree needed to be founded in a party with its own security apparatus. Moreover, while acknowledging that a limited degree of internal autonomy was needed to make Marxist–Leninist theory applicable to specific conditions, the Chairman ac-

---

166. Three people formed a division of labor to draft the statement according to their individual strengths after the top leaders decided to write the article: Hu Qiaomu wrote the first section (the common lessons of the Soviet experience) and the introduction and conclusion; Wu Lengxi drafted the second section (the evaluation of Stalin) and the fourth part (on socialist internationalism), while Tian Jiaying was responsible for the third part on anti-doctrinarianism and revisionism. After numerous revisions by politburo members, the Chairman in particular, the manuscript was eventually finalized under Mao's direction on 28 December 1956. See Wu Lengxi, "Yu Jiaying gongshi de rizi, shang" [Remembering the days I worked with Tian Jiaying, Part 1 of 2], *Dang de wenxian* [Party Documents], no. 4 (1996): 85.

cepted the political and ideological correctness of reestablishing a general framework to bind a bloc of states together.[167]

The Chinese delivered their verdict on the October events and Tito's interpretation of them in a lengthy article entitled, "More on the Historical Lessons of the Proletarian Dictatorship." This article, published on 29 December in *RMRB* after eight revisions, was based on a one-month-long CCP politburo discussion convened by Mao. In Mao's words, this statement set out to "pass criticism both on Tito and the Soviet Union, as a means of achieving [bloc] unity." The Chairman recommended the use of traditional Chinese writing methods to make the article persuasive, according to which in order to criticize someone or something, one must first affirm his positive aspects, and in order to defend someone or something, one must first concede his mistakes. The first method applied to Tito and the latter to Stalin.[168] On Tito's attack on Stalinism and the gaggle of Stalinist leaders, the Chinese side thought that although "the Yugoslav comrades' . . . particular resentment of Stalin's mistakes" was "understandable," it was absolutely wrong for Tito to relate Stalin's personal mistakes to Stalin's socialist ideas and the Soviet system and denounce Stalinism on those terms. From the CCP leaders' perspective, "Stalin's mistakes did not originate in the socialist system" and therefore "it is not necessary to 'correct' the socialist sys-

---

167. The changing perception of Mao Zedong (and that of the central leadership largely influenced by him) on the essence of the Polish–Hungarian crises can be reconstructed and understood via a comparative reading of the official records of the Central Party's decision-making process in three different time spans: post–CPSU Twentieth Congress, 1956 to early November 1956; November 1956 to May 1957; May 1957 to early 1958. For the Chinese Communist leadership's view on how to evaluate Stalinism and separate the personal mistakes of some Stalinist leaders, such as Rákosi, from their correct belief systems and political ends, see "Hungarian Embassy in Beijing to the Hungarian Foreign Ministry about Liu Shaoqi's Statements on the Hungarian Problem (3 December 1956)," H00016, MOL, XIX-J-1-z, Beijing, 1945–1964, 12. doboz, 5037/1956. For the ideas formulated about the "class struggle" essence of the Hungarian events and the "appropriate" policies to control the situation as perceived by the Chinese Communist leadership, see "Session of the HSWP Executive Committee on the Chinese leadership's Advice to the Hungarian Leadership with Regard to the Political Consolidation of the Kádár Regime (16 November 1956), H00014, MOL, M-KS f. 288, cs. 5, oe. 2.

168. Wu, *Shinian lunzhan*, 64–65.

tem in order to correct these mistakes." Even if people must speak of "Stalinism," as Mao concluded, this could only mean, in the first place, "communism and Marxism–Leninism," or to be more exact, "imperfect Marxism–Leninism." In the Chairman's eyes, while the CPSU Twentieth Congress had been helpful in correcting some of Stalin's mistakes, it was improper for Khrushchev to seek to negate the Stalinist legacy entirely. By putting up the erroneous slogan of "de-Stalinization," the Chinese statement asserted, some Communists "have helped to foster a revisionist trend against Marxism–Leninism," which "can only lead to a split in the communist movement." During the discussion of writing this article, Mao made it very clear that the cutting edge of this statement should be directed against this trend of revisionism.[169]

To contain the influence of excessive diversity in ideology and practice after Warsaw and Budapest, the Chinese party leadership under Mao's construction summarized the basic laws of the Soviet experience in its December statement, claiming them as "all universally applicable truths of Marxism–Leninism." The Chinese position was thus markedly different from the Yugoslav insistence on the existence of many pathways of practical and ideological implementation toward socialism. Essentially on the ground of this disagreement, the Chinese listed five points they understood in the guise of "the fundamental experience of the Soviet Union in revolution and [the] construction [of socialism]." These points could be recapitulated as a number of phases of socialist development as outlined in the article. First, the advanced members of the proletariat organize themselves into a Communist party that based itself on Marxism–Leninism; the party builds itself up through democratic centralism, establishes close links with the masses and educates its party members and the masses in Marxism–Leninism (by means of mass line or mass campaigns and party rectification). Second, under the leadership of the Communist party (CP), the proletariat takes state

---

169. For the record of CCP politburo meetings for writing this editorial, see Wu, *Shinian lunzhan,* 62–82; "More on the Historical Lessons of the Proletarian Dictatorship," editorial in *RMRB,* 29 December 1956.

power from the bourgeoisie *by means of revolutionary struggle* (my emphasis here and below). Third, after the victory of the revolution, the proletariat, under the leadership of the CP, *rallies the broad mass of the people* on the basis of a worker–peasant alliance, establishes a dictatorship of the proletariat over the landlord and capitalist classes, crushes counterrevolutionary resistance, and carries out the nationalization of industry and the step-by-step collectivization of agriculture. This eliminates the system of exploitation, private ownership of the means of production and classes. Fourth, the state, led by the proletariat and the CP, leads the people in the planned development of a socialist economy and culture, on this basis gradually raising people's living standards and actively preparing for the transition to communist society. All the while, fifth, the state resolutely opposes imperialist aggression, recognizes the equality of all nations, and defends world peace and proletarian internationalism, appealing to laboring and oppressed people of all nations.[170] The Chinese Communists in this article offered a common ideological standard defining the genuine Marxist–Leninist path, reserving for the party itself a directive and organizational role in socialist development. Those who refused to follow any of these general principles, described by the Chinese as a "broad road which the proletariat of all countries must travel to gain victory," would automatically fall into the category of revisionism.[171]

The purpose for Mao and his comrades in summing up certain common laws of the Chinese "correct learning from the Soviet experience" and of Marxism–Leninism was twofold: externally, such a restatement of socialist doctrine defended Stalin and the Soviet experience by generalizing its political and ideological pattern as a prototype for the Soviet Bloc, while internally, it recapitulated Chinese history and offered guidelines for future domestic revolution and socialist construction. The CCP promised that its undefined "active preparations and work" would lead the people all the way to

---

170. "More on the Historical Lessons of the Proletarian Dictatorship," *Communist China 1955–1959*, 260.
171. Ibid.

the realization of socialism (as discussed in the next chapter). From Mao's point of view, in a situation in which the Stalinist formula was being questioned inside the bloc, only China was in a position to vindicate the Soviet model on the basis of "some new methods"— that is, Chinese forms of socialist construction—that bore out "the lessons of the Soviet experience."[172] Given their self-assumed position of arbiter, the Chinese appeared to hold to a middle line, reiterating their earlier warning against "certain great-nation chauvinist tendencies" while at the same time criticizing the "nationalist tendencies in smaller countries," which could not be taken as "a pretext for opposing the general interest" of "the international proletariat solidarity." By December, the Chinese regime had apparently shifted its focus from Stalinist doctrinism or big-power chauvinism to the disintegrative trends in the bloc and the need to restore the hierarchical structure of the Communist commonwealth with the Soviet Union as its core.[173]

It is noteworthy that, as Wu Lengxi recalls, the CCP still had reservations not only on the crude Soviet dissolution of Stalin's legacy but also on the notion of peaceful transition to socialism brought up during the CPSU Twentieth Congress. Using the Hungarian case as a good example, the Chairman told his colleagues that "class struggle is an objective presence that won't be transformed according to people's will," affirming the Stalinist political system as generally correct in its analysis that class struggle was fundamental to socialism. Mao also stressed repeatedly that "the fundamental conflict of the modern world is the antagonistic contradiction between the imperialist force and the socialist power," meaning that on a large scale any "settlement of contradictions within the ranks of the people" had to be conducted within "the class struggle between Capitalism and Socialism" worldwide. Following this logic, any type of non-

---

172. Ibid.
173. On 23 and 24 December, Mao reemphasized that the statement should stress a combination of "patriotism" and "internationalism"; the continuous reiteration of Soviet primacy inside the bloc and opposition to the "multicentric" theory promoted by the international Communist movement. See Wu, *Shinian lunzhan*, 62–82.

violent parliamentary or capitalist democratic device could only lead socialist revolution up a dead end. In the immediate run-up to the Chinese declaration's publication, the draft of the article still contained a section expressing the CCP's different views on this issue of peaceful transition. Probably to avoid further confusion inside the bloc, however, Mao eventually ordered the deletion of this consideration, emphasizing instead the "common laws of the Soviet experience" as a bulwark against "revisionism" or "nationalist tendencies."[174]

The shared Soviet and Chinese consciousness of the dangers involved in the acceptance of new ideological and institutional diversity without a proper framework post-Budapest had the effect of bringing Beijing and Moscow closer together. *Pravda* immediately published the Chinese statement in full on 30 December. Further, according to the Chinese source material, not only the top Soviet leaders but also diplomats, party theorists, and students wholeheartedly embraced the CCP's declaration. Despite ongoing internal disagreements in Moscow, the Kremlin leaders all seemed happy with the Chinese doctrine to replace full-dress Stalinism. The CPSU presidium member Shepilov told Liu Xiao, then Chinese ambassador in Moscow, that "the article demonstrated the mutual understanding and the unanimity reached between us on ideological and theoretical cognitions"; it was "the best new year present" for the Soviet leaders. Khrushchev, who may be thought to have received a priceless lesson in the vagaries of political diversity in 1956, found himself toasting Stalinism as the orthodox form of Marxist–Leninism in his New Year's party of 1957. Both Khrushchev and Molotov told Liu Xiao, invited by the former to sit between them in the politburo session, to send their word to Chairman Mao and Liu Shaoqi that they "totally agreed with" the opinions expressed in the 29 December Chinese article, which resounded with "the magnificent voice of the Chinese people."[175] Any

---

174. Wu, *Shinian lunzhan,* 80.
175. "Reponses of various countries to the 'More on the Historical Lessons of the Proletarian Dictatorship' article," edited and delivered by the Secretariat Bureau of the CCP's Central Party Office to commissions and ministries of the Cen-

hidden divergences between the two socialist giants notwithstanding, the Soviet leaders claimed the Chinese ideological pattern would be of service in addressing their existing problems.

CONCLUSION

From a geopolitical viewpoint, the crises in Poland and Hungary, a thousand miles away from the Middle Kingdom, could not pose a direct threat to the PRC. Nevertheless, Mao attached great importance to the Polish and Hungarian events on account of their indicative or symptomatic significance for the future destinies of all socialist states as they sought to navigate a course to some degree independent of the USSR. Should the Eastern Bloc gain more autonomy, the existing Stalinist interbloc relationships, hierarchically organized, would come under pressure, a development toward which the Chinese Communists entertained rather complicated feelings. First and foremost, the Chairman evidently viewed the Soviet difficulty in dealing with the foul-ups in its Eastern Bloc as a chance to redefine China's position in the camp, which Mao repeatedly complained had been downgraded or diminished by the Kremlin. There is no doubt that the Chinese leaders judged the Soviet management of the Polish and Hungarian crises, including that of Khrushchev personally, as heavy-handed in managing socialist international relationships, notably in balancing the Stalinist legacy with their less "leftist" line of intended development. In these respects, the CCP's leadership perceived itself as far more capable and far-sighted than the CPSU's, which further strengthened the Chairman's consciousness of Beijing's potential to inherit Moscow's central position inside the camp.

This is not to suggest, however, that Mao felt his country was ready to displace Moscow as the strategic center of the world pro-

---

tral Party, state and local party organizations, military organizations, party committees of provinces (cities) and municipalities [...] on 15 January 1957, copy stored in Hunan Provincial Archives (HPA), vol. 856, catalog 1, no. 141, 146–53.

letarian revolution by October 1956. While opposing the presumption of Soviet dominance and of the dependence of all other socialist nations, in theory, and of Stalinist big-power chauvinism" in practice, Mao was necessarily constrained by the Soviet lead in technology and economics, deferring to the success of the Soviet model in building socialism in quick order (Mao had been anxious to plan for faster and better socialist development at home from late 1955 onward). Furthermore, Soviet political and military leverage in the Eastern Bloc was something the Chinese Communists knew they could not hope to emulate over the short run. Ultimately, the Chinese leaders perceived the Hungarian crisis through a prism of cold war defensiveness. Hungary's ideological and political uncertainties warned Mao against the possible disintegrative impact that the demise of Stalinism as the principle of bloc relations would have on the general unity of the camp. The Chairman and his colleagues therefore oscillated in their political objectives from the very start of the Budapest upheavals between an adjustment of Stalinist general principles regulating Soviet-centered relations between fraternal parties and a restoration of Communist camp unity, blown about as they were by their uncertainty over the nature of the Hungarian uprising.

Within this context, the Chinese leaders decided which factors in the Hungarian case were ideologically salient and which they could safely ignore. This made certain questions permissible in China, while consideration of others, concerning the more fundamental tendency of state socialism in small and weak bloc countries and the essential problem of interbloc relations based on hierarchical principles, remained outlawed. In the Chairman's eyes, the permanence of Soviet autocratic rule was improper, while at the same time it was only reasonable that the strongest socialist state should head up an armed socialist camp. The Chinese were interested in determining, for instance, whether Nagy's Hungarian government was able to control domestic disturbances as Gomulka's had done in Poland, or whether popular revolt was going to spin out of governmental control. Their interpretation of the Hungarian developments thus became a key criterion for the Chinese side to shift its policy preferences in the period from 26 October to 29 October. It seems highly likely that Mao's dramatic change of attitude on 29 October, when he suggested that the Soviets deal with satellite states on the basis of the five Bandung principles, i.e., that they issue a declaration allowing the Eastern Bloc states more autonomy to choose their way to socialism, indeed amounted to a bold bid on Mao's part to sap Soviet political and military dominance in Eastern Europe. This line was only facilitated by his judgment that the Hungarian events would pose no fundamental threat to the overall unity of the Communist camp after a new leadership in Budapest had been installed. Chairman Mao's explicit support for the Polish and Hungarian aspirations for autonomy was no more than a pragmatic tactic pushing at the Soviet-centered bloc pattern, paving the way for the Chinese junior partner to displace its senior in the foreseeable future.[176]

Against Mao's expectation, though, Nagy failed to put a lid on Hungary's domestic events. Beijing's immediate change of position to advocate Soviet military intervention demonstrated that the Chinese Communist leadership took the integrity and unity of a centralized Communist camp as fundamental to its interest, and that in the final analysis, Beijing interpreted its own independent distinctiveness in the Communist hierarchical organization as not applicable elsewhere. As far as China's diplomatic and political involvement in the Soviet decision to intervene in Hungary for the second time, the Chinese side did not overall play a significant role in the Soviet Union's determination to return to the scene of the Budapest riots. Although the CCP's leaders affirmed the need to save Hungary from a reactionary crisis by 30 October, urging the Soviet leadership to keep its troops in place, they were wary of showing their cards over Hungary before they had ascertained the nature of the Hungarian party and government. Without having formed any

---

176. This seems to have been the first time Mao ever proposed the application of principles designed for dealing with nonaligned states to relations between the Soviet Union and its satellites.

view of the intentions and capacities of the new Hungarian leader Imre Nagy, the Chinese side was unable to press its position at the moment when it saw the Soviet leaders already at a point of consensus over pulling military forces out of Hungary. Once Beijing received the telegrams from the Chinese embassy in Budapest on the worsening Hungarian situation from 28 to 30 October, backed by Chinese diplomats' comments on the shakiness of the new government from a doctrinaire Marxist viewpoint after 31 October, Mao was content to play power politics by openly supporting the Kremlin's use of force in subjugating the Eastern Bloc once more.

The Hungarian crisis and Soviet military intervention triggered further debate on the evaluation of Stalin and Stalinism, occasioning severe disagreement not only in the socialist states but within Communist parties in the West. Tito's Pula speech underlined the fact that global Communism was anything but monolithic, thereby checking the fundamental momentum of the united international Communist movement and throwing into doubt the moral justification of many states, like China, which relied heavily on mass ideological and political mobilization institutionalizing Stalinist-type principles. This perception of the form of their own Communism led the Chinese to defend the Stalinists and the Soviets, even as they perhaps appreciated a greater multiplicity of causal factors in Hungary than the Soviets were prepared to do themselves. Any hidden divergences between the two socialist giants notwithstanding, the shared Soviet and Chinese consciousness of the dangers involved in the acceptance of new ideological and institutional diversity without a proper framework post-Budapest had the effect of drawing Beijing and Moscow closer together.

Interestingly, if we change our angle of examination, the Hungarian crisis, together with the Polish, can be judged as indirectly helping the Chinese achieve a greater measure of equality, however ill-defined, with the Soviet Union, boosting its prestige in the Communist camp. The fact that the statement defining the form of Communist interrelationships originated from Beijing instead of Moscow and the Kremlin's complete acceptance of it meant a much greater role for China and an admission of China's position inside the Soviet bloc, which as some scholars had pointed out was "a development the Soviets would later regret."[177] After the Polish and Hungarian crises, the Chinese party continued to play an important role in mediating relations between the Soviet and the Eastern European parties. Zhou Enlai's trip to the Soviet Union, Poland, and Hungary in January 1957 brought China's political thought on correctly managing relations among the socialist states (the five principles) outside Asia to Europe for the first time. China's political influence on the Eastern Bloc increased, providing at least some PRC leverage where none had existed previously.

In terms of their implications for domestic policy, though, insofar as the two crises enabled Chinese leaders to grasp various structural contradictions within state socialism, they were construed as bearing positively on indigenous problems. In this respect, although Mao and his comrades steadfastly remained votaries of international Communism, their perspectives always remained bound by domestic politics. As soon as the Soviet armed forces suppressed the riots in Hungary, the Chinese leaders exerted great effort in trying to apply their lessons to their own situation.[178]

---

177. Joseph L. Nogee and Robert H. Donaldson, *Soviet Foreign Policy Since World War II* (New York: Pergamon Press, 1984), 219.
178. Bo, *Huigu,* 2: 597–99.

CHAPTER 4

The Impact of the Hungarian Crisis on Chinese Domestic Politics
(1956–1957)

The Polish–Hungarian crises were not only important events in terms of Cold War geopolitics but they also had highly significant consequences for the development of socialism in China. The Chinese delegation returned from Moscow on 1 November, with the top leadership waiting no more than a few hours before the CCP politburo standing committee meeting convened later that evening to hear detailed reports by Liu Shaoqi and Deng Xiaoping on the state of affairs in Hungary and Poland. Two enlarged politburo standing committee sessions were subsequently called for 2 November and then 4 November, in the wake of the reentry of Soviet troops into Budapest and mounting unrest within the Eastern Bloc. The general expectation in China at the time was that the riots in Eastern Europe would be quickly suppressed without incurring mainstream popular resentment. Mao's view was that, whatever the outcome, the task of consolidating socialism in Hungary would necessarily remain a long-term effort. It was already not feasible for the Hungarians to press on with the old formula that had held before the outbreak of the crisis, Mao's view being that party leaders had to grope their way toward a new pattern, in which search they would be supported by the Chinese. It seemed to Mao and his lieutenants that the Polish and Hungarian crises might even be of benefit to the Chinese in helping them, in the first instance, better appreciate the distinctive features of political problems in China.[1]

By November, the Chinese Communist leaders had come to the view that Nagy's Hungarian leadership had lost control of events, leading to alarming outbreaks of antiparty and general violence throughout the country. Worst of all, Nagy and his men, Communist leaders properly charged with fortifying the people against reactionaries in such a crisis, had called on the masses to take up arms against the Soviet army, announcing Hungary's withdrawal from the Warsaw Pact and the restoration of a pre-1945 model of multiparty government. The Hungarian decision posed for Mao and his lieutenants a number of novel theoretical and practical questions concerning the danger of a reversion to capitalism not only in the economic sense but also in political, ethical, and social functions even after the revolutionary establishment of a socialist state. As explored more fully later, Mao was concerned with investigating the political and ideological implications of this potential backsliding for Chinese domestic development. The other top leaders, however, were more concerned with systematic problems in party organization and economic crises in food and other forms of production at home in the aftermath of the bloc crises. In hindsight, Mao had no intention of carrying out a fundamental reform in his party and bureaucratic architectures. However, he was bolder than his colleagues in aiming to line up the majority of the Chinese population behind the Maoist version of socialism. With the party cadres resisting the Hundred Flowers (HF) policy after Hungary, Mao decided that he could prevent a Hungarian-type crisis from happening at home by adopting soft means of governance in trying to win over marginal groups to the ideology of Communism. This meant a continuation of the HF

---

1. Wu, *Shinian lunzhan*, 59. Wu Lengxi was then director of Xinhuashe (New China News Agency) and editor-in-chief of *RMRB*; he attended several politburo standing committee meetings, discussing the de-Stalinization issue and the Polish–Hungarian crises. Also see Pang and Jin, *Maozhuan*, 604–5; for an overview of Chinese politics and economy, 1956–1957, see David Bachman, *Bureaucracy, Economy, and Leadership in China: The Institutional Origins of the Great Leap Forward* (New York and Cambridge: Cambridge University Press, 2006), 13–28.

policy and the opening of the party to the "rectification" of the criticism of non–party members. The dramatic cancellation of the HF campaign and mutation of rectification into an Anti-Rightist Campaign represented, then, the failure of the Maoist experiment.

THE HUNGARIAN REVOLT AND CHINESE DOMESTIC PROBLEMS

By the latter half of the 1950s, China's national economy and its people's standard of living quickly began to show the strains imposed by the radical Maoist form of socialization. By the end of the First Five-Year Plan (FFYP) in late 1956, in response to shortages of food and consumer goods, mass demonstrations had taken place in a number of Chinese provinces from around September 1956 to March 1957. Within the first six months of 1957, around ten thousand workers' strikes, both large- and small-scale, and a similar number of student strikes were held nationwide.[2] Many groups, furthermore, withdrew from the agricultural collectives in the countryside, some even calling publicly for a revolt inspired by the Hungarian Revolution.[3] A central committee directive delivered on 25 March 1957 says: "In Northeast China, Northern and Northeast China, South Central, Northwest, and Southwest China, strikes and demonstrations took place in all these regions."[4] Another party

---

2. "Zhonggong Zhongyang guanyu chuli bagong, bake wenti de zhishi" [Central Committee's directive on how to solve the problems of demonstrations by students and strikes by workers] from Zhongguo renmin jiefangjun guofang daxue dangshi dangjian zhenggong jiaoyanshi, *Cankao ziliao*, 22: 8; also see Pang and Jin, *Maozhuan*, 610.

3. "Zhonggong Henan shengwei nongcun gongzuobu guanyu chuli bufen diqu bufen nongye shengchan hezuoshe fasheng naoshe tuishe qingkuang de jianbao" [Country work department of the Henan provincial party committee's briefing on the situation of managing some cases of troubles or withdrawals from the practical agricultural collectives in certain regions], from Zhongguo renmin jiefangjun guofang daxue dangshi dangjian zhenggong jiaoyanshi, *Cankao ziliao*, 22: 12.

4. See "Report made by the Party Organization of the Chinese National General Labourers' Union on the situation of the strikes of workers," *HPA*, 141-1-840, 16.

memo reads: "It is worth noting that among those demonstrations, some were led by party members and youth league members; chairmen of the primary work unions participated in some; some were provoked by the private capital representatives of certain firms and in some cases demonstrations were stirred up by counterrevolutionaries. In many cases, the masses' blood was up, with even some administrative leaders yelling '[we] have to fight till the end,' 'the troops cannot be withdrawn until [the] success [of our protest] is sure,' and '[we'll] denounce the low ranking [officials] and then turn to the higher ones.' A few workers were even heard to proclaim, 'as [we] see, there's no other way for us other than to learn lessons from Hungary!'"[5] Although the unrest of 1956 had begun months before the October crises and most participants' grievances were economic, rather than in any sense ideological or informed by an accurate appraisal of Warsaw or Budapest, the Polish and Hungarian events apparently had the undesirable consequence of suggesting to the Chinese grassroots that the domestic demonstrations and strikes could have external sources.

In trying to face down the effect of the Eastern European crises both diplomatically and domestically, the Chinese leaders actually sat together and went over point by point their interpretations of the underlying causes of the Polish and Hungarian uprisings and of the methods required for solving the problems they embodied. From 10 to 15 November, the second plenary session of the eighth party central committee convened, with the European uprisings a top item on the agenda. Liu Shaoqi made a key report on the current situation, which summarized the central leadership's evaluation of the genesis of the troubles in the Soviet Bloc. Admitting that the Polish and Hungarian events were both "large-scale anti-Soviet campaigns which should be regarded as [emerging out of] contradictions among the people," Liu was careful nonetheless to distinguish between the two cases: while the Polish simply featured "some non-Marxist [politically or ideologically incorrect] factors," "the

---

5. Ibid., 18. Also see Bo Yibo, *Huigu*, 2: 589; Jin, *Liuzhuan*, 810.

counterrevolutionaries [had] already seized power ... taking up a dominant position during a certain period of the [mass] campaign" in Hungary. As regards the historical origins and immediate causes of "the severest events inside the Communist camp," Liu cited three historical origins and three further immediate causes: (1) both Poland and Hungary had been liberated by the Soviet army, meaning that the masses as workers and peasants had never been sufficiently politicized or organized in the struggle against landlords and capitalists; their class consciousness was as a consequence deficient. Problems with national self-determination in both countries meant that class politics were less defined than they might be, with many struggles rather assuming the appearance of interstate rivalries. Local students admired the West and disliked socialism, being further tutored by intellectuals who had never taken to communism. Last, specific mistakes in political purges had made good men suffer but left the real counterrevolutionaries unpunished. (2) Further, the state apparatuses in both countries had invested excessively in heavy industry, ignoring light industry and agriculture. As a result, people's standards of living had not risen. Local leaders' privileges, meanwhile, aroused popular discontent. (3) Local regimes had lost confidence and become disheartened once the shortcomings of their aping of the Soviet experience had become apparent; at the same time, Soviet intervention into the countries' domestic affairs hurt their national pride. (4) Hungarian and Polish adherents, party members and masses alike, were confused after the CPSU Twentieth Congress's condemnation of Stalin's mistakes. (5) The Soviets had mismanaged the early stages of both crises, in particular (6) Protest campaigns in Poland and Hungary were spurred by Yugoslav agitation.[6] These six points in fact represented the CCP core leadership's (namely Mao and the other standing committee polit-

---

6. Liu Shaoqi's report delivered during the second plenary session of the CCP Eighth Congress, 10 November, 1956. This report was partially published with the title "Yao fangzhi lingdaorenyuan teshuhua" [To avoid the "Leadership as privilege philosophy" (title added by the editor)] (hereinafter Yaofangzhi) in *Dang de wenxian* [Party's Documents] 5 (1988): 2–4. An on-the-spot written record is quoted by Shen, "Fanying he sikao," 76.

buro members) clear attitude toward Poland and Hungary in the immediate aftermath of the Soviet second intervention in Budapest. The Chinese condemnation of the Yugoslavs' role in provoking the Poles and (even more so) Hungarians into nationalist ambitions fully reflected Mao and his colleagues' eventual support of a Communist camp hierarchy.

The CCP central leadership's analysis of the crises reflected a purely, or at least a very heavy, understanding of Maoist doctrine, which would go on in turn to shape the formation of Chinese domestic policy. Possibly the most notable example of this tendency was Liu's implicit reference to the CCP's successful experience of political and social reconstruction in the initial stage of socialist state-building, in which it had mobilized the workers and peasants as participants in the class struggle, in so doing (apparently) remolding the ideology of the intelligentsia and so eliminating most of the real and potential class enemies. This Chinese ideological perspective on political struggle notwithstanding, the CCP top leaders still recognized some faults in the Eastern Bloc regimes' more specific management of state socialism, especially in the areas of party organization and economic policy, which should exert a cautionary effect on the Chinese leadership in forewarning them of certain policy hazards.

On the question of how to avoid similar upheavals in China, Liu suggested, first and foremost, to dig into possible contradictions and sources of political failure within the party. In his eyes, the fundamental issue was to avoid bureaucratic mismanagement within the party's leadership, according to which individuals would pursue personal or sectarian interests at the expense of identification with the masses and with the spirit of the revolution.[7] As the developments in the Eastern Bloc states had demonstrated, Liu asserted, it was possible for cadres to appear as and to become "a privileged class" within a socialist party's leadership. The tendency among some Chinese cadres in the party and government organizations to see their leadership roles in terms of power and privilege

---

7. Jin, *Liuzhuan*, 807–8; Bo, *Huigu*, 2: 590.

rather than responsibility could potentially lead to the formation of a Chinese "new aristocratic class" as had happened in Poland and Hungary. In Liu's view, if necessary measures were not taken in time, the example of Hungary proved that a divorce of practical interests between the party and the masses could have very dangerous results. The gap between the two, as Liu saw it, might be bridged by, on the one side, educating the masses and, on the other, educating the party.[8] Liu's prognosis was that under the leadership of the CCP, more effective state organization and the cultivation of political constituencies through the better provision of public services could allow the party to hold onto people's allegiances despite changes in their circumstances and possibly in Communism's international context.[9]

In seeking to resist bureaucratism and make the party work more efficiently, Liu took the view that the authority of leaders and the party cadres should be constrained, so that the CCP could "exercise [a] democracy of the people." By hemming in senior party figures, Liu further expounded, "there should be a framework of power defining to what extent a party member may use his authority to determine a certain issue, i.e., the limits of officials' scales of function and power [should be defined]." The internal threats to socialist development, Liu believed, could be headed off by ending the life tenure of party cadres, which he anticipated would reduce income gaps among different sections of the population following the example of Western democratic countries. Liu recalled in support of this initiative the names of George Washington, Dwight Eisenhower, and George Marshall, quoting Mao's words back at him that "some of the [means of] capitalist democracy, in particular those adopted during the initial stage of its establishment, are more developed than the ones we are using." [10] The fact that Liu had re-

---

8. Jin, *Liuzhuan*, 808.
9. Lowell Dittmer, "Review: The Past Recaptured," *China Quarterly* 97 (March 1984): 126–34; *Liu Shaoqi and the Chinese Cultural Revolution* (New York: M.E. Sharpe, 1998), 3–5.
10. Zhongyang dang'anguan, *Zhenguidang'an*, 1: 515–18; Shen, "Fanying he sikao," 75–89.

course to the early expression of Mao's own views in promoting his own policy preference in curbing cadre bureaucracy demonstrates the unchallenged centrality of Mao to decision-making, even during a period in which the Chairman deliberately created a relaxed and democratic atmosphere in the center. At the same time, it appears unlikely that Mao would have been willing to sanction any proposal that could harm his absolute authority inside the party, even if the majority of his leadership agreed to it. We will return to this topic later when considering the steps the party actually took in ensuring the continuity of the revolution.

At the same time, Liu underlined the need for mass participation in governance and for officials' supervision by the people: "Our country is a democratic dictatorship of the people, meaning that dictatorship can only be used to deal with counterrevolutionaries while democracy should be exercised among the people."[11] Liu's emphasis on the role of the masses on restraining cadres' freedom of operation reflected a Maoist orthodoxy in seeking to rid the party of the bureaucratization, corruption, and deviation from a common interest, which had already aroused popular dissatisfaction according to briefings received at the center from lower levels of party organization. Liu Shaoqi's concerns were apparently focused in a practical way on preventing the consolidation of a system of hierarchical privilege, which would alienate the party and government from the masses, as the lessons of Stalin's Soviet Union and the Eastern Bloc socialist meltdowns had shown.

However, the central discussion of curtailing party privileges and introducing certain forms of popular moderation and check into socialist government only circulated within the highly restricted ambit of the party's leadership, in accordance with Mao's notions of democratic-centralism. As a highly disciplined and intelligent Leninist, Liu also shared Lenin's skepticism over the possibility or efficacy of spontaneous mass activity. "Democracy" in China, in Liu's interpretation, "could merely be democracy under the leadership [of

---

11. Liu Shaoqi, "Yao fangzhi," 25.

the party] rather than, as some had advocated, a 'big democracy' or some form of 'democracy' without proper political leadership."[12] Liu later dubbed this Chinese form of democracy "limited democracy," designating a restriction of popular participation in and supervision of Chinese politics for situations where the ideological and directional role of the party was not under serious threat. On the whole, as one scholar has pointed out, Liu was willing to experiment on pragmatic grounds in organizational or economic realms alone, while standing in principle for the ideological purity of the Communist Party.[13] He later made it clear that a mode of "extensive democracy," namely "bourgeois" electoral and parliamentary arrangements, "is unsuitable" for China.[14] Insofar as it refused to deviate from state dirigisme, top-down CCP reform was in essence a self-regulative attempt to avoid Polish- or Hungarian-style disorders, rather than any genuinely self-critical attempt at political transition.

At the end of his report, Liu talked briefly about Eastern European economic problems, tactfully expressing his own view that domestic industrialization courted obvious difficulties if conducted at a breakneck pace. Agreeing with the position of Chen Yun, the party's chief economic planner for both the first and second five-year plans, for Liu the "speed of economic construction" should be "slower" and "steadier." Industry should be brought forward at a "sound and reliable" pace, balancing the demand for efficient and rational management with a call for increased enthusiasm in production. But "[w]hat is a 'sound and reliable' pace [of development]? . . . By this we mean that [our economic policy] should not lead the people to go out to the street or to mount a mass disturbance; at the same time, it should maintain the initiative and enthusiasm of the masses."[15] Alongside Zhou Enlai's later much more assertively

---

12. Zhongyang dang'anguan, *Zhenguidang'an*, 515–16; Shen, "Fanying he sikao," 76–77; *Sikao yu xuanze*, 426.

13. Dittmer, "Review: The Past Recaptured," 130.

14. "Address to the 1957-Class Graduates of the Peking Institute of Geology," May 1957, cited in Dittmer, "Review: The Past Recaptured," 129.

15. Zhongyang dang'anguan, *Zhenguidang'an*, 516; Shen, "Fanying he sikao," 76–77; *Sikao yu xuanze*, 426–27.

worded report on economic problems, Liu's argument about fitting industrial development to China's economic means was much more cautious and moderate.

Liu's circumspection doubtless owed to the identification of his "rightist" mistakes in the sixth plenum of the CCP Seventh Congress in 1954 and his effectively being placed on his best ideological behavior by Mao's presence. Mao responded to Liu's view that right was better than left on the question of keeping to a "sound and reliable" pace in economic construction by saying, "It depends what sort of rightism is involved." After Liu circumscribed his rightism just to the speed of construction, Mao replied that this kind of rightism was acceptable, implying that Liu's 1950s flirtation with capitalism remained firmly off-limits. In Liu's case, his political ambiguities were probably less a matter of taking a truly middle line in evaluating China's economic difficulties than of acting rationally in avoiding offense to the Chairman and his radical plan for socialization.[16] On the other hand, the Chairman's implicit warning to the central party against excessive reforms that ventured too far to the right indicated that Mao preferred restrictive policy adjustments after the Hungarian events, whose unexpected political consequences emphasized the need for a restrained approach in dealing with domestic problems.

For Zhou Enlai, Chen Yun, and the other top economic leaders who had overseen the First Five-year economic plan based on the Soviet model, the uprisings in Poland and Hungary represented a

---

16. Shen Zhihua interprets the final section of Liu's speech on economic matters to connect the lessons learned from the Eastern bloc to "the relationship between heavy industry and light industry and that of accumulation and consumption" as laying the groundwork for a following discussion of domestic economic problems on the basis of the Polish–Hungarian events. Shen's interpretation is arguably misleading in giving the impression that Liu Shaoqi, Chen Yun, and Zhou Enlai presented a united front in opposing "rash advances," even forming a bloc on the matter of economic policy. In fact, although Liu was apparently sympathetic to a "sound and reliable" economic policy, as against a radical move forward, he was far from a leading figure in setting out an "anti-rash advance" policy, which was spearheaded instead by the more unambiguously sound ideologues Zhou and Chen. See Shen, "Fanying he sikao," 76–78; *Sikao yu xuanze*, 426–27.

historic opportunity to question the applicability of Stalinist development strategy to Chinese conditions. On the one hand, the top economic planners saw that the Soviets themselves were suffering from the emphasis they had placed on heavy industrialization efforts at the expense of a concentration on agriculture and light industry. On the other, they realized that the massive uprisings in East Germany, Poland, and Hungary reflected "the serious consequences of enforcing this [Soviet or Stalinist] policy," which did not appear, further, to be universally sound ("Stalin's economic theory has [left] something open to doubt," they noted).[17] Knowing that China's development in the first half of the 1950s was in fact established on the Stalinist pattern, people like Zhou Enlai feared that if further adjustments were not made to rectify the "modern industry-centered" policy, China risked a fate similar to that of Poland and Hungary. The premier therefore called for a special focus on existing problems of socialist construction in a standing committee meeting of the State Council on 9 November: "The recent international development affords us lessons that merit attention: ever since the CPSU Twentieth Congress's denunciation of Stalin, many problems with socialist construction have been exposed with the consequence of social and political instabilities making themselves felt from Poznan to the Hungarian October. There are still hidden problems in other [socialist] countries. All these should be taken as an objective lesson for our country."[18] Up to this point, the premier felt it important for a wider range of party cadres to arrive at a common view on the necessity for a change in the country's development strategy. Zhou thus decided to appeal, in a stronger and more direct way than he did in the CCP's Eighth Congress, to his central party colleagues to recognize mistakes in their previous economic policies on the basis of lessons learned from the Polish and Hungarian crises.

---

17. Zhongyang Wenxian, ZNP, 1: 629–30.
18. "Zhou Enlai's Speech Record, Meeting of Standing Committee of the State Council, November 9, 1956," in Zhonggong Zhongyang wenxian yanjiushi, ed., *Chen Yun zhuan* [Biography of Chen Yun] (CYZ hereinafter) (Beijing: Zhongyang wenxian, 2005), 1: 1036.

As a result, when it was the premier's turn to deliver his speech on national economic planning for 1957, Zhou addressed the main agenda item of the economic plan by drawing attention to the unbalanced economic policies in Poland and Hungary. Based on ideas formulated in a series of discussions with his State Council colleagues about Poland and Hungary's economic problems and how they might relate to Chinese domestic conditions, Zhou in fact offered his colleagues two resolutions for readjusting economic policies at home, the first underlining the need to raise people's standards of living and the other advocating a moderate, well-balanced prospectus for the Second Five-Year Plan. Carefully stating that socialist industrialization was "designed for people's long-term interest," Zhou made the case that light industry and agriculture were more directly related to people's immediate interests. "If people had been placed under undue stress to tighten their belts, that is, if people's living standards had not risen or they had been asked to give up basic goods," Zhou said, "then it would have been impossible to arouse people's enthusiasm, let alone to increase capital accumulation." Following this logic, Zhou warned that "development of heavy industry would have had to come to a halt even had it been further advanced." At this point in history, then, Zhou came to the conclusion that it was necessary to slow down the pace of industrialization, even claiming that the economic index formulated in the CCP Eighth Congress and the forty-article Draft Program for Agricultural Development of January 1956 on Mao's initiative were "merely suggestions" capable of revision. Backing up his arguments, Zhou reminded his audience that "the events [that] took place in some Socialist countries should serve as a grave warning to us."[19]

In order to push the 1957 annual plan in the direction of greater moderation, the premier again raised the issue of FFYP evaluation, repeating his theme of the August CCP Eighth Congress. This time, however, Zhou's review of the FFYP pressed harder on "defects and errors" than previously, taking the line that the CCP's "achieve-

---

19. "Zhou Enlai's Report to the Second Plenary of the 8th Central Committee of the CCP, November 10, 1956," in Zhonggong Zhongyang wenxian yanjiushi, ed., *Zhou Enlai xuanji* (Beijing: Renmin, 1980), 2: 229–58.

ments are tremendous, but there have also been *some* defects and errors in our work which we must strive to correct." In rowing back to a position where Communist development had only been "generally" correct, Zhou took aim at the so-called rash advance tendency, which between 1953 and 1956 had blundered in setting unrealistically optimistic targets, something that had to be corrected in the 1957 planning. On the 1957 proposal, the premier called everybody's attention to the necessity of "a general lowering [of the economic targets]," otherwise "[our economy] will be unstable and have negative impact on our currency, goods and materials, labor and salaries." The party should not "allow [something like] Poznan to happen in China, leading to several hundred thousands or several millions of people standing on the streets and demonstrating."[20] Despite Zhou's boldness and persistence in advocating for a balanced economy while opposing a rash advance, the premier's address was still a political balancing act: industrialization and socialization remained "primary" and in "the long-term interests of the people" as defined by the Chairman.[21] However, the substantive message was a sober one: unless something was done to solve the real problems of people's livelihoods, China would court the same falling-out with the masses as in Hungary.

Following the premier's report, Chen Yun made a speech on the themes of food and nonstaple foodstuff supplies.[22] Shortages in all

---

20. Ibid. Zhou Enlai told Szall, the Hungarian chargé d'affaires to China, that the economic difficulties in socialist countries were caused by [the leaders and policymakers'] lack of experience in making balanced economic policies and admitted that China had made very serious mistakes in this respect. With a combined effort, Zhou then encouraged the Hungarian diplomat, "We [Communist leaders] can correct this type of mistake." "Hungarian Chargé d'Affaires to China, Szall's Report on Zhou Enlai's Introduction to the Progress of Hungarian Government's Credit-Based Borrowing from China," 6 May 1957, Szobolevszki, *Magyar-Kínai Kapcsolatok*, 190.

21. Mao moderated his emphasis on heavy industry as primary by agreeing to balance investment between heavy industry and light industry in April 1956; see his "On the Ten Major Relationships" (25 April 1956), in Michael Y. M. Kau and John K. Leung, eds., *The Writings of Mao Zedong, 1949–1976* (Armonk, NY: M.E. Sharpe, 1986), vol. 1: 46–47.

22. The first five-year planning period got underway in 1953 with Zhou Enlai and Chen Yun as the chief persons responsible. After Gao Gang had been promoted to lead economic planning in late 1952, Chen Yun ceded his leading posi-

comestibles, especially pork and cooking oil, had become particularly acute, causing the issue to rise up the plenary agenda, prompting reassessment of the top of the CCP development strategy. Chen Yun reported that there would be a 2.5 billion kilograms deficit in supplies the following year, predicting "a mess," which should mean a cutting of forecasts now rather than later. Chen further suggested a role for the free market in rural areas in stimulating agricultural production and encouraging a flow of commodities, notably in nonstaples like pork, to towns.[23] Together with Liu Shaoqi's speech on bureaucratism in the party system, Zhou's concern over the economic and societal validity of the Soviet model and the widespread perception that people's livelihoods in China were not improving as anticipated, Chen's report struck a chord, focusing party attention in the subsequent small discussion sections on shortages in housing, power generation, steel, and other daily necessities. Local representatives further connected the entrenched privilege of cadres at home with the lessons learned from Eastern Bloc states and questioned the applicability of the heavy industry development pattern to Chinese conditions. Zhu De, a member of the Standing Committee of the CCP Politburo, stated that "it appears that the problems [at home] are serious," coming into line behind a more balanced development strategy. Dong Biwu, politburo member and head of the People's Supreme Court, commented that unless the rash-advance ideology had been put in its place, problems were sure to emerge in the Second Five-Year Plan. The Northwest group (divided between different geographical locations) reported during discussion that supply was unable to meet the demand in its regional market, resulting in shortfalls of both food and clothing in Lanzhou, the capital city of Gansu province. If the situation contin-

---

tion in the FFYP to Gao. The first year saw the emergence of the Gao-Rao affair, leading to the Chairman's nomination of Chen Yun to head up the FFYP (Zhonggong zhongyang wenxian yanjiushi), *Chen Yun zhuan*, 2: 873–916.

23. Chen Yun's report, records of the Second Plenary of the 8th Central Committee, 11 November 1956, cited in Shen, "Fanying he sikao," 77. For an analysis on the origin of the food supply and agricultural raw materials problem from an economic perspective, see Eckstein, "Economic Growth," 214–15.

ued, suggested the cadres from this region, something like Poznan would be hard to head off.[24]

Evidently, a large number of the leading cadres who attended the sessions, either from the center or from the provinces, already realized that the East European problems in the realms of economic and party organization emphasized the danger of letting similar problems fester at home, resolving on the necessity of further reforms in China. Moreover, encouraged by the inner-party détente promoted by Mao since early 1956, the top elites must have felt safer to express their real attitudes toward domestic problems, considering they were answering the Chairman's call for collective wisdom and effort in spearheading internal reform. It seemed that both Premier Zhou and Chen Yun believed their advocacy for an adjustment of the Stalinist model of economical development was politically in line with Mao's desire to specify and cultivate the specifically Chinese characteristics of socialist construction on the basis of a critical review of the Soviet experience. Yet the degree to which Mao would allow criticism of the Stalinist model remains very much in doubt; such criticism may have been especially unwelcome if it could be taken to cast doubt on the achievements of China's socialization, as identified with Mao, and even on the legitimacy of his past policies. Therefore, no matter how the central party cadres may have called for further reforms to prevent a Poznan or Hungary from happening in China, Mao's own interpretation of the meaning of Communist Bloc crises and their possible impact on domestic developments has to hold a central place in our analysis of the possible direction of any policy changes post-Budapest.

---

24. Briefing and small-group discussion records, the Second Plenary of the 8th Central Committee, 11 November 1956, cited in Shen, "Fanying he sikao," 78; also see Shen, *Sikao yu xuanze*, 429. For the Hungarian investigation of Chinese domestic problems, together with the change of Chinese foreign policy in the post-Polish–Hungarian crises atmosphere, see "Hungarian Embassy in Beijing to the Hungarian Foreign Ministry about the CCP's Policies after the Polish and Hungarian Events" (25 January 1957), H00021, MOL, XIX-J-1-j China, 1945–1964, 7. doboz, 5/c, 00986/1957.

Mao's views on the economic issues discussed in the second plenum appear to have been complex and contradictory. All the same, we can discern his viewpoint on two interrelated but distinct questions: China's broad development strategy and current imbalances and failures in execution. On the specific economic problems at hand, the Chairman continued pragmatically to acquiesce in moderate economic policy adjustments.[25] The Chairman's discussion of economic policies in fact allowed his lieutenants to ratchet down expectations, "arrang[ing] the reduction problem rationally to avoid disturbances from occurring." "[Since we only have] this limited amount of money and material," Mao stated, "it is necessary to make appropriate reductions from 1956 levels and to guarantee the implementation of key construction projects while ensuring that people's livelihood continues at an acceptable level." Mao further advised that "when materials are not sufficient, [they should be] first and foremost sent to support necessary production; at the same time, the balance [in material supply] should also be noted."[26] There can be no doubt that Mao was fully apprised of the financial and resource restrictions on rapid industrialization, as his comments on economic policy in fact broadly support the State Council's reduction proposal for 1957. At the same time, it is also plausible that, in Mao's mind, these moderate measures were no more than transitional means for getting around the bottleneck on resources prior to a fresh round of industrialization. On the basic problem of the applicability of a heavy-industry-centered economic model to Chinese conditions, Mao does not appear to have wavered from his belief in industrial modernization, parting company with Zhou's immediate post-Hungary doubt on this matter.

This determined differences between the two men over both tone and strategy, with Mao taking exception to Zhou's emphasis on defects and errors in the party's economic work, which Mao feared as potentially jeopardizing the enthusiasm of the party cadres and

---

25. For a well-documented historical narrative of the anti–rash-advance policy and Mao's attitudes toward it in the summer of 1956, see Shen, *Sikao yu xuanze*, 169–212.

26. Zhongyang wenxian, *Mao wenji*, 7: 160.

masses for ongoing socialist revolution, or even worse, encouraging misgivings about the basic correctness of the party's policies. The Chairman therefore summoned a meeting of the small-group heads, closing the session on the fifteenth by apparently offering a corrective to Zhou's excessively pessimistic take on economic development work. Without standing against purely tactical adjustments in the speed of construction and specific economic policies, Mao in fact put in a bottom line for any moderation attempts: in no circumstances should the achievements of socialism be underestimated or the party's success bad-mouthed. Mao rehearsed the old 1955 case of Deng Zihui, though without specifically bringing up Deng's name, to warn Zhou and others off similar mistakes: "[We] should protect the enthusiasm of the cadres and masses and not pour cold water on them. Some people once poured cold water [on them] on the issue of agricultural socialization and formulated a 'pro-retreat committee.'" In the interests of retaining "the enthusiasm of the cadres and masses," Mao revised the wording "safe and reliable" for the economic guideline from the State Council budget report to "sufficient and reliable." For Mao, keeping to the "correct" political consciousness fired by the revolutionary enthusiasm of the party and his people always took priority over tactical demands for economic course-trimming.

There is also reason to believe that Chairman Mao harbored implicit reservations on Zhou and Chen's argument for giving a high priority to people's livelihood in reviewing economic conditions both at home and in the East European satellite states. Their emphasis on living standards worried Mao, because it seemed to impugn the authority of the development goal he had himself set up for his country. With the fundamental political struggle largely won, priority was now given to economic development with the aim of, as Mao made clear, "wiping out China's economic, scientific and cultural backwardness within a few decades and getting rapidly abreast of the most advanced nations in the world."[27] In the Maoist

---

27. Mao Zedong, "Speech to Supreme State Conference" (January 1956), cited in Teiwes, *Politics and Purges*, 167.

scheme of values, it was definitely the modern heavy-industry sector, rather than food or light industry production, that constituted the principal determinant of national power.[28] Following the Chairman's logic, once his country achieved the goal of modernization (or industrialization as defined by Mao), people's living standard would naturally rise in tandem with the increase in China's productive power. Yet in getting to this stage, it was necessary to direct the majority of resources into industrial development. This motivated Mao's words to his colleagues that "the improvement of people's living standard must be a gradual process" and "[if] the masses make unrealistic demands or raise what seem to be insoluble problems, [we] should explain [this] to the public openly and repeatedly." Mao's conclusion was that "most of the investment in capital construction and other projects in 1956 was sound, and only a portion of it inadequate," attempting to bear out the general correctness of his economic strategy, however congruent this was with a Stalinist mode that had been put in doubt.[29] This line differs markedly from that of Zhou and others, who had misgivings about the development strategy in general.

In short, although Mao accepted the specific economic plan for 1957 and did not oppose his colleagues' "cool-down" policy in the aftermath of the Eastern European uprisings, the Chairman must have felt that Zhou and the other economic leaders lacked the vision to identify the key problems actually revealed by the incidents. Mao's mind, at this stage in the middle of 1956, was more preoccupied by the political and ideological considerations prompted in the aftermath of the Polish October and abortive Hungarian Revolution than by their specifically economic character. To a significant degree, Mao Zedong agreed with Liu's argument that the government and the ruling party's alienation from the people lay at the root of the Hungarian public's discontent, in particular the disaffection of the peasants, workers, intellectuals, and students. At the

---

28. Anthony M. Tang, "Agriculture in the Industrialization," 1118.
29. Mao Zedong, *Mao Zedong xuanji* [Selected Works of Mao Zedong] (Beijing: Renmin, 1977), 5: 313–29.

same time, the weak leadership of the Hungarian party made it possible for reactionary forces at home and abroad to exploit otherwise justifiable popular unhappiness, fundamentally changing the class character of their protest.[30] Nonetheless, Mao apparently had no intention of accepting Liu's proposals of restricting the power of the inner party in the name of curbing bureaucracy, given that he believed that Communist rule made policy deliberations and the consolidation of power at the center more, rather than less important. Instead, Mao set out to instigate a procedure of reforming thinking by soft means, seeking thereby to displace the incorrect ideas, including those of a bureaucratic stamp, that had come to light together with the lessons pointed out by the Eastern European events. Nevertheless, the political climate at home in the wake of Poland and Hungary was particularly volatile, with participants never able to feel sure that the Chairman would stick to noncoercive means in framing his agenda for Chinese Communism.

THE HUNGARIAN REVOLT AND THE RECTIFICATION PLAN

The events in Hungary, even more so than the Polish October, stimulated domestic debates, in the first place among upper- and middle-ranking cadres in Beijing and, at both central and local levels, among senior intellectuals and democratic party members.[31] The major issues discussed were the nature and origin of the uprisings in Hungary, the perils of weak leadership, the legitimacy of the Soviet military intervention, and the relevance of the events to the CCP's governance. The initial reactions of these groups of the population seem to have been a mixture of shock and confusion caused

---

30. Bo Yibo, *Huigu*, 598–99; Jin, *Liuzhuan*, 807–8.
31. The latter two groups could also get access to more information on Hungarian events through the dissemination of inner-circle party documents on account of the liberal political atmosphere during the HF campaign and "mutual supervision" of the CCP and the democratic parties' policies since early 1956.

by their knowledge of violent and violently suppressed antigovernment demonstrations taking place in a Soviet Bloc state, which eventually needed the intervention of Soviet troops. The masses may have been particularly bewildered by the contradictory conclusions drawn by the Chinese state newspaper on the nature of the Hungarian uprisings (as discussed in Chapter 3: the *RMRB* [People's Daily] initially dubbed the Hungarian case a "riot," changing this to an "incident," before the events' later redesignation as "counterrevolutionary" in early November). This begged the question of why so many Hungarian civilians participated in the uprisings if these events were "rebellious and counterrevolutionary" as eventually defined by the CCP.[32]

Moreover, the events did nothing to dispel the uncertainties by certain groups of people over the wisdom of adopting the Stalinist legacy: some pointed out that both the Polish and Hungarian revolts grew out of local parties' bureaucratism and could be understood as attempts on the parts of the masses to get the party to heed their voices. As the Hungarian people lost confidence in the solidarity of their leaders, they began to express dissatisfaction; and when the party again stood aloof from the mass line, they revolted. Notably, in the views of some analysts, the Hungarian case was caused by internal party splits, echoing the Gao-Rao affair in China. All these debates and discussions among party and nonparty people supposed, without explicitly articulating more sensitive questions concerning possible institutional flaws in the Communist Party and its patterns of governance.[33]

Collected official information suggests that while popular responses continued to be largely positive toward the role of the Chinese central leadership, they also indicated a growing sense of apprehension among more thoughtful groups or individuals. Even those who appraised the CCP top leadership as "wise and correct in Marxism–Leninism" recognized that party work was liable to cer-

---

32. *Neican* (2 November 1956): 61; (5 November 1956): 127.
33. *Neican* (6 November 1956): 167–68.

tain defects, which, they were careful to specify, "should only be blamed on lower echelons who had mistakenly carried out the central policy." As an instance of this disquiet, teachers and students in Jiangxi Normal College questioned the superiority of the socialist system, with some cadres and intellectuals implicitly suggesting that "China should draw a lesson from the Polish-Hungarian events" as they effectively indicted "errors in the work of [the socialist] party and government."[34] A senior student at Beijing University wrote a letter directly to *RMRB* on 27 October 1956 to criticize its embargo on international news. This letter sets out an understanding of "democracy and freedom," proclaiming that only someone who had established his ideas on the basis of "real knowledge about existing events" could be regarded as a "man of free thinking." Only a "free press" (under the dictates of the party), then, could truly respect "human rights and personal dignity" in informing China's citizens appropriately.[35] Besides these discussions, a number of reactionary slogans appeared on the wall of the dining hall of the Beijing Steel Institute, calling students to "Oppose the Current Regime," saying "We Need Democracy and Freedom," and setting forth the analyses "The Chinese People Are in a Miserable Situation; Youth, Take Action!," "Support the Polish and Hungarian Peoples' Struggles!"[36]

These scattered and unsystematic ideas inside and outside the party in the aftermath of the Hungarian events were collected by central and local party organizations and submitted to the center. According to Mao's mass line, the leadership of the CCP was under an obligation to respond to local currents of thought. The central leadership was thus impelled to conduct a thorough "investigation and study" of peoples' views in which it would "seek truth from facts" (that is, carry out phases of understanding and evaluation) before any specific policy could be set.[37] Alerted by their interpreta-

---

34. *Neican* (5 November 1956): 122–23, 129; (1 November 1956): 5.
35. *Neican* (10 November 1956): 295–98.
36. *Neican* (6 November 1956): 167–68.
37. For an in-depth analysis of the mass line in Chinese politics, see Graham Young, "On the Mass Line," *Modern China*, 6, no. 2 (April 1980): 225–40.

tion of Hungary to the possible existence of so-called residual and active class-enemy elements stirring up insurrection within China, the top leaders, Mao in particular, thus had to decide to what extent these manifestations were in essence counterrevolutionary, rather than popular, and evaluate to what extent the consciousness of the cadres and of various groups of people was appropriate before seeking to direct them systematically. At first glance, this Maoist mass line method resembles a statesmanlike policy emphasizing the leadership's awareness of local support and popular opinion as the only conceivable basis for bringing large populations around to a policy. The contrast with centralizing Stalinist methods would appear stark. In essence, though, Mao, the inventor of the democratic method, never let up on his insistence on the elite's absolute and ultimate authority to examine the ideological and political "correctness of popular demands, deeming it inappropriate to bow to whatever the people seemed to want. Mao's approach was more un-Stalinist in form than content.

Mao was immediately restive with "some democratic party members' negative comments" on "the policies of suppression taken against the counterrevolutionaries" in the immediate aftermath of Hungary. Materials available from the second plenum suggest that democratic outsiders did not cast direct doubts on the correctness of specific policies but rather took issue with the legitimacy of paying too high a human price to realize revolutionary ideals.[38] But in Mao's understanding, these democratic party people were nakedly throwing down a challenge to the authority of the Communist policy of "beating down those notorious landlords, bad gentry, and counterrevolutionaries," which the Chairman had considered as indispensable to consolidating the victory of the revolution. Therefore, when Liu talked about the Vietnamese government's concern over an excessive numbers of deaths in its land reform campaign and political

---

38. For Mao's allusion to democratic party members' comments on the CCP's policy in suppressing counterrevolutionaries, see *Mao Zedong xuanji*, 5: 313–29; see also Liu Shaoqi's report written for the Second Plenum of the 8th Central Committee in Shen, "Fanying he sikao," 73–78.

purge on 10 November 1956, the Chairman gave his view, as connected to the Eastern European developments: "We put seven hundred thousand to death [in political campaigns], or 0.13 percent of the total [Chinese] population of six hundred million. There has not been much killing [of counterrevolutionaries and enemies] in Eastern Europe. This [kind of killing] is revolution!"[39] Later in his closing speech on the fifteenth, Mao took up this theme again, jibing that the democratic party members "had always taken a different tone than we do on this matter [of the elimination of counterrevolutionaries]."[40] As Mao saw it, the democrats' inclination toward clemency was a sign of their lack of the proper political and ideological consciousness, a mistaken view that he vowed should not cause any confusion among the Communist cadres. His own assessment, meanwhile, was that the fundamental problem in the Hungarian crisis was a failure to bind the masses to socialism brought about by an insufficient waging of class struggle against counterrevolutionaries. Hungary became in these terms a useful negative example with which the Chairman could counterattack democratic commentators and educate the party.

Mao was likewise exercised by some commentators' call for a big democracy, or political reform on the Western democratic model, both from within and outside the party. It appears that Mao never understood more by "democracy" than a revolutionary means toward the end of achieving ultimate political goals, such as the instigation of mass campaigns against political enemies or supposed counterrevolutionary classes. Mao's democratization campaigns—the land reform, "Three Antis, Five Antis," and purges in 1955—

---

39. Shen, *Sikao yu xuanze*, 430. If Eastern Europe's most severe problems in late 1956 came about as a result of transplanting the Stalinist model, North Vietnam's most acute problems originated from its imitation of mass Chinese campaigns and political purges. Land reform in Vietnam was modeled on Chinese practices, in which any better-off peasant could be labeled a landlord, sent to people's court, and even publicly executed without any legal process, with sympathizers facing severe punishment. See Cheng Yinghong, "Beyond Moscow-Centric Interpretation."

40. Mao, *Mao Zedong xuanji*, 5: 317.

never had anything to do with democratic political reform. Mao's closing speech set out his viewpoint unequivocally: "There are some intellectual cadres on the levels of *si* (department) and *ju* (bureau), who advocate *daminzhu* (big democracy) since a little one is far from enough. This so-called big 'democracy' would adopt the Western capitalist parliamentary system and copy the Western style of 'parliamentary democracy,' 'free press,' and 'free speech.' Their ideas are wrong, deficient from a Marxist standpoint and do not set out a class position."[41] In other words, the Chairman now became aware that admitting political elements from capitalism into China's socialist regime was theoretically and practically beyond his pale in the post-Hungary atmosphere. The "intellectual cadres" Mao referred to in his speech were most likely Wang Fei and Li Shenzhi, then director and vice director, respectively, of the international department of the New China News Agency.[42]

In early November, Mao sent his personal secretary Lin Ke to consult Wang Fei and Li Shenzhi for their opinions on the international issues. Li and Wang's jobs had kept them better informed of the actuality of the Polish and Hungarian riots than other pressmen so there was little strange in Mao's wanting to sound out the political and ideological understanding on post–CPSU Twentieth Congress issues of two such well-informed intellectuals.[43] Li recalls being deeply stirred by the denunciation of Stalin and the outbreak of Polish October and the Hungarian crisis, furthermore nurturing great hopes that Mao's famed tolerance and open-mindedness

---

41. The official record of Mao's speech delivered on 15 November 1956 in the second plenary session of the CCP Eighth Central Committee remains unavailable. For a record of Mao's comments on big democracy, see Mao Zedong, *Mao Zedong xuanji*, 5: 323. In Pang and Jin, *Maozhuan*, 605–6, two paragraphs quote Mao's speech.

42. Lin Ke, *Lin Ke riji* [Lin Ke's diary] (unpublished written draft, personal collection), 15; Li Shenzhi, *Fengyu*, 105.

43. In Li Shenzhi's account, he and Wang "were the two figures who came into contact with the situation [of the international disturbances in 1956] the most." Li Shenzhi, *Fengyu*, 105–17; also see Wang Qixing (Wang Fei's son), "Wang Fei, Li Shenzhi yu Maozhuxi mishu tan minzhu" [Wang Fei, Li Shenzhi talked about democracy with Mao's secretary], *Yanhuang chunqiu*, 8 (2010): 26–29.

would be able to draw the correct lesson from the incidents and change the course in China. Li and Wang used the terms "big" and "small" democracy to forward their ideas of how China's political system should develop through Lin Ke to Mao. Moreover, Li suggested that the central party draw up a five-year plan for returning "political power back to the people," setting up courses in the national constitution and in citizenship at the primary-school level, and establishing a constitutional court. Li was possibly emboldened in these suggestions in that he had learned of some of the Chairman's liberal ideas from Wu Lengxi, who sat in politburo meetings regularly in the fifties, perhaps believing further that Mao was receptive to ideas of democratizing China's political system after class enemies in China had generally been eliminated. Li thought he was "anxious about what the Chairman is anxious about" and supposed his contributions might make a difference, though it turned out that these were fond hopes on his part.[44]

Nonetheless, the terms "big" and "small" democracy as used by Li and Wang were of some service to the Chairman in helping him define two opposing approaches to current problems: "Since the language of big and small democracy is easily imagined, let us borrow these [two] terms."[45] In reviewing recent popular criticisms against inner-party bureaucratism, Mao spoke up for "big democracy," which he redefined as strikes, popular parades, and demonstrations as proper methods for forcing the cadres to correct their mistakes.[46] He summed up the origin of the workers' and students'

---

44. As Li recalled, Wu Lengxi had always come to him for the latest international news before he went to sit in the politburo meetings; Wu also told Li about some of the issues discussed during the politburo meetings, particularly the Chairman's major concerns and ideas, giving Li hints about what type of news to collect for the Center. Li Shenzhi, "Guanyu 'daminzhu' he 'xiaominzhu' de yiduan gong'an" (hereafter Gong'an) [On the intricate case of 'Big Democracy' and 'Small Democracy'], *Bainianchao*, 5 (1997): 49.
45. Mao Zedong, *Mao Zedong xuanji*, 5: 323.
46. After the second plenum, Lin Ke went to see Li Shenzhi to make sure that he had conveyed Li's messages to Mao correctly. Li explained that by his term "big democracy" he did not mean "taking to the streets" but rather the instigation of democratic reforms against the background of the triumph of the revolution. Mao responded to Li's assertion that in his eyes "congress democracy and free press

strikes as lying in their dissatisfaction with bureaucratism, noting "there are more than several hundred thousand cadres whose levels are above the county party committee level, [and] the nation's fate is held in their hands. Had [these cadres] not exerted themselves to their utmost ability and skill in the completion of their tasks, the workers, peasants, and students would have reasons to disapprove of them. We have to be on our guard against officialdom and the formation of an aristocratic class whose interest deviates from that of the people. The masses have the right to dismiss and replace those [cadres] whose officialdom is problematic, who always do not solve the difficulties of the people but rather scold and suppress them."[47] Notably, although both Liu Shaoqi and Chairman Mao advocated political measures taking aim at intraparty bureaucratism, the former's ideas largely concerned party discipline and systemic improvements, while the latter envisaged corrective action taken by the masses in the form of strikes; once cadre bureaucratism had been decisively identified by protests, it was acceptable to appeal directly to the masses and to use large-scale violence against the party.

However seriously or closely Mao formulated his idea of big democracy as a solution to inner-party problems, in the Chairman's overall assessment of the domestic situation in the immediate aftermath of Hungary, *"xiaominzhu"* (small democracy), that is, the traditional party rectification (i.e., thought reform) strategy, was good enough to deal with current problems. On the one hand, Mao understood big democracy as a measure more suitable for power struggles against longstanding class enemies or in the event of a domestic emergency (as the later Cultural Revolution against inner-party capitalist enemies represented by Liu Shaoqi). At this point in late 1956, the Chairman still demonstrated a willingness to adopt peaceful and persuasive methods in the correction of mistakes, seeking to convene a united front, which as he understood it might best facili-

---

advocated by them [Li and Wang] are in no sense different from taking to the streets." See Li, "Gong'an," 49; Wang Qixing, "Wang Fei, Li Shenzhi," 27.

47. Pang and Jin, *Maozhuan*, 611.

tate his grand vision of social and economic development. His session talk could thus declare: "From now on, all problems among the people and inside the party are to be solved by means of rectification, by means of criticism and self-criticism, and not by force."[48] On the other hand, Mao saw the ideas of Western democratic reforms expressed by the leading journalists "not merely [as] problems among a few people, but [as] a wave of thought" that should be corrected now rather than later.[49] With these words, Mao announced a rectification campaign to deal with subjectivism in thinking, sectarianism in organization, and bureaucracy in working style to commence the following year, that is to say, in 1957.[50] Mao then interpreted the Hungarian riots as demanding urgent full-scale rectification within the party. Of his trio of evils to be overcome, the subjectivism bespoken by politically and ideologically incorrect thoughts inside the party was at the top of the list, with the Chairman's definition of objective and subjective in party orthodoxy being flexible or just opportunistic enough to respond to different practical situations.

In the following weeks, although Mao and his colleagues were preoccupied with fraying of the Eastern Bloc (as discussed in Chapter 3), the Chairman seems not to have taken his eye off developing issues at home. In *More on the Historical Lessons of the Proletarian Dictatorship*, published in December 1956, Mao expressed a thesis on two types of contradictions within established socialism: first, a

---

48. For Mao's session talk, see Pang and Jin, *Maozhuan*, 605, 612–13.

49. After the plenum, the Chairman told Wu Lengxi "not to criticize them (Wang and Li), they are good comrades." This statement, however, was balanced by his assessment that the opinions expressed by Wang and Li represented a whole tendency that would need to be denounced. Li Shenzhi, "Mao zhuxi shi shenme shihou jueding yinshe chudong de [When did Mao decide to draw a snake out of its hole?]" in Han Niu and Deng Jiuping, eds., *Liuyuexue: Jiyizhong de fanyoupai yundong* [Snow in June: Remembering the Anti-Rightist Campaign] (Beijing: Jingjiribao, 1998), 124–25; see also Li Shenzhi, "Gong'an," 47–49; Wang Qixing, "Wang Fei, Li Shenzhi," 27–29.

50. The original text is from Mao's speaking notes for the session of 15 November 1956. Since most of the resources quoted in *Maozhuan* are from the Beijing central archives, very few people are permitted to read and study these materials, meaning much trust has to be placed in their interpretation. For Mao's session talk, see Pang and Jin, *Maozhuan*, 605, 612–13.

set of contradictions between "us" and "enemies" based on the inevitable persistence of class differences after the success of the revolution, and second, further contradictions within the ranks of the people. With his thinking bearing directly on both international and domestic realities, the Chairman made it clear that any solution to contradictions within the people should be "subordinate to overarching interests in the struggle against the enemy," not least because of his recognition that "a certain contradiction among the people can gradually come to take on the character of an antagonism," a view that from mid-1957 on would set China on a path of continual self-criticism and revolution.[51] The theme of continuing contradictions in socialist society had already been identified as potentially throwing up obstacles to Chinese socialism before the Hungarian crisis, but Mao's view of the possibility of intractability of these contradictions was sharpened in late 1956 by a new perception that, unchecked, they could incite popular revolt.

It is noteworthy that the editorial to the *Historical Lessons* included a special paragraph on the correct understanding of "socialist democracy." Although admitting that "a broad basis of democracy" was needed to cement a socialist political system, the editorial however pointed out that "socialist democracy should in no way be pitted against the dictatorship of the proletariat; nor should it be confused with bourgeois democracy." Using the communist intellectuals' reaction to the Hungarian events as a case in point, it further stated that setting up a representative democracy in the absence of a dictatorship of the proletariat (the party's leadership, to be more specific) ran the risk of directly countering socialism: "Some people, however, do not see things that way. Their reaction to events in Hungary has revealed this most clearly. . . . Communist intellectuals in some countries . . . came out with declarations that

---

51. *RMRB* Editorial Department, ed., "Zailun wuchanjieji zhuanzheng de lishi jingyan" [More discussion on the historical lessons of the proletarian dictatorship], written according to the discussions of the CCP Central Committee's expanded session, *Xinhua banyuekan* [New China semimonthly], 2 (1957): 1–10; Zhongyang wenxian, *JMW,* 6: 283–85. Also see *Cankao ziliao,* 21: 549–62. "On the historical lessons of the proletarian dictatorship" is in the same volume, 249–54.

the counterrevolution in Hungary was a 'revolution' and with demands that the Worker–Peasant Revolutionary Government extend 'democracy' to the counterrevolutionaries! . . . These people are, in effect, asking for capitalism and opposing socialism, though many among them may themselves be unaware of that fact." While the main target of this analysis was Communist intellectuals in Hungary, the Chairman's criticism of "some Communist intellectuals'" illusion about capitalist democracy in his 15 November closing remark found domestic implications for the highlighting of internal dissenters as well.[52]

The Hungarian events presented Mao with a frightening version of the possible mutation of contradiction from an evolving, dialectically generative antagonism between different classes to a form of outright conflict between the people and their imperialist foe. As early as the start of 1957, Mao noticed the role of the Petőfi circle in challenging the legitimacy of the Hungarian government, which to some extent may have reawakened his suspicion of intellectuals' loyalty.[53] Therefore, in the meeting of provincial-level secretaries held on 18 January 1957, the Chairman gave the question of recent ideological trends among different groups of people the highest priority. Noting that some places had openly solicited a "Hungarian Revolution," Mao also advertised his cognizance of "several strange discussions among professors, saying things like 'we can't get on with this Communist party,' 'Communism is no good,' etc." These intellectuals "thought that they were not permit-

---

52. In his late March speech to the Shanghai cadres on his HF policy, Mao was asked by some cadres, "What's to be done if there is poison [in the HF campaign]?" Mao replied: "Speaking of poisonous things, there is an article titled 'More on the Historical Lessons of the Proletarian Dictatorship.' . . . In this article there is a passage that says that under democratic centralism . . . criticism 'should be made only for the purpose of consolidating [the center] and strengthening the leadership of the party.' This is correct and very well said. You should discuss this article with the democratic personages." MacFarquhar et al., *The Secret Speeches*, 338–39.

53. Mao mentioned the role of the Petőfi circle in organizing the student strikes in Hungary in his speech delivered on 27 February 1957. See his speaking note "On the Correct Handling of Contradictions among the People" in MacFarquhar et al., *The Secret Speeches*, 144.

ted to state their view before, but when the Hundred Schools Contending [policy] came out, they began to vent these [bad] words." Again, Mao chided the Communist intellectuals who had wavered politically since Khrushchev's denunciation of Stalin while expressing enthusiasm for October and the Hungarian riots. In Mao's eyes, these party insiders were making mistakes similar to those of the non-Communist professors in their fixation on the European events: "Whatever they say, it's all about Poznan and Hungary; whatever they do, it's just to follow Gomulka's direction: once Gomulka called for 'big democracy,' they also advocated it [in China]."[54] The role of the intellectuals and revisionist Communists as provocateurs in the Polish and Hungarian upheavals warned Mao against the possibility that similar groups at home would seek to take advantage of international tensions and the domestic détente in questioning the legitimacy of the Communist regime.

As a result of this political concern, Mao thus emphasized the need to get the party well prepared to deal with domestic small-scale riots, calling for a continuous ideological remolding of intellectuals and democratic members in the process of the HF campaign. The intellectuals and democratic outsiders were blamed by Mao in inner-circle meeting as sowing confusion on the question of "democratic political reform" and the "CCP's policy of eliminating counterrevolutionaries." Summarizing events at home and across the Communist camp, the Chairman concluded that "last year was a year of many troubles; internationally, it was Khrushchev and Gomulka who carried on agitation; internally, it was a period of vehement socialist transformation. Now is still a period of trouble with all kinds of thoughts emerging or being exposed."[55] It was within this context that Mao again asserted the necessity to press on with the HF policy. But his emphasis shifted from positive participation of the intelligentsia in further domestic economic and scientific development to the utility of the policy in strengthening the power of

---

54. Mao Zedong, *Mao Zedong xuanji*, 5: 330–62; Pang and Jin, *Maozhuan*, 615.
55. Zhongyang wenxian, *MWJ*, 7: 198; Mao Zedong, *Mao Zedong xuanji*, 5: 330–62.

party artists, writers, commentators, and professors in their cultural struggle against the "harmful views" or "poisonous weeds" (*ducao*), in Mao's words, that needed to be cut down on a year-by-year basis. In this way the Chairman wanted to make sure that his relaxation rule would not get out of hand.[56]

Nonetheless, the Chairman's response to the events of October and November 1956 at this point (at least not immediately) was that intellectuals in general had to be left out of any process of moving toward a rapid socialist construction. As Mao saw it, years of class struggle and intellectual reeducation has reshaped the intellectuals into what the party termed "middle forces," namely, people who without necessarily subscribing in full to the CCP's philosophy had gradually separated from their class origin. These forces should be placated and in the long run assimilated so that the next phase of socialist construction could tap their knowledge and expertise.[57] Furthermore, as Mao said with some confidence in the meeting, since Chinese policies in the rural and urban areas were all correct, "big riots like those that took place in Hungary won't happen in China. Perhaps only a few will make a fuss here and there and advocate big democracy." On the question of how to deal with a small group of diehard bad elements and their poisonous views, the Chairman told his colleagues not to be afraid of the words "big democracy," or of political challenges from suspect individuals who sooner or later would reveal their hand. After all, "If there is anyone who wants to use big democracy of whatever form to oppose the Communist system, to overthrow the leadership of the Communist party, we should exercise the dictatorship of the proletariat on him."[58] Holding on firmly to ultimate power, Mao could afford to be optimistic with respect to the political situation domestically, inti-

---

56. Zhongyang wenxian, *MWJ*, 7: 195–96; Pang and Jin, *Maozhuan*, 614–16; Teiwes, *Politics and Purges*, 182; see also Mao Zedong, *Mao Zedong xuanji*, 5: 330–62.
57. Benjamin Schwartz, "Thoughts on the Late Mao—Between Total Redemption and Utter Frustration," in MacFarquhar et al., *The Secret Speeches*, 30.
58. Mao Zedong, *Mao Zedong xuanji*, 5: 330–62; Pang and Jin, *Maozhuan*, 615.

mating all the while that repression would be the penalty for anyone in the center party who dared test the limits of his political tolerance.

Thinking more specifically about Mao's policies toward the intellectuals and nonaligned democrats as social fractions, in the immediate post-Hungary aftermath the Chairman still considered it better to be lenient, relying on rectifications behind closed doors to remold the mentality of party outsiders and those of the wrong class origin. In November 1956, the China Democratic National Construction Association (CDNCA), largely a businessmen's party, held the second plenary session of the first central committee. This was the association's first central meeting after the period of socialist reform (the period of the Chinese socialist reform ran from 1949 to 1956).[59] Huang Yanpei, chairman of the CDNCA, wrote to inform the Chairman of the "political progress" of his party members: the members of CDNCA had heatedly debated issues such as the "two-sidedness" of the national capitalist class (that is, the possible contribution it could make to socialism juxtaposed to its innately counterrevolutionary character), the proper role and position of the capitalist class in society, and the relationship between workers and capitalists.[60] Huang reported that CDNCA members had entered

---

59. Founded in December 1945, the CDNCA is mainly composed of patriotic national business entrepreneurs and intellectuals from business circles. The major eight democratic parties have a varied history, but all date back to the pre-Communist period when they made up a small and disunited "third force." The most important one was, and remains, the (China) Democratic League (CDL), of which Luo Long-ji and Zhang Bojun were deputy chairmen at the time of the launch of the rectification campaign. They were both identified as leading rightists in late 1957.

60. Huang Yanpei (1878–1965), born in Jiangsu, founded the League of Chinese Democratic Political Groups (LCDPG) in March 1941 and also led the CDNCA; the league adopted its current name—the China Democratic League (CDL)—in September 1944. After the establishment of the PRC in 1949, Huang was elected vice premier of the Government Administration Council and vice head of the National People's Congress, posts he held for many years. For Huang's involvement in the educational movement in the early twentieth century, see Peter Schwintzer, "Education to Save the Nation: Huang Yanpei and the Educational Reform Movement in Early Twentieth-Century China" (PhD diss., University of Washington, 1992).

fully into Communist methods of self-criticism, reeducating themselves into a unanimous conformity with the central party's line. Expressing delight with the outcome of the session, on 4 December Mao wrote back to Huang, congratulating him "on your successful sessions. It is really great news that criticism and self-criticism, as it gradually refines itself, was taken up in your group, among businessmen nationwide and among high-level intellectuals."[61] While there is nothing evidently disingenuous in either Mao's or Huang's praise of self-criticism, it seems likely that after Hungary, as a battle-scarred politician and rigid Marxist–Leninist, Mao would not allow his attention to be distracted from class differences and of the possible persistence, even after the triumph of socialism, of class struggle.

Chairman Mao's views on class relations as expressed in his letter to Huang in fact reflected his cautious reevaluation of the ideological and political conditions in socialist China post-Hungary: "Society is full of contradictions, even in the socialist and communist world; only the essence of the contradictions and [the names of] the class societies vary. As long as there is contradiction, it has to be revealed and resolved." There are two methods, Mao said, by which contradictions could be dealt with: "One is to come to grips with the foe [which here refers to spies and saboteurs] and the other is to work with the people (including the problems within the party and those between parties). The first means uses suppression and the second, persuasion, that is, some form of criticism." It is clear from Mao's letter that he foresaw the persistence of class difference in Chinese society in people's "ideological perspectives for a very long time. At the same time, a small number of secret agents will be with us for a long time too." With these words the seasoned revolutionary politician expressed his concern that a long-term ideological indoctrination of people both within and outside the party would be necessary to buttress CCP rule. Partly to reassure non–party members and partly to reveal his political intentions, he made

---

61. For the published version, see Zhongyang wenxian, *MWJ* 7: 164–66. For two pages of the handwritten version, see Pang and Jin, *Maozhuan*, 613.

it clear to Huang that he wanted to unite the majority "through criticism and self-criticism." He did not state his more ulterior purpose in fostering self-critical sessions, that is, to induce "a small number of enemies" (or "poisonous weeds") to show their hands and effectively offer themselves up as candidates for elimination.[62]

After all, the message Mao drew from the Hungarian events was that rule through repression remained a last resort and that the Communist party would be ineffective if it sought to deal with popular riots only through relying on rigid policies and coercion. As Mao understood it, the main reason for Rákosi's being forced out of office lay in the Hungarian Communist leader's ineptitude in "the art of governing," in failing to divide the rioters and manage the situation peacefully. To avoid Rákosi's blunders, Mao told his colleagues that "both inside and outside the party, all sorts of discussions, strange words, or contradictions are better off disclosed. [We] should find out the contradictions and then resolve them."[63] Following the logic of this Maoist tactic of "temporary indulgence for better investigation and control," the central party should in the first place leave those people either dissatisifed with or critical of the CCP's policies at large, the better to understand their purposes and intentions. Far from waiting passively for the popular discontent or dissidence to accumulate and turn into a real threat to the regime, as in Rákosi's case, Mao deliberately let people air their views, appearing to let down his vigilance as part of a concealed scheme to "divide, steer, and educate" the majority. Mao told his cadres to accept opinions that sincerely pointed out shortcomings in the work, which they should revise accordingly; when they were critiqued on political grounds, however, they should denounce their attackers. Meanwhile, in regard to "a very small section who intend to cause counterrevolutionary riots like those in Hungary," Mao's attitude was firm: "[We] must exercise the dictatorship of the proletariat on them." In laying down these guidelines, however, Mao made avail-

---

62. Ibid.
63. Mao Zedong, *Mao Zedong xuanji*, 5: 330–62; Pang and Jin, *Maozhuan*, 615.

able no precise criteria by which to assess the character of outsiders' criticisms; furthermore, no clear boundaries were laid down limiting the involvement of non–party members in political participation and the review of policy. Both these vague areas would leave the cadres in a position where they could not reliably execute Mao's wishes, meaning that often they construed policy with confusion, passively waiting for more specific policies from the center.

In this period from November 1956 to January 1957, Mao was engaged in a continual process of redefining his policy line toward both cadres and the non-Communists, seeking to balance apparently irreconcilable elements (or to square intellectual contradictions) to meet very immediate preoccupations. Mao's positions were highly capricious during this period, though in retrospect we can identify certain persistent preoccupations. First of all, Mao in fact brooked no doubt as to the essential correctness of his plans for socialist state-building in both the political and economic realms. In consequence, any criticism that the Chairman perceived as tainting his core ideology was considered intolerable and in need of rectification at some stage. Second, and very much relatedly, while the Chairman had enthusiastically advocated genuine Chinese socialist methods, endorsing and supporting ideological and political relaxation throughout 1956, he never displayed an awareness of the real problems in the Chinese socialist system, making him blind to the need for any essential political or economic reforms. In this sense, the Chairman learned little from Poland and Hungary vis-à-vis the value of Chinese socialism as such or the feasibility of his revolutionary vision. Moreover, despite the political thaw promised by the Chairman himself in early 1956, his long-lasting suspicion of intellectuals and non-Communists did not retreat overnight, especially when these people began to be more vocal with dissenting (or pluralistic) views with regard to CCP policies following the outbreak of the Hungarian Revolution. Notwithstanding this suspicion, there is little evidence to suggest that the Chairman intended to reverse the previous relaxation of controls by undertaking repressive measures immediately after Hungary. In a slightly different context, though, spurred by the increased theoretical and ideological uncertainty in the Communist Bloc, Mao seems to have backed off his emphasis on pluralism in developing policy as expressed by the early months of his HF campaign, focusing more on using the softer methods of the HF campaign to effect the ideological reorientation of unaligned classes toward socialism. Within only two months of this campaign's onset, in fact, the Chairman began to orchestrate the HF liberalization together with the Rectification Campaign, inviting outsiders to criticize party errors, in the teeth of entrenched opposition from his own party. Was this a genuine attempt to broaden the CCP's skills and intellectual base or a ruse to draw out residual class opposition? This question must preoccupy us in the following examination of how Mao conducted his rectification policies.

INVITING THE DEMOCRATIC PARTIES TO PARTICIPATE IN RECTIFICATION

In the wake of the Hungarian revolt, Mao's warning against revisionism on the part of the Chinese had provided a good opportunity for the cadres to express publicly their suspicion of the HF, a view that found support with many local cadres. Perhaps unsurprisingly, Mao's HF policy and innovation in mutual supervision, letting party outsiders (bourgeois intellectuals and members of the so-called democratic parties) criticize the highly power-centralized CCP from May 1956, did not receive a warm response from within the party: after years of class struggle and the dismantling of the old state during the transformation phase, party cadres would undoubtedly feel bitter to be subject to the criticisms of those social groups they had defeated and, in ideological terms, surpassed.[64] The center's new move especially stimulated the middle-ranking officials in propaganda and education departments to air their views against

---

64. Gansu Provincial Party Committee's report on cadres' responses to HF policy, Jilin Provincial Archives (JPA), 1-13/1-1957.72, 3-5; on reports from Heilongjiang, Shanxi, Zhejiang, see JPA, 1-13/1-1957.72, 19–21, 10–12, 18–21.

previous liberal policies toward the intellectuals.[65] On 7 January 1957, Chen Qitong, deputy head of the People's Liberation Army (PLA) propaganda department, Ma Hanbing, and two other cadres published an article in the *RMRB* critical of the trend of satirizing intraparty machinations and bureaucracy in a vein of imaginative literature that had been allowed to flourish in the period of "blooming and contending." The authors feared this tendency in literature would lead to an erosion of political values as comic squibs came to be valued more highly than socialist dogma. The authors warned that "If we do not take action . . . politics will be at an end."[66] In fact, only a few flowers had bloomed on political soil under Mao's HF policy in 1956. Wang Meng's short story, "Young Newcomer to the Organization Department," was perhaps the most famous and bold in its cynical exposé of bureaucratic problems at the center of the party. Published in September 1956, the story was about an idealistic youth who struggled against the entrenched bureaucracy in a party district office in Beijing.[67] In their article, Chen and the other three cadres took Wang Meng's style of writing to task; the authors more generally feared that, in a more relaxed political atmosphere, their ideological and political control of society in general would come under threat.[68]

Besides propaganda departments in the military sector, many local party committees only grudgingly fell in with the new line. The Beijing municipal party committee, to take a notable example, submitted in response to "On the Correct Handling of Contradic-

---

65. MacFarquhar et al., *The Secret Speeches*, 7, 10–12, 49–53, 44–45.
66. *RMRB*, 7 January 1957. Summary of this article cited in Teiwes, *Politics and Purges*, 183.
67. Merle Goldman, "Mao's Obsession with the Political Role of Literature and the Intellectuals," in MacFarquhar et al., *The Secret Speeches*, 44; for party cadres' attacks on this novel and the author, 44–46, 51.
68. Pang and Jin, *Maozhuan*, 615, confirm that "ever since the Chairman had tabled the 'Hundred Flowers Blooming, Hundred Schools Contending' thesis, reservation and even a head of opposition had been building up toward this HF policy." For an analysis on the CCP cadres' rural orientation and revolutionary experiences, and their effects on the process of nation-building, see Lee Hongyung, *From Revolutionary Cadres to Party Technocrats in Socialist China* (Berkeley: University of California Press, 1991), 43–56.

tions among the People" that "until Chairman Mao's report in the [twelfth enlarged] Supreme State Council Conference (held on 27 February 1957), we [the Beijing municipal party committee] have not held a systematic discussion on how to carry out the Hundred Flowers coexistence and mutual supervision policies since these were raised by the Central Party... many comrades held different views or did not completely agree with these [HF and coexistence and mutual supervision] policies, and a considerable number of comrades, including some principals of the Beijing municipal party committee, were in agreement with the views raised by the article by Chen Qitong and others."[69] There is much other evidence of foot-dragging among the cadres.[70] Taking stock of this ill-feeling and inertia within the party, the central party put off the formal launch of the rectification campaign until 1958, deciding that in 1957 "the Central Committee must hold a session [and] issue a directive" preparing the cadres and people for change.[71] Notwithstanding the

---

69. This was a central party document circulated to the provincial party committees. The Beijing party committee's response (7 May 1957), submitted to the central committee of the CCP and marked "Chen No. 16," may be found in *HPA*, 141-1-850, 72–76. In a meeting summoned by Mao in Hangzhou in early April to investigate the local cadres' response to his new policy, the chief propagandists for Shanghai, Jiangsu, Anhui, Zhejiang, and Fujian all reported various levels of uncertainty over and passive resistance to the HF campaign among middle-ranking party members. See the record of this meeting in Pang and Jin, *Maozhuan*, 652–59.

70. "The Beijing Party Committee's Response, Submitted to the Central Committee of the CCP (7 May 1957)," "Transmitting a Version of the Reports on the Correct Handling of Contradictions among the People, Hubei Provincial Party Committee (8 May 1957), Sichuan, Guangdong, Gansu Provincial Party Committee (15 May 1957)," *HPA*, 141-1-850, 72–76, 77–83, 84–99. Kang Sheng noted "three factions in relation to this (rectification) policy of the Central Committee: a Left faction represented by Chen Qitong and Ma Hanbing, suspecting the policy is bad and believing it should stopped at once; a Right faction, obsessed with the policy and finding it advantageous to stir things up in the newspapers; and a middle, who recognize the policy as good but are not certain in their minds and fear difficulties... [for instance,] the army cadres are confused about this policy." MacFarquhar et al., *The Secret Speeches*, 264.

71. An article in the 16 January issue of *Zhongguo qingnian* [Chinese Youth] revealed that the rectification campaign would get under way in 1958 (rather than 1957 as Mao announced in mid-November); cited in MacFarquhar, *Origins of the Cultural Revolution: Contradictions*, 1: 76. Later in the talk with literary and art circles held on 8 March 1957, the Chairman announced the de facto postponed

cadres' opposition, though, Mao's later complaints that his attempts at reform in the HF were dogged by bureaucratic obstruction should be treated with caution. One crucial but usually ignored factor for this loss of a mass basis to the HF, in Mao's own phrase, is the slowness of the central and local officials' response to the coexistence and mutual supervision initiatives formulated in the early months of 1956. This dilatoriness largely came about as a result of the absence of any systematic directive from the center—that is, from Mao—regarding the execution of his liberal ideas, which perhaps indicated the emperor's own half-heartedness in drawing up a specific action plan over the period. Within the more restrictive post-Budapest atmosphere, meanwhile, many cadres may have felt emboldened to attack external critics, thinking they were in tune with the Chairman's antirevisionist line.[72]

In the light of the party cadres' open criticism of Wang Meng's novel and their apparent reluctance to submit themselves to scrutiny, the misgivings of many nonparty outsiders over the consistency of the central party's decompression become understandable. And to a significant extent, the intellectuals were also full of worries about the real intention of this HF policy. "The Intellectuals' Early Spring Weather," the title of an article written by the noted sociologist Fei Xiaotong, vividly demonstrates the prevailing mood among the Chinese intellectuals. On the one hand, when "early spring came to the Earth," that is, when the political atmosphere began to thaw in the spring of 1956, the intellectuals began to hope for a period of greater leeway and freedom than they had enjoyed during Communism's very early consolidation phase. But on the other, the relaxation resembled the easily changing weather of early spring, as Fei indicated in his article, and could hardly be trusted as a genuine

---

schedule of rectification: "Within the party [we] have proposed criticizing subjectivism (the focus is on doctrinairism), bureaucratism, [and] sectarianism. [The policy] has not been implemented yet. The Central Committee must hold a session [and] issue a directive, [ordering] preparation this year [and] beginning [the campaign] next year." Pang and Jin, *Maozhuan*, 631; for an English version, see MacFarquhar et al., *The Secret Speeches*, 220.

72. HPA, 141-1-850, 72–76, 77–83, 84–99.

opportunity to begin to voice distinct nonorthodox positions. Without proper political assurance from those in power, as attested by Fei's article, the Chinese intellectuals dared not "bloom," although most were strongly disposed to participate in various debates and discussions.[73]

Dissent inside the party over the HF campaign, together with doubts over the CCP's sincerity over relaxation, put the Chairman in the position of having to defend his own policy. With certain ideas formulated in his mind, Mao summoned several small-scale talks within the central party propaganda circle (such as the central party's newspaper agencies, writers' associations under the party's auspices, youth leagues) to explain his positions as a prelude to convincing the cadres to mend their ways.[74] The Chairman began with the question on how to evaluate Wang Meng's novel in revealing the institutional bureaucratism of the central party, enunciating the line that "the view that says that the shortcomings of the Communist party can't be exposed is incorrect." Although Wang's story is marred by a "bourgeois ideology" and the author himself "does not have enough experience," Wang himself "represents a newborn force" whose courage in speaking up when others were silent is wholly praiseworthy. Once again, however, the novel "has its one-sidedness," in failing to balance negative characters with positive, with the result that "both praise and denunciation of Wang Meng's writing are one-sided in nature."[75] On the matter of Chen's article

---

73. *RMRB*, 24 March 1957; Fei's article was written before Mao had delivered his famous "On Correctly Handling Contradictions" speech on 27 February. See Pang and Jin, *Maozhuan*, 616; for Fei's article (partial) in English with analysis, see MacFarquhar, *Origins of the Cultural Revolution*, 1: 24

74. The first was the January talks, and the second the talk at Yiniantang held on 16 February, before the Supreme State Conference, when the Chairman summoned a small-scale supreme state conference of thirty-seven participants. All these talks homed in on recent political and ideological trends and on Mao's ideas about how to identify and deal with contradictions among the people. Pang and Jin, *Maozhuan*, 617; for an English version of "Talk at Yiniantang," see MacFarquhar et al., *The Secret Speeches*, 113–28.

75. Mao's original words are: "He [Wang] should be protected. The articles criticizing him have not set out to do that." MacFarquhar et al., *The Secret Speeches*, 116. A complete reading of Mao's analysis of Wang's case strongly suggests that the

and the cadres' criticisms against Wang, the Chairman expressed the judicious position that "many comrades have not actually understood the policy on how to handle mistakes among the people."[76] Mao's comments on Wang's story imply that the Chairman thought, given the broad correctness of party policy, that there was some advantage to fostering a literary mode of critiquing the party, if only to sugarcoat CCP propaganda.[77] Wang Meng's one-sided fictional criticism did not quite meet the bill of the good and persuasive articles that the party should choose to encourage; it was too one-sided and lacked positive exemplars of party action. Nevertheless, though, to a large degree, Mao was prepared to countenance Wang's satire, not least because its attack on bureaucratism in the capital coincided with Mao's immediate political purposes. The young man's story came out at a time when Mao needed a typical case to defend his HF policy and clarify his intentions.[78]

Clearly for Mao, many cadres' opposition to blooming and contending was caused by "fear [of] a Hungarian incident."[79] In Mao's view, however, "the Hungarian incident was not necessarily bad" insofar as it pointed out the lesson for him that one-sided propa-

---

Chairman's emphasis on protection of young people like Wang was based on his belief in the possibility of remolding their thoughts via persuasive means.

76. Here Mao referred to Chen Qitong's article and other cadres' criticisms against Wang Meng's novel, quoted from "Speech Note of Mao in the Meeting with Heads of Central Party Newspapers and Journals, Writers' Associations, Academy of Sciences and Youth Leagues, 16 February 1957," Pang and Jin, *Maozhuan*, 617; for the English version, see MacFarquhar et al., *The Secret Speeches*, 116.

77. For Mao's complaining about his lack of mass basis, see MacFarquhar et al., *The Secret Speeches*, 364.

78. Mao had left an ambiguous comment on Wang: "Wang Meng has a dual nature: One is his good points; the other is his shortcomings." He then said that Yao Wenyuan's article in the Wenhui bao "is very good," as Yao's argument of "dogmatism and principle" "is very convincing"; MacFarquhar et al., *The Secret Speeches*, 123. Yao Wenyuan was a young Shanghai literary critic who later became a leading polemicist of the Gang of Four, and whose attack on the historian Wu Han initiated the Cultural Revolution. This article may have first brought him to Mao's attention; MacFarquhar et al., *The Secret Speeches*, 123 ft. 28.

79. As commented on by cadres from Shanxi province, "80% of the college students are from families of exploitation, they would become cadres after graduation. How can Chairman Mao not learn lessons from the Hungarian crisis [and let the party outsiders criticize us]?" JPA, 1-13/1-1957.72, 19–21.

ganda promoting party polices or suppressing dissidents risked estranging the masses and provoking national disturbance. The Chairman therefore concluded it was useless continually to call on dogmatism to criticize others, especially since noncoercive persuasive measures stood a better chance of "help[ing] others refashion their views so that we can achieve true unity."[80] This line of thought guided Mao's critique of Chen's article as unconvincing and dogmatic in seeming to say that "since the adoption of the Hundred Flowers policy, everything has gone wrong." In other words, Mao took exception to the article for casting doubt on his policy. Even so, Chen Qitong and his fellow writers were "loyal and devoted to the Party and the people," an appraisal in effect confirming many cadres' judgment that dogmatism was better and safer than rightism.[81] A careful reading of Mao's words to the heads of central party newspapers, writers' associations, the science academy and youth leagues on 16 February suggests that the Maoist HF experiment represented little more than a tactic to appease immediate social dissatisfactions, remaking the highly centralized and uniform party indoctrination pattern into a more diversified and persuasive one so as to unite the broadest forces possible for future economic and social construction without sacrificing the long-term Communist goal of ideological purity.

There is little evidence that Chairman Mao had anticipated a significant degree of resistance within the party to his HF policy in the post–Hungarian Revolution atmosphere. From the commanding height of his ruling position, Mao thought his persuasive strategy was designed to set the one-party state on a firmer and more

---

80. MacFarquhar et al., *The Secret Speeches*, 117.
81. In Mao's original words, these four writers were *"zhongxin genggeng, weidang weimin"*; see Wang Ruoshui, *Zhihui de tongku* [The bitterness of intellect] (Sanlian shudian: Hong Kong, 1989), 319–27; Mao said in the 6 March meeting: "I have said on several occasions in supplementary remarks that 'these few comrades are loyal and devoted to the party, that [they] are committed to the party's undertakings; but [their] article cannot [serve as] advice.' This [last qualifying] phrase was cut out [when transmitted down]." MacFarquhar et al., *The Secret Speeches*, 210.

unified political basis than achieved by the Soviets and Communists in Eastern European states. For the party officials in the central propaganda apparatus and cadres in the provinces, however, this Maoist relaxation for better control was a paradox, reasonable-sounding in theory but impossible in practice, especially when the Chairman was reluctant to set up specific principles, leaving officials to be tormented by unlimited criticisms from previous suspect groups. In the absence of specific HF policies, the cadres, then, went on the offensive in rejecting the policy. Playing one force off against another in his typical style, the Chairman found it opportune to encourage party outsiders to participate in politics more broadly, goading the cadres to accept his line.[82]

Although the Chairman did not even mention mutual supervision in his call for rectification in the late November 1956 central party meeting, he pushed the blooming and contending policy much further than one could have expected in the first half of March after the enlarged session of the Eleventh Supreme State Conference and the CCP's national propaganda meeting. In the first conference, Mao delivered a lengthy speech "On the Correct Handling of Contradictions among the People" on 27 February to 1,800 leading Communists and non-Communists, in which he elaborated in detail his views as they had been developing over the past year concerning the two types of conflicts in China's new society. Notably, the Chairman spoke in a reflective, even philosophical vein, in touching on the need for HF and "mutual supervision" policies, reminding his audience that Marxism had come of age in engaging with capitalist ideas to which it was a "newborn force," while they simply denoted "old objects, old things."[83] If we look at Mao's original speech notes for this talk, there seems to be no difference in principle between this

---

82. Mao was more than able to manipulate court politics in the context of the socialist transition policy from 1951 to 1953; one only need consider the Gao-Rao affair and the dramatic small leap forward from late 1955. For my broad take on the formation of Mao's socialist China, see Chapter 1; for an analysis of Mao's changed position in pushing for blooming and contending, see Teiwes, *Politics and Purges*, 183–84.

83. MacFarquhar et al., *The Secret Speeches*, 162–74.

passage and Mao's views as outlined in his previous small-scale talks. Yet his speech has been described as "rambling and full of bizarre associations of ideas," which makes it difficult for readers (let alone audience participants) to grasp its essentials.[84] However, records suggest that most of the non-Communists who either attended the meeting or listened to the speech on record were struck by the Chairman's humor and frankness, reporting feeling inspired or rejuvenated at such a great show of communication between the party leader and his followers.[85] These favorable responses from the non-Communists encouraged Mao to convene a national propaganda meeting from 6–13 March to further promote his "contradictions among the people" doctrine.[86]

To make sure that his message reached the targeted groups, the Chairman broke the rule of closed-door party meetings and invited more than 160 non-Communist scientists, literary and artistic intellectuals, professors, journalists, and publishers; in all, one-fifth of the total number of participants to take part in inner-party discussions. All the participants were able to listen to a recording of Mao's "contradictions" speech before being summoned by the Chairman separately for group meetings. During these free discussions, the Chairman generally listened to the issues raised by others and put himself at their disposal in answering queries about the HF policy and rectification. Mao devoted considerable attention to problems such as teaching in schools and intellectuals' ongoing fear of party trickery in developing his blooming and contending policy. Mao had two main intentions in opening up these policy sessions to outsiders: he wanted further to propagandize the blooming and contending policy, and more importantly, to investigate non-Communists' views of the party's work, especially over

---

84. See Benjamin Schwartz's comments on the style of Mao's speeches in "Thoughts on the Late Mao," 20–21. This speech, in fact, was recorded and delivered to a wider range of non-Communists during the national propaganda meeting held in early March; Pang and Jin, *Maozhuan*, 629–39.
85. Zhang Yihe, *Wangshi bingbu ruyan* [The past is not like smoke] (Beijing: Renmin, 2004), 37; MacFarquhar, *Origins of the Cultural Revolution*, 1: 86–87.
86. Pang and Jin, *Maozhuan*, 629–40.

the HF, which he imagined might win over significant numbers to his project.[87]

Having collected enough information on the thoughts of intellectuals, Mao made a closing speech on 12 March 1957, taking pains to ease any post-Hungary anxieties among this group. Kicking off with an overall assessment of the situation in the spring of 1957, Mao asserted that in China: "We find ourselves in a period of social transition, in which the old system has been overthrown and a new socialist one has been established. . . . But we currently still haven't shifted to a consolidation phase, and I think it may still take five years to consolidate this socialism in our country before we see a future, in which we build our country into an industrialized one on the basis of this socialist system." This judgment, moreover, reflected a view that the phase of "*large-scale* (italics added) class struggle had concluded and the main problem we have to deal with now is contradictions among the people." These words can be taken as conveying the reassurance that class had been removed from the top of the CCP's political agenda and that "problems concerning the bourgeois class" would hereafter be downgraded to "contradictions among the people." Furthermore, Mao declared that "the five million intellectuals are our nation's property" and the "people's teachers," redesignating these as "workers" and putting their intellects at the service of the workers and peasants. While this praise was perhaps received as an unexpected favor from the great leader, the nonaligned figures in Mao's audience had reason to withhold their unquestioning allegiance to the HF on the grounds of Mao's insistence on the need to remold intellectuals' ideology and his critique of one-sidedness in the speech, taking issue with the tendency either to embrace or eschew Communism wholesale. At the same time as holding out the prospect for more nuanced ideological commentary, though, Mao restated his view that ultimately there were only two schools, Marxism and capitalism, and that those

---

87. MacFarquhar et al., *The Secret Speeches*, 191–274; also see Pang and Jin, *Maozhuan*, 629–39.

siding with the latter would set themselves up as enemies of the state.[88]

Although Mao had repeatedly warned his veteran cadres against the "weeds" coming up alongside "the fragrant flowers" in inner-party discussions on HF, the tone of the Chairman's speech was distinctly encouraging to outsiders, seeming to testify to Mao's view that blooming would not fundamentally harm his country, nor would the HF precipitate another Hungary.[89] Mao had reason to suppose that most counterrevolutionary elements had been eliminated in China after the victory of socialism in a way they had not in Poland, Hungary, and Vietnam.[90] Furthermore, as Mao later claimed in an inner-party session, "China is not Hungary; here the Communist party and the People's Government enjoy a high reputation among the people."[91] A further important contributory factor to Mao's sanguine outlook was his evaluation of China's intellectuals. Despite his longstanding distrust, he took the line that since the source of the intellectuals' social power—the landlords, rich peasants, and the bourgeoisie—"have been cut off," this starved the space for a Petőfi Circle to emerge in China.[92] Retaining a strong commitment to his HF experiment, the Chairman thus made his attitude clear: "Should we still 'bloom' or should we 'rein in'? It is a problem

---

88. Pang and Jin, *Maozhuan*, 633–39; this concluding speech is not included in MacFarquahar et al., *The Secret Speeches*. Pang and Jin, *Maozhuan*, provided a summary of Mao's speech, which is good enough for us to grasp the main ideas expressed to the party outsiders. Jian Bozan, a noted Marxist historian, wrote an article commenting on the HF policy published by *RMRB* on 20 April 1957, which represented a section of intellectuals' continuous doubts about the sincerity of the bloom and contend policy even after Mao's contradictions and propaganda conferences. Jian Bozan's comments, as argued by MacFarquhar with evidence, apparently offended Mao and probably led to the Chairman's rush to rectification at summary *Origins of the Cultural Revolution*, 1: 209. Jian's article was translated in part in MacFarquhar, *The Hundred Flowers Campaign* (London: Praeger, 1960), 27–28. For a well-documented historical narrative of the HF campaign, see Shen, *Sikao yu xuanze*, 239–42, 252–60, 275–77.
89. Pang and Jin, *Maozhuan*, 633–39.
90. MacFarquhar et al., *The Secret Speeches*, 299–300, 329.
91. Ibid., 338.
92. Ibid., 336.

of policy. The Center's opinion is we must 'bloom.'"[93] In this speech, Mao announced an incremental start to the rectification campaign in 1957, with "Non-Party people [being invited] to take part on a voluntary basis."[94]

Mao's speech on the continuing social contradictions in Communism made a profound impact on certain groups of non-Communist members of his audience. After hearing Mao, the famous writer and translator Fu Lei (who committed suicide with his wife during the Cultural Revolution) wrote to his son: "Chairman Mao's speech was kind and easy in rhythm and phrase; it was full of humor. [He spoke] no indoctrinatory words, but took care to pause at the right places. I cannot express my feelings just by noting down what he said.... He stressed several times that the fact that contradictions remain among the people is a new problem for the Party. This means that the Party needs to talk with nonparty people. It is good to combine inside and outside elements when studying this problem. [This kind of discussion and study] should be organized annually within the coming three to five years." Fu Lei went on to praise Mao's open-mindedness, saying that such a man as the Chairman would have no difficulties in managing public affairs. In Fu Lei's eyes, the very freedom with which Mao handled Marxist categories (understood as slovenly or incomprehensible by a Western scholar on the basis of reading Mao's speech notes) demonstrated that "his [understanding of] Marxism already reached perfection." Fu took Mao's inconsistencies (or ambiguities) as a deliberate strategy concealing the logic of his view, which proved him to be "the master of art." Fu Lei's reaction to Mao's overtures is not atypical of the politically inexperienced intellectuals' response to the Chairman's late March speech, which seems in many instances too dazzling for them to think closely about what the emperor might actually have meant by any of his words.[95]

---

93. Pang and Jin, *Maozhuan*, 638.
94. Ibid., 635; Zhongyang wenxian, *MWJ*, 7: 190.
95. Fu Lei, *Fu Lei jiashu: Zengbuben* [Family letters of Fulei: Appended version] (Beijing: Sanlian, 1994), 158; Pang and Jin, *Maozhuan*, 639–40. For other

If Mao had stopped at rectification of the party and conducted his blooming and contending policy separately, the PRC's history might have been very different. However, describing the causes of the Hungarian crisis as "a pustule that will burst sooner or later!" the Chairman resolved to eradicate bureaucratism or subjectivism not merely within the inner-party circle but more systematically, by initiating a campaign of rectification through the old method of relaxation and self-correction, which had its roots in the Yan'an era.[96] Though this general approach to organizational management was a staple of the party's conduct of its own evolution, in the fifties Mao wrought a variation on traditional party policy by allowing the nonparty intellectuals and democratic party members to play the role of licensed internal censors, criticizing and supposedly spurring the CCP's reform.[97] On the one hand, the Chairman wanted to brush aside any doubts, especially those from party outsiders, of his ability to mobilize his party for an open-door rectification; on the other, he was averse to allowing disagreements to persist within the party once he made his attitudes clear. As a matter of fact, in April 1957, when Mao was enthusiastically launching the rectification and HF

---

intellectuals' positive reactions to Mao's speech, see *RMRB* 24: 16 March, 25 April; Zhang, *Wangshi*, 37; Xu Zhucheng, *Xu Zhucheng huiyilu* [Xu's memoir] (Beijing: Sanlian, 1998), 265; and his *Qinli 1957* [Experiencing 1957] (Wuhan: Hubei renmin, 2003), 17–18 (Xu was chief editor of non–Communist Party *Wenhui bao* in 1957). For Benjamin Schwartz's comments on the style of Mao's secret speeches, Schwartz, "Thoughts on the Late Mao," 20–21.

96. MacFarquhar et al., *The Secret Speeches*, 281. For a detailed analysis on the origin and tradition of the CCP's rectification doctrine established in the Yan'an era, see Teiwes, *Politics and Purges*, 13–46; for the relationship between the formation of Yan'an rectification doctrine and the process of Mao's rising to the top in the late 1930s to early 1940s, see Gao, *Hongtaiyang*, 81–109, 211–60, 605–46. For CCP documents during the Yan'an rectification period, see Boyd Compton, *Mao's China: Party Reform Documents, 1942–44* (Seattle: University of Washington Press, 1952).

97. MacFarquhar et al., *The Secret Speeches*, 133–38. In Mao's eyes, both democracy and dictatorship were useful means to consolidate his political regime; when and how to use these tools mostly depended on the concrete situation and the current political need. He also emphasized a choice between big democracy (*da minzhu*) and small democracy (*xiao minzhu*). On the original arguments for big and small democracy (*da xiao minzhu*), see Li, *Fengyu*, 105–17. For resemblances between the two campaigns see MacFarquhar, *Origins of the Cultural Revolution*, 1: 169.

campaigns, he himself made an *ex post facto* complaint that a majority of the CCP members were not supportive enough of the campaign—bemoaning the fact that "I have no mass base" among the apparatus he was trying to move. Mao had thus to devote much of his effort to persuading the inner-party members to support his upcoming campaign. After the national propaganda conference, the Chairman toured Tianjin, Jinan, Nanjing, and Shanghai to convene meetings with local party cadres, turning himself, in his own words, into "a wandering lobbyist." Within the short period from 17 to 20 March, Mao made four speeches to local leaders and party members, in which he called on the provincial cadres to participate in his general project of universal emancipation through unity. Interestingly, in his later speech in March, Mao emphasized the positive side of the Hungarian crisis, which he described as educational in the sense that it imparted an urgency to his personal desire to implement his new policy.[98]

While pressing the rectification and big-tent reforms, Mao, however, continued to assure the local cadres that China was different from Hungary and had no plans to deviate from socialism. No Petőfi Circle, that is, no capacity on the part of students and intellectuals to mobilize the people against a weakened socialist government, was possible in China. The intellectuals would be bound to a narrow definition of patriotism and have a crimped freedom of maneuver; democratic party members (who in Mao's mind were largely intellectuals) would *not* be at liberty to question the fundamental themes of socialism. On the problem of winning over intellectuals' hearts and minds to "our" side, Mao conceded that it would take a long time to educate intellectuals of capitalist origins.[99] Further-

---

98. MacFarquhar, *Secret Speeches*, 193, 209, 217, 249, 281, 364. For the Chinese version, see Zhongyang wenxian, *MWJ*, 7: 186, 204, 245, 249, 260, 267.

99. Mao, in fact, also analyzed the situation of intellectuals in China and concluded that those who truly supported Marxism constituted perhaps only 10 percent of all Chinese intellectuals. The wavering centrist faction took up 70 to 80 percent; giving up on the remainder, the party's task was to win the centrists over. MacFarquhar, *Origins of the Cultural Revolution*, 337. Also see Pang and Jin, *Maozhuan*, 644, 649, 655.

more, Mao understood his experiment of a small democracy in China to emerge in an unforced way from national conditions—explaining why he placed so much emphasis on the coordination of the HF with his essentially Chinese scheme of rectification. Properly managed, then, he considered that his steps toward liberalization would forestall, rather than foment, a Hungarian incident in China.[100]

Once Mao had promoted his post-Hungary open-door policy of rectification among the party outsiders, and the local cadres had determined that the policy had to be carried out without hesitation, the touchy side of the Chairman's personality began to manifest itself. Mao was in fact deeply frustrated with *RMRB* for not actively attacking the four PLA writers' article and for failing to publish articles in support of the blooming and contending policy; he singled out Deng Tuo, the head of the *RMRB* news agency, as deliberately opposing his relaxation. The Chairman severely rebuked Deng, explicitly urging the *RMRB* to publicize his new policy in a meeting with the editor and senior journalists in early April, which directly led to the formal launch of open-door rectification in late April.[101] Even if Mao's judgment that Deng harbored reservations about the HF was correct, the Chairman seems to have deliberately overstated the extent and effect of the editor's diffidence. Having for years kept his ear to the ground in the *RMRB*, a classic Communist propaganda organ that institutionalized communications under the direct control of the central party, Deng is unlikely to have misconstrued Mao's actual intentions, most probably just believing that the

---

100. Zhongyang wenxian, *JMW*, 6: 457–61; Pang and Jin, *Maozhuan*, 651. The source material from the Hungarian side also reflected Mao's optimistic attitudes toward China's situation compared with that of Hungary at this moment; see "Hungarian Embassy in Beijing to the Hungarian Foreign Ministry about Ambassador Sandor Nogradi's Conversation with Mao Zedong (22 May 1957)," H00023, MOL, XIX-J-1-j China, 1945–64, 2. doboz, 1/c, 002759/1957.

101. On 10 April, *RMRB* published an editorial criticizing the Chen Qitong group and other opponents of the blooming and contending policy, also taking itself to task for not having criticized them earlier, given that Mao had stated his determination to push ahead with the new policy. See *RMRB*, 10 April 1957; MacFarquhar, *Origins of the Cultural Revolution*, 1: 201.

Left was more in tune with Mao's real line, so that it was ultimately safer to side against the rectificationists. Unlike Chen and his colleagues, who openly questioned the political feasibility of blooming and contending in the post-Hungary atmosphere, Deng seems to have imagined that any opening-wide policy would necessarily be followed by a corrective suppression.[102] However, insofar the Chairman made his attitude clear that he wanted immediate rectification, the party in general, including the media, had no alternative but to follow his course.[103]

Indeed, the Communist Bloc crises in the latter months of 1956 were crucial in bringing Mao round to a sense of the reality of the problems he faced at home, as can be seen in two related if not necessarily reconcilable views he held with respect to policy in that year. The first concerns the modification of the party's ruling methods, the other ideological remolding. If the Soviet reevaluation of Stalin in early 1956 stimulated Mao to repair the relationship between the Communist party and the party outsiders, the intelligentsia in particular, the Hungarian Revolution alerted Mao to the danger of isolating himself from broad popular sentiment, as might well happen if the political consciousness of various groups (those with an intellectual background in particular) was allowed to develop independently of the party's scrutiny and guidance. The his-

---

102. On Mao's dissatisfaction with *RMRB*'s failure to respond to his speeches on contradictions and his dislike of Deng Tuo, see Merle Goldman, "Mao's Obsession," 49–58; for a detailed record of Mao's harsh criticism of Deng Tuo in a small-circle meeting with the journalists and pressmen and of the central propaganda organization's wariness in publicizing the Chairman's blooming and contending policy in the early months of 1957, see Wang Ruoshui, *Zhihui de tongku*, 319–27; further, an abridged official meeting record can be found in Pang and Jin, *Maozhuan*, 661–66.

103. Largely due to Mao's dissatisfaction with the propaganda and educational departments' inefficiency in advocating his policies, *RMRB*'s editorial on 13 April declared that party committees of all levels, especially their first secretaries, should take ideological and political work to the masses, downgrade the authority of the propaganda departments of the party and the educational departments of the government, and strengthen the authority of local party committees, which were under direct control of Mao's central party committee. See *RMRB*, editorial, 13 April; English translation; MacFarquhar, *Origins of the Cultural Revolution*, 1: 202.

torical consequences of Stalin's crude purges and Rákosi's heavy-handed leadership reaffirmed Mao's belief in the need to soothe short-term social dissatisfaction toward the regime via persuasive measures, all the while striving to assess whether or not the disturbances were anti-Communist. In terms of practical policy, then, Mao therefore advocated an inner-party rectification against bureaucratism and sectarianism, opening the CCP up to external participation through the HF. At the same time, the emergence of "pro-liberal Westernization" views inside the party and an increase of incorrect criticisms from outsiders strengthened Mao's fears of the unsettling effect of ideological deviationists even within a stable socialist system. This fear lay behind Mao's choice of subjectivism as the main target of the forthcoming rectification throughout late 1956 and into early 1957; the reference of this term subtly changed from its pre-Hungary designation to point to the ongoing class animus of the party's enemies. Mao was consistent throughout this period in desiring the remolding of the thought of intellectuals and students, and also consistent in thinking that the relaxation would be propitious in bringing bad elements to light.

While Mao's controversial effort to link rectification and the HF in the spring of 1957 could be interpreted as a genuine attempt to square these policy orientations, the shift of his short-term priority from insiders' subjectivism to the party's relationship with the masses in fact was largely in reaction to the party cadres' resistance to critics from outside and to party outsiders' suspicion of his intentions in apparently opening up. Mao was nettled by the resistance to the HF and wanted to revive mutual supervision as an exemplary means of reform. In doing so, Mao intended to deal with the problems that had led to the party's alienation from the masses in the first place, using the pressure of the party outsiders' political involvement to overcome the inner obstacles to his grand rectification plan. On Mao's initiative, therefore, in the announcement of the rectification campaign published in *RMRB* on 1 May, the central party listed the evils to be corrected in order, placing correcting bureaucratism and sectarianism before subjectivism as the highest priorities of the party's new movement.¹⁰⁴ A very crucial precondition for the Chairman to be willing to change his priorities was his sanguine assessment that the class struggle was over in China as it had proved not to be in Hungary.¹⁰⁵ With the capitalist class largely eliminated and political power tightly controlled in the Communist center, as Mao estimated, most of the non-Communist groups would perforce attach themselves to the Communist regime in the long run.

ABOUT FACE: FROM BLOOMING AND CONTENDING TO THE ANTI-RIGHTIST CAMPAIGN

As Benjamin Schwartz pointed out, as a politician Mao was perhaps unduly optimistic, with a tendency to construct best-case scenarios in the early months of 1956.¹⁰⁶ But if Mao, as Schwartz suggests, came later to place the best possible construction on his sweeping HF and rectification campaigns after Hungary, his optimism was always balanced by his clear awareness that there could still exist a small group of antagonist elements among the intellectuals and that poisonous weeds would also emerge alongside the fragrant flowers.

---

104. See the rectification directive published on 1 May 1957, *RMRB*; MacFarquhar, *Origins of the Cultural Revolution*, 1: 202; Teiwes, *Politics and Purges*, 186–87.

105. On 30 April 1957, Mao told his forty-four audience members, which included party and state leaders, the leaders of democratic parties, and non–party-affiliated persons, that he had chosen not to accept his reappointment as chairman of the state the following year. On the second day of the gathering, Chen Shutong and Huang Yanpei cosigned a letter to Liu Shaoqi and Zhou Enlai, in which they expressed their disappointment at Mao's withdrawal. Mao asked Deng Xiaoping to circulate this letter, along with Mao's marginal annotations, among the high- and middle-ranking cadres, and representatives of non-Communists. It was in this letter that Mao stated with confidence, "Now that [we] have the basic consolidation of [this socialist] country, this country cannot be overthrown. With regard to absolute consolidation [of this country], according to Soviet experience, [we] may need another fifteen to twenty years." See Zhongyang wenxian, *JMW*, 457–61; also see Pang and Jin, *Maozhuan*, 671; about Mao's plan to retire from state chairmanship, see MacFarquhar, *Origins of the Cultural Revolution*, 1: 105–7.

106. Schwartz, "Thoughts on the Late Mao," 25–26.

Underneath his tolerance, moderation, and even openness to "liberal" and new ideas, Mao always intended to prohibit incorrect utterances but emphasized that the Communists should not enter into disputes hastily or be badly prepared in terms of argument: "We need to collect sufficient materials [before we write articles], we do not meet an enemy attack in a hurry; we do not meet an enemy attack with no certainty [of success]."[107] This is also why the Chairman kept revising his contradiction speech in line with his changing perceptions of the domestic situation, limiting the diffusion of his speech-notes between February and April to a select circle.[108] Moreover, the Chairman's consistent rejection of definitive restrictions on blooming either for insiders and outsiders made any critique of the party a dangerous game for all potential dissenters. Indeed, Mao had formed a very clear picture of the domestic causes that led Hungary, an established Communist bloc state, to the verge of disintegration. Foremost among these were the failures to check ideological dissent to party hegemony and to stamp out challenges to an established Communist leadership. With the passive resistance to HF inside the party largely overcome by the end of April, and inner-party rectification underway, the Chairman began to spend more time and energy on supervising the behavior of the non-Communist intellectuals, seeking to ward off any unpleasant side effects of cohabitation.[109]

If we examine the wording of the official and unofficial materials on Chairman Mao's policy guidelines made for party outsiders'

---

107. Pang and Jin, *Maozhuan*, 617; MacFarquhar et al., *The Secret Speeches*, 123–24. In MacFarquhar's English-language collection, Mao's words in the same conference were recorded as: "We do not meet an enemy attack in a hurry; we do not write articles in a hurry."

108. *Zhongyang gongzuo jianbao* [Briefing on the Central Party's work], an inner-circle bulletin, published the draft of a speech made by Zhang Bojun conveying the main content of Mao's speech made on 30 April at the Supreme State Council Conference to his party members. One member accused both Zhang Bojun and Ye Duyi of rightist guilt for their distortion of the main spirit of Mao's speech on 30 April 1957. Ye Duyi, *Suijiusi qi youweihui* [Still do not regret though suffered severely] (Beijing: Beijing shiyuewenyi, 1999), 88–89.

109. Pang and Jin, *Maozhuan*, 683.

participation in the rectification campaign in the first week of May 1957 carefully, we find that Mao's attitude to blooming and contending had gone through a process of change corresponding to his shifting perceptions of the development of the criticisms put forward by outsiders. Noteworthy is that in the Supreme State Conference held on 30 April, the Chairman stated that the non-Communists' formal participation in the rectification to find faults in the party's work should be traced back to February 1957; of course, this may simply be regarded as a small change with no significant political meaning.[110] However, only four days later, in referring to the critical views expressed by the nonparty people either in forums or via the press "in the recent two months," the Chairman made clear in the inner-circle central directive of 4 May that "when critics are not correct, or we come across incorrect opinions in one certain article, we should refute them rather than allow the mistaken thoughts to prevail and go unanswered (but we should think closely about the timing of our answers and the tone in which we speak, which should be fully persuasive)." To avoid any unnecessary confusion about the central party's position immediately after the launch of the new campaign, Mao added that "most of the outsider critics are cogent and are beneficial to unification enhancement and work improvement." Nevertheless, we see a revival of his January emphasis on the utility of blooming to uncover poisonous weeds as the Chairman pointed out in particular: "Even those mistaken critics [do us some kind of service] in exposing the real nature of some people, so we can see that they have a valuable contribution for us to help these people in carrying through ideological reforms in the future." Although Mao insisted that the CCP rectification be continued for a period during which the outsiders' major roles remained at offering advice and criticism to the party, he apparently placed more hopes on the extension of the rectification pattern to the whole society to educate and unify the thoughts of various groups once "our party succeeds in rectification" and "wins absolute

---

110. Ibid., 669; Ye Duyi, *Suijiusi qi youweihui*.

initiative [in moving to the next stage]." The first targeted group of the forthcoming societal rectification, as the Chairman said explicitly in this directive, should be the intelligentsia.[111] The 4 May directive showed that Mao, after encouraging the nonparty intellectuals to participate in the rectification process for about two months, began to pave the way for putting a restrictive gloss on the open-door rectification experiment.

By the early days of May 1957, Mao was prepared to lop off a few blooms in order to avoid unexpected consequences of soliciting outsiders' input. In the same directive of 4 May, requesting party committees at all levels to arrange forums for party outsiders to air their criticisms of the party, Mao sanctioned the CCP's United Front Work Department to meet in circles with urban intellectual elites from 8 May to 3 June in all the chief cities, especially in Beijing and Shanghai.[112] The purpose of these meetings, as stated by the central committee, was to solicit suggestions and opinions regarding the CCP's work to assist the party in its ongoing processes of self-criticism. The campaign, though, was not necessarily only innocent in motivation. In hindsight and whatever Mao's intentions, it is clear that the forums had the effect of subjecting the non-Communist elites' political activities to the surveillance of the party. Possibly alerted by the dangers of letting the intellectual elites disseminate their views to society unrestrained as demonstrated in the Hungarian events, the Chairman moved first to place these people under the supervision of the party bureaucracy. Furthermore, given the reactionary behaviors of the elites in the Hungarian uprising and the emergence of some suspicious and mistaken views among Chinese intellectual groups after Hungary, Mao considered that the Chinese intelligentsia had to pass a test of political loyalty before

---

111. "Zhongyang guanyu jixuzuzhi dangwai renshi dui dangzheng sufan cuowu quedian zhankai piping de zhishi" [Central Party's directive on keeping on organizing the party-outsiders to criticize party and government's mistakes and shortcomings], *Cankao ziliao*, 22: 17–18.

112. Pang and Jin, *Maozhuan*, 683.

the regime could use it in future development. While Mao took it upon himself to be the sole planner, manipulator, and arbiter of this examination, his criteria of what constituted loyalty changed markedly with his view of domestic events.[113]

It is evident that by early May Chairman Mao still believed, despite his potential worries, that China was different from Hungary since the engagement between the party and its outside critics would, in the Middle Kingdom, follow the prescribed script of criticism and self-criticism coming together to secure unity. It only took a week for the Chairman to revise his view, coming to rest on the position that the center would reserve for itself the right to truncate outsiders' censure of the CCP at the appropriate moment.[114] On 14 and 16 May, two enlarged CCP politburo emergency meetings were held under Mao's auspices, reassessing the political implications of the domestic blooming and contending. Although the contents of these two meetings will possibly never be known in

---

113. In a meeting with a Polish delegation held on 8 April 1957, Mao told the Polish leaders that, in his understanding, the Hungarian events that took place in October 1956 were in essence different from the Polish movements. The Hungarian events were orchestrated by the Petőfi circles, while the Polish events were controlled by the Polish Communist Party. In Hungary, tens and thousands of the masses took to the streets and put the party center in an embarrassing situation; within the Hungarian Communist Party, meanwhile, there were two factions, one represented by Nagy, who was for revisionism on the strength of previous connections with the Petőfi circles. Without proper leadership from the party, the Hungarian incident degenerated into a mass riot, leading to the disintegration of the party, government, and military forces. Mao's words indicated that he learned at least one lesson from the Hungarian crisis: the Communist party had to organize and control domestic movements to head off deviation. See "Summary of Chairman Mao's Meeting with the Polish Government Delegation," *CFMA* 204-00040-03, 1–14. In referring to some intellectuals' worries that the HF blooming was aimed (by the center) at "fishing" or uncovering wrong thinking, Mao stated, "It depends on how to understand [the HF]: is 'blooming' a means or an end? In order to know the truth, it [HF policy] can be interpreted as a way of 'fishing,' but [we are] uncovering two type of fish, one is Marxist, the other is non-Marxist." Record of Mao's talks, 6 May 1957, in Ye Duyi, *Suijiusi qi youweihui*, 36.

114. Mao's judgments on the progress of HF can be reflected by his revising drafts of the "On Contradictions" speech from 24 April to 7 May; Pang and Jin, *Maozhuan*, 674–83.

the stated absence of any records, the wording of the directives issued on 14 and 16 May reflect the top leadership's decision-making processes. They indicate that the central party's attitude toward criticism had already hardened, suggesting that the central leadership now only intended to make short-term concessions to external critics to reap future benefits. Tactically, the party believed that a certain type of criticism would only serve to make clear the real features of the rightists (a word first used in the directive of 14 May) to the masses.[115] By mid-May 1957, therefore, failure to suppress or shut down criticism that the center judged incorrect or poisonous did not so much indicate that the party was listening, as that it was waiting for the democrats to overplay their hand. Those changes directly paved the way for the transformation of rectification and HF into an Anti-Rightist Campaign in early June 1957, about two weeks after rectification had actually begun. The leading question thus becomes why and how Mao's attitude changed so dramatically in such a short period of time, especially regarding the intellectuals at home.

The change of tone in the center's directives circulated among high-ranking cadres during this period allows us to identify at least two domestic developments that possibly shook Mao's basic assumption that a well-managed rectification could resolve the divergent or contradictory interests of social fractions, which, in his analysis, had exacerbated the Hungarian revolt. All the available evidence would indicate that the suggestions raised by the non-Communists by the middle of May were concerned largely with how to repair the relationship of the party with nonparty people, with little evidence that they were moved by any policy of supplanting the CCP leadership. However, Mao's understanding of the political implications of the outsiders' words was undoubtedly decisive in reorienting policy.[116] First and foremost, as the Chairman

---

115. Liu Shaoqi, Zhou Enlai, Zhu De, Chen Yun, Deng Xiaoping, Peng Zhen, Li Weihan, Kang Sheng, and Lu Dingyi attended the meeting; *Cankao ziliao*, 22: 18–19; Pang and Jin, *Maozhuan*, 688–91.

116. Parts of these speeches made by the nonparty leading figures' were pub-

possibly perceived, the outsiders' criticism of the CCP shortcomings began to touch upon some sensitive issues that went beyond his limit of tolerance, such as their harking back to the injustices inflicted on the counterrevolutionaries during the campaign to establish Communism (as some of them did in early 1957) with particular reference to typical cases such as the suppression in 1955 of "counterrevolutionary" Hu Feng's "literary faction."[117] Another factor that significantly aroused Mao's concern was the non-Communist newspapers' active political involvement in the campaign to criticize the ruling party's policies and disseminating dissenters' opinions to the students and the masses.[118] As noted previously, the party's relaxation of control over the press (nonparty papers in particular) had constituted an important part of the Chairman's post-CPSU Twentieth Congress reforms, designed by the center to diversify Chinese journalism to serve the underlying purpose of broadening Communism's appeal. The press reforms allowed outsiders unprecedented discretion in crafting messages critical of the party's policies and broadcasting these, especially to the elites and the young, in a way unforeseen by the center. By mid-May, Mao seems to have weighed the pros and cons of relaxation, coming to the view that he had underestimated the strength, ability, and

---

lished on a daily basis by *RMRB* throughout May 1957; for the editor's comment and reports on the first week meetings, see *RMRB*, 9–12 May 1957. For detailed speech records, see *Cankao ziliao*, 22: 21–92; Pang and Jin, *Maozhuan*, 683–87.

117. *Guangming ribao* (Guangming daily) published intellectuals' charges against the purge movement and their doubts about the legal reliability of Hu Feng's case as early as 11 May 1957. For the intellectuals' charges against the purge movement and their doubts about the legal reliability of mass campaigns in general, see "Selected Files of the Blooming and Contending," Shandong Provincial Archives (SPA), 123-40-47, 31–33, 35–43. For parts of these nonparty leading figures' speeches published throughout May 1957 see *RMRB*, 9–12, 14, 16, 17 May 1957; *Guangming Ribao*, 8, 11 May 1957; *Cankao ziliao*, 22: 21–92; *Neican*, 9 May 1957, 19–20.

118. It is known that Chairman Mao read newspapers such as *Guangming* and *Wenhui bao*, which had been run by non-Communist intellectuals in the short period from early 1957 to the summer of the same year, viewing the content and style of articles on these papers as key indicators of the party outsiders' political development. See MacFarquhar, *Hundred Flowers*, 66; Pang and Jin, *Maozhuan*, 664–66, 684, 687–88, 692–93.

especially the desire of residual bourgeois elements among the intellectual class to disrupt socialism and oust the Communists.[119]

The party outsiders' request for real power in a coalition government and their resourcefulness in expanding their political influence among a wider range of people via the press all owe their inception to the center's promotion of HF policies against the party bureaucrats' passive resistance in the early months of 1957. Performing a volte-face (in appearance), the Chairman understood these initiatives as some democratic rightists' alleged effort to "seize the leadership of the press, cultural, education and scientific fields in the first instance."[120] On the basis of the Chinese Communists' rich experience in using propaganda to win over the masses, and their appreciation of the importance of the media in fomenting counterrevolutionary insurrection in Hungary, Mao and his colleagues could be in no doubt that "the rightists in journalism intend to incite the working-man and peasant against the government."[121] In general, Mao and his lieutenants must have already decided on 14 May that a counterattack against revisionism and rightism had to be organized shortly, while strategically opting to let latent rightists and enemies inside and outside the party run amuck before the party reasserted its authority. Mao's tactics are reminiscent of the advice that the Chinese side gave the Soviet leadership in dealing with the Hungarian reactionaries at the end of October 1956, namely, to conceal its real intentions and make temporary concessions in order to obtain enough legitimacy to allow it to move forcefully.

---

119. Teiwes, *Politics and Purges*, 210-13, 217-19; Pang and Jin, *Maozhuan*, 689-90.

120. For democratic party members' complaints about inequalities between Communists and non-Communists and their request for equal rights and real power in practice, see *RMRB*, 14 May 1957. For Mao's interpretation of the political and ideological intention behind these outsiders' words, see "Shiqing zhengzaiqibianhua" (Things are changing), Zhongyang wenxian, *JMW*, 6: 469-76. In fact, the Chairman began to write this article on 15 May and had revised it several times according to his changing perceptions of the domestic development before circulating it within the party on 12 June 1957.

121. Pang and Jin, *Maozhuan*, 690.

While the domestic situation in China in 1957 differed in many respects from that in Hungary in 1956, with the central party itself instigating forums and printing a series of prorectification articles in *RMRB*, many non-Communist elites came to feel they were playing a role very similar to the Hungarian Petőfi Circle, pointing out the party's errors and offering salutary advice for the state's reform.[122] Critically reviewing the Communist-organized political movements since the establishment of the regime, besides the 1955 purge and Hu Feng's case, many intellectuals further sought to revisit abuses from the "Three and Five Anti" campaigns and various thought reforms.[123] At the same time, some began to question the validity of the official evaluation of the overall achievements of the socialist transformation as they became more and more aware of the economic consequences wrought by a rigid application of Stalinist development policies.[124]

Within the fraught, heady atmosphere of liberalization in the second half of May, the political ideas emerging from both the democratic press and *RMRB* in the midst of its Anti-Rightist and HF campaigns enthused university students to join in blooming- and -contending attacks on the "three evils" of party work on 19 May, with impromptu demonstrations held in Beijing, Shanghai, and other major cities. With no obvious party intervention in the initial period, the student movements soon developed a momentum of their own, beginning to touch upon some sensitive political topics in China through flyers, unofficial publications, debates, and interschool visits. In particular, top party officials became concerned by students debating the correctness of cadre denunciations of Hu Feng and his faction as counterrevolutionary and of the Gao-Rao group as antiparty and antipeople without open trials and support-

---

122. For example, see *RMRB*, 19 May editorial and *RMRB*, 21 May on blooming and contending in Shanghai with the encouragement of Ke Qingshi, the first secretary of the Shanghai party committee and a close follower of Chairman Mao.
123. For an introduction to China's political campaigns in the early 1950s, see MacFarquhar and Fairbank, *CHOC*, 14: 51–91.
124. Shen, *Sikao yu xuanze*, 568–83.

ing evidence.¹²⁵ Largely idealistic, demonstrators did not appear to consider the idea that their rectification impulses could go down badly with the party leadership, imagining that these disputes originated at a lower level of party organization.¹²⁶

One female activist from Renmin University (the People's University) even declared that the Chinese movements "were different from the Hungarian events in essence" since "we [Chinese Communists] haven't made serious mistakes like that of Rákosi and Gerő in Hungary.... I do not see the recent developments at Peking University as dangerous, even if some 'mistaken views' have emerged since no one intends to overthrow socialism." She dubbed those officials concerned about the recurrence of the Eastern Bloc riots in China "nervous masters," aligning herself with "the Party center and Chairman Mao" and against the university authorities in willing "a thorough rectification."¹²⁷ Unbeknown to the students, however, Mao was all too well aware of his role in recent political bloodletting and mindful of the effect that rehabilitating Rajk had had on the Rákosi regime, leading him to treat the Chinese student demonstrations with extreme caution.

The university students' voluntary participation in the big blooming and contending event represented another unexpected consequence of the central party's ruse to smoke out their enemies as agreed in mid-May. The Chairman later admitted that, unlike the non-Communist forums, the students' movements were not arranged by the party committees and proceeded like a "violent storm," which "actually had a flavor of ... the Hungary incident in miniature."¹²⁸ In this light, it becomes easier to understand the depth of uncertainty and frustrated annoyance felt by Mao and his top lieutenants imme-

---

125. "Materials on Rectification in Colleges," SPA, 123-43-38, 10–17; "Collected Materials on Political and Ideological Problems of the College Students Participating in Rectification," 123-43-472, 1–11. Also see *Neican* (20 May 1957): 3–10, (23 May 1957): 3–16, (25 May 1957): 3–5, (27 May 1957): 14–18, (29 May 1957): 14–17, (31 May 1957): 7–10.
126. *Neican* (23 May 1957): 19–21.
127. Ibid.
128. Lin Ke, *Lin Ke riji*, 44–45.

diately after the unanticipated escalation of student blooming and contending in late May. The Chairman responded to the agitation by sending people to collect firsthand information on the latest developments among the students in the four principal universities Peking, Qinghua, Beijing Normal, and Renmin University. Several months later, Mao declared that "before [I] got to the root of [the student movements] in the four universities, I dispatched personnel to read the big-character newspapers [to figure out] how significant the influence of the Hungarian incident was. Only after 20 May when [I] found out the real situation did [I] truly stop worrying."[129] By "real situation," the Chairman perhaps meant that after pooling information on the disturbances and assessing their nature at a high level, the party concluded that the influence of student movements was still limited, so that the campus campaigns could be sealed off from the rest of society and other major groups such as the workers and peasants. That is, they posed no threat to the CCP's dominant status.[130]

Consequently, in the directive issued on 20 May, the central leadership clearly stated that "in order to avoid disturbances," the local cadres should make sure not to expand blooming and contending movements to the students and workers, since these groups, once they had made one with the campaign, "would bring up too many specific requirements," making reform unmanageable for the CCP. The (party-controlled) press should not cover riots among students, workers, and peasants, nor publish debates on economic or remuneration policies. In contrast to the optimistic attitude that the Chairman had toward the domestic situation in the early months of 1957, viewing a certain degree of student and peasant demon-

---

129. Pang and Jin, *Maozhuan*, 694.

130. The Chairman should have summoned a politburo standing committee meeting around 19 or 20 May to analyze and discuss the unexpected developments on campus in the capital. The directive issued on 20 May is a specific action guidance to the local cadres out of their policy discussion in these days. General Office of the CCP CC, ed., "Situation Briefing, on Rectification, Part 1," SPA, 123-43-466, 1–60. On Deng Xiaoping's and Liu Shaoqi's recollections of these highest-level meetings in an enlarged politburo meeting on 23 May, see Pang and Jin, *Maozhuan*, 694.

strations as salutary in stimulating the cadres to put more effort into their work, Mao adopted an entirely contrary position, moving to preempt wider social groups' involvement in criticisms of the party. This change of attitude suggests that the Chinese leader may himself at this stage have come to share many cadres' fears of repeating the Hungarian Communist regime's mistakes in China, i.e., losing control of developments at home and being sabotaged by hidden enemies and rightists both inside and outside the party.[131]

By the end of May, Mao already regretted having co-opted the bourgeois intellectuals and nonparty members in such a sensitive political issue as the party's criticism and self-criticism movement. The side-effect of open-door rectification, in inducing students to question the Communist party's policies, fundamentally shook the Chairman's assertion from early 1957 that "Communist Party has great power, . . . [we] do not fear riots in the world since this [Communist] world [already] cannot be led to turmoil."[132] It turned out that intellectuals were unworthy of the party's trust, particularly since, Mao recalled, it was the Petőfi circles, with the help of revisionists like Nagy inside the Hungarian Communist Party, that stoked the Budapest riots: "There are some people who have erroneous revisionist or rightist opportunist thought," as Mao said of the situation in China, doubtless referring to liberal intellectual-cadres of the kind headed by Li Shenzhi, who advocated big democracy in early 1957. "They long for bourgeois liberalism and negate everything; they are linked to the bourgeois intellectuals in society in a hundred and one ways."[133] Therefore, as the Chairman understood the Chinese situation at this stage, the reactionary and rightist elements had merely remained concealed in the bourgeois intel-

---

131. *Cankao ziliao*, 22: 19–22.
132. Mao probably wrote this sentence in his "On Correct Handling" article in early 1957 and deleted it in early May when his assessment of the domestic situation changed; Pang and Jin, *Maozhuan*, 682.
133. "Things Are Beginning to Change," 15 May 1957; see Zhongyang Wenxian, *JMW*, 6: 469. Mao had revised this article throughout the period from mid-May to 12 June after his judgments on domestic politics changed dramatically by late May. For an English translation, see Kau and Leung, *Writings of Mao Zedong*, 547–48.

lectuals, students, and CCP members, who had had their own reasons for affiliating themselves with Mao's reforms and professing adherence to party principles.

In making these diagnoses, Mao more than ever positioned himself as almost stranded between two camps. On the one hand, Mao was disappointed with the behavior of the intellectuals' and the students' during the campaigns, starting to view them with deep distrust. Consideration of the Hungarian crisis only brought home to the party the continuing danger for the regime of cadres nursing bourgeois ideology within itself, especially when it was connected to the supposed rightist deviationism outside. Going back on his mixed or positive February interpretation of the Budapest events, Mao began to stress their negative aspects, especially insofar as they provided a parallel with a conceivable case in China. Mao therefore turned to the unquestioned loyalty of the mass of the Chinese people, calling for a campaign to vanquish class enemies. Ever since a segment of the nonparty intellectuals and later student activists had become vocal in questioning the legitimacy of the party's policies in the political realm, Mao had been uncomfortable with potential opposition to his own revolutionary way and its implicit challenge to his personal authority. Budapest allowed Mao to paint the skeptics of the essential correctness of the central party's politics with strokes of rightism or revisionism, opening up a political front that broke the compromise he had previously accepted. All the remarks and written materials made by the democratic intellectuals and students from late May to early June thus became hard evidence that Mao's party used to charge these groups of people with rightist and revisionist political intentions to overthrow the regime in the following Anti-Rightist Campaign.[134]

---

134. Up to early June, the thrust of the criticisms made by outsiders of the party had been directed more to the systematic political origins of the party's shortcomings than to the superficial sectarian or bureaucratic mistakes made by the middle- and low-ranking cadres. Available evidence shows that a number of prominent democrats began to view the excessive concentration of power in the center, seeing "the world belongs to the party," as the key problem underlying the Eastern Bloc crises and the Chinese Communist regime's alienation from the peo-

CONCLUSION

The Hungarian crisis and Soviet military intervention threw socialism, or at least Stalinism, in doubt across the socialist world. States began to question the legitimacy of using radical methods to transform society in pursuit of socialism, critically probing the moral justification for mass ideological and political mobilization. In China, several middle-ranking party members were naive enough to suggest to the center that the CCP consider promoting political reform modeled on the Western experience of liberal democratization. At the same time, top CCP leaders such as Liu Shaoqi, Zhou Enlai, and Chen Yun became clearly committed to a critical review of Stalinist bureaucratic organization, embedded as it was in a sys-

---

ple. One intellectual named Huang Sha later confessed that "after the Hungarian incident, I came to the conclusion that the party itself should change." For Huang Sha's confession, see MacFarquhar, *Hundred Flowers*, 72–73. Chu Anping, the chief editor of *Guangming ribao*, the party organ of the Democratic League (Chu had been newly appointed to the position in early 1957 and Guangming under his direction became one of the most active non-Communist newspapers to cover and make comments on the developments of rectification), made a speech entitled "Allow Me to Offer Some Opinions to Chairman Mao and Premier Zhou" in one forum organized by the party on 1 June. Chu claimed the key to the problem of the party's alienation from the people in recent years lay in the idea that "the world belongs to the party" and pointed out that it was far from enough only to criticize "the young monks," namely, the officials in lower echelons, without questioning anything about "the old monks," i.e., the leadership represented by Mao and Zhou. For the Chinese version (complete speaker notes) see *Cankao ziliao*, 22: 81; also see Zhang Yihe, *Wangshi*, 48–50; for an English translation (incomplete), see MacFarquhar, *Hundred Flowers*, 51–53. For a well-documented narrative and analysis of the Chinese intellectuals' critical review of the CCP's nation-building in the first half of the 1950s, see Shen, *Sikao yu xuanze*, 535–61, 568–83. For writings and literature of this period translated into English, see Mu Fusheng, *The Wilting of the Hundred Flowers: Free Thought in China Today* (London: Heinemann, 1962); Nie Hualing, *Literature of the Hundred Flowers: Criticism and Polemics*, vol. 1 (New York: Columbia University Press, 1981). The report of the Hungarian diplomat in Beijing who was an eyewitness of the radical change of CCP policy from May to July 1957 can be found in "Hungarian Embassy in Beijing to the Hungarian Foreign Ministry about the Internal Situation in China (3 August 1957)," H00032, MOL, XIX-J-1-j China, 1945–1964, 8. doboz, 5/c, 003835/1957. It is notable that this high-ranking Hungarian diplomat in Beijing suggested to his leadership that the anti-rightist activities and their developments in China could provide useful experience to the other [socialist] states.

tem of hierarchical privilege underpinned by the development of heavy industry. The central and local senior party membership attending the second plenary session of the CCP Eighth Congress were for the first time broadly united in their disagreement with the Stalinist model in political and organizational terms, sensing the necessity for reform as a precondition to future socialist development. Notably, Liu Shaoqi and Zhou Enlai, top colleagues of the Chairman, along with many middle-ranking cadres and intellectual outsiders, were sure that their concerns were essentially in agreement with Maoism and even with the trajectory of the Chairman's thought in seeking to go beyond Stalin. Even during a period in which the Chairman deliberately created a relaxed and democratic atmosphere in the center, as seen in the process of policy discussion and domestic situation interpretation, Mao's centrality to decision-making endured no challenge. In the post-Hungary atmosphere, Mao's interpretation of the ideological confusion swirling around the form of his own Communism was, however, much more complex than both insiders and outsiders could correctly divine.

If we say that Mao began to recognize some problems with the Stalinist model in both the political and economic realms in the aftermath of Hungary, taking the opportunity to shed much of the personal mythology and institutional appurtenances clinging to Stalin, his mind was nevertheless preoccupied by the political and ideological considerations of defending his own Communism and past policies, which were so closely associated with the Soviet model. By reform, Mao never meant to curb bureaucracy by restricting the power at the center, let alone changing the existing one-party system as some intellectual cadres had wrongly suspected; nor did he invite any doubt as to the essential correctness of his past policies in consolidating power or putting in place a socialist state in both the political and economic realms. In theorizing democracy and dictatorship in late 1956 and early 1957, Mao made clear within his inner circle that he was not prepared to tolerate the advocates of so-called big democracy, which he presumed to be active in the aftermath of the Hungarian crisis. At the same time, although Mao accepted the specific economic plan for 1957 and did not oppose his colleagues' cooling-off policy in the aftermath of the Eastern European uprisings, the Chairman did not appear to have wavered from his belief in industrial modernization and the core features of the Stalinist economic pattern. In Mao's understanding, these moderate measures were no more than transitional means for getting around the bottleneck on resources prior to the emergence of a fresh phase of industrialization.

In the end, the message Mao drew from the Hungarian events was that rule through repression *after* the establishment of socialism would undermine the ideological and political legitimacy of a Communist regime; he thus chose to instigate a procedure of determining residual contradictions in China and solving these by soft or peaceful means. By "contradictions," the Chairman referred to people's discontent with shortcomings of the party's work, dissidence from the party's political policies, and the counterrevolutionary views of a few suspicious groups. The divergent interests of the businessmen and intelligentsia trained in the West would present formidable obstacles to the project of unity, meaning that continuing class struggle in China was inevitable. It was thus central to Mao's plans that nationalist agents and political enemies standing against the regime would be executed or imprisoned. The vast majority of the Chinese intellectuals, it was anticipated, could be won over by persuasion. In order to achieve his broad goal of a socialist leap forward, Mao seems to have been sincere in believing that the support of the Chinese intelligentsia would be of great value to the CCP in securing universal popular support. From a purely prudent standpoint, the intellectuals' support would have a number of advantages: intellectuals' technical expertise was needed in the construction of socialism, and they would add considerable luster to the party. So long as the CCP retained control of all administrative functions, a hundred flowers might bloom and schools of thought contend.

While Mao's controversial effort to link rectification and HF in the spring of 1957 could be interpreted as a genuine attempt to accommodate these two policy orientations, his dramatic decision to push forward an open-door rectification, inviting outsiders to criticize party errors, largely was in response to the cadres' passive resistance to his HF policy and to party outsiders' suspicion of his intentions in seeming to open up. One of the key reasons why the party organizations—the cultural, educational, and propaganda departments in particular—were reluctant to implement the Maoist soft policies of unification and investigation was that these projects not only put these bureaucrats' interests and security under threat, but also wrested from them their accustomed political and ideological functions, i.e., the party officials now had to receive criticism from people of the backward class whom they had been used to rectifying and even suppressing. The intellectual outsiders' role in the Hungarian events and the Chinese antirevisionist posture taken on the international front after the October crises encouraged the Chinese cadres to be open about their reservations about blooming and contending. To a large extent, then, the Chairman's efforts to encourage party outsiders to participate in inner-party rectification were aimed at goading the cadres into accepting his line.

This outcome of his movement of blooming and contending made Mao question afresh the institutional bases upon which any future reform of Communism could be carried out.[135] After having pushed through rectification and HF against strong internal opposition, Mao found himself in the position of having to confront the fact that his initiatives had yielded results opposite to those he had anticipated.[136] Far from consolidating the intellectual elites' confidence in the party, the campaign had driven a wedge between them and the party. In addition, Mao's personal preeminence and judgment had been subjected to, in his eyes, a new level of hostile criticism. One can imagine both how furious and depressed Mao was in May and early June 1957. His "gentle breeze and mild rain" had

---

135. Bo, *Huigu*, 2: 634–37; Pang and Jin, *Maozhuan*, 693–94.
136. See Li Zhisui, *The Private Life of Chairman Mao: The Memoirs of Mao's Personal Physician* (London: Arrow Books, 1996), 200; in it he described Mao's health after the unexpected turning of the rectification and HF campaigns: "He stayed in bed, depressed and apparently immobilized, sick with the cold."

turned into a full-blown gale. It was in this mood that Mao's thoughts on contradiction adapted themselves to the suspicion that a fifth column element might be persistently operative within China itself. As Mao sought to manage the dissent that rectification had aroused, he was particularly concerned about reconciling the divergent or contradictory interests of social fractions, which, in his analysis, had exacerbated the Hungarian revolt.

Conclusion

The 1956 Hungarian Revolution had a profound impact on the orientation of China's international policies. Even more importantly, the Chinese leaders', particularly Mao's, interpretation of the crisis shaped the development of domestic policy from late 1956 to the end of 1957 in a way that, while probably undertreated in historiography, is certainly consequential. Maoism adopted radical policies after Hungary to salvage the revolutionary dogma apparently jettisoned by Moscow and to push forward the famous 1958 Great Leap Forward campaign. These developments prompted a crisis in the relationship between China and the Soviet Bloc and a second crisis in the Chinese leaders' belief that they had found a valid path toward socialism within their own country. This double crisis led to the Chairman's committing himself to an extreme revolutionary path, resulting in the country turning its back on the world for the best part of the next twenty years.

The CCP leadership—party chairman Mao Zedong in particular—by the end of the mid-1950s began to conceive of a great Chinese revolution in modernization, that is, industrialization and socialist consolidation. On the basis of a self-consciousness about China's potential to lead the Communist Bloc in the near future, the Chinese central leadership under Mao took the Kremlin's denunciation of Stalin in early 1956 as a once-in-a-lifetime opportunity to strike out on a more valid path toward socialization (and the realization of Communism) within its country. At the same time, in trying to clear up ideological confusion among the Communist camp states by issuing declarations rehabilitating Stalin and publicizing the peculiar Chinese experience of revolution and socialization, the Chinese regime gained considerable prestige in the Soviet Eastern Bloc after Khrushchev's secret speech. After Poznan, the Poles took the lead in approaching Beijing, looking for Chinese support in navigating a course to some degree independent of the USSR. For a while, Mao and his colleagues found themselves in such a unique historical position that they were able to initiate domestic reform that accelerated the process of industrialization while intervening actively on the Eastern European scene, challenging the Stalinist formula of bloc order without troubling the presupposition of bloc unity. In retrospect, a key question emerged out of this reformist posture in relation to Stalinism throughout the period from early 1956 to early 1957: To what extent could Mao allow himself to question Stalin and operate beyond the Stalinist framework, at home and abroad, when his worldview and political inspiration were derived so closely from Stalinist dogma? Stalinism tended to pose issues in a black-and-white way, rendering the USSR incapable of bending itself to the subtleties of the Hungarian crisis and its dramatic repercussions. As such, the crisis put Chinese reformism to a severe test, ultimately proving that central-led reform on either an economic or political front under Mao was destined to exhaust itself unproductively.

In the field of interbloc diplomacy, China's sharp criticism of Soviet big-power chauvinism immediately after the outbreak of the Hungarian upheavals agitated the collective Kremlin leadership in mounting a challenge to their primacy. It was hard for Khrushchev and his colleagues to deny the pertinence of the criticisms: they could hardly seek to revise domestic and interbloc Stalinism without conceding past big-power errors. The disapproval of China, the junior partner, no doubt discomfited a side habituated to taking its superiority in the camp for granted. Therefore, although Khrushchev made the effort to restrain his top colleagues from reacting with unnecessary emotion to Chinese accusations, it seems that the top Soviet leaders had little interest in pursuing the theme of big-power chauvinism, let alone thinking seriously about changing Soviet–satellite relations in line with Chinese suggestions.

The Soviets had not anticipated having to return to Hungary after their first withdrawal, but found their hand forced by the unexpected strength of liberals inside Budapest. Up until 29 October, the Chinese were able, without damage to their self-image of neo-Stalinist orthodoxy, to mediate between the Poles and the Soviets, asking the Poles to make concessions on external affairs and pressuring the bloc masters to concede to a greater degree their mismanagement of interbloc relations. This allowed the Chinese strategically to displace the Soviet Union's image as the center of international revolution, while contributing to facing down insurrection in Eastern Europe. The unanticipated escalation of violence in Hungary after 30 October, combined with the strong Chinese suspicion of the counterrevolutionary character of the events, however, forced Mao and his colleagues to drop their plan of criticizing the Soviets in order to save the Soviet Bloc system from collapse.

After the Chinese had been so helpful in rallying bloc unity and stressing Moscow's leading role inside the camp post-Budapest, the Soviet leaders found no difficulty in accepting China's highly theoretical prescriptions for party and bloc unity once the fires had died down. The Soviet leadership itself also became aware of the danger in abandoning Stalin in symbolic terms, taking Mao up on his suggestion of maintaining a Stalinist ideological orthodoxy as the glue of an international Communist movement. This reaffirmation of Stalinism brought the partners together in a fraternal union in late 1956. But the Chairman's desire to surpass the Soviets and enhance China's status in the revolutionary camp did not diminish with Hungary, posing future problems for the Sino–Soviet relationship and the general structure of the Communist commonwealth once the two had later broken over a mutually acceptable formula both for domestic socialist construction and international relations.

In the domestic context, senior party officials' interpretations of the Hungarian events were likewise instrumental in the evolution of social policy and governance in the sense that Stalinism had been open for criticism ever since the CPSU Twentieth Congress. The

Hungarian Revolution intimated to Chinese party leaders that an established Communist regime might fracture on account of socioeconomic tensions and the corruption and ossification of its party organization. This was an unprecedented insight for the Chinese leaders. Central party leaders like Liu Shaoqi, Zhou Enlai, and Chen Yun clearly gave themselves over to a policy of adjusting the Stalinist model in terms of both economic and party organization and were further tacitly applauded by a large number of leading cadres from both the center and the provinces. Prior to 1956, although the Chinese Communist regime had gone through a very brief period of New Democracy, when some central leaders believed that private and capitalist economies should be tolerated and even developed in a run-up period to the flowering of a mature Soviet-style socialism, no one in the center had ever doubted the vision that the "Soviet's today is our tomorrow." In other words, the essential applicability of the Soviet model to China in building a new socialist society was unimpugned. Even in the face of Chairman Mao's divide-and-rule strategy as he aimed to reshape and unite the thinking of the central leaders under his radical line, the top party officials' political and ideological belief in the ultimate legitimacy of Stalinism and its applicability to China was undoubtedly decisive in allowing them to work with Mao in achieving socialism. Only after the Polish and Hungarian crises, the latter in particular, did the top elites awaken to the necessity of reforming to avoid another Hungary in China. Within the inner-party democratic atmosphere promoted by Mao from early 1956, the leading cadres apparently felt that their advocacy for deepening the internal reform of the Stalinist model was politically congruent with Mao's desire to specify and cultivate specifically Chinese characteristics of socialist construction on the basis of a critical review of the Soviet experience.

Nevertheless, Mao, from the very beginning of his formulation of modifications to the Soviet experience, coupled all references to reform with an assurance that the party's past policies (largely his own) were correct, and that great achievements of China's socialization stood beyond reproach. After Hungary, it is evident that Mao became gradually aware of the danger of denigrating the Stalinist model in a context where it was nearly indistinguishable from the foundations of China's own state order. Consequently, the Chairman repeatedly emphasized orthodox Stalinism as a basic standard in evaluating Chinese domestic policies. This standard inclined Mao to disagreements, however implicit, with leading economists' diagnoses of defects and errors in the party's economic work and with their prescriptions that socialist planning should grant a high priority to people's livelihoods. Although Mao accepted the specific economic plan for 1957, declining to oppose his colleagues' cooling-off policy in the aftermath of the Eastern European revolts, he does not appear to have wavered from his belief in the ultimate applicability of a heavy-industry-centered economic model to Chinese conditions, parting company with his top colleagues' doubts on this score. In regard to the severe problems of the party's alienation from the people as revealed by Hungary, Mao apparently had no intention of accepting Liu's proposals of restricting the power of the inner-party top cadres in the name of curbing bureaucracy, believing instead that Communist government made policy deliberations and the consolidation of power at the center more, rather than less, important. In sum, the thought that his established socialist system might be economically or institutionally defective was absolutely unacceptable to the Chairman, stymieing any essential political or economic reforms of the Stalinist pattern.

Hungary stimulated unwanted political debate in China, raising politically sensitive questions of possible institutional flaws in the country's state architecture. Tolerated by Mao's relaxation policy, to Mao's disquiet, some non-Communist intellectuals' queried the repressive line taken against class enemies, falling in with some cadres' call for a political big democracy, or political reform on the Western democratic model. The first type of opinion touched on the correctness of radical Maoist class struggle policies, which as understood by Mao were central to the legitimacy of using revolutionary means to accomplish socialist transformation. The problem of big or small democracy, in the Chairman's eyes, pertained to the basic ideological character of his regime; the question here was whether the Chinese people should choose a proletarian route or a bourgeois Western one. Mao undoubtedly regarded these opinions as utterly wrongheaded and in need of rectification sooner or later. But what made Mao different from Rákosi or other Stalinist leaders in the Eastern Bloc was his choice not to clamp down at once on internal dissent or to use coercive means to silence wrong ideas, which Mao interpreted as a last resort in restoring unity to an established socialist society. Instead, Mao set out to displace incorrect ideas through an institutionalized policy of ideological suasion, which targeted both right and bureaucratic left deviationism as these had come to light in the wake of the Eastern European events.

The tale of Chairman Mao's orchestration of the HF liberalization together with the rectification campaign, inviting outsiders to criticize party errors, is by and large that of Mao's personal efforts to defend his own policy in the face of unexpected internal dissent over the HF campaign, piqued perhaps by doubts about the CCP's sincerity over relaxation after Hungary. Before the emergence of explicit inner-party resistance to the HF policy, the Maoist HF experiment represented little more than a tactic to appease immediate social dissatisfactions, transforming highly centralized and uniform party indoctrination into a more diversified ideological scheme so as to make socialism as attractive as possible to as many as possible. Nettled by resistance to his relaxation policy, Mao thus decided to prove that China was different from Hungary insofar as his softer methods would not provoke side effects comparable to the Budapest upheaval—which had arisen in Hungary on account of its political dependence on the Soviet Union in the absence of a large-scale social transformation leading to a successful socialist revolution. The fact that the Chairman encouraged party outsiders to participate in the party rectification campaign and to criticize party officials' work allowed him to urge party cadres to implement his line and silence any doubts from outside.

In the process of soliciting nonparty members' suggestions, the party and the intelligentsia found themselves at cross-purposes.

Historically, the Chinese scholar–bureaucrats have more or less formed a cadre, content to serve new political dynasties in the traditional spirit of their predecessors. Further, possibly influenced by the Western political theories influential among the Chinese intelligentsia during the early twentieth century, quite a few middle-aged and senior intellectuals likely believed deep down that their social function was not to exercise governmental power, but to check the negative tendencies of whatever government existed—that is, they believed that they bore responsibility for the supervision of state governance and, where necessary, for the reform of the system. These liberal concepts dictate that the ideal Chinese intellectual be honest, disinterested, principled, conscientious, and capable of self-sacrifice in the face of unjust power. While the motives of the non-Communists attending the forums were doubtless mixed, patriotism and enthusiasm for more active political participation, showcasing their social values, would seem to have played a larger role in the cadres' resistance to Mao than political opportunism. Moreover, the majority of the Chinese intellectual elites did not bear any hostility toward Marxism or Chinese socialism but wished rather to take a more active role in politics to help the CCP build a more scientific socialism theoretically reconcilable with liberalism, democracy, and humane values.

Within the fraught, heady atmosphere of liberalization in the second half of May, many non-Communist elites and then students came to feel they were playing a role very similar to the Hungarian Petőfi Circle, pointing out the party's errors and offering beneficial advice for the state's reform. However, the domestic situation in China in 1957 differed in many respects from that in Hungary in 1956, with the central party itself instigating forums, which subjected the non-Communist elites' political activities to the surveillance of the party. Although the party had relaxed its control over the press (nonparty newspapers in particular), its tight hold of the main communication channels to the masses guaranteed that the forums and the press could not become breeding grounds for a Hungarian-type campaign that could mobilize a broad popular (and particularly youth) following. Both the non-Communist intellectuals and students were too politically inexperienced to make out the center's preoccupations. By mid-May, Mao was all too well aware of the danger of reform to Stalinism at home, which would sooner or later pose a direct threat to his own authority and legitimacy, as Rákosi had found in Hungary. Disappointed with the intellectuals' and the students' behavior during the campaigns, the Chairman's mind turned against them, as he gave up on his plan of inviting in the well-educated to contribute to the next phase of socialist construction. Mao's recourse was to the unquestioned loyalty of the mass of the Chinese peasants, changing the direction of his ideological campaigns to develop the revolutionary consciousness of the population at large by calling for a ramped-up effort at socialist construction. This, Mao thought, would be genuinely characteristic of a distinctively Chinese path to modernization.

In November 1957, Chairman Mao paid his second visit to Moscow. Compared with his embarrassment of eight years ago, and from his perspective, Mao's second trip was surprisingly fruitful. Necessarily constrained within the Stalinist socialist framework, Mao was brimful of confidence in his Chinese version, for which he believed the people, unlike the Russians, had retained their enthusiasm. Just as Khrushchev had committed the USSR to overtaking the United States in industrial production within a fifteen-year period, in keeping with the traditional Chinese precept that both the East and West Wind could not be strong, Mao pledged China to meet and surpass the output of the United Kingdom within a similar timeframe. Establishing in this way a motivating target for the efforts of the Chinese people, he readied the country for a forthcoming Great Leap Forward, setting China on a more radical path of socialist revolution that was to continue unchecked for decades. Within this context, it is understandable that Mao would decisively terminate the most hopeful period of economic reform since the establishment of the PRC, which was perceived by him to be at odds with the vigorous onward march of orthodox socialism (Stalinist in essence, Maoist in formula).[1] This radical Maoist domestic line, rendered in the slogan as "Uninterrupted Revolution," would become a key feature of the ideological and political conflicts between the Chinese and the Soviet Communists in the coming years.

However, the most important lesson that the Chairman and his successors learned from Hungary was the risks of surrendering any measure of political and ideological control, however limited, over popular conceptions of the regime's legitimacy. Power and success, in apparently forging a socialist polity, had for a short period bred overconfidence in Mao. It led him to believe that the reform of Stalinism would be made possible from within by innovative noncoercive means: that is, the political rationality of socialism could be retained without its inefficient bureaucratism. All the while, state totalitarianism and Mao's personal dominance would continue unchallenged. However, in the face of a growing sense of disillusionment with Communism among the more thoughtful intellectuals and students—in many ways parallel to Budapest—the Chairman's instincts saw outside critics as another Petőfi Circle, impudently contesting the leadership of the CCP and by extension that of Mao himself. The collapse of the rectification and HF policies into the repressive Anti-Rightist Campaign represented a failure of Mao's liberal policy, which was inevitable given that Mao and the inner party could not countenance any suggestion that their hold on

---

1. For the formulation of the Great Leap Forward line and Mao's apparent reservations concerning the anti–rash economic policy in the latter half of 1957, as communicated in stinging criticisms passed on to Zhou Enlai and Chen Yun throughout early 1958, see Pang and Jin, *Maozhuan,* 763–77; Chen Hongxun, "Luelun Mao Zedong pipan fanmaojin de zhengzhi yinsu" [Briefly commenting on the political factors in Mao Zedong's criticisms against Anti-Rash Advancement], *Dangshi jiaoxue yu yanjiu* [Party history teaching and research], 2 (2002): 34–36; Liu Wusheng, "Zhou Enlai yu maojin, fanmaojin, fanfanmaojin" [Zhou Enlai and Rash-Advancement, Anti-Rash Advancement and opposing Anti-Rash Advancement], *Zong Heng* [Length and breadth], 5 (2004): 4–13. For the process of Mao changing the anti–rash economic policy back to the radical line that had been set up in the second half of 1955, see Shen, *Sikao yu xuanze,* 768–73; Teiwes, *China's Road to Disaster,* 82–110.

power was not in the best interests of the Chinese people. Thereafter, Hungary became a symbolic event, its name repeatedly invoked by the Soviet Union to shore up bloc unity and by the CCP to insist on the ideological rectitude of Communism. After Budapest, the CCP's political centralization became impregnable.

Bibliography

Bachman, David. *Bureaucracy, Economy, and Leadership in China: The Institutional Origins of the Great Leap Forward*. New York and Cambridge: Cambridge University Press, 2006.
Banac, Ivo. *With Stalin against Tito: Cominformist Splits in Yugoslav Communism*. Ithaca, NY: Cornell University Press, 1988.
Békés, Csaba. "New Findings on the 1956 Hungarian Revolution," *CWIHP Bulletin* (hereinafter *Bulletin*) 2 (1992): 1–3.
———. "The 1956 Hungarian Revolution and World Politics," *Hungarian Quarterly* 36 (1995): 109–21.
Békés, Csaba, and Malcolm Byrne. *The 1956 Hungarian Revolution: A History in Documents*. Budapest and New York: Central European University Press, 2002.
Békés, Csaba, Christian F. Ostermann, and Malcolm Byrne, eds. *The Hidden History of Hungary 1956: A Compendium of Declassified Documents*. Budapest; Washington DC: National Security Archive, 1996.
Bernstein, Thomas P. *Leadership and Mass Mobilisation in the Soviet and Chinese Collectivisation Campaigns of 1929–30 and 1955–56: A Comparison*. Cambridge: Cambridge University Press, 1967.
———. "Cadre and Peasant Behavior under Conditions of Insecurity and Deprivation: The Grain Supply Crisis of the Spring of 1955," in *Chinese Communist Politics in Action*, edited by Arthur Doak Barnett. Seattle: University of Washington Press, 1969.
Bo Yibo. *Ruogan Zhongda juece yu shijian de huigu* [Review on a certain number of crucial decisions and events]. 2 vols. Beijing: Remmin, 1997.
Borhi, László. *Hungary in the Cold War, 1945–1956: Between the United States and the Soviet Union*. Budapest: Central European University Press, 2004.
Brzezinski, Zbigniew. *The Soviet Bloc, Unity and Conflict*. Cambridge, MA: Harvard University Press, 1960.

———. *The Grand Failure: The Birth and Death of Communism in the Twentieth Century*. New York: Scribners, 1989.

Cheek, Timothy, and Tony Saich. *New Perspectives on State Socialism in China*. Armonk, NY: M.E. Sharpe, 1997.

Chen Hongxun. "Luelun Mao Zedong pipan fanmaojin de zhengzhi yinsu" [Briefly commenting on the political factors in Mao Zedong's criticisms against anti-rash advancement], *Dangshi jiaoxue yu yanjiu* [Party history teaching and research], 2 (2002): 34–36.

Chen Jian. "The Sino-Soviet Alliance and China's Entry into the Korean War." CWIHP Working Paper 1. Washington, DC: Woodrow Wilson International Center for Scholars, 1992.

———. *China's Road to the Korean War: The Making of the Sino-American Confrontation*. New York: Columbia University Press, 1994.

———. *Mao's China and the Cold War*. Chapel Hill, NC, and London: University of North Carolina Press, 2001.

———. "A Response: How to Pursue a Critical History of Mao's Foreign Policy," *China Journal*, no. 49 (January 2003): 137–42.

Cheng Yinghong. "Beyond Moscow-Centric Interpretation: An Examination of the China Connection in Eastern Europe and North Vietnam During the Era of De-Stalinization." *Journal of World History* 15, no. 4 (2004): 487–518.

Cliver, Robert. "Mao and the Economic Stalinization of China, 1948–1953." *Business History Review* 82, no. 4 (2008): 908–10.

Compton, Boyd. *Mao's China: Party Reform Documents, 1942-44*. Seattle: University of Washington Press, 1952.

Cox, Terry, ed., *Hungary 1956—Forty Years On*. London: Frank Cass Publishers, 1997.

Crampton, Richard John. *Eastern Europe in the Twentieth Century—and After*. London: Routledge, 1997.

Crockatt, Richard. *The Fifty Years War: The United States and the Soviet Union in World Politics, 1941-1991*. London and New York: Routledge, 1995.

Dai Maolin and Zhao Xiaoguang. "Shixi 'Gao-Rao shijian' fasheng de yuanyin" [An attempt on analyzing the origin of the "Gao-Rao affair"], *Dangshijiaoxue yu yanjiu* [Party history teaching and research], 6 (2003): 65–68.

Dai Qing. *Liang Chuming, Wang Shiwei, Chu Anping*. Jiangsu: Jiangsu wenyi, 1989.

Deng Xiaoping, *Deng Xiaoping wenxuan* [Selected works of Deng Xiaoping], vol. 3 (Beijing: Renmin, 1993).
Deng Zihui. *Deng Zihui wenji* [Collective works of Deng Zihui]. Beijing: Renmin, 1996.
Dimitrov, Georgi. *The Diary of Georgi Dimitrov, 1933–1949*. New Haven, CT: Yale University Press, 2003.
Dittmer, Lowell. "Review: The Past Recaptured." *China Quarterly*, no. 97 (March 1984): 126–34.
———. *Liu Shaoqi and the Chinese Cultural Revolution*. Armonk, NY: M.E. Sharpe, 1998.
Du Runsheng. "Yi wushiniandaichuqi wo yu Mao Zedong zhuxi de jici huimian" [Recollecting the meetings I had with Chairman Mao Zedong in the early 1950s]. In *Mianhuai Mao Zedong* [*Recollecting Mao Zedong*], edited by Mianhuai Mao Zedong editing group, 370–81. Beijing: Zhongyang wenxian, 1993.
Dzis. "Kiryluk's Telegram to Gomulka: Mao Zedong's Attitude to the Polish Events." *Dzis*, no. 10 (1996): 124–26 (Chinese translated version).
Eckstein, Alexander. "Conditions and Prospects for Economic Growth in Communist China." *World Politics: A Quarterly Journal of International Relations* 7, no. 1 (October 1954): 255–83.
———. "National Income and Capital Formation in Hungary, 1900–1950." *Review of Income and Wealth* 5, no. 1 (1955): 152–223.
———. "Economic Growth and Change in China: A Twenty-Year Perspective." *China Quarterly* 54, no. 1 (1973): 211–41.
Eisenhower, Dwight D. *The White House Years: Mandate for Change 1953–1956*. New York: Doubleday & Company, 1963.
———. *Waging Peace: The White House Years, A Personal Account, 1956–1961*. London: Heinemann, 1966.
Esherick, Joseph W. "Ten Theses on the Chinese Revolution in Modern China." *Modern China* 21, no. 1 (1995): 45–76.
Fehér, Ferenc, and Agnes Heller. *Hungary 1956 Revisited: The Message of a Revolution—A Quarter of a Century After*. London: George Allen & Unwin, 1983.
Feng Xigang. "Maoci shuangbi: Yongxueci yu youyongci [Two: Praise snow and on swimming]." *Suibi* [Essay], no. 3 (2007): 13–17.
Freeland, Noble, ed. *Documents on International Affairs, 1956*, Oxford: Royal Institute of International Affairs, 1959.
Frucht, Richard C. *Encyclopedia of Eastern Europe: From the Congress of*

Vienna to the Fall of Communism. London: Taylor & Francis Group, 2003.

Fu Dazhang. "Guanyu Mao Zedongtongzhi 1953nian2yue shicha Anqingshi jianghua de huiyi" [Recollection of Mao's speech given in February 1953 during his visit to Anqing]. *Lilun zhanxian* [Theoretical Front] 96 (1981).

Fu Lei. *Fu Lei jiashu: Zengbuben* [Family letters of Fulei: Appended version]. Beijing: Sanlian, 1994.

Fursenko, Aleksandr, and Timothy Naftali. *Khrushchev's Cold War: The Inside Story of an American Adversary*. New York; London: W.W. Norton & Company, 2006.

Gabriel, S.J. "Book Review: Mao and the Economic Stalinization of China, 1948–1953." *Choice: Current Reviews for Academic Libraries* 43, no. 11/12 (2006): 2043.

Gaddis, John Lewis. *We Now Know: Rethinking Cold War History*. New York: Oxford University Press, 1997.

Gao Wenqian. *Wannian Zhou Enlai* [Zhou Enlai's later years], vol. 86. Hong Kong: Mirror Books, 2003.

Gao Hua. *Hongtaiyang shi zenyang shengqide* [How did the sun rise over Yan'an? A history of the rectification movement]. Hong Kong: Chinese University of Hong Kong, 2000.

Garver, John W. *Chinese-Soviet Relations, 1937–1945: The Diplomacy of Chinese Nationalism*. New York: Oxford University Press, 1988.

——. "The Opportunity Costs of Mao's Foreign Policy Choices." *The China Journal*, no. 49 (Jan. 2003): 127–36.

Gati, Charles. *Failed Illusions: Moscow, Washington, Budapest, and the 1956 Hungarian Revolt*. Stanford, CA: Stanford University Press, 2006.

Gibianskii, Leonid. "Soviet-Yugoslav Relations and the Hungarian Revolution of 1956." *Cold War International History Project Bulletin* 10 (1998): 139–48.

Gluchowski, Leszek. "Poland, 1956: Khrushchev, Gomulka and the 'Polish October.'" *Cold War International History Project Bulletin* 5 (1995): 38–49.

Gluchowski, Leszek, and E.J. Nalepa. "The Soviet-Polish Confrontation of October 1956: The Situation in the Polish Internal Security Corps." CWIHP Working Paper 17, Woodrow Wilson International Center for Scholars (1997).

Goldman, Merle. "Hu Feng's Conflict with the Communist Literary Authorities." *China Quarterly*, 12 (1962): 102–37.

———. "The Party and the Intellectuals." In *The Cambridge History of China*. Vol. 14. *The People's Republic, Part 1: The Emergence of Revolutionary China, 1949–1965*, edited by Roderick MacFarquhar and John K. Fairbank. Cambridge: Cambridge University Press, 1987, 218–58.

———. "Mao's Obsession with the Political Role of Literature and the Intellectuals." In *The Secret Speeches of Chairman Mao: From the Hundred Flowers to the Great Leap Forward*, edited by Roderick MacFarquhar, Timothy Cheek, and Eugene Wu, 39–58. Cambridge MA: Harvard University Press, 1989.

Goldstone, Jack A. *Revolution and Rebellion in the Early Modern World*. Berkeley, CA: University of California Press, 1993.

———. "The Problem of the 'Early Modern' World." *Journal of the Economic and Social History of the Orient/Journal de l'histoire economique et sociale de l'Orient* 41, no. 3 (1998): 249–84.

Goncharov, Sergei, John Lewis, and Litai Xue. *Uncertain Partners: Stalin, Mao, and the Korean War*. Stanford, CA: Stanford University Press, 1993.

Gough, Roger. *A Good Comrade: János Kádár, Communism and Hungary*. New York: I.B. Tauris, 2006.

Granville, Johanna. "Hungary, 1956: The Yugoslav Connection." *Europe-Asia Studies* 50, no. 3 (1998): 493–517.

———. "From the Archives of Warsaw and Budapest: A Comparison of the Events of 1956." *East European Politics & Societies* 16, no. 2 (2002): 521–63.

———. "1956 Reconsidered: Why Hungary and Not Poland?" *Slavonic and East European Review* 80, no. 4 (2002): 656–87.

———. *The First Domino: International Decision Making During the Hungarian Crisis of 1956*. College Station, TX: Texas A&M University Press, 2004.

Guojia nongye weiyuanhui bangongting [National Agricultural Committee administration office], ed. *Nongye jitihua zhongyao wenjian huibian* [A selected edition of the important documents on agricultural collectivization]. 2 vols. Beijing: Zhonggong zhongyang dangxiao, 1981.

Guo Simin. *Wo yanzhong de Mao Zedong* [My perceptions of Mao Zedong]. Shijiazhuang: Hebei renmin, 1990.

Gyarmati, Gyorgy, and M. Janos Rainer. *A Captive Nation in the Soviet Empire, 1944-1989*. Boulder, CO: East European Monographs, 2008.

Györkei, Jenö, and Miklós Horváth, eds. *Soviet Military Intervention in Hungary 1956*. Budapest: Central European University Press, 1999.

Hanhimäki, Jussi M., and Odd Arne Westad. *The Cold War: A History in Documents and Eyewitness Accounts*. Oxford and New York: Oxford University Press, 2003.

Hao Deqing. "Waijiaogongzuo sanshinian" [Thirty years of my diplomatic career]. In *Dangdai Zhongguo shijie waijiao shengya* [Diplomatic careers of contemporary Chinese envoys], edited by Pei Jianzhang, 65–70. Beijing: Shijie Zhishi, 1995.

Harrison, Hope M. *Driving the Soviets up the Wall: Soviet-East German Relations, 1953-1961*. Princeton, NJ: Princeton University Press, 2003.

———. *Driving the Soviets up the Wall: Soviet-East German Relations, 1953-1961*, 2nd ed. Princeton, NJ: Princeton University Press, 2005.

Harvard University, Center for International Affairs, and East Asian Research Center Harvard University. *Communist China 1955-1959: Policy Documents with Analysis*. Vol. 10. Cambridge, MA: Harvard University Press, 1962.

———. *Communist China, 1955-1959: Policy Documents with Analysis*. Cambridge, MA: Harvard University Press, 1971.

Hegedüs, András. *A Törtenelem a Hatalom Igézetében: letrajzi Elemzések* [In history and struggles, memoir of Andras Hegedüs]. Budapest: Kossuth, 1988.

———. *Hegejusi huiyilu* [Hegedüs's memoir]. Trans. Chen Zhiliu and Chai Pengfei. Beijing: Shijie zhishi, 1992.

Horváth, Miklós. "Soviet Aggression against Hungary in 1956: Operations "Wave" and "Whirlwind." In *The Ideas of the Hungarian Revolution, Suppressed and Victorious, 1956-1999*, 67–69, edited by Lee Congdon and Bela Király. Bradenton, FL: East European Monographs, 2003.

Hsu, Immanuel C.Y. *The Rise of Modern China*, 3rd ed. Oxford: Oxford University Press, 1992.

Hu Bo. "Lengzhan yinying xia de Xiongyali shijian" [The Hungarian crisis under the shadow of the cold war]. PhD diss. East China Normal University, 1999.

———. *Lengzhan yinying xia de xiongyali shijian: Daguo de yingce yu hudong* [The Hungarian crisis under the shadow of the Cold War: Great powers' responses and interactions]. Beijing: Zhongguo shehuikexue, 2004.

Hu Sheng, ed. *Zhongguo gongchandang de qishinian* [The Chinese Communist Party's seventy years]. Beijing: Zhonggong dangshi, 1980.

Huang Daoxia. *Jianguo yilai nongye hezuohua shiliao huibian* [Collected historical documents of the agricultural collectivization since the establishment of the PRC]. Beijing: Zhonggong dangshi, 1992.

Hughes, Trevor, and Det Luard. *The Economic Development of Communist China*. Cambridge: Cambridge University Press, 1961.

Hunt, Michael H. *The Genesis of Chinese Communist Foreign Policy*. New York: Columbia University Press, 1996.

Huszár, Tibor. *Kádár János Politikai Életrajza* [A political biography of János Kádár]. Budapest: Szabad Tér Kiadó-Kossuth Kiadó, 2001.

Izsák, Lajos. *Magyarország Miniszterelnökei, 1848–1990* [The prime ministers of Hungary, 1848–1990], 2nd ed. Budapest: Cégér Kiadói Kft., 1993.

Jin Chongji, ed. *Liu Shaoqi zhuan* [A biography of Liu Shaoqi], vol. 2. Beijing: Zhongyang wenxian, 1998.

———. "Zai Liu Shaoqi shengping he sixiang yantaohui shang de jianghua" [Speech delivered at the closing session of the seminar on Liu Shaoqi's life and thoughts, 23 November 1998], *Dang de wenxian* [Party documents], 1 (1999): 51–55. Jingji ziliao bianji weiyuanhui [Economic materials editing committee], ed. *Nongye shehui zhuyi gaizao wenji*, vols. 1, 2. Beijing Zhongguo caizheng jingji, 1955.

———, ed. *Nongye shehui zhuyi gaizao wenji*, vol. 3. Beijing Zhongguo caizheng jingji, 1957.

———, ed. *Nongye shehui zhuyi gaizao wenji*, vol. 4. Beijing Zhongguo caizheng jingji, 1958.

Junshi Kexueyuan et al., eds. *Mao Zedong junshi wenji* [Mao Zedong's selected works on military affairs], vol. 5. Beijing: Junshikexue; zhongyang wenxian, 1993.

Kau, Michael Y.M., and John K. Leung, eds. *The Writings of Mao Zedong: 1949–1976*. 2 vols. Armonk, NY: M.E. Sharpe, 1986, 1992.

Keith, Ronald C. *The Diplomacy of Zhou Enlai*. New York: St. Martin's Press, 1989.

Kelkar, Govind S. "The Chinese Experience of Political Campaigns and Mass Mobilization." *Social Scientist*, vol. 7, no. 5 (December 1978): 45–63.

Kemp-Welch, Anthony. *Poland under Communism: A Cold War History*. Cambridge: Cambridge University Press, 2008.

Kertesz, Stephen D. *Diplomacy in a Whirlpool: Hungary between Nazi Germany and Soviet Russia*. Notre Dame, IN: University of Notre Dame Press, 1984.

Khrushchev, Nikita. *Khrushchev Remembers*. Translated by Strobe Talbott. Boston: Little, Brown, 1970.

———. *Khrushchev Remembers: The Last Testament*. Translated by Strobe Talbott. New York: Bantam Books, 1974.

———. *Khrushchev Remembers: The Glasnost Tapes*. Translated by Jerrod L. Schecter with Vyacheslav Luchkov. Boston: Little, Brown, 1990.

———. *Heluxiaofu huiyilu, quanyiben* [Nikita Khrushchev, Khrushchev remembers, a complete version]. 3 vols., vol. 3. Beijing: Shehui kexue wenxian, 2006.

Khrushchev, Sergei. *Khrushchev on Khrushchev: An Inside Account of the Man and His Era*. Translated by William Taubman. Boston: Little, Brown, 1990.

Király, Bela. "The United Nations Organization and the Hungarian Revolution." In *The Ideas of the Hungarian Revolution: Suppressed and Victorious 1956–1999*, edited by Lee Congdon and Bela Király. Bradenton, FL: East European Monographs, 2002: 142–66.

———, ed. *The First War between Socialist State: The Hungarian Revolution of 1956 and Its Impact*. New York: Brooklyn College Press, 1984.

Kissinger, Henry. *Diplomacy*. New York: Simon & Schuster, 1994.

Kong Hanbing. *ZhongSu guanxi jiqi dui Zhongguo shehui fazhan de yingxiang* [Sino-Soviet relationship and its impact on the development of the Chinese society]. Beijing: Zhongguo guoji guangbo chubanshe, 2004.

Kovács, Imre. *Facts about Hungary: The Fight for Freedom*. New York: Hungarian Committee, 1966.

Kovrig, Bennett. *The Myth of Liberation: East-Central Europe in US Diplomacy and Politics since 1941*. Baltimore: Johns Hopkins University Press, 1973.

———. *Communism in Hungary: From Kun to Kadar*. Vol. 211. Stanford, CA: Hoover Institution Press, 1979.

Kramer, Mark. "Hungary and Poland, 1956: Khrushchev's CPSU CC Presidium Meeting on East European Crises, 24 October 1956." *Cold War International History Project Bulletin* 5 (1995): 50-51.

———. "New Evidence on Soviet Decision-Making and the 1956 Polish and Hungarian Crises." *Cold War International History Project Bulletin* 8–9 (1996/1997): 358–84.

———. "The 'Malin Notes' on the Crises in Hungary and Poland, 1956," *Bulletin*, 8–9 (1996/1997): 393–410.

———. "The Early Post-Stalin Succession Struggle and Upheavals in East-Central Europe: Internal-External Linkages in Soviet Policy Making (Part 3)." *Journal of Cold War Studies* 1, no. 3 (1999): 3–66.

Kuo, Mercy A. *Contending with Contradictions: China's Policy toward Soviet Eastern Europe and the Origins of the Sino-Soviet Split, 1953–1960.* New York: Lexington Books, 2001.

Lan, Hua R., and Vanessa L. Fong. *Women in Republican China: A Sourcebook.* Asia and the Pacific. Armonk, NY: M.E. Sharpe, 1999.

Ledovsky, Andrei. "Mikoyan's Secret Mission to China in January and February 1949." *Far Eastern Affairs*, no. 6 (1995): 72–94.

———. "Migaoyang de fuhua mimi shiming 1949nian 1-2yue" [Mikoyan's secret mission to China in January and February 1949]. Trans. by Li Yuzhen. *Dangde Wenxian* [Party Documents], no. 6 (1995): 81–84.

———. "Mikoyan's Secret Mission to China in January and February 1949." *Far Eastern Affairs*, no. 3 (1995): 74–90.

———. "Migaoyang de fuhua mimi shiming 1949nian 1-2yue" [Mikoyan's secret mission to China in January and February 1949]. *Dangde wenxian* [Party documents], no. 1 (1996): 90–96.

———. "The Moscow Visit of a Delegation of the Communist Party of China in June to August 1949 (First Installment)." *Far Eastern Affairs* no. 4 (1996): 64–86.

———. "The Moscow Visit of a Delegation of the Communist Party of China in June to August 1949 (First Installment)." *Far Eastern Affairs* no. 5 (1996): 84–97.

Lee, Congdon, and Bela Király. *The Ideas of the Hungarian Revolution: Suppressed and Victorious 1956–1999.* Bradenton, FL: East European Monographs, 2002.

Lee Hongyung. *From Revolutionary Cadres to Party Technocrats in Socialist China.* Berkeley, CA: University of California Press, 1991.

Lee, Steven Hugh. *Outposts of Empire: Korea, Vietnam, and the Origins of the Cold War in Asia, 1949–1954.* Montreal: McGill-Queen's University Press, 1996.

Leffler, Melvyn P. "The Cold War: What Do 'We Now Know'?" *American Historical Review* (1999): 501–24.

——. *For the Soul of Mankind: The United States, the Soviet Union, and the Cold War*. New York: Hill and Wang, 2007.

Lendvai, Paul. *One Day That Shook the Communist World: The 1956 Hungarian Uprising and Its Legacy*. Translated by Ann Major. Princeton, NJ: Princeton University Press, 2010.

Levenson, Joseph R. *Confucian China and Its Modern Fate*, 3 vols., vol. 1. Berkeley and Los Angeles: Routledge and Kegan Paul. Vols. 2 and 3, Berkeley, CA: University of California Press, 1958.

——. *Confucian China and Its Modern Fate: The Problem of Intellectual Continuity*, vol. 2. Berkeley and Los Angeles: University of California Press, 1964.

——. *Confucian China and Its Modern Fate: A Trilogy*. Berkeley and Los Angeles: University of California Press, 1968.

Li Hua-Yu. "The Political Stalinization of China: The Establishment of One-Party Constitutionalism, 1948–1954." *Journal of Cold War Studies* 3, no. 2 (Spring 2001): 28–47.

——. *Mao and the Economic Stalinization of China, 1948–1953*. Harvard Cold War Studies Book Series. Lanham: Rowman & Littlefield, 2006.

——. "The Political Stalinization of China: The Establishment of One-Party Constitutionalism, 1948–1954." *Journal of Cold War Studies* 3, no. 2 (2001): 28–47.

Li Huaiyin. "The First Encounter: Peasant Resistance to State Control of Grain in East China in the Mid-1950s." *China Quarterly* 185, no. 1 (2006): 145–62.

Li Rui. *"Da Yuejin" qinliji* [Personal experience during the "Great Leap Forward"]. Shanghai: Yuandong chubanshe, 1996.

Li Shenzhi. "Guanyu 'Daminzhu' he 'Xiaominzhu' de yiduan gong'an" [On the intricate case of 'Big Democracy' and 'Small Democracy.'" *Bainianchao* 5 (1997): 47–49.

——. "Mao zhuxi shi shenme shihou jueding yinshe chudong de [When did Mao decide to draw a snake out of its hole?]." In *Liuyuexue: Jiyizhong de fanyoupai yundong* [Snow in June: Remembering the Anti-Rightist Campaign], edited by Han Niu and Deng Jiuping, 117–25. Beijing: Jingjiribao, 1998.

——. *Fengyu canghuang wushinian—Li Shenzhi wenxuan* [Fifty years of upheaval and chasm—Selected texts by Li Shenzhi]. Hong Kong: Mingbao, 2004.

Li Weihan. *Huiyi yu yanjiu* [Recollections and studies], vol. 2. Beijing: Zhonggong dangshiziliao, 1986.

Li Xiaobing and Hongshan Li. *China and the United States: A New Cold War History*. Lanham, MD: University Press of America, 1998.

Li Zhisui. *The Private Life of Chairman Mao: The Memoirs of Mao's Personal Physician*. Translated by Tai Hung-chao. London: Arrow Books, 1996.

Liao Xinwen, Huaxuan Xiong, and Yangyong Chen. *Zouchu guomen de Zhou Enlai* [Zhou Enlai who stepped out of China]. Shijiazhuang: Hebei renmin, 2001.

Liang Zhi, Xia Yafeng, and Ming Chen, "ECNU-WWICS Occasional Paper: Recent Trends in the Study of Cold War History in China." Cold War International History Project, Woodrow Wilson International Center for Scholars (October 2012), occasional paper 1.

Lin Ke. *Lin Ke riji* [Lin Ke's diary]. Unpublished written draft, personal collection.

Litván, György, J.M. Bak, L.H. Legters, G. Schöpflin, and P. Kende. *The Hungarian Revolution of 1956: Reform, Revolt, and Repression, 1953–1963*. London: Longman, 1996.

Liu Congwen and Shaotao Chen, eds. *Liu Shaoqi nianpu (1898–1969)* [The chronicles of Liu Shaoqi (1898–1969)]. 2 vols. Beijing: Zhongyang wenxian, 1996.

Liu Jianping. "Sugong yu Zhongguo gongchandang renmin minzhu zhuanzheng lilun de queli" [The communist party of the Soviet Union and the formation of Chinese communist people's democratic dictatorship theory], *Lishi yanjiu* [History studies], 1 (1998): 78–96.

Liu Shaoqi. *Liu Shaoqi xuanji* [Selected works of Liu Shaoqi], vol. 1. 2 vols. Beijing: Renmin, 1981.

———. *Liu Shaoqi xuanji* [Selected works of Liu Shaoqi], vol. 2. Beijing: Renmin, 1985.

———. "Yao fangzhi liangdao renyuan teshuhua" [To avoid the 'leadership as privilege' philosophy (Title added by the editor)]. Dang de wenxian [Party's documents], no. 5 (1988): 24–25.

———. "Report at the 1st Meeting of the 2nd Plenary Session of the Eighth Central Committee." In Shen Zhihua, *Sikao yu xuanze: Cong zhishi-*

fenzi huiyi dao fanyoupai yundong [Reflections and choices: The consciousness of the Chinese intellectuals and the Anti-Rightist Campaign (1956–1957): The history of the People's Republic of China], vol. 3, 75–85. Hong Kong: Chinese University of Hong Kong, 2008.

Liu Wusheng. "Zhou Enlai yu maojin, fanmaojin, fanfanmaojin" [Zhou Enlai and rash-advancement, anti-rash advancement and opposing anti-rash advancement], *Zong heng* [Length and breadth], 5 (2004): 4–13.

Liu Ying. "Buxunchang de dashi: yi Zhangwentian chushi Mosike [Unusual ambassador: Recollecting Zhang Wentian as an ambassador to Moscow]." In *Dangdai Zhongguo shijie waijiao shengya* [Diplomatic careers of contemporary Chinese envoys], edited by Pei Jianzhang, 1–29. Beijing: Shijie zhishi, 1995.

Liu Yu. "Why Did It Go So High? Political Mobilization and Agricultural Collectivization in China." *China Quarterly* 187 (2006): 732.

———. "From the Mass Line to Mao's Cult." PhD diss., Columbia University, 2006.

Liu Zhende. *Wo wei Shaoqi dang mishu* [Being personal secretary of Liu Shaoqi]. Beijing: Zhongyang wenxian, 1994.

Lomax, Bill. "The Hungarian Revolution of 1956 and the Origins of the Kádár Regime." *Studies in Comparative Communism* 18, no. 2 (1985): 87–113.

Lu Dingyi. "Duiyu zhanhou guoji xingshizhong jige jiben wenti de jieshi" [Explanations of several basic problems concerning the postwar international situation], *Jiefang ribao* [Liberation daily], 4 January 1947.

———. *Lu Dingyi wenji* [Collection of Lu Dingyi's writings]. 2 vols. Beijing: Renmin, 1992.

Luo Yisu. "1956nian 'Bolan shijian' he Zhongguo de zhengce" [The 1956 "Polish Incident" and Chinese policies], *Waijiao xueyuan xuebao* [Chinese foreign affairs university bulletin], issue 3 (1997): 41–42.

Lüthi, M. Lorenz. *The Sino-Soviet Split: Cold War in the Communist World* Princeton, NJ, and Oxford: Princeton University Press, 2008.

MacFarquhar, Roderick. *The Hundred Flowers Campaign and the Chinese Intellectuals*. London: Praeger, 1960.

———. *The Origins of the Cultural Revolution: Contradictions among the People 1956–1957*, vol. 1, London: Oxford University Press, 1974.

———. *The Origins of the Cultural Revolution: The Great Leap Forward 1958–1960*, vol. 2. London: Oxford University Press, 1983.

MacFarquhar, Roderick, Timothy Cheek, and Eugene Wu, eds. *The Secret Speeches of Chairman Mao: From the Hundred Flowers to the Great Leap Forward*. Cambridge, MA: Harvard University Press, 1989.
MacFarquhar, Roderick, and Michael Schoenhals. *Mao's Last Revolution*. Cambridge: Cambridge University Press, 2006.
Makowski, Edmunda. *Poznański Czerwiec 1956: Pierwszy Bunt Społeczeństwa W Prl*. Poznań: Wydawn. Poznanskie, 2001.
Malashenko, Yevgeny I. "The Special Corps under Fire in Budapest: Memoirs of an Eyewitness." In *Soviet Military Intervention in Hungary 1956*, edited by Jenö Györkei and Miklós Horváth. Budapest: Central European University Press, 1999.
Malin, V.N. "The 'Malin Notes' on the Crises in Hungary and Poland, 1956." In *Cold War International History Project Bulletin 8–9*, edited by Mark Kramer, 385–410. Washington DC: Woodrow Wilson International Center for Scholars, 1996/1997.
Mao Zedong. *Selected Works of Mao Tse-Tung*, vol. 4, Beijing: Foreign Languages Press, 1969.
———. *Mao Tse-Tung Unrehearsed: Talks and Letters, 1956–71*. Translated by John Chinnery and Tieyun and Introduced by Stuart Schram. London: Penguin books, 1974.
———. *Mao Zedong xuanji* [Selected works of Mao Zedong], vol. 5. Beijing: Renmin, 1977.
———. *Mao Zedong xuanji* [Selected works of Mao Zedong], vol. 2. Beijing: Renmin, 1991.
———. "Resolution of the Second Plenum of the Seventh CCP CC (13 March 1949)." In *The Rise to Power of the Chinese Communist Party: Documents and Analysis*, edited by Tony Saich and Benjamin Yang, 1342–44. Armonk, NY: M.E. Sharpe, 1996.
Meisner, Maurice. *Li Ta-Chao and the Origins of Chinese Marxism*, vol. 27. Cambridge, MA: Harvard University Press, 1967.
———. *Mao's China and After: A History of the People's Republic*. New York: Free Press, 1999.
———. *Li Ta-Chao and the Origins of Chinese Marxism*, vol. 27. Cambridge, MA: Harvard University Press, 1967.
Meray, Tibor. *Thirteen Days That Shook the Kremlin: Imre Nagy and the Hungarian Revolution*. New York: Praeger, 1959.
Mićunović, Veljko. *Moscow Diary*. Translated by David Floyd. Garden City, NY: Doubleday Books, 1980.

Mitter, Rana. "An Uneasy Engagement: Chinese Ideas of Global Order and Justice in Historical Perspective." In *Order and Justice in International Relations*, edited by Rosemary Foot, John Gaddis, and Andrew Hurrell, 207–35. Oxford: Oxford University Press, 2003.
———. *A Bitter Revolution: China's Struggle with the Modern World*. Oxford: Oxford University Press, 2005.
———. *Modern China*. New York: Sterling Publishing, 2009.
Mo Zhibin, and Teshui Chen. *Gen Mao Zedong xuedushu* [Learn how to select and read books from Mao Zedong]. Beijing: Zhongyang wenxian, 2003.
Mu Fusheng. *The Writing of the Hundred Flowers: Free Thought in China Today*. London: Heinemann, 1962.
Nagy, Imre. *On Communism, In Defense of the New Course*. New York: Praeger, 1957.
Nie Hualing. *Literature of the Hundred Flowers: Criticism and Polemics*, vol. 1. New York: Columbia University Press, 1981.
Niu Dayong and Zhihua Shen. *Leng zhan yu Zhongguo de zhoubian guanxi*. Beijing: Shijie zhishi, 2004.
Niu Jun. *Cong Yan'an zou xiang shijie—Zhongguo gongchandang duiwai guanxi de qiyuan* [From Yan'an to the world: The origins of CCP foreign relations]. Fuzhou: Fujian renmin chubanshe, 1992.
———. "Xin Zhongguo waijiao de xingcheng jiqi zhuyao tezheng" [The formation of diplomatic policy in China and its characteristics]. *Lishi yanjiu* [History studies], no. 5 (1999): 23–42.
Nogee, Joseph L., and Robert H. Donaldson. *Soviet Foreign Policy since World War II*. New York: Pergamon Press, 1984.
Ochab, Edward. *Rozmowa z Edwardem Ochabem, Teresa Toranska*. Warszawa: Oni, 1989.
Pang Xianzhi and Jin Chongji, eds. *Mao Zedong zhuan (1949–1976)* [Biography of Mao Zedong 1949–1976], vol. 1. Beijing: Zhongyang wenxian, 2004.
Pei Jianzhang, ed. *Zhonghua renmin gongheguo waijiaoshi: 1949–1956* [Diplomatic history of the People's Republic of China], vol. 1. Beijing: Shijie zhishi, 1994.
———, ed. *Zhonghua renmin gongheguo waijiaoshi: 1957–1969* [Diplomatic history of the People's Republic of China], vol. 2. Beijing: Shijie zhishi, 1998.
———. "Maozhuxi dushu shenghuo wojian wowen: Jiangsu zhenshi de

Mao Zedong" [The reading life of Mao Zedong: What I saw and what I heard of the real Mao], *Tebie cehua* [Special report] (2006): 39–43.

Person, James F. "The Myth of Factional Struggle within the Korean Workers' Party, 1945–1956" (Preliminary draft delivered in International Workshop on The Cold War and the Korean Peninsula: The Domestic Politics and Foreign Relations of North and South Korea, Beijing University, PRC, 18 May 2007.

Pons, Silvio. "Stalin and the European Communists after World War Two (1943–1948)." *Past & Present* 210, suppl. 6 (2011): 121–38.

Radványi, János. "The Hungarian Revolution and the Hundred Flowers Campaign." *China Quarterly* 43 (1970): 121–29.

———. *Hungary and the Superpowers: The 1956 Revolution and Realpolitik*, vol. 3. Stanford, CA: Hoover Press, 1972.

Rainer, Janos. "The Yeltsin Dossier: Soviet Documents on Hungary, 1956." *CWIHP Bulletin*, 5 (1995): 22.

RMRB Editorial Department, ed. "Zailun wuchanjieji zhuanzheng de lishi jingyan" [More discussion on the historical lessons of the proletarian dictatorship], written according to the discussions of the CCP CC's expanded session. *Xinhua banyuekan* [New China semimonthly], 2 (1957): 1–10.

Rowiński, Jan, ed. *Polski Październik 1956 W Polityce Światowej*. Warszawa: Pism, 2006.

Saich, Tony, and Benjamin Yang. *The Rise to Power of the Chinese Communist Party: Documents and Analysis*. Armonk, NY: M.E. Sharpe, 1996.

Salisbury, Harrison E. *The New Emperors: China in the Era of Mao and Deng*. New York: Little, Brown, 1992.

Schaller, Michael. *The American Occupation of Japan: The Origins of the Cold War in Asia*. New York: Oxford University Press, 1987.

Schram, Stuart. "The Party in Chinese Communist Ideology." *China Quarterly* 38 (1969): 1–26.

———. *The Thought of Mao Tse-Tung*. Cambridge: Cambridge University Press, 1989.

Schram, Stuart, ed. *Chairman Mao Talks to the People: Talks and Letters: 1956–1971*. New York: Pantheon Books, 1974.

Schurmann, Franz. *Ideology and Organization in Communist China*. Berkeley, CA: University of California Press, 1966.

Schwartz, Benjamin. "Marx and Lenin in China." *Far Eastern Survey*, 18, no. 15 (1949): 174–78.

———. *Chinese Communism and the Rise of Mao*. Cambridge, MA: Harvard University Press, 1951.

———. "Modernisation and the Maoist Vision—Some Reflections on Chinese Communist Goals." *China Quarterly* 21 (1965): 3–19.

———. "China's Developmental Experience, 1949–72." *Proceedings of the Academy of Political Science* (1973): 17–26.

———. "Thoughts on the Late Mao—Between Total Redemption and Utter Frustration." In *The Secret Speeches of Chairman Mao: From the Hundred Flowers to the Great Leap Forward*, edited by Roderick MacFarquhar, Timothy Cheek, and Eugene Wu, 19–38. Cambridge, MA: Harvard University Press, 1989.

Schwintzer, E. Peter. "Education to Save the Nation: Huang Yanpei and the Educational Reform Movement in Early Twentieth Century China." PhD diss., University of Washington, 1992.

Selden, Mark. *The Yenan Way in Revolutionary China*. Cambridge, MA: Harvard University Press 1971.

———. *China in Revolution: The Yenan Way Revisited*. Armonk, NY: M.E. Sharpe, 1995.

Shao Kuokang. *Zhou Enlai and the Foundations of Chinese Foreign Policy*. Houndmills, Basingstoke, Hampshire: Palgrave Macmillan, 1996.

Shen Zhihua. "XinZhongguo jianlichuqi Sulian duihua jingji yuanzhu de jiben qinghuang—laizi Zhongguo he Eluosi de dang'an cailiao" [Basic information regarding Soviet economic aid to China in the early years of new China—archival material from China and Russia]." *Eluosi yanjiu* [Russian study], no. 1 (2001): 53–66.

———. "XinZhongguo jianlichuqi Sulian duihua jingji yuanzhu de jiben qinghuang—laizi Zhongguo he Eluosi de dang'an cailiao" [Basic information regarding Soviet economic aid to China in the early years of new China—archival material from China and Russia]." *Eluosi yanjiu* [Russian study], no. 2 (2001): 49–58.

———. "Dui ZhongSu tongmeng jingji Beijing de lishikaocha" [A historical investigation into the economic background of the Sino-Soviet alliance—studies on Sino-Soviet economic relations, 1948–1949, Part I]. *Dang de wenxian*, no. 2 (2001): 53–64.

———. "Jianguo chuqi Sulian duihua yuanzhu de jiben qinghuang" [The Soviet economic assistance to communist China in its early years: A general introduction]. *Dangshi yanjiu ziliao* [CCP history research materials], no. 3 (2001): 1–16.

———, ed. *Sulian lishi dang an xuanbian* [Selected historical Soviet archives]. 34 vols. Beijing: Shehui kexue wenxian, 2002.

———. *Mao Zedong, Sidalin yu Chaoxian zhanzheng* [Stalin and the Korean War]. Guangzhou: Guangdong renmin chubanshe, 2003.

———. "Sugong ershida fei Sidalinhua jiqi dui ZhongSu guanxi de yingxiang" [The Soviet Party's twentieth congress, de-Stalinization, and their impacts on Sino-Soviet relations: A study based on recently declassified Russian archives]. *Guoji lengzhanshi yanjiu* [Cold War international history studies], no. 1 (2004): 29–69.

———. "1956nian shiyue weiji: Zhongguo de juece he yingxiang—'BoXiong shijian yu Zhongguo yanjiu zhi yi'" [China's role and influence in the revolts in Poland and Hungary in 1956: Studies on Polish and Hungarian crises and China, Part 1]. *Lishi yanjiu* [Historical studies], 2 (2005): 119–43.

———. "China's Role and Influence in the Incidents in Poland and Hungary in 1956." *Social Sciences in China* 26, no. 3 (Summer 2005): 3–16.

———. "Mao and the 1956 Soviet Military Intervention in Hungary." In *The 1956 Hungarian Revolution and the Soviet Bloc Countries': Reactions and Repercussions*, edited by M. János Rainer and Katalin Somlai, 24–37. Budapest: Institute for the History of the 1956 Hungarian Revolution, Historical Archives of Hungarian State Security, 2007.

———. "1957nian zhengfeng yundong shi ruhe kaishi de?" [How was the rectification movement in 1957 started?]. *Zhonggong dangshi yanjiu* [Chinese Communist Party history studies], no. 6 (2008): 72–83.

———. *Sikao yu xuanze: Cong zhishifenzi huiyi dao fanyoupai yundong* [Reflections and choices: The consciousness of the Chinese intellectuals and the Anti-Rightist Campaign (1956–1957). The history of the People's Republic of China], vol. 3. Hong Kong: Chinese University of Hong Kong, 2008.

———. *Sulian zhuanjia zai Zhongguo, 1948–1960* [Soviet experts in China, 1948–1960], 2nd ed. Beijing: Xinhua, 2009.

Shen Zhihua and Li Danhui, eds. *ZhongSu guanxi: Eguo dang'an fuyinjian huibian (weikan)* [Sino-Soviet relations: Collected copies of Russian archives: Unpublished version]. Center of Cold War History Studies: China East Normal University, 2002.

———. "The 1956 Polish Crisis and Sino-Polish Relations: Sources from the

Chinese Archival Documents and Inside Reports." In *The October 1956 Events in Poland in International Relations*. Warsaw: Poland, 2006.

———. "1956nian Bolanweiji yu ZhongBo guanxi—Laizi Zhongguo dang'an wenxian he neibu baodao" [1956 Polish crisis and Sino-Poland relations: From the perspective of Chinese archives and inner-circled reports]. *Eluosi yanjiu* [Russian studies], no. 3 (September 2006): 46–58.

———. "Zhongguo dui dong'Ou shiyue weiji de fanying he sikao—'Boxiong shijian yu Zhongguo' yanjiu zhi er" (hereinafter Fanying he sikao) [On the October crises in Eastern Europe: China's reaction and reflection—A study of the Polish and Hungarian incidents and China, Part 2]. *Shixue yuekan* 1 (2007): 75–85.

Shen Zhihua and Zhongyang yanjiuyuan jindaishi yanjiusuo. *Chaoxian zhanzheng: Eguo dang'anguan de jiemi wenjian* [Korean War: Declassified Russian archives]. Zhongyang yanjiuyuan jindaishi yanjiusuo shiliaocongkan. 3 vols. Taibei: Zhongyang yanjiuyuan jindaishi yanjiusuo, 2003.

Shi Jingtang, ed. *Zhonguo nongye hezuohua yundong shiliao* [Materials on the history of the movement for the cooperativization of agriculture in China]. 2 vols. Beijing: Sanlian, 1957, 1959.

Shi Yinhong. "The Hungarian Incident and American Policy." *Nanking University Journal* 1 (1998): 97–111, 122.

Shi Zhe. *Zai lishi juren shenbian: Shi Zhe huiyilu* [At the side of historical giants: Shi Zhe's memoirs], edited by Li Haiwen. Beijing: Zhongyang wenxian, 1996.

———. "Boxiong shijian yu Liu Shaoqi fangsu" [The Polish–Hungarian incident and Liu Shaoqi's visit to the Soviet Union]. *Bainian cao* [Tide of the century], 2 (1997): 11–17.

———. *Wo de yisheng* [My Life]. Beijing: Renmin, 2001.

———. *Shi Zhe koushu: ZhongSu guanxi jianzhenglu* [Shi Zhe's oral recollection: My own experience of the Sino-Soviet relations], edited by Li Haiwen. Beijing: Dangdai Zhongguo, 2005.

Shi Zhongquan, ed. *Zhonggong badashi* [History of the eighth national congress of the Chinese Communist Party Central Committee]. Beijing: Renmin, 1998.

Short, Philip. *Mao: A Life*. New York: Holt Paperbacks, 2001.

Shurmann, Franz. *Ideology and Organization in Communist China.* Berkeley, CA: University of California Press, 1966.
Skocpol, Theda. "States and Social Revolutions: A Comparative Study of France, Russia, and China." Cambridge: Cambridge University Press, 1979.
Snow, Edgar. *Red Star over China: The Classic Account of the Birth of Chinese Communism.* New York: Grove Press, 1994.
Spence, Jonathan. "On 'Chinese Revolutionary Literature.'" *Yale French Studies*, 39 (1967): 215–25.
———. *The Search for Modern China.* New York: W.W. Norton, 1999.
———. *The Search for Modern China*, 2nd ed. New York and London: W.W. Norton, 1999.
Stokes, Gale. *From Stalinism to Pluralism: A Documentary History of Eastern Europe since 1945.* New York: Oxford University Press, 1996.
Stykalin, Alexander. "The Hungarian Crisis of 1956: The Soviet Role in the Light of New Archival Documents." *Cold War History* 2, no. 1 (2001): 113–44.
Szobolevszki, Sándor, and István Vida, eds. *Iratok a Magyar-Kínai Kapcsolatok Történetéhez: Magyar-Kínai Kapcsolatok: 1956–1959; Dokumentumok* [Hungarian-China relations, 1956–1959: Documents]. Budapest: MTA Jelenkor-kutató Bizottság, 2001.
Szvák, Gyula. *Magyar Századok*: A Huszadik Század Története [One hundred years of Hungary series. Jeno Gergely-Lajos Izsak, history of the twentieth century]. Budapest: Pannonica Kiadó, 2000.
Tang, Anthony M. "Agriculture in the Industrialization of Communist China and the Soviet Union." *Journal of Farm Economics* 49, no. 5 (1967): 1118–34.
Teiwes, Frederick C. *Politics and Purges in China: Rectification and the Decline of Party Norms, 1950–1965.* Armonk, NY: M.E. Sharpe, 1993.
———. *The Politics of Agricultural Cooperativization in China: Mao, Deng Zihui, and the "High Tide" of 1955.* Armonk, NY: M.E. Sharpe, 1993.
———. *China's Road to Disaster.* Armonk, NY: M.E. Sharpe, 1999.
———. "Establishment and Consolidation of the New Regime." In *The Cambridge History of China.* Vol. 14. *The People's Republic, Part 1: The Emergence of Revolutionary China, 1949–1965*, edited by Roderick MacFarquhar and John K. Fairbank, 114–15, 167–68. Cambridge: Cambridge University Press, 1987.

———. "Politics at the 'Core': The Political Circumstances of Mao Zedong, Deng Xiaoping and Jiang Zeming." *China Information* 15, no. 1 (2001): 1–66.
Teiwes, Frederick C., and Warren Sun. *China's Road to Disaster: Mao, Central Politicians, and Provincial Leaders in the Unfolding of the Great Leap Forward, 1955–1959*. Armonk, NY: M.E. Sharpe, 1999.
Tong Yanqi. *Transitions from State Socialism: Economic and Political Change in Hungary and China*. Lanham: Rowman & Littlefield, 1997.
Tottossy, Magdolna. *A Magyar Népi Szövetség Története 1944–1953*. [History of the Hungarian People's Party, 1944–1953], vol. 1. Budapest: Pallas-Akadémia, 2005.
Townson, Duncan. *A Dictionary of Contemporary History: 1945 to the Present*. Oxford: Blackwell, 1999.
Valuch, Tibor, and Gyorgy Gyarmati. *Hungary under Soviet Domination: 1944–1989*. Boulder, CO: East European Monographs, 2010.
Vàmos, Pèter. "Evolution and Revolution: Sino-Hungarian Relations and the 1956 Revolution." *Cold War International History Project, Working Paper No. 54*, 56 (2006). Published electronically November 2006.
———. *Kína Mellettünk? Kínai Külügyi Iratok Magyarországról, 1956* [Is China with us? Chinese diplomatic records on Hungary, 1956]. Budapest: MTA Történettudományi Intézete, 2008.
Varsori, Antonio. "Reflections on the Origins of the Cold War." In *Reviewing the Cold War: Approaches, Interpretations, and Theory*, edited by Odd Arne Westad, 281–302. London and Portland, OR: Frank Cass, 2000.
Verona, Sergiu. *Military Occupation and Diplomacy: Soviet Troops in Romania, 1944–1958*. Durham, NC: Duke University Press, 1991.
Wang Dong. *The Quarrelling Brothers: New Chinese Archives and a Reappraisal of the Sino-Soviet Split, 1959–1962*. Washington, DC: Cold War International History Project, Woodrow Wilson International Center for Scholars, 2005.
Wang Qixing. "Wang Fei, Li Shenzhi yu Maozhuxi mishu tan minzhu" [Wang Fei, Li Shenzhi talked about democracy with Mao's secretary], *Yanhuang chunqiu* 8 (2010): 26–29.
Wang Ruoshui. *Zhihui de tongku* [The bitterness of intellect]. Hong Kong: Sanlian shudian, 1989.
Wang Yan, ed. *Peng Dehuai nianpu* [A chronicle of Peng Dehuai]. Beijing: Renmin, 1998.

Werblan, Anderzej. "Chiny a Polski Pazdziernik 1956," *Dzis*, no. 10 (1996), 124–26.

———. "1956nian de Bolan shiyue: Chuanshuo yu xianshi" [October 1956 in Poland: Legends and realities]. Translated by Wang Yan. *Lengzhan guojishi yanjiu* [Cold War international history studies] 4 (Fall 2006): 74–95.

Westad, Odd Arne. *Cold War and Revolution: Soviet-American Rivalry and the Origins of the Chinese Civil War, 1944–1946*. New York: Columbia University Press, 1993.

———, ed. *Brothers in Arms: The Rise and Fall of the Sino-Soviet Alliance, 1945–1963*. Palo Alto, CA: Stanford University Press, and Washington, DC: Woodrow Wilson Center Press, 1998.

———. *Reviewing the Cold War: Approaches, Interpretations, and Theory*. London and Portland, OR: Frank Cass, 2000.

———. *Decisive Encounters: The Chinese Civil War, 1946–1950*. Palo Alto, CA: Stanford University Press, 2003.

Westad, Odd Arne, Sven G. Holtsmark, and Iver B. Neumann. *The Soviet Union in Eastern Europe, 1945–89*. New York: St. Martin's Press, 1994.

Wu Lengxi. *Yi Mao Zhuxi: Wo qinsheng jingli de ruogan Zhongda lishi shijian pianduan* [Memory of Chairman Mao: Some important historical incidents of which I have firsthand knowledge]. Beijing: Xinhua, 1995.

———. "Yu Jiaying gongshi de rizi, shang" [Remembering the days I worked with Tian Jiaying, Part 1 of 2]. *Dang de wenxian* [Party documents], no. 4 (1996): 83–61.

———. *Shinian lunzhan, 1956–1966: ZhongSu guanxi huiyilu* [Ten-year polemical debate, 1956–1966: A memoir on Sino-Soviet relations]. Beijing: Zhongyang wenxian, 1999.

Xia Yafeng. "The Study of Cold War International History in China: A Review of the Last Twenty Years." *Journal of Cold War Studies* 10, no. 1 (2008): 81–115.

Xin Jianfei. *Mao Zedong's World View: From Youth to Yan'an*. Oxford, New York: University Press of America, 1995.

Xinhua tongxunshe, ed. *Xinhuashe xinwengao* [New China news report draft], vol. 2322. Beijing: Xinhua, 1956.

Xu Zehao. *Wang Jiaxiang nianpu 1906–1974* [A chronicle of Wang Jiaxing 1906–1974]. Beijing: Zhonggong zhongyang wenxian, 2001.

———. *Wang Jiaxiang zhuan* [A biography of Wang Jiaxiang]. Beijing: Dangdai Zhongguo, 2006.

Xu Zhucheng. *Xu Zhucheng huiyilu* [Xu's memoir]. Beijing: Sanlian, 1998.
———. *Qinli 1957* [Experiencing 1957]. Wuhan: Hubei renmin, 2003.
Yang Kuisong. *Makesi zhuyi Zhongguohua de lishi jincheng* [The historical process of China's nationalizing Marxism]. Kaifeng: Henan renmin, 1994.
———. "Mao Zedong weishenme fangqi xinminzhuzhuyi—guanyu Eguo moshi de yingxiang" [Why did Mao Zedong give up New Democracy?—On the influence of the Soviet Model], *Jindaishi yanjiu* 4 (1997): 139–53.
———. *Mao Zedong yu Mosike de en'en yuanyuan* [Past kindness and grudges between Mao Zedong and Moscow]. Jiangxi: Jiangxi renmin, 2002.
———. *Zhonghua renmin gongheguo jianguoshi yanjiu* [Historical study of the formation of the People's Repulic of China], vol 2. Nanchang: Jiangxi renmin, 2009.
———. *"Zhongjian didai" de geming: Guojida Beijing xia kan Zhonggong chenggong zhi dao* [Revolution in the intermediate zone: On the success of the Chinese Communist Party in the international setting]. Taiyuan: Shanxi renmin, 2010.
———. "Guanyu Zhongguo chubing Chaoxian de yishixingtai yinsu" [On the ideological factors in China's military involvement in the Korean War]. http://www.yangkuisong.net/ztlw/wjsyj/000122_2.htm. accessed on 1 July 2008.
Ye Duyi. *Suijiusi qi youweihui* [No regrets despite severe suffering]. Beijing: Beijingshi yuewenyi, 1999.
Young, Graham. "On the Mass Line." *Modern China* 6, no. 2 (1980): 225–40.
Zhang Shuguang. *Deterrence and Strategic Culture: Chinese-American Confrontations, 1949–1958*. Ithaca, NY: Cornell University Press, 1992.
Zhang Shuguang and Chen Jian. "The Emerging Dispute between Beijing and Moscow: Ten Newly Available Chinese Documents, 1956–1958." *Cold War International History Project Bulletin*, no. 6–7 (Winter 1995/1996): 148–206.
Zhang Wenxiong et al., eds. *Jujiao zhuxitai: Zhidian jiangshan (1949–1976)* [Focusing on the rostrum of the Chinese chairman: To set China the right way]. Changsha: Hunan renmin, 2004.
Zhang Yihe. *Wangshi bingbu ruyan* [The past is not like smoke]. Beijing: Renmin, 2004.

Zhen Derong, Fulin Bo, and Zuoshen Wang, eds. *Mao Zedong sixiang fazhanshi* [The history of the development of Mao Zedong thought]. Jilin: Jilin University Press, 1990.

Zhonggong hebeisheng dangshi yanjiushi [CCP Hebei province party history research office], ed. *Lingxiu zai Hebei* [The Leader in Hebei province]. Beijing: Zhonggong dangshi, 1993.

Zhonggong hubeisheng dangshi ziliao weiyuanhui [CCP Hubei provincial party historical materials committee], ed. *Mao Zedong zai Hubei* [Mao Zedong in Hubei]. Beijing: Zhonggong dangshi, 1993.

Zhonggong zhongyang dangshi yanjiushi [CCP central committee document research office], ed. *Mao Zedong nongcun diaocha wenji* [Collection of essays on Mao Zedong's countryside investigations]. Beijing: Renmin, 1982.

———, ed. *Jianguo yilai Liu Shaoqi wengao* [Liu Shaoqi's manuscripts since the founding of the People's Republic of China], vols. 1–4. Beijing: Zhongyang wenxian, 2005.

———, ed. *Zhongguo gongchandang lishi dashiji, 1919.5–2005.12* [Major events of the Chinese Communist Party, 1919.5–2005.12]. Beijing: Zhonggong dangshi, 2006.

———, ed. *Jianguo yilai Liu Shaoqi wengao* [Liu Shaoqi's manuscripts since the founding of the People's Republic of China], vols 5–7. Beijing: Zhongyang wenxian, 2008.

———, ed. *Zhongguo gongchandang lishi: Diyijuan (1921–1949)* [History of the Chinese Communist Party, 1921–1949], vol. 1. Beijing: Zhonggong dangshi, 2011.

———, ed. *Zhongguo gongchandang lishi: Diyijuan (1949–1978)* [History of the Chinese Communist Party, 1949–1978], vol. 2. Beijing: Zhonggong dangshi, 2011.

Zhonggong Zhongda shijianjishi bianweihui [Central Committee historical record editing group], ed. *Zhongguo gongchandang Zhongda shijian jishi* [On-the-spot report of the crucial events of the CCP]. Inner-Mongolia: Inner-Mongolia Publishing House, 2001.

Zhonggong zhongyang wenxian yanjiushi [CCP Central Committee Document research office], ed. *Zhou Enlai xuanji* [Selected works of Zhou Enlai], vol. 1. Beijing: Renmin, 1980.

———, ed. *Zhou Enlai xuanji* [Selected works of Zhou Enlai], vol. 2. Beijing: Renmin, 1980.

———, ed. *Zhongguo gongchandang dibaci quanguo daibiao dahui wenjian huibian* [Eighth National Congress of the Communist Party of China: Documents translated in English]. Beijing: Foreign Languages Press, 1981.

———, ed. *Zhu De xuanji* [Selected works of Zhu De]. Beijing: Renmin, 1983.

———, ed. *Mao Zedong xinwengongzuo wenxuan* [Selected articles of Mao Zedong's works on press]. Beijing: Xinhua, 1983.

———, ed. *Zhou Enlai waijiao wenxuan* [Selected diplomatic papers of Zhou Enlai]. Beijing: Zhongyang wenxian, 1990.

———, ed. *Jianguo yilai Mao Zedong wengao* [Mao Zedong's manuscripts since the founding of the People's Republic of China], vol. 6. Beijing: Zhongyang wenxian 1992.

———. "Liu Shaoqi, 'Letter to Stalin on Mao's Plan of China's Transition to Socialism'" [title added by the author], *Jianguo yilai zhongyao wenxian xuanbian*, vol. 3 (Beijing: Zhongyang wenxian, 1992).

———, ed. *Mao Zedong nianpu* [A chronological record of Mao Zedong]. 3 vols. Beijing: Renmin, 1993.

———, ed. *Mao Zedong waijiao wenxuan* [Selected diplomatic papers of Mao Zedong]. Beijing: Shijie zhishi, 1994.

———, ed. *Mao Zedong wenji* [Collected works of Mao Zedong], vol. 5. Beijing: Renmin, 1996.

———, ed. *Zhou Enlai nianpu, 1949–1976* [A chronological record of Zhou Enlai, 1949–1976], vol. 1. Beijing: Zhongyang wenxian, 1997.

———, ed. *Mao Zedong wenji* [Collected works of Mao Zedong], vol. 7. Beijing: Renmin, 1999.

———, ed. *Zhou Enlai waijiao wenxuan* [Selected diplomatic papers of Zhou Enlai]. Beijing: Zhongyang wenxian, 2000.

———, ed. *Chen Yun nianpu* [A chronological record of Chen Yun]. Beijing: Zhongyang wenxian, 2000.

———. *Liu Shaoqi zizhuan* [Liu Shaoqi's memoir]. Beijing: Jiefangjun wenyi, 2003.

———, ed. *Chen Yun zhuan* [Biography of Chen Yun]. 2 vols., vol. 1. Beijing: Zhongyang wenxian, 2005.

———, ed. *Zhongguo gongchandang dangshi dashiji: 1919.5–2005.12* [Record of the CCP historical events: May 1919–December 2005]. Beijing: Zhonggong dangshi, 2006.

Zhongguo renmin jiefangjun guofang daxue dangshi dangjian zhenggong jiaoyanshi [National Defense University of the Chinese People's Liberation Army], ed. *Zhonggong dangshi jiaoxue cankao ziliao* [Chinese Communist Party history teaching and research materials], vols. 19–24. Guofang daxue chubanshe, 1986.

Zhongyang dang'anguan [Central archives], ed. *Gongheguo wushinian zhenguidang'an* [Fifty years precious archival collection of the People's Republic of China], vol. 1. Beijing: Zhongguo dang'an, 1999.

Zubok, Vladislav. "Look What Chaos in the Beautiful Socialist Camp! Deng Xiaoping and the Sino-Soviet Split, 1956–1963." *Cold War International History Project Bulletin*, 10 (1998): 150–55.

———. "Deng Xiaoping and the Sino-Soviet Split, 1956–1963." *CWIHP Bulletin*, no. 10 (Spring 1998).

———. *A Failed Empire: The Soviet Union in the Cold War from Stalin to Gorbachev*. Chapel Hill: University of North Carolina Press, 2007.

Zubok, Vladislav, and Constantine Pleshakov. *Inside the Kremlin's Cold War: From Stalin to Khrushchev*. Cambridge, MA, and London: Harvard University Press, 1996.

Index

Agricultural Producers' Cooperatives (APCs), 29, 40, 40n50, 42
Agricultural reforms
    Collectivization, 21–22, 29, 29n25, 30, 35, 36, 36n41
    Chen Yun role, 41
    Gao Gang role, 32n32
    Liu Shaoqi role, 27, 32, 37
    Deng Zihui role, 40n49, 41–42, 43
    Mao Zedong role, 22–23, 27–33, 29n25, 32n32, 36n41, 41–43, 41n52
    peasant resistance to, 40n50
    Zhou Enlai role, 28, 32
Andropov, Yuri, 66, 66n38, 69, 70n52, 118n5, 120n10, 121, 122n16
An Ziwen, 34n35

Beria, Lavrenti, 77n66, 146
Bierut, Boleslaw, 59, 70, 71
Bo Yibo, 2n5, 32n31, 34n35, 36, 37n43, 136
bourgeois, 19, 24, 26n19, 43, 45, 47, 187, 203, 222, 230, 234, 239, 240, 254, 258, 259, 270
bureaucratism, 201, 208, 219, 220, 233n71, 234, 235, 242, 246, 273

Chen Qitong, 231, 232, 232n70, 235, 236, 244n101 (*see also* Ma Hanbing)
Chen Yun
    reevaluation of the Soviet model, 206–209

    on economic policy after Hungary, 203, 207–208, 208n23
    on socialist transformation, 34n35, 207n22
China Democratic National Construction Association (CDNCA), 226, 226n59
    Huang Yanpei as the head of (*see* Huang Yanpei)
    the second plenary session of the first central committee, 226–227
Chinese Communist Party (CCP)
    Eighth Party Congress, 92, 95n103, 96–98, 100n112, 110, 129, 130, 199n6, 205–206, 261
    relations with the Eastern European Communist parties, 52–55
    mass line tradition, 36n41, 79, 186, 214, 215, 215n37, 216
Central Committee of the Chinese Communist Party (CC)
    Rural Work Department of, 40, 41, 43, 58
    relations with the Eastern bloc communist parties, 92, 93n97, 106–107, 125, 171
    analysis of Polish October 1956, 105–107
    the second plenary session of the eighth CCP CC, 130, 198, 199n6, 218n41, 261
Communist Information Bureau (Cominform), 52n3, 64n32
    Stalin's suggestion for Asian Cominform, 53n5

Deng Tuo, 244–245, 245n102
Deng Zihui
  agricultural collectivization role (*see* Agricultural collectivization)
  background, 33n33
  national manufacturing role, 32n32
  China-Eastern Bloc states' relations (1954) role, 58–59, 59n22
  Mao's criticism of, 43, 211
Deng Xiaoping
  background, 33n33
  China's involvement in Hungarian crisis, 8n16, 106, 107, 109n139, 124, 125, 169, 171, 172, 195 (*see also* PRC involvement in Hungarian crisis)
  1957 domestic changes role, 247n105, 252n115, 257n130
  on socialist transformation, 28, 34n35
  on Soviet "big power chauvinism," 51, 97

East Germany, 4n8, 54, 104n148, 182n164, 205

Fu Lei, 241, 241n95

Gao Gang
  agricultural collectivization role (*see* agricultural collectivization)
  background, 33n33, 207n22
  national manufacturing role, 32n32
  relationship with Mao, 22, 29n25, 33–34, 32n32
  relationship with Liu Shaoqi, 21, 29
Gao-Rao affair, 28n23, 29n24, 40, 207n22, 214, 237n82, 255
Geneva Conference (1954), 40n48, 57
Gerő, Ernő
  political career and Soviet Union, 64n31, 66–67, 68, 68n45, 69, 69n51, 113
  as first secretary of the Hungarian Communist party, 68, 69
  relationship with Tito, 69, 69n51
  Hungarian crisis role, 70, 118–119, 118n5, 120, 120n10, 122, 123, 139, 140n58, 153, 155, 179n158, 256
Gomułka, Władysław
  China's Policies to Poland role, 90, 91, 92, 92n96, 94, 105, 106–107, 125, 127, 133, 134, 136n48, 139, 145, 146–147, 148, 149, 150, 162, 191, 224
  political career and Soviet Union, 70, 72n59, 73, 120, 122
  political role before 1956, 70, 90
  rehabilitation of, 71–72, 93, 93n98, 100
  political policies 1956, 72, 99–100, 103–104, 120
  Polish-Soviet relations policies, 72, 100, 103
  relationship with Khrushchev (*see* Khrushchev)

Hao Deqing, 3n7, 65n34, 84n80, 140, 141, 142, 142n62, 143n63, 172n134, 172n135, 176, 177
Hegedüs, András, 58, 59, 118n5, 120n10, 157n91
Hu Feng, 43, 44, 44n58, 44n59, 253, 253n117, 255
Huang Yanpei, 41n52, 226. 226n60, 247n105
Hungary
  American policy during October crisis, 175, 175n143
  debate among Communist parties after October crisis, 180–183, 181n161, 181n162
  domestic situation before October 1956, 5, 14, 49, 62n26, 64, 66–67, 70, 72–73, 82, 84n77, 84n80, 85, 111

Index

domestic situation in October crisis, 2, 5, 5n8, 6n10, 14, 15, 140, 141, 143–144, 140n59, 155–156, 165–166, 174
relations with China, 4n7, 7, 8, 9, 10, 16, 51, 52n2, 59, 77, 84n80, 85n82, 85–87, 89n91, 98 (see also People's Republic of China)
Soviet policies to, 6n11, 7, 8, 8n17, 67n40, 69, 95, 98, 104, 115, 119, 120, 120n10, 121, 121n11, 122, 126, 127, 152, 152n80, 152n81, 154, 156–159, 166–167, 168, 171n127, 173, 173n136, 175n144, 178, 182 (see Soviet Union)
UN and the October crisis, 8n17, 158, 158n95, 178
Hungarian Communist Party, 64n32, 258, Central Committee divisions and factionalization, 69, 251n113
Hungarian crisis impact on Chinese domestic politics
and Mao's reemphasis on class struggle, 196, 200, 247–248, 254, 256, 264, and Mao's open-door rectification policy, 249–250, and CCP's supervision of non-communists, 250, 271, and Mao's analysis of Hungary, 251n113, 251, 254, 259, 272–273, and Mao's reassessment of open-door rectification, 251–252, 253n118, 254, 254n120, and Mao's Anti-Rightist policy, 254, 257–259, 258n132, 258n133, 272
domestic problems and Hungary, 197–198, 201, 204–207, 209, 213–215, 213n31, 255, 256, 260, 269, 273
and Mao's analysis of, 99, 196, 200, 211–213, 216–217, 218, 222, 247–248, 251, 251n113, 254, 256, 259, 261, 264, 272–273, and Mao on democracy, 217–218, 219–221, 221n49, 222, 223n52, 224, 225, 242n97, 244, 258, 261, 269–272 (see also Li Shenzhi, Wang Fei), and Mao's policy of rectification, 2, 4n7, 12, 196–197, 220, 221, 226, 229, 232n71, 243, 244, 245, 246, 247, 250, 251–252, 254, 270
and CCP's supervision of non-communists, 250–251
and Mao's anti-rightist policy, 254, 257–259, 272
and Chinese intellectuals, 255, 270–272, and student movements, 256, 272
Hundred Flowers policy (HF) policy
HF policy and campaign, 3, 3n6, 12, 15, 16, 35, 44n58, 86n85, 87, 87n85, 243n96
and intellectuals' doubts over, 233–234, 234n73, 238, 240n88, 251n113
Party Cadres' resistance to, 196, 230, 230n64, 231, 231n68, 232, 232n69, 233, 237, 244–245, 263 (see also Chen Qitong, Ma Hanbing), and Mao's suspicion of intellectuals' loyalty, 223–224, 243n99, 245, 248, 250–251, and Mao's reevaluation of HF policy, 223n52, 224, 230, 236
and Mao's analysis of Hungary, 225–227, 228, 230, 235, 240, 242, 243, 262, and Mao's defense of HF policy, 234, 234n74, 234n75, 235, 235n76, 235n77, 235n78, 236, 236n81, 237, 238, 239, 240, 242, 246, 252–253, 253n117, 254, 254n120, 259n134, 263, 271 (see also Fu Lei), and Mao's HF open-door rectification policy, 242, 244, 244n101, 245, 246, 247, 251n113, 251n114, 252, 262–263, 270, and social responses to, 255, 256, 270–272, change of HF to anti-rightist campaign, 252, 254, 256–257, 258–259, 264

Hundred Flowers policy (HF) policy (*continued*)
  leadership's association of with domestic problems, 195–196, 197–199, 200, and analysis of genesis of domestic troubles, 201–204, and reevaluation of Stalinist model, 205, and policy reforms, 203–204, 206–209, 207n20, 208n23, 210n25, 260, 267–268 (*see also* Chen Yun, Liu Shaoqi, Zhou Enlai), and Mao's attitudes, 209, 210n25, 210–213, 262, 268–269
  Mao's reemphasis of class struggle, (*see* Mao Zedong)
  Maoist version of socialism, 213, 262, 265, 270, 272
Hungarian Workers' Party, 66, 123

Iudin, Pavel, 98, 101, 102, 106, 107, 109, 170, 170n127

Kádár, János, 7, 7n15, 68, 156, 157, 157n92, 172n135, 178, 178n152, 178n154, 179n158, 181, 181n162, 185n167
Kang Sheng, 232n70, 252n115
Khrushchev, Nikita. *See also* Soviet Union
  China policies, 38, 55–56, 55n11, 56n12, 58, 60, 61, 190
  denunciation of Stalin by, 2, 14, 16, 46, 49, 63, 64
  economic policies, 62, 62n26, 65
  expectations on China during Polish-Hungarian crises, 116–117, 117n2, 126–127, 132, 175, 266
  relationship with Tito, 62–63, 69, 69n51, 83, 83n77, 95, 181, 181n162, 182, 182n163, 182n164, 183, 185
  relationship with China, 56, 60, 61, 73, 74, 74n61, 97, 98, 189
  1956 Polish events role, 71, 72, 93n98, 99–100, 100n114, 101n118, 102–103, 103n125, 104, 115, 117, 132, 133
  1956 Hungarian crisis role, 8, 66, 67, 67n40, 68, 69, 70n54, 118–119, 120, 120n10, 122, 122n15, 157, 157n97, 158, 159, 163, 163n108, 165, 166–167, 170, 172, 173, 175, 178, 179n158 (*see also* Soviet Union)
  pursuit of bloc unity, 96, 115, 116–117, 117n2, 153–154, 160, 163, 178
Kiryluk, Stanislaw, 90, 145, 146, 148, 149, 150, 160n99 (*see also* Gomulka, Mao Zedong)
Korean War, 30, 30n26, 31n28, 31n29, 32, 38, 39, 39n47, 84

Lashchenko, Pyotr Nikolayevich, 121
Lenin, 21n10, 24, 25, 25n16, 26n18, 78, 97, 118, 171n127, 202
Leninism, 183
Li Shenzhi, 218, 218n43, 219n44, 219n46, 221n49, 258 (*see also* Wang Fei)
Lin Ke, 218, 218n42, 219n46, 219, 256n128
Liu Shaoqi
  background, 26
  China's involvement in Hungarian crisis role, 124, 124n21, 124n22, 126, 127, 128n31, 129, 130, 131, 133, 134, 137, 145, 147, 160, 163, 163n107, 169, 170, 170n127, 171, 174, 185n167, 195 (*see also* PRC involvement in Hungarian crisis)
  reevaluation of the Soviet model, 199, 203–205
  on New Democracy line, 25–26

Index 305

on party organization reforms after Hungary, 200–203
on economic policy after Hungary, 203–204, 204n16
on socialist transformation line, 34n35, 27–28, 204
relationship with Mao, 28, 34n35, 37, 204
Lu Dingyi, 39n46, 252n115

Ma Hanbing, 231, 232n70 (*see also* Chen Qitong)
Malashenko, Evgenii, 121, 122n13
Malenkov, Georgi, 56, 157n91, 158, 181n162
Mao Zedong
  analysis of Stalinism, 79, 80, 82, 108–109, 111, 112, 113, 114, 118, 127–129
  designed new pattern for bloc unity, 111, 113, 116, 125, 125n23, 126, 130, 135, 136–137, 144–147, 148n73, 148, 149, 150–152, and Hungarian crisis, 159–160, 161, 162, 163–164, 167, 168
  evaluation of Khrushchev's secret speech, 2, 4n7, 74, 75, 76n66, 79–80, 82, 83, 97, 112, 186
  evaluation of Twentieth Congress of the CPSU, 74–75, 74n61
  initiative to lead international communism, 82, 110, 113, 125–126, 127–129, 130, 131, 190–191
  initiative to resign as chairman of state, 247n105
  knowledge of Hungary, 58–59, 61–62
  knowledge of Poland, 59–60, 61–62
  Maoist version of socialism, 74, 75–76, 81, 112–113, 213, 262, 265, 270, 272
  Marxist-Lenist beliefs, 24, 24n16
  on Gomulka, 46, 48, 91, 92, 92n96, 94, 106, 108, 125, 127, 133–134, 146, 149, 162, 191, 224
  on Hundred Flowers policy in 1956 (*see* Hundred Flowers policy)
  "On the Correct Handling of Contradictions among the People" speech, 223n53, 232n70, 237–238
  on Nagy, 161, 161n103, 162, 163, 164, 170, 170n127, 172, 172n134, 172n135, 173, 173n139, 174, 177, 191, 196, 251n113, 258
  on Soviet "big power chauvinism," 96, 97–98, 100, 101n117, 106n132, 107, 107n135, 110, 125, 126, 128, 128n31, 129, 132, 133, 135n47, 144, 147, 160n99, 188, 191, 266 (*see also* PRC (1956–1957))
  ruling style, 23, 23n13, 23n14, 28, 237n82, 238–239, 244–245
  Polish October policies of, 106–109, 110–111, 134, 146–150
  pursuit of bloc unity, 146–150, 184–185, 186–188, 188n173, 193, 198–200
  Hungarian crisis policies of, 116, 124n22, 134, 135–137, 136n49, 144–145, 148–150, 151, 159, 160, 163–164, 167, 169, 170, 170n127, 171, 171n129, 172, 172n134, 172n135, 174, 174n139, 175–176, 177, 178, 179, 179n157, 179n158, 183, 184, 190–193
  relationship with Liu Shaoqi (*see* Liu Shaoqi)
  on Rákosi, 59, 95, 99, 185n167, 228, 246, 256, 272
  Soviet model adaptations, 27–28, 28n22
  speech on Ten Relationships, 87, 87n85, 90, 92, 96, 96n106, 113
  support of Khrushchev by, 56, 97

Marxist-Leninism, 23n13, 26, 47, 78, 79, 80, 104, 186, 187, 189, 214
Mićunović, Veljko, 65n33, 67n40, 95
Mikoyan, Anastas
   1956 Hungarian crisis role, 67, 68–69, 120, 122, 120n7, 120n9, 152, 152n80, 152n81, 153, 156, 157, 158, 165, 175, 175n144 (*see also* Suslov)
   Sino-Soviet relations role, 20n8, 39n46, 96–99, 110
   intervention in North Korean politics with Chinese, 51–54
Molotov, Vyacheslav, 56, 56n13, 127n28, 157n91, 160, 166, 167, 171, 189
"More on the Historical Lessons of the Proletarian Dictatorship" article, 124n21, 185, 186n169, 187n170, 189n175, 221, 223n52
Münnich, Ferenc, 177, 177n151, 178, 178n152

Nagy, Imre
   admiration of China's five principles of coexistence, 85, 85n82, 86
   as prime minister, 65–66, 65n34, 123
   Communist beliefs, 65, 65n34, 86, 86n83
   Hungarian crisis role, 138, 149, 155–156, 161, 166, 174, 176, 178
   life of as a citizen (1955), 65
   New Course reform role, 65, 122
   political career and Soviet Union, 65, 65n34, 70, 70n54, 73, 120, 122, 122n16, 123, 156, 157–158, 159, 171, 174, 175n144, 178
   relations with intellectuals and the youth, 66
   reputation of as a nationalist leader, 70
Neibu cankao (*Neican*), 54n8, 85n81, 89, 91n93, 94n101, 94n102, 102n121, 105n130, 107n137, 123n19, 138n52, 214n32, 214n33, 215n34, 215n35, 215n36, 253n117, 256n125
New Course, 62–63, 62n26, 65, 86, 86n83, 122

Ochab, Edward, 71, 72, 72n59, 92–94, 92n95

Pancha Shila (five principles of coexistence), 162, 162n105, 163–164, 167
People's Republic of China (PRC) consolidation, reconstruction (1949–1952)
   Anti-Revolutionaries Suppression Movement, 31–32, 31n29
   collectivization (*see* agricultural reforms)
   divisions, factionalization of the leadership, 22, 23
   leadership's policies toward the Soviet bloc states, 52
   Mao's policies, 22–24, 23n13, 28, 28n22, 29, 29n25, 30–36, 36n41, 37–39, 42–43, 45–47
   New Democracy line, 19n5, 20, 20n9, 21, 22, 25–26, 26n19
   policy disputes among the leadership, 28–29, 32n32, 32–33
   relations with Soviet Union, 50–53
   relations with Soviet bloc states, 51–53, 53n5, 53n6, 54 (*see also* Stalin)
   relations with Yugoslavia, 52n3
   socialist transformation line, 22, 33–37
   Stalinization in China, 30n27
PRC socialist construction, transformation (1953–1955)
   fifth anniversary of the establishing of, 57–60

Index

leadership's policies toward the Soviet bloc states, 54n8, 57–60, 61–62
relations with Council for Mutual Economic Associate (CEMA), 60–61
relations with Soviet Union, 55–57, 60–61
relations with Soviet bloc states, 49, 53–55, 53n7, 57, 58–62
socialist transformation, 39–40, 45–46, 54, 54n8, 76
PRC involvement in the Hungarian crisis (1956)
Chinese embassy in Budapest, 140–144, 142n62, 143n63
delegation to Moscow 1956, 106, 173n136,
agenda of, 107, 160n99, and analysis of Stalin, 118–119
and analysis of Polish October, 127, and criticism of Soviet "big power chauvinism," 125, 126, 128–130, 128n31, 131, 266, and Soviet reaction to Chinese criticism, 129, 130, 131–132, 133, 132n39, pursuit of bloc unity, 130, 133–134, 135, analysis of Hungarian crisis, 116, 169 (*see also* PRC socialist adaptations)
influence on Soviet policy, 119, 127n28, 163, 165–167, 167n116, 168–169
leadership's policies to Hungarian crisis 1956, 116, 124n22, 134, 135–137, 136n49, 144–145, 148–150, 151, 159, 160, 163–164, 167, 169, 170, 170n127, 171, 171n129, 172, 174, 174n139, 175–176, 178 (*see* CC of CCP; Mao Zedong); and perception of Hungarian crisis as counterrevolutionary, 172n134, 172n135, 176, 177, 178–179, 179n157, 179n158, 183, 184, 190–193, and policies toward Soviet bloc states, 184–185, 186–188, 193, and reevaluation of de-Stalinization, 185–186, and association of Hungary with domestic unrest, 136, 136n49, 194
leadership's information sources on Hungary, 77n68, 123n19, 124n20, 124n21, 137, 138, 138n53, 138n54, 138n55, 139, 139n57, 140–144, 143n65, 155n86, 161, 165n111, 169, 170, 170n125, 170n126, 172n134, 176n148, 177, 177n150, 177n151
first soviet military intervention role, 123–124, 124n21, 127
second soviet military intervention role, 115, 136n49, 169, 170–171, 171n127, 171n129, 172, 172n134, 172n135, 173, 174, 175, 178n154, 191–193, 267
PRC socialist adaptations (1956–1957)
foreign policy making, 89–90, 123–126, 123n19, 124n20, 124n21
Great Leap Forward policy, 265, 272, 273n1
leadership's analysis of Twentieth Congress of the CPSU, 46, 74–75, 74n61, 85, 86n85, 88, 94, 110, 113, 186, 188, 199, 205, 218, 253, 267
leadership's analysis of Soviet "big power chauvinism," 96, 97–98, 100, 101n117, 106n132, 107, 107n135, 110, 125, 126, 128, 128n31, 129, 132, 133, 135n47, 144, 147, 160n99, 188, 191, 266 (*see also* Mao Zedong)
leadership's policies toward Soviet bloc states, 87–88, 89–92, 94–95, 109–111, 113, 144–145, 146–150, 151–152, 190 (*see also* Mao Zedong)

PRC socialist adaptations (1956–1957) (*continued*)
leadership's association of with domestic problems, 195–196, 197–200, and analysis of genesis of domestic troubles, 201–204, and reevaluation of Stalinist model, 205, and policy reforms, 203–204, 206, 207, 207n20, 208, 208n23, 209, 210n25, 260–261 (*see also* Chen Yun, Liu Shaoqi, Zhou Enlai), and Mao's attitudes, 209, 210, 210n25, 211–213, 261–262, 268–269
relations with Soviet Union, 189–190, 193–194, 267, 272–273
relations with Soviet bloc states, 50, 89n91, 266 (*see also* Poland; Hungary)
Petőfi Circle, 66, 66n35, 66n36 (*see also* Rákosi)
influence of on Mao's thought, 223, 223n53, 240, 241, 243, 251n113, 258, 273 (*see* Hungarian crisis)
influence of on China's domestic politics, 255, 271
Pravda, 71n57, 71n58, 129, 129n32, 131, 182n163, 189
Poland, 5n8, 14, 83, 85, 87, 88, 89, 89n91, 90, 93, 111, 120, 138, 182n164
Poznan uprising, 66, 66n36, 71, 71n57, 72, 73 (*see also* Gomulka)
Polish October, 73, 100, 103
relations with China, 49, 51, 53n6, 57, 58, 60, 84–85, 85n82, 94, 95, 113 (*see also* Gomulka, Ochab)
Polish United Worker's Party (PUWP), 71, 72, 92, 93, 100n114, 101, 107, 113, 124n20
Polish-Soviet relationship 1956, 6n10, 93, 93n98, 100, 101n118, 102n119, 103, 103n125, 104, 126, 133, 136n48

China's role, 4n7, 8, 9, 10, 72n59, 73, 95, 98, 101, 102n118, 105, 106, 106n132, 107, 114, 124, 124n20, 125, 127–128, 134–135, 136n48, 139, 146–152, 160, 162, 164, 170n127, 190, 191, 194

Rajk, László, 59n21, 64, 64n32, 67, 69, 256
Rákosi, Mátyás, 64n31, 161, 179
Petőfi Circle role, 66, 66n35
political career and Soviet Union, 65–66, 67, 67n40, 68, 69, 99
rehabilitation of Rajk, 59n21, 64, 64n32
relations with China, 12, 59, 61n25, 95, 99, 142, 185n167, 228, 246, 256, 270, 272 (*see also* Mao Zedong)
schemes against Nagy, 65, 66, 65n34, 122, 122n16
Rao Shushi, 22, 33n33, 34n35
Renmin ribao (RMRB, People's Daily), 44, 75, 78, 78n69, 88, 161, 161n101, 162, 178–179, 179n157, 179n158, 182n164, 185, 186n169, 214, 215, 222n51, 231, 231n66, 234n73, 240n88, 242n95, 244, 244n101, 245n102, 245n103, 246, 247n104, 252n116, 253n117, 254n120, 255, 255n122
Rokossovsky (Rokossowski), Marshal Konstantin, 72, 100, 100n114, 101, 102, 103, 125, 133, 145, 148, 150, 151, 160

Soviet Union. *See also* Stalin; Khrushchev
Soviet China policy after Stalin, 96
influence on Chinese socialist transformation, 13, 20–21, 20n8, 28 (*see also* Stalin)
influence of on Mao, 28, 28n22, 30, 47, 61, 78, 97, 247n105

Index   309

leadership's policies to 1956 Polish events, 71, 72, 102–104 (see Poland, Khrushchev)
leadership's policies to 1956 Hungarian crisis (see Hungary), 152, 152n80, 152n81, 154, 156–159, 166–167, 168, 171n127, 173, 173n136, 175n144, 178, 182
leadership's pursuit of bloc unity 1956, 68, 96, 104, 115, 116–117, 117n2, 153–154, 160, 163, 178, and China's role, 168–169, 182–183
Mao's analysis of, 77–78
purges in Eastern European Communist parties supported by, 64n32 (see Stalin)
Stalin, Joseph
death of and China, 14, 36, 37, 38, 47, 48, 52–53, 57
policy recommendations to China (1948–1953), 19, 19n5, 20n8, 26n18, 30, 33–34, 34n35, 35, 35n38, 38, 46
influence of on Mao Zedong, 19n7, 20n9, 21n10, 24, 25, 28, 28n22, 29n25, 38, 38n45, 45, 47, 78, 183
Sino-Soviet bloc relations role, 48, 52, 53, 53n4, 53n5
suggestion for an Asian Cominform, 53n4
purges in Eastern European Communist parties led by, 21, 21n11, 64n32
Stalinism, 38, 56, 76, 79, 82, 83, 84, 88, 111, 114, 118, 135, 181, 182, 182n163, 183, 185, 185n167, 186, 189, 191, 193, 260, 267, 268, 269, 272, 273
Suslov, Mikhail, 122, 122n15, 152, 152n80, 152n81, 153, 155, 156, 165, 166, 167, 169 (see also Mikoyan)

Tito, Joseph, 62–63, 64n32, 67, 67n40, 68, 69, 83, 83n77, 95, 99, 137n51, 180, 180n160, 181, 181n161, 181n162, 182, 182n163, 182n164, 183, 185, 193
Twentieth Congress of the Communist Party of the Soviet Union (1956)
de-Stalinization influence on Soviet bloc, 2, 14, 49, 63, 71, 73, 82, 83, 88, 111–112
de-Stalinization influence on China, 2, 14, 16, 46, 49, 74–75, 76, 77n67, 77n68, 82, 84, 86n85, 110, 111, 185n167, 186, 188, 199, 205, 218, 253, 267
Yugoslav's role in Soviet bloc after, 83, 95, 181n162
China's role in Soviet bloc after, 85, 87, 90, 92, 94, 113, 137
Chinese leadership's reaction, see PRC (1956–1957)
Chinese leadership's analysis of, see PRC (1956–1957)

Wang Fei, 218, 218n43, 220n46, 221n49
Wang Jiaxiang, 53n5, 97, 147
Wang Meng
cynical short story, 231
CCP cadres' criticism of, 231, 233
Mao's analysis of, 234, 235, 235n76, 235n78 (see also Mao Zedong)
Wang Ruoshui, 236n81, 245n102
Warsaw Pact, 148, 149, 150, 160, 162, 167, 168, 174, 179, 181, 196
Wu Lengxi, 2n4, 78n70, 89n91, 101n118, 106, 106n132, 125n24, 136n48, 171n129, 173n136, 183, 183n165, 184n166, 188, 196n1, 219, 219n44, 221n49

Xi Zhongxun, 33n33, 34n35
Xie Wenqing, 91n93, 105, 105n130, 107n137, 142

Yao Wenyuan, 235n78
Yan'an era, 12, 12n25, 23n13, 24, 32n30, 242, 242n96
Yang Shangkun, 34n35
Yugoslavia
  relations with China, 52n3, 95n103, 100n112, 185, 186, 199, 200
  relations with Soviet Union, 53, 53n5, 63, 83, 84
  relations with Soviet bloc states, 69n51, 83, 84, 84n77, 95
  1956 Hungarian crisis role, 181, 181n162, 182, 182n163

Zhang Wentian, 26, 97, 145

Zhukov, Georgy, 119, 122n15, 157n91, 158
Zhou Enlai
  background, 26
  foreign policy role, 51n1, 55, 57, 86, 162n105, 194
  reevaluation of the Soviet model, 203, 204, 204n16, 205, 206, 207, 207n20, 208, 209, 260, 261, 268
  on socialist transformation, 32, 34n35, 36
  relationship with Mao, 22, 37, 37n43, 273
  Sino-Soviet bloc relations role, 57–58, 94n103, 106, 107, 145

CORNELL EAST ASIA SERIES

4 Fredrick Teiwes, *Provincial Leadership in China: The Cultural Revolution and Its Aftermath*
8 Cornelius C. Kubler, *Vocabulary and Notes to Ba Jin's Jia: An Aid for Reading the Novel*
16 Monica Bethe & Karen Brazell, *Nō as Performance: An Analysis of the Kuse Scene of Yamamba.* Available for purchase: DVD by Monica Bethe & Karen Brazell, "Yamanba: The Old Woman of the Mountains"
18 Royall Tyler, tr., *Granny Mountains: A Second Cycle of Nō Plays*
23 Knight Biggerstaff, *Nanking Letters, 1949*
28 Diane E. Perushek, ed., *The Griffis Collection of Japanese Books: An Annotated Bibliography*
37 J. Victor Koschmann, Ōiwa Keibō & Yamashita Shinji, eds., *International Perspectives on Yanagita Kunio and Japanese Folklore Studies*
38 James O'Brien, tr., *Murō Saisei: Three Works*
40 Kubo Sakae, *Land of Volcanic Ash: A Play in Two Parts,* revised edition, tr. David G. Goodman
44 Susan Orpett Long, *Family Change and the Life Course in Japan*
48 Helen Craig McCullough, *Bungo Manual: Selected Reference Materials for Students of Classical Japanese*
49 Susan Blakeley Klein, *Ankoku Butō: The Premodern and Postmodern Influences on the Dance of Utter Darkness*
50 Karen Brazell, ed., *Twelve Plays of the Noh and Kyōgen Theaters*
51 David G. Goodman, ed., *Five Plays by Kishida Kunio*
52 Shirō Hara, *Ode to Stone,* tr. James Morita
53 Peter J. Katzenstein & Yutaka Tsujinaka, *Defending the Japanese State: Structures, Norms and the Political Responses to Terrorism and Violent Social Protest in the 1970s and 1980s*
54 Su Xiaokang & Wang Luxiang, *Deathsong of the River: A Reader's Guide to the Chinese TV Series Heshang,* trs. Richard Bodman & Pin P. Wan
55 Jingyuan Zhang, *Psychoanalysis in China: Literary Transformations, 1919–1949*
56 Jane Kate Leonard & John R. Watt, eds., *To Achieve Security and Wealth: The Qing Imperial State and the Economy, 1644–1911*
57 Andrew F. Jones, *Like a Knife: Ideology and Genre in Contemporary Chinese Popular Music*
58 Peter J. Katzenstein & Nobuo Okawara, *Japan's National Security: Structures, Norms and Policy Responses in a Changing World*
59 Carsten Holz, *The Role of Central Banking in China's Economic Reforms*
60 Chifumi Shimazaki, *Warrior Ghost Plays from the Japanese Noh Theater: Parallel Translations with Running Commentary*
61 Emily Groszos Ooms, *Women and Millenarian Protest in Meiji Japan: Deguchi Nao and Ōmotokyō*

62 Carolyn Anne Morley, *Transformation, Miracles, and Mischief: The Mountain Priest Plays of Kyōgen*
63 David R. McCann & Hyunjae Yee Sallee, tr., *Selected Poems of Kim Namjo,* afterword by Kim Yunsik
64 Hua Qingzhao, *From Yalta to Panmunjom: Truman's Diplomacy and the Four Powers, 1945-1953*
65 Margaret Benton Fukasawa, *Kitahara Hakushū: His Life and Poetry*
66 Kam Louie, ed., *Strange Tales from Strange Lands: Stories by Zheng Wanlong,* with introduction
67 Wang Wen-hsing, *Backed Against the Sea,* tr. Edward Gunn
69 Brian Myers, *Han Sōrya and North Korean Literature: The Failure of Socialist Realism in the DPRK*
70 Thomas P. Lyons & Victor Nee, eds., *The Economic Transformation of South China: Reform and Development in the Post-Mao Era*
71 David G. Goodman, tr., *After Apocalypse: Four Japanese Plays of Hiroshima and Nagasaki,* with introduction
72 Thomas Lyons, *Poverty and Growth in a South China County: Anxi, Fujian, 1949-1992*
74 Martyn Atkins, *Informal Empire in Crisis: British Diplomacy and the Chinese Customs Succession, 1927-1929*
76 Chifumi Shimazaki, *Restless Spirits from Japanese Noh Plays of the Fourth Group: Parallel Translations with Running Commentary*
77 Brother Anthony of Taizé & Young-Moo Kim, trs., *Back to Heaven: Selected Poems of Ch'ŏn Sang Pyŏng*
78 Kevin O'Rourke, tr., *Singing Like a Cricket, Hooting Like an Owl: Selected Poems by Yi Kyu-bo*
79 Irit Averbuch, *The Gods Come Dancing: A Study of the Japanese Ritual Dance of Yamabushi Kagura*
80 Mark Peterson, *Korean Adoption and Inheritance: Case Studies in the Creation of a Classic Confucian Society*
81 Yenna Wu, tr., *The Lioness Roars: Shrew Stories from Late Imperial China*
82 Thomas Lyons, *The Economic Geography of Fujian: A Sourcebook,* Vol. 1
83 Pak Wan-so, *The Naked Tree,* tr. Yu Young-nan
84 C.T. Hsia, *The Classic Chinese Novel: A Critical Introduction*
85 Cho Chong-Rae, *Playing With Fire,* tr. Chun Kyung-Ja
86 Hayashi Fumiko, *I Saw a Pale Horse and Selections from Diary of a Vagabond,* tr. Janice Brown
87 Motoori Norinaga, *Kojiki-den, Book 1,* tr. Ann Wehmeyer
88 Chang Soo Ko, tr., *Sending the Ship Out to the Stars: Poems of Park Je-chun*
89 Thomas Lyons, *The Economic Geography of Fujian: A Sourcebook,* Vol. 2
90 Brother Anthony of Taizé, tr., *Midang: Early Lyrics of So Chong-Ju*
92 Janice Matsumura, *More Than a Momentary Nightmare: The Yokohama Incident and Wartime Japan*
93 Kim Jong-Gil tr., *The Snow Falling on Chagall's Village: Selected Poems of Kim Ch'un-Su*

94 Wolhee Choe & Peter Fusco, trs., *Day-Shine: Poetry by Hyon-jong Chong*
95 Chifumi Shimazaki, *Troubled Souls from Japanese Noh Plays of the Fourth Group*
96 Hagiwara Sakutarō, *Principles of Poetry (Shi no Genri)*, tr. Chester Wang
97 Mae J. Smethurst, *Dramatic Representations of Filial Piety: Five Noh in Translation*
98 Ross King, ed., *Description and Explanation in Korean Linguistics*
99 William Wilson, *Hōgen Monogatari: Tale of the Disorder in Hōgen*
100 Yasushi Yamanouchi, J. Victor Koschmann and Ryūichi Narita, eds., *Total War and 'Modernization'*
101 Yi Ch'ŏng-jun, *The Prophet and Other Stories*, tr. Julie Pickering
102 S.A. Thornton, *Charisma and Community Formation in Medieval Japan: The Case of the Yugyō-ha (1300-1700)*
103 Sherman Cochran, ed., *Inventing Nanjing Road: Commercial Culture in Shanghai, 1900-1945*
104 Harold M. Tanner, *Strike Hard! Anti-Crime Campaigns and Chinese Criminal Justice, 1979-1985*
105 Brother Anthony of Taizé & Young-Moo Kim, trs., *Farmers' Dance: Poems by Shin Kyŏng-nim*
106 Susan Orpett Long, ed., *Lives in Motion: Composing Circles of Self and Community in Japan*
107 Peter J. Katzenstein, Natasha Hamilton-Hart, Kozo Kato, & Ming Yue, *Asian Regionalism*
108 Kenneth Alan Grossberg, *Japan's Renaissance: The Politics of the Muromachi Bakufu*
109 John W. Hall & Toyoda Takeshi, eds., *Japan in the Muromachi Age*
110 Kim Su-Young, Shin Kyong-Nim, Lee Si-Young; *Variations: Three Korean Poets;* trs. Brother Anthony of Taizé & Young-Moo Kim
111 Samuel Leiter, *Frozen Moments: Writings on* Kabuki, *1966–2001*
112 Pilwun Shih Wang & Sarah Wang, *Early One Spring: A Learning Guide to Accompany the Film Video* February
113 Thomas Conlan, *In Little Need of Divine Intervention: Scrolls of the Mongol Invasions of Japan*
114 Jane Kate Leonard & Robert Antony, eds., *Dragons, Tigers, and Dogs: Qing Crisis Management and the Boundaries of State Power in Late Imperial China*
115 Shu-ning Sciban & Fred Edwards, eds., *Dragonflies: Fiction by Chinese Women in the Twentieth Century*
116 David G. Goodman, ed., *The Return of the Gods: Japanese Drama and Culture in the 1960s*
117 Yang Hi Choe-Wall, *Vision of a Phoenix: The Poems of Hŏ Nansŏrhŏn*
118 Mae J. Smethurst and Christina Laffin, eds., *The Noh* Ominameshi: *A Flower Viewed from Many Directions*
119 Joseph A. Murphy, *Metaphorical Circuit: Negotiations Between Literature and Science in Twentieth-Century Japan*

120 Richard F. Calichman, *Takeuchi Yoshimi: Displacing the West*
121 Fan Pen Li Chen, *Visions for the Masses: Chinese Shadow Plays from Shaanxi and Shanxi*
122 S. Yumiko Hulvey, *Sacred Rites in Moonlight: Ben no Naishi Nikki*
123 Tetsuo Najita and J. Victor Koschmann, *Conflict in Modern Japanese History: The Neglected Tradition*
124 Naoki Sakai, Brett de Bary, & Iyotani Toshio, eds., *Deconstructing Nationality*
125 Judith N. Rabinovitch and Timothy R. Bradstock, *Dance of the Butterflies: Chinese Poetry from the Japanese Court Tradition*
126 Yang Gui-ja, *Contradictions,* trs. Stephen Epstein and Kim Mi-Young
127 Ann Sung-hi Lee, *Yi Kwang-su and Modern Korean Literature:* Mujŏng
128 Pang Kie-chung & Michael D. Shin, eds., *Landlords, Peasants, & Intellectuals in Modern Korea*
129 Joan R. Piggott, ed., *Capital and Countryside in Japan, 300–1180: Japanese Historians Interpreted in English*
130 Kyoko Selden and Jolisa Gracewood, eds., *Annotated Japanese Literary Gems: Stories by Tawada Yōko, Nakagami Kenji, and Hayashi Kyōko* (Vol. 1)
131 Michael G. Murdock, *Disarming the Allies of Imperialism: The State, Agitation, and Manipulation during China's Nationalist Revolution, 1922–1929*
132 Noel J. Pinnington, *Traces in the Way: Michi and the Writings of Komparu Zenchiku*
133 Charlotte von Verschuer, *Across the Perilous Sea: Japanese Trade with China and Korea from the Seventh to the Sixteenth Centuries,* Kristen Lee Hunter, tr.
134 John Timothy Wixted, *A Handbook to Classical Japanese*
135 Kyoko Selden and Jolisa Gracewoord, with Lili Selden, eds., *Annotated Japanese Literary Gems: Stories by Natsume Sōseki, Tomioka Taeko, and Inoue Yasushi* (Vol. 2)
136 Yi Tae-Jin, *The Dynamics of Confucianism and Modernization in Korean History*
137 Jennifer Rudolph, *Negotiated Power in Late Imperial China: The Zongli Yamen and the Politics of Reform*
138 Thomas D. Loooser, *Visioning Eternity: Aesthetics, Politics, and History in the Early Modern Noh Theater*
139 Gustav Heldt, *The Pursuit of Harmony: Poetry and Power in Late Heian Japan*
140 Joan R. Piggott and Yoshida Sanae, *Teishinkōki: The Year 939 in the Journal of Regent Fujiwara no Tadahira*
141 Robert Bagley, *Max Loehr and the Study of Chinese Bronzes: Style and Classification in the History of Art*
142 Edwin A. Cranston, *The Secret Island and the Enticing Flame: Worlds of Memory, Discovery, and Loss in Japanese Poetry*
143 Hugh de Ferranti, *The Last Biwa Singer: A Blind Musician in History, Imagination and Performance*

144 Roger des Forges, Minglu Gao, Liu Chiao-mei, Haun Saussy, with Thomas Burkman, eds., *Chinese Walls in Time and Space: A Multidisciplinary Perspective*

145 Hye-jin Juhn Sidney & George Sidney, trs., *I Heard Life Calling Me: Poems of Yi Sŏng-bok*

146 Sherman Cochran & Paul G. Pickowicz, eds., *China on the Margins*

147 Wang Lingzhen & Mary Ann O'Donnell, trs., *Years of Sadness: Autobiographical Writings of Wang Anyi*

148 John Holstein, tr., *A Moment's Grace: Stories from Korea in Transition*

149 Sunyoung Park in collaboration with Jefferson J.A. Gatrall, trs., *On the Eve of the Uprising and Other Stories from Colonial Korea*

150 Brother Anthony of Taizé & Lee Hyung-jin, trs., *Walking on a Washing Line: Poems of Kim Seung-Hee*

151 Matthew Fraleigh, trs., with introduction, *New Chronicles of Yanagibashi and Diary of a Journey to the West: Narushima Ryūhoku Reports from Home and Abroad*

152 Pei Huang, *Reorienting the Manchus: A Study of Sinicization, 1583–1795*

153 Karen Gernant & Chen Zeping, *White Poppies and Other Stories by Zhang Kangkang*

154 Mattias Burell & Marina Svensson, eds., *Making Law Work: Chinese Laws in Context*

155 Tomoko Aoyama & Barbara Hartley, trs., *Indian Summer by Kanai Mieko*

156 Lynne Kutsukake, tr., *Single Sickness and Other Stories by Masuda Mizuko*

157 Takako U. Lento, tr. with introduction, *Tanikawa Shuntarō: The Art of Being Alone, Poems 1952–2009*

158 Shu-ning Sciban & Fred Edwards, eds., *Endless War: Fiction & Essays by Wang Wen-hsing*

159 Elizabeth Oyler & Michael Watson, eds., *Like Clouds and Mists: Studies and Translations of Nō Plays of the Genpei War*

160 Michiko N. Wilson & Michael K. Wilson, trs., *Of Birds Crying by Minako Ōba*

161 Chifumi Shimazaki & Stephen Comee *Supernatural Beings from Japanese Noh Plays of the Fifth Group: Parallel Translations with Running Commentary*

162 Petrus Liu, *Stateless Subjects: Chinese Martial Arts Literature and Postcolonial History*

163 Lim Beng Choo, *Another Stage: Kanze Nobumitsu and the Late Muromachi Noh Theater*

164 Scott Cook, *The Bamboo Texts of Guodian: A Study and Complete Translation, Volume 1*

165 Scott Cook, *The Bamboo Texts of Guodian: A Study and Complete Translation, Volume 2*

166 Stephen D. Miller, translations with Patrick Donnelly, *The Wind from Vulture Peak: The Buddhification of Japanese Waka in the Heian Period*
167 Theodore Hughes, Jae-yong Kim, Jin-kyung Lee & Sang-kyung Lee, eds., *Rat Fire: Korean Stories from the Japanese Empire*
168 Ken C. Kawashima, Fabian Schäfer, Robert Stolz, eds., *Tosaka Jun: A Critical Reader*
169 John R. Bentley, *Tamakatsuma—A Window into the Scholarship of Motoori Norinaga*
170 Dandan Zhu, *1956: Mao's China and the Hungarian Crisis*

eap.einaudi.cornell.edu/publications

Lightning Source UK Ltd.
Milton Keynes UK
UKHW011816260123
416025UK00001B/119